D1550472

THE LIBERAL TEMPER IN
GREEK POLITICS

39-35

THE
LIBERAL TEMPER
IN
GREEK POLITICS

by

ERIC A. HAVELOCK

YALE UNIVERSITY PRESS:
NEW HAVEN AND LONDON

First published in 1957.
Second printing, August 1964.
Printed in the United States of America by
The Carl Purington Rollins Printing-Office of the
Yale University Press, New Haven, Connecticut.

Originally printed in Great Britain.

CONTENTS

Preface to the Paperbound Edition

IT WAS PREDICTED by friendly critics of this work when it first appeared that it could not expect to win acceptance from professional scholarship for at least ten years. I am all the more grateful to Yale University Press for risking an anticipation of this prophecy by issuing a paperbound edition at this time. Nevertheless, in fairness to my more skeptical reviewers, admission should be made that several difficulties stand in the way of easy acceptance of the conclusions here argued. Mental distance which has intervened since the period of composition has made it easier for me, I hope, to see what some of these are.

This work seeks to demonstrate not one but several theses which are unfamiliar. They could feasibly have been presented separately in independent monographs to facilitate digestion, before being assembled into that pattern of interconnection which is here identified as a body of liberal political theory. They have been documented and the documents translated in full for the English reader. But it is evident from critical comment that the quality of the documentation is not really the issue—few even considered this part of the problem—but rather the unfamiliarity of the theses themselves, those intellectual constructs which were inferred from the documents and built upon them.

Thus it is proposed here that early Ionian science included as a central element in its speculations a fairly coherent theory of the origins of human society, technology, and civilization, itself based upon a theory of the development of man as a species out of previous species, a theory which can fairly be described as naturalist and evolutionary, in sharp contrast to the typological reasoning of Plato and Aristotle. This combined department of biological and cultural history I have labeled Greek anthropology. Though not unobserved by specialists, as noted in the first four appendices, it has received scant attention in the standard textbooks and none at all in the general histories of early Greek science and philosophy. It is as though this area of knowledge and the evidence for it, when presented to the attention of classical scholarship, has encountered a blind spot. This aspersion may be justified if one takes note, in contemporary scholarship of the pre-Socratics, of the very different status of metaphysical concepts attributed for example to the Milesian philosophers. Here, where original documentation does not exist, attention is lavished on speculative possibilities which seem to reflect more a bias of modern scholarship than conclusions enforced by philology.

A second demonstration attempted in these pages supports the thesis that in Periclean Athens there existed a body of political theory which could fairly be labeled democratic and egalitarian, a theory designed to support the practices of what has been called in modern times an open society. Such a proposition would perhaps have been accepted more readily two generations ago, before the disillusionments and defeats of two world wars had rendered us reluctant to consider the evidence for it.

But when it is further argued, as it is in this volume, that this body of political theory received direct speculative support from the Ionian science of man and society, this indeed strikes harshly upon the sensibilities of the Hellenist, who by instinct and training has been schooled to look for the theoretic basis of the free citizenship of the Greeks in the pages of Plato and Aristotle. It is argued here, on the contrary, that it was the view of man as an animal species, consisting of individuals whose common biological characteristics were descriptively more important than their social differences, which furnished essential theoretical support for a doctrine of political equality. The conclusion is drawn that, long before the Hellenistic age, Greek political theory was prepared to indicate the ground rules for a society in which the city-state was incidental, not essential, in which law was built up by human convention and rendered viable by the historical process, rather than derived from divine archetypes; a society in which language functioned as a vehicle of communication and of persuasion, by which men working on each other continually formulated common goals and purposes. The very different theories of Plato and Aristotle, so far from being a summation of previous Greek thinking in this department, were designed to counteract its effects, or more properly to call up the forces of an older order of Greek ideas to correct the balance of the new.

If this book speaks any truth about the Greek mind in its

formative phase, that mind was not really the kind of mind that it became in the Hellenistic age, when, under the combined influence of the Academy, the Lyceum, and the Stoa, it molded into shape what we now style "the great tradition" of the West. That tradition is much more conservative and metaphysical, aspirational and moralistic, than is the message of these pages. It can be replied that this "great tradition" is the one that is attested and defended fully in the philosophical writers and that if any earlier world-view existed, we cannot now be sure what it was. The documentation of what, for want of a better word, I have styled the Greek "liberal" position, is admittedly tortuous and difficult. But that there was such a position, in whatever variety of versions, is attested by one central fact, and that is the vehemence with which Plato and Aristotle sought to discredit it. To take their polemics at face value is, as I have written elsewhere, equivalent to accepting an estimate of the philosophy of Hume as that philosophy is refracted through the arguments of Kant.

As for the documentation, it is not inconsiderable, extending as it does over the pages of Democritus, of Plato's *Protagoras,* of Antiphon, and of the reports included by Aristotle in his *Ethics* and *Politics,* as I have spread these before the reader.* But, to repeat, I have concluded that the issue is not the documentation. In writing the history of early Greek philosophy and thought, a process of selection takes place in the mind of the modern historian which seems to reflect the obscure needs of our own time rather than the evidence contributed by original sources. Thus a historian who will dismiss or ignore the political aphorisms of Democritus finds no difficulty in reporting the organized beliefs of, say, the Pythagoreans, and in attributing these to the fifth and sixth centuries, though they remain wholly unsupported by any contemporary quotation. Objections taken to the proposition that a political theory of the sort described in these pages did actually exist seem to have less to do with philology, but a great deal to do with the preservation of certain sacred cows of the classical discipline.

It seems to be a fact that, within the confines of the world of classical scholarship, there is a perceptible tendency abroad to

---

*For an addendum to these, see now A. T. Cole, "The Anonymous Iamblichi and His Place in Greek Political Theory," *HSCP* 65 (1961).

concentrate attention upon the more traditional and even reactionary aspects of Greek culture. The things we look for as most significant in the Greek experience are no longer rationalism but religion, no longer reality but myth, not democracy but order (or its frequent breakdown), not experiment, often dangerous, but existentialist assurance, not tolerance but heroic affirmation.

Moreover, while scholarly resources have been multiplied, their use in research need not automatically guarantee a clear and distinct perspective upon Periclean ways of thinking. The metropolis of the mind inhabited by the Hellenist of today is not Athens but Alexandria. In terms of materials, the world of classical scholarship has indeed become an affluent society, well designed to protect its possessors against thinking subversive thoughts. It was in a simpler epoch of plainer living and high thinking that Democritus observed, "Poverty under a democracy is as much to be preferred to what men of power call prosperity, as is liberty to bondage."

E. A. H.

New Haven, Connecticut
April 1964

PREFACE

THE possibility of this book, though not yet its design, began to shape itself in my mind fifteen years ago, when I was still at the University of Toronto. Leisure for the teacher in the universities of North America is a commodity hardly bought, and my gratitude is due to the Guggenheim Foundation for giving it to me at that time. Bread then cast upon the waters has indeed returned only after many days, and in a form unforeseen, but it has returned. My second debt is to that great university I now serve, which as it gave me the freedom to lecture on this subject gave me also the opportunity to put it in order. The compilation of those bibliographical materials which are analysed in the appendices was materially aided by the services of my former pupil, Samuel De Merit.

As the processes of note-taking and translation and exegesis and bibliography gathered momentum, I began to seem to myself involved almost unwillingly in a task of restitution, an enterprise which would render historical justice to a group of forgotten men. In the fall of 1954 I resorted to solitude in New Hampshire in order to write out the story of their thought, and they can be said to have followed me there, as I sought to live with their memory, sitting beside a wood stove and composing the entire first draft in a sort of sustained fury of composition.

I could not remain unaware as I wrote that these men had a message which is contemporary, though a work of scholarship should, I suppose, do its best to ignore the fact. They argued that political and even moral convictions were negotiable, that the path of duty does not run counter to self interest, and that in cases of doubt it is better to prefer amity above justice. Since Kant and Hegel, these beliefs have not been fashionable. Rejecting them, we have preferred to train ourselves and our children to believe in moral and political absolutes, to the point where the two major powers of modern times now confront each other across the world, in what look suspiciously like two Platonic systems of complete and mutual intolerance. If Russia and America and their dependencies do indeed draw back from the atomic abyss, and allow themselves the luxury of survival, they will have listened at the eleventh hour to that tolerant and empirical kind of wisdom which in politics was promulgated twenty-three hundred years ago by those forgotten men, the Greek 'liberals'.

Tamworth, New Hampshire
  December, 1956

INTRODUCTION

THE boundaries of the word liberal, when used in a political context, are perhaps broad enough to justify its use in the title of this book. Its precise application to a given group of political theorists, who flourished in classic Greece, is described and defended in the first chapter.

Nevertheless, a difficulty of nomenclature remains. The doctrines of this group were developed in complete independence of the teachings of Plato and Aristotle. Their foundations were laid before Plato was born; the completed structure must already have been in existence to confront Aristotle when he composed his *Ethics* and his *Politics*. In short, what is here styled Greek liberalism grew and flowered in an intellectual climate which lay outside those walls with which Plato's idealism and Aristotle's teleology surrounded the Greek citizen and his city-state. Liberalism is a part of the intellectual history of classic Greece, but it is not part of those political concepts which have hitherto been accepted in the West as classic, as typically Greek, as the expression, definitive and complete, of a unique Greek experience of citizenship in the city-state.

Because the walls of that state, ideologically speaking, collapsed with Alexander's conquests, it has always been remarked that the physical setting of this supposedly classic system of concepts was already becoming antiquated even as it was being written. The history of western political theory from the Stoics to Karl Marx has a perceptible continuity, which disappears when one takes a step backward and in company with Plato and Aristotle enters the gates of the Greek *polis*. But political theory, just because it is theory, is never just a photograph of the particular institutions with which it may be dealing. In the West it has always used a set of intellectual frameworks, a series of leading concepts dealing with man and society, which have been employed as archetypes of explanation. As these have slowly changed and evolved, they have exhibited their own laws of intellectual progression. The originals were all, or nearly all, seeded in the writings of Plato and Aristotle. One can say that whenever western man has directed his thinking towards those problems created by his relation to his fellowmen, problems of society in general, of the state in particular, of government and law, of rights and responsibilities, of duties, of constitutions, of citizenship, he has consciously or otherwise used the political and often the moral vocabulary supplied to him by the two masters. This has meant that where he forms his own vision of what the political problems are, when he selects the issues which he thinks need treatment, his mind and hand are still guided under their remote control. This is as true of Marx as it was of Locke.

The words liberal and liberalism, from the time when they were applied politically in Europe in the latter half of the nineteenth century, and up to the period of their present use, with some difference of emphasis, in America, cannot escape this law of classic control.[1] To call Democritus and Protagoras, Antiphon or Lycophron, 'liberals' is unconsciously to identify them with ideological battles for intellectual positions won, lost and recaptured, in a battleground chosen for us by the two masters.

For reasons which, as we shall argue, had nothing directly to do with the political life as such, both Plato and Aristotle gave first priority to problems of political authority. This is not to say these were not vital problems. But it meant that at the level of practical application they concentrated almost exclusive attention on the mechanisms of power; at the theoretic level they devoted the energies of their joint genius to establishing a valid source, philosophically respectable, for the use of political power. They found this either in the eternal ideas outside time and space, or in the equally eternal forms inherent in the political process itself. The thinking of both, despite their differences, is committed to the proposition that society is a fixed quantity, or reaches towards a fixed quantity, or should do so. Both share a parallel conception of the human soul as itself a little cosmos, a closed system or an essence, either itself an eternal idea, or the final form of a natural process which becomes a fixed quantity, if it does not begin as such. These two determinate systems, the ideal closed society, and the completely organized soul, are then fitted together into an air-tight system of politics and morals. The act of organization as applied either to society or to the soul is not spontaneous nor is the system automatic. It requires discipline in the person and in the state to hold both the soul and the state in a condition of harmony and perfection. Hence the problem of building an intelligent authority over the whole had automatic priority in their thinking as against the disposition and behaviour and autonomy of the separate parts.

According to this type of thinking, then, man, society and law are all theoretically fixed quantities. An examination of historical process and environmental conditions is relevant only as it illustrates the presence of such fixed quantities in history. When history makes it difficult to identify them, it is better to ignore historical man altogether. The theory taken as a whole might remind one of an abstract painting—a likeness of the city state so simplified as to leave out of account the neighbouring territory, the ports and docks, the flow of seaborne commerce, and nations and territories beyond the horizon line.

When the walls of the city-state fell down, Stoicism used the materials to refurbish a larger conception of man and society which yet retained an almost fatal likeness to the original. For the new citizen of the world-state was discovered to be living in a community wholly designed for him by the same intelligence which had presided over the ideal city-state. He lived under a system of natural law founded on those same *a priori* principles which had supported the ideas and the forms, or had given structure to Aristotle's system of ends. As for himself, he remained an immortal essence structurally designed to live in harmony with this same system. Providence and nature in replacing the city-state had assumed all the status and fixity and the non-historical permanence characteristic of what had been replaced. Human brotherhood was now theoretically possible, and also a law of nations, superseding local custom and usage, but always and only under the authoritarian aegis of these majestic controls. Stoicism accordingly became the fitting intellectual instrument of that authoritarian system necessary to a world-empire. Any other forms of government, a democracy for example, remained by definition unthinkable.

As the Christian church assumed these intellectual responsibilities, the concept of intellectual authority was wedded to the parallel tradition of Hebrew monotheism and Mosaic Law. The theocratic community, with its orders and classes, its hierarchies temporal and spiritual, its guiding idea of a harmony of rulers and ruled in a chain of obedience which suspended itself from the worship of the creator of the universe, simply conserved in a rather extreme form the political theory of the two Greek masters.

But there was the conception of the soul, essentially Greek, and now in Christian theology married to Hebrew monotheism. In this new combination intellectual strains and stresses were set up which had not existed in the classic originals. For the soul had now become the personal creation of its maker, while still retaining its substantial and eternal reality. This meant it reached perfection as it obeyed its maker's will and established a completely intimate and organic relationship with him. But, in the classic representation, the soul and the state had remained as complementary systems whose harmonization was by definition taken for granted.

In this shift, slight but significant, there might lie some peril of collision at some future date between the personal soul of man and his society. At least it created two *foci* for man's loyalty – there was himself and his own salvation, and yet again there was his church, his society or his nation to which, as representing the divine intelligence, he also owed duty and obedience. A split was about to develop which the Greek mind would have had difficulty in conceptualizing.

The order of priorities in political thinking had been security and authority, law and order first, and liberty, freedom of choice, individual decision a bad second. When under pressures historical and economic the emphasis began to shift towards the second, it could do so only under the aegis of concepts derived from the first. The Renaissance, the Protestant Reformation, the English and French and American Revolutions, introduced a host of new political demands, all of them generally slanted in favour of a greater freedom for man at the expense of an increasing limitation of the political powers placed over man to govern him. But even if we discern in these demands the first programme of a future liberalism, none of them were framed in independence of the previous classic tradition. Human society and the human individual remained ideally fixed quantities. Aspirations for personal liberty, demands for commercial freedom, and rebellions to gain religious and national independence still sought to ground themselves on conceptions of morality and society which derived man and society from *a priori* principles, outside time and space and historical inspection. Thus the Natural Law of Grotius, as it heralded a dawning conception of an international commercial system which might reunite the scattered elements of medievalism in a new allegiance, and though it appealed to human reason at the expense of divine revelation, still clung to the postulate that the principles discoverable by that reason as they are inherent in human nature are unchallengeable and incontrovertible because human nature is a fixed quantity. The kind of physical universe disclosed by the science of Copernicus and Newton did nothing to weaken what was essentially a classic Greek position. When Locke thought he had found a foundation for the claims of the subject against his despot in that right to property with which all individuals are endowed in a state of nature, his projection backwards into primitive time of the theoretically complete personality is wholly Platonic as well as Christian. And so, when the cause of liberty was fought for in France and America under banners inscribed with the doctrine of the rights of man, the battle was conducted on behalf of those same convictions about the eternal nature of man's soul. The majestic language of the Declaration of Independence, appealing to the testimony of self-evident truths as before a bar of eternal justice, still used the formulas congenial to men who believed in a natural law written in the heavens and wished to use it to support the equally metaphysical conviction that all men as individuals have innate and inalienable rights.

Metaphysics in politics is perhaps no bad thing when used to serve such a cause, but it is a double-edged tool, more readily placed at the disposal of authority than liberty. And that perhaps is why the liberalism which from these intellectual seeds arose in the nineteenth century in response to the new needs of an industrial society often spoke with an ambiguous voice. The problems and the vocabulary were still Platonic and Aristotelian. It is possible that Hume's empiricism and naturalism, if wedded to the utilitarianism promoted by Bentham, could have provided support for a different and more effective type of defence of liberty, equality, and democracy than any which actually emerged. But Hume's influence was swamped and his distinction between reason and passion, and between fact and value, which could have eliminated the classic metaphysics from morals and politics, was obliterated by the idealist reaction which set in with Kant and Hegel. Once more man's personal life was placed under the control of imperatives beyond his own natural condition, though now apprehensible by his intuition, and his moral destiny was made dependent upon a corporate spiritual essence represented by that national society in which he lived and to which he now owed patriotic allegiance. Mill's perception of the spiritual health and strength conferred on the community by the unfettered exercise of free thought and speech reflected a powerful but isolated intuition of his moral sense, bearing little relation to his systematic principles. For any available principles of politics, being all stamped with the same colour of the classical, could never be accommodated to the proposition that raw 'opinion', individual, untutored and unorganized, could have any moral or social relevance. The main influence in political and moral theory lay with the German idealists, not with the English empiricists and utilitarians, nor with Mill. That the frame of reference for politics was once more metaphysical was convincingly demonstrated in the neo-idealism of the Oxford school, as formulated under Hegel's influence by T. H. Green, Bradley, and Bosanquet. This school, correctly representing perhaps the growing interest of the rising middle class in social conservatism, reasserted the Platonic postulate of the individual's moral dependence on the state and the identification of his own ends with the larger ends expressive of the spiritual substance of the continuing community. Meanwhile Marx, living in dingier surroundings than any envisaged by an Oxford don, was constructing a second memorial to Hegel's metaphysics, a system which swept away pragmatism and empiricism and individualism in order to place history under the tight control of a new form of natural law wholly authenticated by the operation of the dialectical reason; and even reintroduced that teleological fantasy of classicism, according to which all historical process reaches its completion in the perfect society, this time not the Greek city-state, but the classless industrial utopia.

Liberalism today is a temper, a state of mind, not easily identifiable with any particular school of political philosophy. But so far as it has concepts of its own, so far as the liberal mind tends to rally itself round preferred issues which it selects for emphasis, these are perceived and shaped within the conceptual limits set by the whole classic tradition. Thus *laissez faire* in economics presupposes a system of natural law, certainly not perceptible by the senses, which magically harmonizes the competing interests of individuals in a synthesis which becomes the common interest of all. The contrary policy whereby a welfare state devises organs of central authority to restrain the strong and protect the weak seeks to adapt more obviously the classic conceptions of the community to modern industrial conditions. As for the insistent protection of the civil and legal liberties of the individual against all organs of government, legislative and executive, which in America is the single most prominent characteristic of the liberal mind, this purpose carries the implication that individual men are inviolable essences, ends in themselves, who cannot be 'forced to be free'. Such doctrine, going back as it does directly to the letter and spirit of the American Bill of Rights, would be incomprehensible without many centuries of acceptance of the dogma that all individual personalities have an independent metaphysical status and have 'rights' which enjoy a metaphysical authority independent of the community.

Greek liberalism as it is to be discovered in the following pages was conceived in a wholly different intellectual climate. It was incapable of conceiving of human behaviour as obeying the control of a law of nature, single, universal and timeless, the same at all times and under all circumstances for all men. It was equally incapable of thinking of individuals with inalienable natural rights received from their creator or inherent in the structure of their personalities, for the simple reason that Platonism had not yet invented the basis for this notion of personality. Nor did it polarize its findings round the opposing claims of authority *versus* liberty, for Plato and Aristotle had not yet made the constitution of authority the central issue in politics. The Greek liberals occupy positions which from the vantage point of the long classic tradition can be viewed as intellectually naïve. But their thinking for all its simplicity has a rather formidable quality. Reaching across those barriers in the mind artificially set up by the systems of Plato and Aristotle, they seem to find intellectual company in unexpected quarters. These affinities are very diverse. Their vision of evolution conducted on a cosmic scale might have been approved by Darwin, Huxley and Spencer. But the conception proposed by Democritus of human government as a contract would have been understood best by the pre-feudal societies of northern Europe. Antiphon's violent attack on the tyranny of custom law would have been appreciated by Bentham. The pragmatism and empiricism of Protagoras would have won sympathy from Hume, James and Dewey. The claims put forward for philanthropy and good will as instinctual principles of social order anticipated the intuitions of primitive Christianity.

Where such parallels can be drawn, they are of course historically fortuitous. But it is not fortuitous that they are easiest to perceive where the influence of classicism, so-called, has been weakest. Democritus, Protagoras, Antiphon, and their successors were not 'liberals' in any classic sense of that term, and yet scarcely a better label is devisable for them. For at least the label has been a word of challenge, a banner of faith in the common man, and a plea for hope and philanthropy; a word which has drawn battle lines, rallying friends and identifying enemies. Things were not so very different in ancient Athens when the Sophists taught.

These same historical considerations help to explain why, to a reader with any acquaintance with modern histories of Greece or with modern text-books of political theory, the present treatment may seem unexpected. The history of Greek political theory, as also of Greek politics, has been written in modern times exactly as Plato and Aristotle would have wished it to be written. For the theory describes a morally virtuous state to which its morally virtuous citizens owe complete allegiance, and in which they realize the perfect human life. This is then applied to the facts as exhibited in the career of the Athenian democracy from the days of Cleisthenes to the surrender to Macedon. Since the two patently do not fit, preference is given to theory and the facts are evaluated so as to be placed under the control of the theory, with many moral head-shakings. It would be safe to say that no modern historian, describing the equally complex careers of the French, British, or American democracies in the present century, and the perils they have encountered within and without, would ever take refuge in those platitudes which still find their way into histories of Greece, composed by historians palpably unaware of their own obedience to Platonic canons of historiography.

On the side of political theory, among the ranks of the historians of Greek thought, there have been a few exceptions,[2] but these have registered themselves more as angry protests against the influence of classic political theory as a whole, for it has been assumed that, aside from the idealism and the teleology of Plato and Aristotle, none other seriously existed in Greece.[3] Why has this been so? Why has it been so easy for scholarship to close its ear against any other voice? The answer lies surely not in the lack of critical equipment to evaluate the available testimonies, as these exist both within and without the writings of Plato and Aristotle. There has been a block in the mind, an unconscious unwillingness to use the equipment. Behind every historian of thought, controlling the selection of his evidences and the weighting of his values, stands that cast of moral preferences, that pattern of moral prejudices, which he has inherited from his epoch and which form part of his own intellectual climate. Modern historians of Greek politics and Greek political theory have not written very much in their field which does not reflect the control, direct or remote, of the two systems of thought set up respectively by Kant and Hegel. In England, to repeat, it was these two divergent forms of idealism, personal and political, which contributed the most powerful influence to that synthesis of political theory achieved at Oxford by Green, Bradley and Bosanquet. There is a standard English text-book on Greek political theory[4] which is justly admired for the eloquence with which it expounds the political teachings of the *Gorgias*, *Republic*, *Statesman* and *Laws*. If, in its pages, exposition often reads as though it were fervent apology; if the naturalists and the materialists, the Sophists and the democrats, are treated only as faint and futile voices protesting off-stage; it is surely relevant to observe the ever-present inspiration, in these same pages, of the Oxford school of neo-idealism.[5]

To attempt to resurrect the Greek liberals is an act of historical justice. It can be mistaken for something different, a polemic at the expense of the doctrinal positions of Plato and Aristotle. But this book is not intended as such. At the present date of writing, there is a kind of warfare abroad conducted against the Greek idealists and their influence on social thinking, and more particularly against Plato. Correspondingly, conservative-minded historians are rallying to Plato's defence.[6] The argument of the following pages is not, strictly speaking, addressed to this controversy either *pro* or *con*. It is of course assumed that by any common sense definition of the word liberal as it is applied in politics Plato is not a liberal thinker. His social formulas are completely authoritarian, in the *Laws* as they were in the *Republic*, and Aristotle's hardly less so. But this need not imply a negative estimate of their over-all contribution to the science of society. Their genius had made a social discovery of immense importance, a discovery the implications of which preoccupied them to the exclusion of almost all other interests. This was nothing less than the perception that a system of university education had now become socially indispensable for the progress of western culture. For this they set themselves to devise the institutional forms, the curriculum, the techniques of instruction, and the necessary intellectual discipline. As Rousseau rightly saw, the *Republic* is the greatest single treatise on education ever written. They made the mistake, easy to recognize in retrospect, of identifying the academic apparatus with the state apparatus. It was a mistake natural under the circumstances of the time for men who had the compelling genius to invent the idea of an institution of higher learning as the functional instrument of western culture. They can be forgiven if, in their devotion to such a revolutionary conception, they failed to perceive the precise relationship which history would assign to such an institution in the society which it came into being to serve.

Modern democracy in the West can be said to exhibit, at the level of practical application, a synthesis of the postulates of the Greek liberals on the one hand, and of Greek idealism on the other. Its organs of political power are so framed as to express as far as possible some conformity with the thesis that a common mind exists, that the common men are best judges of their own political interests, that political wisdom is empirical and pragmatic, and that men are naturally more inclined to co-operate than to fight, and that divergent personal opinions can be negotiated to the point of effective decision. This is the kind of political programme which would best represent the liberal temper in Greek politics. But equally, if modern democracies function with administrative efficiency and judicial objectivity, it is because they have adopted those instruments and techniques of training in the skills and the service of government which were first articulated by the two masters of the Greek idealist tradition.

INTRODUCTION

REFERENCES

1 In F. M. Watkins *The Political Tradition of the West* (1948), liberalism is even viewed as "the secular form of Western civilization".

2 see for example Warner Fite *The Platonic Legend* (1934); R. H. S. Crossman *Plato Today* (1937); A. D. Winspear *Genesis of Plato's Thought* (1940); B. Farrington *Science and Politics in the Ancient World* (1940); Karl R. Popper *The Open Society and its Enemies* (2nd edition 1952) Part One.

3 but cf. Winspear (note 2), cap. 5, on "The Progressive Philosophy", where however the basis of this philosophy is represented to be a Greek brand of dialectical materialism.

4 Sir Ernest Barker *Greek Political Theory: Plato and his Predecessors* (1918: 3rd edtn. 1947) and cf. the same author's *Political Thought of Plato and Aristotle* (1906) and *The Politics of Aristotle translated with introduction, notes and appendices* (1946).

5 The fourth chapter of this work deals with 'The Political Theory of the Sophists'. To this the author has added a version of the Antiphon papyrus, but this would appear to have been printed almost as an afterthought, without being allowed to have any effect on the previous exposition.

6 Two such works have recently appeared in the same year: John Wild *Plato's Modern Enemies and the Theory of Natural Law* (1953) and R. B. Levinson *In Defence of Plato* (1953).

THE LIBERAL TEMPER IN
GREEK POLITICS

CHAPTER I

PREFATORY:

THE EDEN MYTH AND THE SCIENCE OF MAN

> The hand of Chance is kind, and I her child
> Naming myself shall not lose dignity.
> She was my mother, and the natural months –
> My brothers and my sisters – brought me up,
> In littleness and greatness measured me.
> Such being my native state, how should I rise
> To something else that would forget to learn
> The secret of my race and what I am?
>
> [*Oedipus Tyrannus*, 1080–1085]

THESE words were spoken by Oedipus the King not many minutes before the revelation of his birth was to strip him of royalty and leave him polluted, blinded, and destitute. There is something occult in what he says. What does it mean that he was mothered in Chance's bosom, that the seasonal months were his familiar kin, that he had a natural estate of which he was proud and which yet required that he know his race and himself?

Factual explanation can be given: he now knows himself to be a foundling; he has lived through many vicissitudes, and feels his achievements can cancel any shame of lowly origin. But this supreme of Greek tragedies operates at more than one level of meaning. Oedipus, born a royal babe in the city of Thebes, had yet been transferred crippled and helpless to the mountainside. There under the weather, in earth's bosom, he had somehow survived, to be transferred back again to an adopted royalty in Corinth. Thence he comes back to Thebes and solves the famous riddle and conquers the Sphinx. He has now become technical, resourceful, and political, exercising a skill of mind which has identified the nature of man and paved the road to political power. Elected king of Thebes, he is the source of her security and the symbol of her law; state and society repose in his keeping. But he is to be returned to the mountain side, to the lonely natural earth whence he came. This is his destiny, and for this he prays in abnegation at the close of the play. Once more he is revealed a child of Chance; his company will be the seasons, the sky and the earth, which allowed him to survive.

There is something in the symbolism of his career, and in the words with which it is memorialized, which is evocative of another drama, played out in the *fifth* century not upon the tragic stage but in the theories and speculations of Greek science. It was a drama which, in the generation when this play was written, the Greek anthropologists were recommending to the intellectual attention of their contemporaries. We know from the *Antigone* that their science had already fascinated the mind of Sophocles, for he had in that play celebrated the marvellous miracle represented by man the tool-user, the thinking reed, the conqueror of nature and the builder of cities. But the historical vision, perceived as in a glass darkly, was complex. Greek anthropology had its hero: he was *homo sapiens*; but he was also variously a worm, a fish, and a savage. Like Oedipus, he had an ambivalent character and a doubtful destiny. He too had been a foundling, discovered on the earth's surface mysteriously alive, whose early existence had been nasty, brutish and brief. Moreover, both in his origin and in his historical development, he seemed to exhibit like Oedipus the two contrary forces of chance and intelligence: his life as an animal organism was a physical thing, biologically determined, yet it could embrace the discovery of technologies, the building and ruling of cities, the moulding of custom and law. How explain this paradox, this cosmic phenomenon? By what complex paths of historical growth had he become what he at present was?

To Plato and to Aristotle the answer was theoretically simple. They denied that there had been any significant development at all. To understand man, you fix your gaze on what he should be. For in a sense this is what he always has been – a species apart from the brutes, rational and moral, intelligent and just. If man's practice did not fit this theory, then man was to be corrected and educated till it did. For the norms by which his behaviour is governed, while they lie within the cosmos, lie outside history and process. They are as eternal as the cosmos itself. If the cosmos had a history, well and good. But it was always a history which exhibited a complete intelligence already present in the beginning.

The anthropologists were not so sure. They tried to look backwards, and to imagine a pre-moral and pre-intellectual condition of man. They felt that what he was now could best be understood by building an historical bridge between the present and the past; and between man and what had been, and still was, not-man. They found man complicated and unpredictable and not always consistent, and they tended to leave him so. Since the two conceptions, idealist and historical, continually collide with and interact on each other, it is difficult to tell the story of the second without paying some attention to the first. In the same moment that we turn to look at Greek anthropology, we have also to give some consideration to Plato's use of it, or his misuse.

But when Greek anthropological science and not Platonic metaphysics is to supply the main theme, the haunting words of Oedipus make a better preface than anything Plato could say. For here speaks a hero who presented himself and spoke and felt like a philosopher king, yet had been a child of nature and perhaps still was. As a little animal he had survived and grown; as a thinking mind he had risen to be king; and all under the presidency of historic chance. His story was not so unlike that of *homo sapiens* himself, that creature of mystery whose historical nature Greek anthropological science was proposing to explore as a dark secret of the past.

There was a degree of impiety in the proposal, for, if man was not a fixed quantity, neither were his morals and his law. Justice itself might be only a creation of history, just as humanity was. To see the archetype of justice written in the heavens for ever, and imitable on earth in the ideal statesman, might, by substituting metaphysics for historical science, create dangerous delusions of grandeur. This is exactly what classical Greek philosophy did. By its standards, Oedipus the King, instrument of salvation for Thebes and source of political authority in the state, is a 'great' man, typical exponent of the eternal norms of justice, political authority and wisdom as applied in a given social context. He is a fixed quantity. If he falls, there is either, in his otherwise perfect virtue, a tragic flaw, an excess or a blindness, some incautious neglect of divine power, which merits exposure; or, if none, then

he leaves the stage with his moral dignity still essentially un-
impaired, a hero to the end, and a hero of the civilized condition. But suppose he is not a fixed quantity? Suppose that his
magnitude is only a present condition of the historical process,
a relative increase upon his previous littleness –

> . . . the natural months –
> My brothers and my sisters – brought me up,
> In littleness and greatness measured me –

Suppose that his kingdom of Thebes, with its religion and laws,
is a pattern of chance configuration that sprang from the putre-
faction of worms, with twisted roots that reached down not to
realms of death but to life and growth, formless, vital, without
prejudice or prejudgment? He was the scientist who had
solved one riddle of the Sphinx, the riddle of the nature of
that human being who starts a helpless babe and returns to a
frail senility. Now in his own life that knowledge is pushed
further and made something like a historical formula: look not
at what I am become, but at what I started from, a small thing
upon the mountainside. To that estate I now return. This is the
goal of the knowledge of science, to know what was not human in
man before it became human, and what was blind and instinctual
before it became intelligent; to trace all the brave show of the
civilized estate to necessities of the biological life and even to the
chance of historical development:

> Such being my native state, how should I rise
> To something else that would forget to learn
> The secret of my race and what I am?

There is a whole school of moral and political philosophy latent
here. This is not the primitivism of those philosophers who saw
in the past a Utopia that had been lost, and imagined man fallen
from a previous grace. Rather it is an empirical sociology based
on historical principles. Viewing man's present technology and
institutions and even his morality as the end-product of a long
process, it is prepared pragmatically to accept them and evaluate
them as inventions of man devised to meet his historical needs. In
later antiquity, this school of political and moral theory came to
be regarded as outside the main stream – and the 'best' stream –
of Hellenic thought. The effect of the exclusion upon the history

of ideas lasted long after the world of pagan antiquity had passed away.

For in the West, at least since the Hellenistic age, it has been the prevailing temper to think of morality and law in *a priori* terms as resting on principles which are independent of time, place, and circumstance, whether these principles are viewed as inherent in the structure of the universe, or as expressions of the divine will and purpose. Plato and Aristotle had taught that man's personal virtue and civic organization should express certain ideal forms of justice and goodness, or be viewed as reaching toward certain ideal ends of human and cosmic development. In the teaching of the church, these forms or ends became expressions of the will of God as revealed in Scripture, which spelled out rules of human behaviour for man in some detail. The united influence of classic Greek philosophy and religious revelation built up the conviction that man has an unchanging spiritual nature which is either itself the source, or is created by the source, of a moral law both timeless and complete.

But there is a radically different conception which views human codes of behaviour less as principles than as conventional patterns, embodying not eternal laws written in the heavens or printed on man's spiritual nature, but rather common agreements elaborated by man himself as a response to collective need. They are the rules of the game by which he finds it convenient to live, and, as such, they are subject to change and development as the game of life itself becomes more complicated. All societies need them in order to live an orderly existence and, indeed, the more primitive the society, the tighter the code seems to be. But in many practical details these conventions represent historical accidents. The various languages themselves, embodying as they do various types of standardized practice in the manipulation of speech sounds, illustrate this accidental quality. Morals and law can be viewed in this way *a posteriori* as a kind of second language, part of the historical process, which like language itself never reaches finality. Their validity is temporal, not eternal.

At bottom, these competing conceptions rest upon competing doctrines of the origin and nature of man himself. According to the first, man must always have existed much in his present form and character. Either he came into existence somehow on the earth as a superior species with special prerogatives, walking upright, able to speak, intelligent, morally conscious and already prepared for social perfection; or else he was created in the image of perfection by God. His spiritual nature rests in either case on metaphysical foundations. This can be called the anti-historical view of man. Civilizations may vary in their material forms, but man the human being has been a constant.

The second and non-metaphysical view of his morality and law is derived from an historical science which argues, first, that the human species emerged from non-human forms of life, by some evolutionary process, so that man's present body and brains represent the end-product of a long series of mutations; and, second, that his moral and social codes have developed since he became intelligent, as a continuation of the evolutionary process, which has now come under the control of his own consciousness. Thus his very language is only a highly developed form of that means of communication open also to the brutes, and his codes of behaviour, like his language, have been 'invented'; they represent successive adaptations to new needs. His developing intelligence continually complicates its patterns of response, and at the same time discovers new needs which evoke the response. This does not imply any necessarily mechanical relationship between man and his environment. Our species seems to have an inner biological motivation which seeks to vary its own forms of expression. Civilization as a historical process can be viewed as both moulding man and as moulded by man. But the only science which can understand it and evaluate it is historical and anthropological; a science which does not shrink from the assumption that man never emerged full-grown upon the earth.

There is no necessary competition here between moralism and immoralism. The historical and evolutionary approach to morals and law is no less likely than the metaphysical to come up with the conclusion that 'mercy, pity, peace and love' have in fact proved to be historically necessary to man's survival and development. Indeed, in the history of the west, the violence done to these virtues has been more often committed by men who professed to march under metaphysical banners.

The Greeks, so far as we know, were the first people to realize that the religious-metaphysical and the biological-historical furnished alternative explanations of the nature of man and man's culture. Hebrew thought had embraced the first alternative exclusively; the older tradition in Greece itself was similar. It received, as we shall see, classic exposition in Hesiod, and was then revived, some two and a half centuries later, in a sophisticated form by Platonism. According to this Greek formula, there is no history, properly speaking, of civilization, no developmental progress in technology and morals. One looks back to a Golden Age now lost, in which man in his unspoilt nature lived in close company with God, in a Greek version of Eden. Perhaps present degeneration can be cancelled and the Age of Gold return; if so, the story of man is cyclical rather than consistently regressive. But in neither case is this conception evolutionary or, indeed, in any strict sense historical at all.

Had Greek culture, like the Egyptian or Hebrew, been centrally controlled by an organized religion, it is improbable that any other notion of man's history would have been allowed to gain currency. But in fact the Greek cults retained only local status as patterns of inherited response, offering a rich and competitive variety, over which no single political control was ever established. Thus follows the familiar fact that the Greeks were never compelled to subscribe to a single orthodoxy of belief.

This allowed Greek science, roughly in the two centuries between Hesiod and Plato, to construct by degrees the outline of what we shall call an anthropology. Different versions might vary in detail, but the governing premiss remained constant. Man is to be viewed in the first instance not as hero or poet, soldier or citizen, tyrant or demagogue, but as a human being, a member of a natural species occupying its place among all the other species of organic life (*phyta* and *zoa*). This species has a history of development. At the biological level, it emerged from a pre-human condition; at the cultural level, the species began its career in savagery, and has mastered the arts of social and technical progress only by slow degrees and painful experiment. There never has been or could have been a Golden Age.

It follows also that there never could have been an original law recognizably moral and political to which man has always owed allegiance. On the contrary, law and justice become recognizable as norms of conduct only as our civilized condition advances, and they are therefore only a facet, even if a very vital one, of our technological progress. No form of social institution has proved historically to be sacrosanct. So far as the scientists of the fifth century could see, from their own foreshortened perspective, there had been a tendency for life to become less savage and more humane, and for forms of government to become correspondingly less autocratic and to rest more on negotiation of opinion.

It is this willingness to take account of man scientifically as a species, with only relative importance in the cosmos, that prepares the intellectual climate for what we shall call in this book the liberal temper in Greek politics. The term *liberal* can mislead; in application it should be carefully qualified. The qualifications, however, will emerge as our portraits of Democritus and Protagoras and Antiphon and their successors are completed. What has to be asserted at the beginning is that, in sum, here is a whole philosophy of man and a point of view towards his morals and politics profoundly different from the classic view so familiar from text-books and printed so deeply on the mind of the west by Plato and Aristotle. For example, in the liberal-historical view, the city-state is a useful form of society, but it can never be viewed as unique, or indeed as ideal; there are too many others. Justice and law can never be placed above or beyond men to regulate them by divine or metaphysical fiat; on the contrary, they are responses to all-too-human needs; they are patently evolved by trial and error, and remain only as imperfect approximations of our wants. Even more fundamentally, justice and law may themselves be evaluated by criteria derived from the methods of science itself. What has been the aim of man's historical development if it is viewed as a whole? The clues seemed to point to a growing preference for agriculture instead of hunting, and for commerce to supplement agriculture; a preference for negotiation instead of war, and for affection (*philanthropia* and *eunoia*) in place of competition (*philotimia* and *philonikia*); for complex political societies in which some adjustment between the powers of the strong and the needs of the many can be worked out. Considered as biological entities, men are all equal to each other, for they have identical desires and needs and organs; and the society required to express this fact would tend to be itself egalitarian. The kind of knowledge required to make political and moral choices cannot be derived from *a priori* forms or changeless principles; it must be drawn empirically from an historical process which is always changing, and applied pragmatically and partially in given situations as they arise.

THE EDEN MYTH & THE SCIENCE OF MAN

These are some examples of the ways in which the liberal temper, as exhibited in Democritus, Protagoras, Antiphon, and their successors in the fourth century, collided head-on with the idealism of Plato and the teleology of Aristotle. Scattered opinions of this sort might arise as individual intuitions in the mind of any thinker exposed to the democratic process of Athens. They might be formulated very differently according as they expressed the confidence of a Democritus or the despair of an Antiphon. But taken together they constituted a way of thinking, a pattern of ideas flexible but recognizably coherent, and rightly regarded by their opponents as dangerous to idealism and to authoritarian forms of political theory.

Since liberalism built its intellectual foundations upon the anthropologies of the pre-Socratics, these have first to be described. Their documentation demands of the historian certain niceties of critical method. Only scraps survive, resembling wreckage left on the shore which, though fragmentary, is curiously shaped and carved, carrying a message so specific as to betray the type of vessel to which it originally belonged. Yet just as the interpreter of such wreckage would have to know something about patterns in shipbuilding of the era to which the scraps belonged, so it is useful in this case to grasp first the uses to which, as a matter of open record, this anthropology was put by others who borrowed it, and on whom we have to rely for testimonies which fill in gaps and supply perspectives. While its impact was still fresh upon the Greek mind, it found its way into three Greek plays by three Greek dramatists, and some outline of its teaching is recoverable from two speeches and a chorus in these plays. It is fortunate that the earliest of the three imitations, by Aeschylus, is the most ambitious, and is rendered in a context which seeks to dramatize the historical grandeur of the conception. The Sophoclean version in the *Antigone*, though briefer and more incidental, does equal justice to this grandeur. A character in Euripides' *Suppliants* borrows the conception mechanically, and subverts it to serve an alien purpose. Nearly four centuries later, after the anthropological approach to history had already been eclipsed through the influence of the two great classical philosophers, it was resurrected by the historian Diodorus in epitomized form as a sort of preface to all history. This Hellenistic echo characteristically survived in an author devoted to the principles of a school of history which had resisted the influence of Plato and Aristotle.

The versions of the three tragedians guarantee a pre-Socratic date for Greek anthropology; the late epitome preserves the essentially naturalistic and non-theological terms in which it was framed. But these reports nevertheless remain only echoes; they are not the work of original thinkers, and their effect upon the record is correspondingly blunted. The structural impact of anthropology upon the history of Greek thought is lost.

This negative result was guaranteed by the next stage in the evidential story which we have to consider. For Plato and Aristotle both 'took up' the anthropology of previous thinkers, and stood it upon its head. To their masterly manipulation we owe the fact of its disappearance, in its original scientific form, from the history of Greek philosophy. Its conquest and elimination were achieved not by frontal polemics, but by absorption of certain elements into an alien but powerfully constructed system of metaphysics, so that the Platonic and Aristotelian versions remained to capture the imagination of posterity and to reinforce idealistic and teleological convictions about man. The 'Darwinian' and 'behaviourist' version (to use a very loose analogy) was crowded off the stage of philosophy; it became unattractive to later antiquity and fell almost wholly into neglect, except where the Epicureans sought for their own purposes to keep it alive.

Thus the problem of reporting on the early Greek anthropologies is inextricably bound up with the manner of their disappearance. Some of what they had to say in detail is found in Plato and Aristotle, but precisely in these contexts is care also taken to obliterate the evolutionary and naturalistic perspective. Since the writings of Plato and Aristotle exist for him who runs to read, the best method to follow might be first to describe their versions, being careful to include the premisses which they are designed to serve, and then to cast backwards and seek to recover the originals as they once existed in a wholly altered philosophical context.

In fact, the method to be followed has to be a little more complicated than this. Plato uses anthropology in two different ways: either he subverts it, turning the whole story backwards to serve a devolutionary and anti-historical conception of man's career; or he manipulates it – and this is much more subtle – to suggest that, while there has been technological development, there has been, strictly speaking, no moral development, nor could there be. For man as citizen, and for the city-state in which he lives, there are certain *a priori* patterns to which both must conform. Somehow the end was also present in the beginning; and there is indeed an end: history stops with the Greek city-state. This compromise of Plato's between evolution and teleology appealed strongly to Aristotle, and he elaborated it to form the basis of his *Politics*.

The first and wholly subverted versions are regressions, though in sophisticated form, to a traditional pattern of Greek thinking which was set by Hesiod, though he presumably did not invent it. These let us report first; then, over against them, should stand the stark contrast and shock offered by that *schema* of human progress which attracted the imagination of Aeschylus and Sophocles, and was summed up by Diodorus. Having thus juxtaposed the two extremes, we are in a position to estimate those compromise versions offered by Plato in his *Protagoras* and in the second book of his *Republic*, and by Aristotle in the first book of the *Politics*, which in fact became dominant in classical thought, and continued to dominate western speculation in this field until modern science forced a complete break with classicism. Only when this evidence is all in does it become possible and proper to consider those authentic scraps of early speculation in this field which survive from the pre-Socratics, or to attempt to organize them in their proper context. By that time it will have become clear to any examiner of this curiously carved wreckage that fashions in naval architecture, so to speak, had undergone a radical change after the close of the fifth century; and he had better be careful to which type of structure he refers the materials that he finds.

CHAPTER II

HISTORY AS REGRESS:

THE *WORKS AND DAYS*, THE *STATESMAN*, THE *LAWS*

T HE *Works and Days* of Hesiod contains the classic Greek statement of the Eden dream:

> In old days the tribes of men used to live upon this earth
> Far, far removed from evils and far from grievous labour
> And far from fell disease which brings on men their dooms.
> [*W.D.* 90-92]

Immunity to hard labour and immunity to bodily ills – these are the regretful yearnings of an early agricultural economy which finds wish-fulfilment by projecting backwards. When we add that for Hesiod this romance of the imagination was ended by the arrival of Woman, the beautiful, the insidious, the foolish and the dangerous [*W.D.* 56-89; cf. *Theog.* 570-613], we get likewise the inevitable note of disillusionment with sex which seems to have been as primal an experience of *homo sapiens* as were his difficulties with the soil.

This nostalgia, be it noted, is in effect a refusal to accept material reality or to come to terms with it. It occurs in a context in which the poet has already strongly hinted at two other connected ideas: first, the loss of such an Eden is part of man's penalty for gaining the use of fire; second, the disaster was the work initially of Prometheus but was compounded by the arrival of Woman, both of them characters who became dangerous to man through their powers of misplaced cunning and guile. Hesiod's narrative conveys the inevitable suggestion that Eden was lost through eating of the fruit of the tree of knowledge. There is no hint of that technology which later theorists linked with the gift of fire. But the whole story implies a moral rejection not only of the material conditions of life, but of the resources of hand and brain by which they could be improved. This way out, says Hesiod in effect, is hopeless. It cannot make men happier or better or more secure; it can only embroil them with Zeus. We can only look back and pray that the good old days will come again.

His form of nostalgia might not have made such a powerful impress if his poem had not proceeded to give it a kind of spurious historicity in the famous account (*logos*) of the five ages of man. This account itemizes the protest against the present uttered by an ethically conscious but unhistorical mind. His objections are disguised in the form of the story of three successive failures of three generations of men. This serves as a framework within which the vices of the present age can be presented cumulatively in a kind of classified series. Against them, at the beginning of his tale, he sets the opposite and ideal condition. This becomes a repetition of his earlier statement of Eden, but now in amplified form. The two conditions of man, in Eden and out of it, in effect define each other by their juxtaposition and their contrast.

The original race of gold: [*W.D.* 109]

1. was created in the age of Kronos [111]
2. lived like gods [112]
3. enjoyed a heart secure
4. was far removed from labour [113]
5. and affliction
6. never grew old but was always physically vigorous [114]
7. and able to enjoy itself [115]
8. died easily like falling asleep [116]
9. enjoyed an abundant food supply [117]
10. which the glebe yielded spontaneously [118]
11. enjoyed a distribution of 'works' [119]
12. which was voluntary and peaceable
13. and was rich in flocks [120]
14. and beloved of the gods.

This catalogue of blessings repeats and expands the two main complaints already made – that we have to work so hard and are also vulnerable to disease. But in items 11 and 12 something else is perhaps added – a muffled protest against economic competition and war, an aspiration for a utopia where co-operative relations would be automatic; significant, this, of a view of social evolution which later authors will convert into speculative form.

The second race of silver: [*W.D.* 127]

1. were far inferior
2. quite different in physique [129]
3. and in sense
4. babyhood and childhood lasted a hundred years [130]
5. but their maturity was short-lived [132]
6. and witless [134]
7. unable to refrain from mutual aggression
8. and indifferent to worship of the gods [135]
9. for this Zeus, in anger, eliminated them [138]

Presumably Kronos' reign has already ended. This catalogue of human frailties over which Zeus presides fastens on an aspect of the human condition which the poet finds peculiarly painful – the protracted helplessness of the infant and child, the long postponement of maturity, which man alone of the animals has to cope with. The poet creates a dramatic exaggeration of this curse, which we still bear, and for which in the previous utopia there had been no necessity, for men apparently sprang full-grown from the soil. But he then proceeds to another and quite independent protest, against that habit of lawless and mutual aggression to which utopia had been immune. This is linked directly with the habit of impiety. The moral sense is already alive, linking religious fear and awe with the pursuit of peaceful relations between man and man.

The third race: [*W.D.* 143]

1. were created of Zeus [144]
2. of bronze but also of ash-trees [144-5]
3. with brazen armour, houses and tools and no iron at all [150-1]
4. not bread eaters [146]
5. with an adamant spirit [147]
6. and huge physical strength [148]
7. war and aggression were their only occupation [145]
8. in fact, a terrible race [148]
9. who however, were likewise eliminated by their own violence. [152]

Conceivably this is a memory of the bronze age of Mycenean Greece, as that memory lingered in the sagas. If so, it is combined with a social critique repeated from the second race: unmitigated violence, already proved dangerous for the men of silver, here becomes self-destructive for the men of bronze, for all their terrible strength.

The fourth race of men: [*W.D.* 157]

1. were created by Zeus [158]
2. were superior and more righteous [159]
3. being the race of heroes – the demigods, so called
4. who fought and fell before Thebes and Troy [161-5]
5. but a few were assigned to the isles of the blest at the ends of the earth [167-71]
6. where they dwell, in heart secure [170]
7. and the glebe yields them its fruit twice a year [172]
8. under the reign of Kronos. [169]

The poet, having put his utopia in the remotest past, as he reaches forward towards the darkening present comes upon an interruption in his descent. He has reached the immediate ancestors claimed by his own audience, the heroes of the Homeric wars. For him they are not a mythical race, a lost Mycenean culture, but a generation which sprang immediately to life from the sagas. So he not only separates them from the men of bronze but seems to reverse the historical descent. These were, after all, great men, and therefore righteous men, even though not the first men, and for a select few he even revives and repeats in the isles of the blest some of the conditions which had characterized his lost Eden.

So we come to the fifth and last: [*W.D.* 174]

1. They are of iron [176]
2. with labour unceasing [177]
3. and care
4. and affliction
5. and destruction [178]
6. children fail to resemble parents [182]
7. or to honour and respect them or repay them [185-8]
8. ties of hospitality, of comradeship and kinship are broken [183-5]
9. and there is no respect for oath, for right, for good [190]
10. only for bad and for deeds of aggression [191]
11. physical violence prevails [189, 192]

39

12. restraint (*aidos*) is not practised [193]
13. the inferior confounds the superior with crooked, dishonest statements [193-4]
14. riotous competition prevails [195-6]
15. cities are destroyed [189]
16. restraint and nemesis abandon men and take refuge with the gods [197-200]
17. leaving no remedy against evil for mankind. [200-1]
18. physical degeneration will shorten the life span [181]
19. until Zeus eliminates them. [180]

The poet may or may not have had difficulty with his own children. At any rate, these complaints against the younger generation are symptomatic. The catalogue, taken as a whole, reads like the perennial and peevish complaint of an ageing conservative whose hardening habits and faculties cannot come to terms with youth or with changing conditions. There is something unmistakably personal about it. Yet for all that, the tone of genuine social and moral critique is not entirely lost. Ruthless competition and dishonesty in contractual obligations, physical violence and war, are all viewed with the intense vision of a man yearning for a better and happier life than the human race has the wit to devise for itself – a life which he so powerfully projected backwards into the age of gold.

If we have lingered over Hesiod before coming to Plato, it is for two main reasons, which explain Hesiod's importance for the history of thought. First, by the very boldness of his contrasts he forecasts for future thinkers what will become a central issue of moral philosophy: there is or should be a good society and it has certain quite definite characteristics. The habit of forming ideal standards of political and social judgment began with him. Second, his fierce rejection of the present order and his grandiose attempt to visualize these standards by projecting them into the past made him the father of all thinkers who said: 'Social standards are indeed divine, have always existed, but have been temporarily lost'. Against this backward vision and this *a priori* epistemology, which was to receive such formidable support from Plato, the anthropology of the scientists was to grapple in an embrace of death.

Plato's dialogue the *Statesman* [*Politicus*] seeks to define the scope and character of the governing authority in a Platonic state. In pure theory, this authority is identified with the wisdom exercised by a benevolent autocrat whose procedures conform to those exact and timeless forms of governmental science by which his temporal decisions are regulated. In actual fact, as Plato recognizes, his task is more complex than this *a priori* epistemology would suggest: he is at once the representative of an ideal formula, independent of time and place, and also the executive who presides over a complex technological society of differentiated functions, engaged in production, distribution and the like. To dramatize this paradox, Plato [at *Polit.* 269cff] tells one of his tales of the olden time, which with some compression can be paraphrased as follows:

This whole world and its contents, animate and inanimate, passes in the course of endless history through alternating periods or cycles, in one of which its motion is perfectly ordered, under the direct control of the ideal intelligence of its creator, and in the other of which the creator lets the world go, the motion is reversed, and the imperfection and the disorder latent in the world's matter begin to gain the upper hand. We live now in such a cycle of disorder: our remote ancestors lived under the ideal cycle in the reign of Kronos. The shift from cycle to cycle, when it occurs, always inflicts cataclysmic shock upon animals and men, leaving only a few survivors to start the new cycle.

In that ideal time, men sprang full-grown from the earth, or could be said to be 'resurrected'. Biological development was in reverse, not towards old age but toward youth and then childhood, till they vanished quite away. This happened to all but a few who were conveyed by God to some other lot [271c2]. It was a spontaneous life, with abundant food, supplied by earth without need of agriculture; even the weather was different. As to social organization, subordinate gods under the direction of the divine ruler governed the various species in departments, and handled their 'distribution' with complete success, with the result that while there were no 'states' in the present sense, there were also no wars, factions or cannibalism [271d-e].

Was it a far happier epoch? If they were able to think and share in the mutual pursuit of knowledge, it certainly was [272b-d]. However that may have been, the time came for the supreme being and his subordinates to let go the helm of the world and its

departments, leaving them to go their own way [272e4]. The shock
destroyed almost all life at first. But once it was absorbed, the
cosmos, with the memory of its creator and teacher still fresh,
started off well [273a-b]. But the distractive and disordered influence of its own "muddy vesture of decay" [273b4] soon increased
to the danger-point [273c-d], until God once more takes over direct
hold; motion is reversed, and still another age of Kronos begins
[273e1]. Our purpose, however, is to understand the kind of epoch
we live in now. God has left our world and us to ourselves; we
therefore begin to propagate our own species from each other.
We no longer spring full-grown as earth-born prodigies, but
begin our career as poor creatures, exposed to the ravages of wild
beasts, deprived of the automatic food-supply of a bountiful
earth [273e4-274c4].

Absence of previous need had discouraged men from gaining
any empirical grasp of material resources in order to provision
themselves; techniques and devices were not available. Accordingly
men had to receive those divine gifts with which we are all familiar,
together with instruction and education in their use: fire and
the technical skills from Prometheus, Hephaestus and Athena, and
agricultural arts from the respective patron deities, who are
responsible for all the equipment which makes human life possible.
For we have to remember that we in the present epoch are on our
own, are responsible for our own concentration-and-supervision
[*epimeleia*] [274c4-d6].

So ends Plato's story. The concept of alternating cycles in
cosmic time is here borrowed from Empedocles, who, though a
pre-Socratic scientist, does not himself seem to have been directly
interested in the history of human civilization. Plato's own
cosmology is not our business, but it is pertinent to notice at once
that his cosmic history is here so framed as to present the divine
and perfect type of government in contrast to the mortal, material
and imperfect. Secondly, although the two epochs are so to speak
balanced and replace each other in apparently endless rhythm,
Plato's moral idealism is reserved wholly for one of them. Only
in the divine period are the motions, major and minor, perfect
or nearly so. Since we live in a non-divine epoch, where present
imperfections are referred wholly to the loss of a previous divine
control, the net effect upon the reader's imagination is less

cyclical than regressive. He is invited to judge the present by reference to a lost Golden Age.

Life in that age has an obvious correspondence with Hesiod's account, even to such details as the retention of vital vigour until painless death supervenes. The earth, for Plato as for Hesiod, was in its ideal condition a spontaneous provider. Still more striking, Hesiod's hint of a peaceful social utopia of distributed functions voluntarily performed is repeated, but with the Platonic addition of divine overseers to handle this, for the science of a divine intelligence is the only possible source for such a way of life.

Were this all, Plato's story would be an interesting imitation of Hesiod, in which the moral intuitions, the protests, the yearnings of the old poet are given a theological and indeed theistic support, but no more than that. But Plato then describes the present age, and here abandons Hesiod's parochialism to turn instead to the scientific anthropologists from whom he borrows the basic conception that man's early life was primitive [*Polit.* 274b-c], exposed and dangerous, until technology furnished him with the means to survive. Technology also had a motive: it came out of man's ability to respond to physical need and to organize provision for himself. For he really is on his own – that is the true picture of man. Then, illogically but necessarily, to suit Plato's own premises, the same techniques and the arts of agriculture are given divine origin [c5-d1], and associated in true conservative style with the traditional deities who patronized them in Greek cult.

What is the total effect that Plato contrives? How does he work on our values? Unmistakably and ingeniously he denatures the achievement of a technological culture and demotes it to the rank of a second-best; it is carried out by man on his own, and man is an imperfect being, in an epoch of increasing moral disorder [273c7-d4 and 274b5-7]. Man's empirical response to natural needs is a poor substitute for the divine guidance of the age of Kronos. Here, too, Plato remains faithful to Hesiod, to the spirit at least of that old story of Prometheus and Pandora. Cunning guile is no match for the wisdom of Zeus. In sum, the poet's regressive and anti-historical nostalgia has been wedded to an *a priori* metaphysical doctrine of the source of knowledge, with formidable results.

In this way a powerful resistance was built against any attempt to trace the growth of man's moral and political nature to its genetic and historical sources. There is evidence that the resistance in Plato grew stronger as he grew older. In the *Protagoras* and *Republic* he could bring himself to accept a kind of compromise between metaphysics and naturalism. In the *Laws*, this has become impossible. Man has fallen; and the lost Age of Kronos haunts Plato's imagination. Perhaps the effect of old age on his mind resembled Hesiod's own experience. At any rate, in the fourth book of that treatise of his last years he repeats in succinct form his basically regressive perspective on history, with considerable poignancy:

Long ago, before any of the present foundations existed, they say that in the time of Kronos there was a government and habitation which was very happy: the best foundations of the present are only imitations of that one. . . . The tradition is that life was pleasant and that the resources with which it was supplied were available in abundance and spontaneously. . . . Kronos knew – a truth we have gone into already – that the nature of man, left in independent management of human matters, is quite inadequate to control its swelling pride, aggressiveness and unrighteousness. Realizing this, Kronos set over our cities kings or rulers, who were not human beings but spirits of a more divine and superior race. . . . God, I say, in his philanthropy set over us the superior race of spirits . . . to look after us and give us peace and reverence and law and abundance of right. Thus on the race of men were conferred internal harmony and happiness.

The lesson of this story continues into the present, saying truly that cities governed not by God but by mortals have no way of evading evils and troubles; what we have to do is to use every contrivance in our power to imitate that traditional life of the time of Kronos; so far as we have something of immortality in us, we should listen to its voice in private and public life and administer our cities accordingly . . . [*Laws* 4.713ff.]

The advantage of citing this much shorter and simpler example is that it so conspicuously establishes the connection in Plato's mind between a regressive concept of human history and an *a priori* morality: you can never understand or clarify the political and moral behaviour of man by referring it to such sources as biological urge responding to the need for progressive advancement of the civilized life. Its causation lies in the immortal: that is, it is outside history, and therefore, to illustrate this fact, history must be written backwards.

As a preface to examining the origin and nature of law itself, Plato offers at the beginning of the third book a more ambitious survey of the past career of man. Though the picture of primitive prosperity is more cautiously drawn, there is no essential difference in principle between the two accounts. Just as it is said in the fourth book: 'The best of our present-day communities only reflect that much earlier form of settled government which so happily obtained in Kronos' reign,' so here 'All our present estate, cities, properties, technologies and law, vice and virtue, are derived from that condition which obtained in those other days.' This slightly ambiguous sentence, while it contains an echo of the evolutionary and genetic language used by the scientific naturalists, is really intended to suggest that the factor of novelty in human history does not exist.

The true character of Plato's account can best be estimated if its items are distinguished and spelled out:

1. All history consists of a series of recurring epochs divided from each other by catastrophes and floods, which leave survivors of our race to make a fresh start on the road to civilization [*Laws* 3.677a].

2. The present urbanized phase of our epoch is comparatively recent, and was preceded by a phase of far longer duration [677d] which was marked by the following characteristics:

3. human beings were mountain-dwellers and wholly pastoral [677b]

4. with no empirical acquaintance with technology, least of all with the urbanized devices which serve competition, greed and wrongdoing [677b]; in fact, their tools had been eliminated and also their inventions, whether applied in statecraft or in other skills [677c]

5. We can infer this to be true from the fact that new inventions have in fact taken place in the recent past. If the inventions had always remained permanent and had never been lost again, there would have been no room for fresh inventions [677c-d]

6. The human condition was one of immense and frightening solitude, with enormous quantities of land available, with some surviving supply of flocks and herds originally quite meagre to support life [677e]

7. with not so much as the memory of urbanized life, polity, legal administration [678a]

8. This condition constituted the source, however, of everything we now have – cities, polities, technologies, law, vice in abundance and also virtue [678a].

9. We can say that men were then not perfect in terms of either virtue or vice [678b].

10. Time, however, progressed; the race increased; matters advanced, not of a sudden but step by step in the course of time [678b].

11. Men for long avoided descent to the plains; their sparseness made them glad to see each other [678c].

12. Means of conveyance by land and sea were not available [678c].

13. Contiguous mutual intercourse was not available [678c].

14. The technologies had vanished; so had iron, bronze and all metals, depriving men likewise of timber-cutting capacity [678d].

15. Any surviving tools were quickly worn out, and they had to await the fresh arrival of the technique of metallurgy [678d].

16. In fact, for an immense period all technologies dependent on iron and bronze, etc., were eliminated [678e].

17. This meant likewise the elimination of faction and war [678e]

18. for two reasons: first, men's solitude made them loving and philanthropic [678e].

19. second, their provision of sustenance was no occasion of fighting, for there was no scarcity [with a few initial exceptions] of distributed pasture, which was their main economic support, nor any lack of milk, flesh and game [679a],

20. clothes, bedding, houses were in plentiful supply [679a],

21. likewise house equipment, both fired and fireless, meaning that the available technologies of pottery and

weaving were in their possession; neither of these require iron [679a].

22. In fact, these two techniques exclusively are God's gift to men to allow growth and development after any disaster [679b];

23. again, the absence of poverty and riches removed the pressure to quarrel [679b],

24. riches being impossible in the absence of gold and silver in that epoch [679b].

25. A community unattended by wealth and poverty is likely to encourage nobility of character and the absence of aggression, unrighteousness and envy. Thus human beings were good and also simple [innocent], uncritical and un-suspicious. They did not have the skill which encourages suspicion [679b-c].

26. In short, then, as contrasted with either our present phase or with the ones that just preceded the last flood, we have here the spectacle of countless generations of mankind living without techniques and without capacity for instruc-tion in techniques, particularly those of war by land and sea and those which in urban life pass by the name of litigation over rights and factional dispute. All devices, verbal and practical, designed to achieve mutual wrongdoing were absent [679d].

27. They were more innocent, courageous, disciplined and in general more righteous [679e].

In the allegory of the *Politicus*, Plato had employed the elaborate construct of a series of cosmic epochs, alternatingly perfect and regressive, and separated by violent cosmic shocks. This mechan-ism is replaced in the present instance by a series of identical historical epochs played out on the earth's surface within each of which primitive perfection is followed by regression. The result is the same in either case. The history of the human race in terms of spiritual and moral values is viewed as a regression from primitive ideals. The Hesiodic nostalgia is in control. It is the conclusion of Plato's story that contains all the clues to its con-struction. Men have lived in a Golden Age of moral equanimity, in completely peaceful co-operation and innocence. It was an age without iron and bronze (items 14, 16, 21) and without the war and violence that accompanies the ages of iron and bronze (items 17, 23, 25, 26). It was an age without voyaging and seafaring (item 12), an age of flocks and herds (items 3, 19), above all an age without those types of skill and calculation that inculcate deceit, treachery and crooked dealing (items 14, 25, 26). To support these moral qualities in man, earth afforded a bountiful sustenance (items 19, 20).

And yet the over-all account conveys an unavoidable impression of a genuinely speculative science applied to history but somehow perverted. How is this? It would seem that Plato has been to school with the scientific anthropologists and has borrowed many of their ideas. Thus for Hesiod's agricultural utopia (still a dominant motif in the *Politicus*) he has now substituted a pastoral one. He is aware of theories which viewed man's agriculture as developing out of a nomadic existence. Hence in his story it is no longer fruit, grain and vegetables which are spontaneously available for the first men, but the untilled pasture, which can support their animals. Various of the technologies are itemized and distinguished, whether as present in or absent from the period, though not necessarily in historical order: transport, navigation, mining, lumbering, and metallurgy; the artifacts of clothing (weaving), pottery; coined money, organized warfare, and the skills of rhetoric and political government. The scientific suggestion is even offered by inference that overpopulation and economic scarcity are the occasions of aggression and war. Above all, the formula is offered of a progressive but very gradual advance in the mastery of technologies step by step in slow accretions through the long advance of time, as invention is added to invention (item 10). Such language is lifted bodily from the true anthropologists.

But the whole scientific perspective on technology is then skilfully and totally corrupted by the wholly unscientific suggestion that weaving and pottery, conducted without benefit of iron, are therefore peaceful and therefore exclusively god-given; and by the equally preposterous hypothesis that these uninitiated primitives had houses and beds and clothing already and were able to maintain them. In short, a set of scientific postulates has been manipulated to serve a wholly non-scientific and non-historical conception, and it is not surprising that Plato cannot quite manage the feat without some inconsistency. Thus an original scarcity of natural resources for man is later supplanted in his account by an original abundance for man, and the saving clause added by the author only glosses over the essential contradiction. More seriously, an Eden of innocence, not perfect in either virtue or vice, is later described as in every respect courageous, disciplined and righteous in a sense that our corrupted period is not. In short, the utopians after all possessed three of the four cardinal virtues complete!

A perverted anthropological science has been put at the service of an *a priori* metaphysic of human morals. The fact becomes plain towards the end, when to clinch his argument Plato substitutes dialectical reasoning for description. A community unattended by either wealth or poverty, he says (item 25), is likely to encourage nobility of character. Hence the connection between utopian economics, primitivism, and moral virtue is established *a priori*. And it is congruent with this metaphysic that Plato's whole conception of history should be static. In item 5, he argues quite naïvely that though new invention has been achieved by man – and he admits the fact as historically attested – it must come to a stop sometime; in fact, it has stopped with our present epoch, which he assumes to be final. Therefore, the tradition of new invention, if true, must be founded on the fact of previous cancellation of invention through catastrophe. The notion of human history as, so to speak, open at both ends is wholly alien to his imagination. Indeed, his convictions about the finite form as alone real and as limiting the formless flux of infinitude effectually prevented his mind from entertaining any other notion about history.

But others before him, naturalists, scientists, historians and empiricists, were pointing in a quite different direction of thought. It is not unfair to say of Platonism as a system that when confronted by the concepts of infinitely extended space and infinitely extended history as offered by the later pre-Socratics, it took up an attitude which betrayed a failure of nerve. This is without prejudice to the fact that Plato's blend of science and metaphysics proved an astonishingly powerful influence upon all similar speculation until Darwin. The hypothesis of an original state of nature, to which political theorists of many different persuasions resorted as to a court of appeal in the seventeenth and eighteenth centuries, is derived from Platonism by direct descent.

Plato constructs this curious mixture of fantasy and history for his own specific purpose, which he states in the conclusion of the anthropology proper. 'Such being our account of these matters, with all that pertains thereto, the purpose of it all is to answer the following question: Did human beings in such an epoch discover the need for laws, and, if so, how? Did they have lawgivers, and, if so, whom?'

The answer as constructed by Plato becomes a formula for the origin of civil society. Though in effect an appendix to his pseudo-anthropology, it acquired great importance in the history of thought because of its effect on the imagination of Aristotle. In brief, Plato argues that in the early dispersed and happy period of man's existence the social unit must have been the household, presided over by the patriarch and governed by wholly unwritten custom law. Subsequently, as settlements descended from the mountains toward the lowlands, households were amalgamated into villages. The conjunction of diverse systems of custom law required the solution offered by an agreed codification of written law. This was carried out by appointed lawgivers and fostered the growth of constitutions, either monarchic or aristocratic. Subsequently, as settlement extended to the plain, urban centres arose of the type exhibited by Troy. In these, as the population swelled by aggregation, all varieties of social form and social pathology were multiplied also.

The neat trilogy of household, village, city, precisely because of its simplicity, was destined to control the genetic aspects of political theory for centuries, mainly as mediated by the first book of Aristotle's *Politics*. It is to be noted at once that in Plato it still conforms to a regressive philosophy of history, and now, as it further defines man's ideal condition in the past, it adds a further item: his forms of government were authoritarian. The city, by contrast, is polymorphic in constitution and behaviour; the note of metaphysical disapproval is unmistakable. This is precisely the charge that Plato levels elsewhere against all democracies. *Per contra*, he looks back nostalgically to the patriarchal authority wielded by the head of the clan, the king, or the council of elders as the proper prototype of government. The growth of complexity in social relations of communication and exchange and in democracy itself is feared and deplored no less than the growth of technology, which, indeed, is a parallel symptom of an identical process.

Before we leave Plato, it is worth adding that in this place he continues his pseudo-historical construction a stage further, to the point where he envisages an early type of confederacy, entered into by three Dorian cities of the Peloponnese, who, he says, formed a common alliance for mutual protection with a common army [*Laws* 3. 683ff.]. Here is the beginning of the concept of the nation (*ethnos*) or social confederacy (*systema*) as a unit larger than the city-state. He never gets as far as exploring the possibility that it might absorb and supplant the city-state. It is an insight he never allowed to develop. He keeps it on the edge of his mind. Plato and Aristotle, in the final analysis, were city-state men; their vision is bounded by its walls. But Plato once at least climbed up the wall and looked over the top of it.

CHAPTER III

HISTORY AS PROGRESS:

THE *PROMETHEUS BOUND*, THE *ANTIGONE*, DIODORUS I

BEFORE the middle of the fifth century, perhaps in the closing years of his life, Aeschylus introduced to the Athenian stage a full-scale dramatization of the doctrines of scientific anthropology. It was an astonishing feat, thus to compose a trilogy the action of which covers not the short span of two mortal generations but the ten thousand years of cosmic history, from *Prometheus Bound* to *Prometheus Unbound*. Our business, however, is only with the surviving first movement of this trilogy and with the testimony it affords of what the scientific anthropologists had already begun to say.

Prometheus himself, addressing the chorus, explains the original motives of Zeus for ordering his crucifixion as follows:

> But as to what you ask, what charge preferred
> Makes him debase me, this will I clarify.
> Directly he his father's throne assumed,
> To divers of the gods he variously
> Prerogatives assigned, and plotted out
> The pattern of his kingdom. Man alone,
> Poor suffering man, meant nothing. His intent
> Was to obliterate and plant fresh stock.
> No one withstood this plan except myself.
> But my nerve did not fail. I rescued man
> From being put away a broken thing.
> Therefore in torments I am bowed, that wring
> Pain from my flesh and pity from your heart.
> Did I who gave man sympathy deserve
> Such fate as even for me cries sympathy?
> So here's the ruthless spectacle you face:
> My education, and Jove's dark disgrace.
>
> [*Prometheus Vinctus* 226-241]

No spectator of the play could avoid remembering his Hesiod nor mistake the intention of the dramatist who already in these lines has offered a drastic correction of the Hesiodic scheme of human history. Zeus has succeeded to the throne of Kronos. According to Hesiod's scheme of the Five Ages, this is when human degeneration began: the silver and bronze and the heroic and the iron ages all perish in turn, Zeus being given personal credit for liquidating the silver and the iron. But in the account given by the Athenian dramatist such a liquidation is prevented. The history of the species has been continuous. Hence there cannot have been five distinct epochs, so the dramatist does not mention them. Moreover the moral reasons which in Hesiod's account either justified these extinctions, or by physical degeneration determined them, are in this play eliminated. Man was perhaps feeble, but certainly to be pitied, a species threatened with an arbitrary and undeserved fate. Though the dramatist's account preserves from the old legend the memory of Zeus' decision, it robs it of any moral validity; it has to be represented as the whim of a cruel and careless despot. In short man has always been 'valuable' and is to be preserved and nursed for greater things to come. What his earliest situation under Kronos had been is not told. The dramatist ignores it because, in his conception, there could not originally have been room for any primeval Utopia.

Prometheus, having become the instrument for the preservation of the species, is to provide also for its progress. If the original service was inspired by compassion, the second is a continuous expression of the same attitude viewed as philanthropy and goodwill:

(Zeus' minister to Hephaestus):
    This was the sin against God, and now the iron
    Of retribution he must undergo,
    That so the lesson be learned: with Jove's absolute power
    To be content, and so give up the road
      That leads to love of man . . .

                           [*P.V.* 8-11]

(Hephaestus to Prometheus):
        This your reward who took the road that leads
          To the love of man.

                         [*P.V.* 28]

(Prometheus' soliloquy):
>   Past the gigantic doors
>   Of Jove's great hall they throng,
>   And turn their back on him whose love
>   For mankind was too strong. . . .
>   [*P.V.* 122-3].

(Prometheus to Chorus):
>   I speak the human race not to condemn
>   But to explain my kindnesses in what I gave to them. . . .
>   [*P.V.* 445-6]

Why did Aeschylus thus underline the philanthropy of the forethinker? He had to go out of his way to do it for the conception of philanthropy was unfamiliar to the Greeks of the classical period. The Hesiodic scheme as it was historically regressive was also morally cynical. Man is at best a fallen creature, at worst a costly mistake. The Homeric notion of him living and dying like the leaves of the trees, the recipient of good and evil in mixed portion or of evil unrelieved by good, is less judgmental than Hesiod's but scarcely more hopeful. These pessimisms were as traditional and as deeply grounded in the Greek mind as in the Hebrew. But in the Promethean drama the values are reversed. Man is worth preserving and worth loving: he is somehow gaining in stature: a challenge is being offered to age-old tradition, one which will deeply affront it, as the outline of man's progress under the aegis of philanthropy is next spelled out.

In Hesiod's folk tale Prometheus had stolen fire from heaven in a hollow fennel stalk and given it to men. The primitivism of this notion about the source of the spark so precious to savages is attested from many parts of the world. Aeschylus preserves the memory of it in one evocative line, but essentially he has no use for it. His hero is a fire-giver only by accident: his significant function is to serve as the channel by which men are endowed with technology:

(Zeus' minister to Hephaestus):
>   And now Vulcan on you
>   Falls the commission of almighty Jove:
>   Here's one that high upon the beetling cliff
>   You must impale. Fetter this criminal
>   In tireless grip of adamantine bonds.

Your triumph of fire, the technological flame
It was that he filched away and transferred to man.

[*P.V.* 3-8]

(Prometheus' soliloquy):

I am the huntsman of the mystery,
The great resource that taught technology,
The secret fount of fire put in the reed
And given to man to minister his need.
This, this the error for which night and day
Nailed up beneath the sky I still must pay.

[*P.V.* 109-113]

(Prometheus and Chorus):

I made their hearts blind citadels of hope –
A brave utility on man conferred –
And more than that, made fire their minister –
Wields now ephemeral man the fervent flame? –
Yes and 'twill teach him all technologies.

[*P.V.* 250-254]

(Prometheus to Chorus):

One sentence short proclaims the truth unique:
Prometheus gave, what man received, technique.

[*P.V.* 505-6]

But even the notion of technique too narrowly defines the dramatist's conception of the influence of his hero upon man's history. Pains are taken in characterizing him to indicate not only his powers of prevision but his habits of exact prognosis, scientific calculation, and rational exposition. The following are only a selection of quotations capable of illustrating this point:

(Hephaestus to Prometheus):

O son of her whose counsels never fail
Intelligence superb and dangerous. . . .

[*P.V.* 18]

(Prometheus' soliloquy):

Yet why these words? of things that are to come
My science is exact nor like fresh news
Will my afflictions happen.

[*P.V.* 101-3]

(Prometheus to Chorus):

Whereat I offered counsels excellent

To the Titan sons of firmament and earth.
But no avail. They scorned the deviousness
Of my device. Their epic pride preferred
What seemed the easy use of simple force.
But she, my mother, who holds the judgment seat,
Even Earth, that entity with many names,
Had often told me, yea had prophesied
The way of it, how not in physical strength
But cunning guile the victory should lie.
But to my explanation of the truth
They did not deign even a moment's heed.
So I in present circumstance thought best
To take my mother and join force with Jove,
A welcome partnership to both of us.
Therefore in Tartarus' black fundament
Saturn the ancient one and his array
Are kept, because my counsels showed the way.

[*P.V.* 204-221]

(Prometheus to Chorus):

My silence is not idle wilfulness.
Pray you believe, my thought's intensity,
Seeing myself abused, gnaws at my heart.

[*P.V.* 436-7]

(Prometheus to Chorus):

Procedures intricate I plotted out
Of the diviner's skill, and how to tell
The waking vision from the idle dream.
Of chance word's augury and journeying sign
The sense obscure did I communicate.
The divers figures of the flights of birds,
Those matched with luck and those made otherwise,
The regimen of their respective groups,
Conjunctions, oppositions, amities,
With strict exactness did I designate.

[*P.V.* 484-492]

Once more Hesiodic values are reversed. Primitive suspicion
of calculation and cunning is converted into acceptance. Indeed
it had to be, if the anthropological vision of man's development
was to be accepted also. In the drama this vision takes shape when

Prometheus undertakes a formal exposition of how the human race had fared under his protective guidance. He begins with something more basic than applied science:

(Prometheus to Chorus):

> Let me rather
> Relate to you the travailing of man:
> How from the silly creature that he was
> I made him conscious and intelligent.
> I speak the human race not to condemn
> But to explain my kindnesses in what I gave to them.
> Seeing they did not see nor hearing grasp
> That which they heard. Like shapes of dreams they lived
> The random planless years all ignorant
> Of houses built of brick to catch the sun
> Or timber fashioning. Like little ants
> They dwelt in holes of sunless cavities.

[P.V. 442-453]

There was then a pre-Promethean stage in the career of the human species. In Darwinian terms the species had an 'origin'. So far from being created by the gods or descended from them it emerged as we now know it from a prehuman condition. Intelligence, the hallmark of *homo sapiens*, was not always within man's competence. He began his career as an animal.

What is the hallmark of his Promethean gifts? It is his ability to articulate meaningful language. His pre-linguistic condition is in the poet's vision viewed from the perspective of his present command of communication; and the one is seen as a caricature of the other, a wordless dream life like that of the gibbering ghosts in a Homeric Hades, blind, deaf and dumb. And then the poet includes a pregnant but ambiguous phrase:

> . . . They lived
> The random planless years

Does this simply indicate the supremacy of blind instinct, the lack of conscious direction, characteristic of the animal condition? Or is he hinting also at the lack of an organized social order of civil society, and therefore does he mean to rank civil society also as a Promethean achievement? Is this why the sentence continues with the building of houses as the first technological achievement, for with the house were to come the household and the village of grouped households? It is impossible to be sure.

At any rate these few lines have already said enough to destroy at a blow the whole Hesiodic perspective and the Platonic metaphysic of history. Man is not historically a constant, emerging full-grown upon the earth, endowed as in Plato with language and the essential arts. His earliest life is not as in Hesiod or Plato a wholly admirable and happy thing. The direction is reversed: devolution has been replaced by evolution even if the evolution is directed by a Prometheus. And it is impossible to avoid the further conclusion that such a scheme was also intended to contradict the moral pessimism, the belief in degeneration, which Plato shared with Hesiod and which requires in both authors a current intervention of catastrophe as a natural consequence or just punishment of degeneration. Our present author has already denied the hypothesis that the species was at any time liquidated by Zeus. But it is equally significant that such a threat existed only in the pre-Promethean condition and was therefore a concomitant not of technical advance but of the total absence of technology. As man gains the Promethean endowment, his survival power increases.

The Promethean account then proceeds to cover as exhaustively as suited the poet's purpose that panorama of achievement which constituted for the Greeks the material basis of their civilization:

(Prometheus to Chorus):

> They had no signs reliable to mark
> Winter and scented spring and harvest-time.
> Mindless was all they did until I showed
> The dubious rise and setting of the stars.
> That triumph next of scientific mind,
> The count numerical for man I find
> And history's instrument, skill of the bard,
> That great compositor, the written word.
> I was the first to yoke the animals
> In service to the strap, and lay on them
> Inheritance of man's excessive toil.
> Between the shafts I led the obedient horse,
> That ornament of luxury and wealth.

HISTORY AS PROGRESS

The gleaming sail that wafts across the sea
The intrepid mariner was my device.
The inventor I, who many a shape did show
Of science to mankind, now do not know
What science will my own release allow.

[P.V. 454-471]

Hear yet again, and marvel what resource,
What science sprang from my intelligence.
Here was the greatest: if a man fell sick,
Where was his remedy of application?
Potions, alembics, messes, poultices –
All were to seek. The sufferer pined and sank
In stark emaciation, till I brought
The soothing unguent and the restoring draught
To man the battlements against disease.
Procedures intricate I plotted out
Of the diviner's skill, and how to tell
The waking vision from the idle dream.
Of chance word's augury and journeying sign
The sense obscure did I communicate.
The divers figures of the flights of birds,
Those matched with luck, and those made otherwise,
The regimen of their respective groups,
Conjunctions, oppositions, amities,
With strict exactness did I designate.
And the smooth look of entrails, and correct
Colour of bile to please the gods withal,
And the prediction of the liver's lobe
Shown in the lineaments' complexities.
By smoke of sacrifice of loin and thigh
Wrapped in the fat I did initiate
Man in a dark and intricate technique,
And the hidden bloodshot eye of the sign by fire
I did unmask, that had been veiled before.
So much for these. Turn next and contemplate
Those great utilities beneath the earth,
Copper and iron, silver and yellow gold.
Who before me dare claim discovery
Of these, unless a madman? None, I trow.

One sentence short proclaims the truth unique:
Prometheus gave, what man received, technique.
[*P.V.* 476-506]

Reduced to its bare components, the account of man's advance yields the following items of civilized achievement:

1. Consciousness
2. Language
3. (Society?)
4. Architecture
5. Woodworking
6. Calendar
7. Numerals
8. Alphabet
9. Domestication of animals
10. Transport (the horse)
11. Navigation
12. Medicine
13. Divination and augury (dreams and birds)
14. Divination (ritual and sacrifice)
15. Mining and metallurgy

Taken as a whole, these read like a list of inventions, and betray unmistakable willingness to interpret human culture in technological terms. The fact that several items which recur in later lists – for example, hunting and agriculture, pottery and weaving – do not happen to occur here is likely to be due to the accident of the poet's selection. Man the tool user (as in architecture, navigation and metallurgy) is conjoined with man the abstract scientist (in numerals, alphabet and medicine) to produce a single perspective upon the character and functions of *homo sapiens*. Whether the poet conceived the order as chronological is hard to say, but it is improbable. Plato, as we saw, argued that woodworking, which is early in Prometheus' list, relied on metal tools, which come last. It is more to the point to ask whether the poet assumes that the historical process has now exhausted its course. It is possible he did so assume, and that the man of his Promethean creation would now be a finished product. And then the drama of the trilogy would be intended to exploit the issues created within the context of this present achievement, rather than focus on problems which might arise from a process still unfinished. The artist working within the limits of tragic form, as against the scientific thinkers from whom he borrowed, was unlikely to find the vistas of infinite time agreeable to his purpose. It could even be argued that he has retained the Hesiodic pessimism, the sense of frustration and failure, and simply given it an altered context in the painful fate to which Prometheus himself is condemned. This however was to be limited, by the terms of the play itself, to a ten-thousand-year span preceding ultimate reconciliation between the protagonist and Zeus. Thus the optimism implicit in the sheer grandiosity of the catalogue of human achievement, and faith that the issues of the historical process will be good and beneficial and happy, are redeemed in the conclusion.

These matters, however, carry us into the mind and purpose of the dramatist himself, and transcend the narrower question which is our present business: namely, the kind of testimony he provides to the anthropological speculation current in his day. One last item in that testimony is worth a second glance. We noted earlier a certain ambiguity in the preamble which might be interpreted as a reference to the origin of civil society. Towards the conclusion Prometheus adds what is almost an excursus on the various practices of divination. It is notable that the speculative Greek temper sees no obstacle to looking at these sacred mysteries simply as technologies, further examples of exact and precise procedure which the mind of man is required to master. The attitude is so to speak secular and is eloquent of the secularization of Greek religion at all levels. There were, as we have said, no centralized priestly institutions which could have prevented the inquiring mind from classifying sacrificial procedure on the same level with building a house or sailing a ship.

The further interesting question arises as to whether the scientific source on which the dramatist is drawing was already prepared to view religion itself and all the institutions of cult as simply another item in that series of achievements which make up the civilized life. We know that within a generation of the assumed date of the play thinkers were prepared to rationalize religion as a useful fiction. Nothing so drastic is here presumed. But when the protagonist says: [*P.V.* 496-8]

> By smoke of sacrifice of loin and thigh
> Wrapped in the fat I did initiate
> Man in a dark and intricate technique,

he seems almost Socratically to suggest that cult sacrifice is after all only a science of propitiation and amenable to the rules of rational procedure. The point is worth making, so far as it suggests that the anthropological source was already prepared to find rational explanations for the most solemn social institutions. Such a mind was surely not far from taking the further step of asking whether even the lawful usage and righteous conduct sanctioned by the gods were not themselves a form of social science designed like other techniques to further the civilizing process.

The anthropologies, in short, were not a mere catalogue of inventions nor was their perspective confined by a kind of vulgar materialism. The play consistently places upon Prometheus' activity a social or humane evaluation: on the one hand it is a reflection of his compassion; on the other it also expresses a purpose which is utilitarian:

(Prometheus to Chorus):

> Turn next and contemplate
> Those great utilities beneath the earth
> Copper and iron silver and yellow gold . . .
>
> [*P.V.* 500-502]

(Io to Prometheus):

> Thou great utility of social man
> His brightest light since history began
> Prometheus, steadfast in your works revealed,
> What spells this punishment, these fetters sealed?
>
> [*P.V.* 613-4]

The first of these quotations classifies the metals as what we would call 'natural resources'. They are related to the context of man's social need. In the second, Prometheus himself is hailed as the 'great utilitarian', the embodiment of the principle of social use and profit. This evaluation pronounced upon him by Io cancels that irony which had been implicit in an earlier comment on him by the chorus:

> I made their hearts blind citadels of hope –
> A brave utility on man conferred!
>
> [*P.V.* 251-2]

And again

> Why such utility for man effect
> Unseasonably, to your own neglect?
> [*P.V.* 507-8]

It is in keeping with this evaluation that the sciences themselves are styled 'resources' which man puts to use:

(Prometheus' soliloquy):

> Giving to man magnificent resource
> Myself I have the iron will of fate.
> I am the huntsman of the mystery
> The great resource that taught technology
> The secret fount of fire put in the reed
> And given to man to minister his need . . .
> [*P.V.* 107-111]

(Prometheus to Chorus):

> Hear yet again, and marvel what resource,
> What science sprang from my intelligence . . .
> [*P.V.* 476-7]

These hints force the historian to confront a problem basic to the play's interpretation. What is intended to be the relation of Prometheus to man? Or, more significantly, what is man's relation to Prometheus? Is he quite other than Prometheus, a mortal under immortal supervision? Is he a mere recipient of divine gifts, a creature arbitrarily and passively at the disposal of decisions which are made in heaven?

On the surface of the drama this is the case. Prometheus cannot even talk about man without assuming that he himself is other than man. After all, is he not immortal, a fact which he feels called upon to underline?

> Trials such as mine you could not even face –
> Mine who 'tis writ must wince, but may not die.
> [*P.V.* 752-3]

But that the problem of man's status vis-à-vis Prometheus is not so simply solved is evident from the following considerations:

1. Prometheus once describes his benefaction as a giving of gifts:

I speak the human race not to condemn
But to explain my kindnesses in what I gave to them.

[*P.V.* 445-6]

This is in the language of religious cult as used later by Plato. The gods of fruit and field in virtue of their desire to do good to men, and their superior power to do so, graciously confer gifts which man unaided could not reach. We have seen Plato specifically stating as much.

2. Aside from this one instance, Prometheus constantly describes himself, and is described by others, as the 'inventor' and the 'researcher' who also *teaches, expounds, explains* and *initiates*. This can only mean that man on his side has been engaged in a prolonged enterprise of learning and instruction requiring the concentration of intellectual powers. The dramatist does not venture to put this enterprise upon the stage: he is compelled by artistic necessity to exploit only one half of the relationship between man and Prometheus. But his language presupposes a historical process of successive human effort to master the secrets made available to him.

Prometheus, in fact, is himself twice sarcastically addressed (at the beginning and conclusion of the play) in very human terms as the 'arch-sophist' or scientist of his day. A Greek audience of this date would associate such a term with the speculative interests of the early philosophers. Prometheus is the embodiment of intelligence. This is the formal identification which he receives as the drama opens. And the language of the play continually adverts to his intellectual powers which are either reviled or applauded. All of which continually tempts the reader to conclude that, despite their dramatic separation, Prometheus is a symbol of man himself; the gulf between his immortality and man's ephemeral condition is easily erased by assuming that he represents man in history, man who has spent many centuries in climbing to his present existence, and will spend many more enduring the mysterious consequences. This consideration of the play's ultimate bearing need not detain us, except so far as it renders plausible the hypothesis that the dramatist's scientific source did not utilize a divine apparatus at all, but that this was the necessary artistic invention of Aeschylus. The play contains only two significant hints that in its author's mind Prometheus and the men he served were not entirely distinct conceptions

> I am the huntsman of the mystery
> The great resource that taught technology.
>
> [*P.V.* 109-110]

And again

> (Chor.) Wields now ephemeral man the fervent flame?
> (Prom.) Yes, and 'twill teach him all technologies.
>
> [*P.V.* 253-4]

Though Prometheus later claims exclusive credit for his discoveries, these two quotations indicate that it is not he but the ministrant fire which is of itself the 'teacher' of man. Is he then but equivalent to the fire he gives and is his instruction only a concrete symbolization of the process of self-instruction employed by men? The chorus, frightened by defiance thus offered to a jealous Zeus, once the anthropological account is concluded, turn to deprecate with appropriate piety the Promethean effort:

> O labour of love thrown away!
> Who now, dear head, shall defend thee?
> Why so unschooled in the state of ephemeral man?
> How feeble he is, how resourceless,
> How like a dream he passes
> Blinded in all his ways and in all his acts prevented!
> Nor, though he still take thought, can the grand design
> By his thinking be circumvented.
>
> [*P.V.* 545-551]

The ambiguity of the last two lines correctly suggests that the contrivance of Prometheus which has brought him to his crucifixion is identical with the vain plan and purpose of mankind.

The above citations do not exhaust those indications supplied in the play that Prometheus the inventor and mankind the discoverer overlap, but they are those that have some philological precision. They are significant for any interpreter who is forced to use the drama as a piece of testimony to the currency in Greece, before 460 B.C., of anthropological speculation couched in purely naturalist and historical terms. For they indicate, if not a formulated doctrine on the dramatist's part, at least a direction in which even his mind is moving. The essential thing from a doctrinal standpoint is not Prometheus' divinity – for that is forced upon the dramatist by past tradition and present artistic necessity – but his humanity. Such a direction of thought betrays the fact that the Greek humane genius is at least open to receive an entirely novel perspective upon its own origin and history. As the gods of Hesiod retreat a little, man himself and the science of man come to the forefront of the stage where man may at least share equal interest with Zeus. For his supposedly divine origins have disappeared and been resolved, perhaps into the raw material of the physical elements, certainly into an evolutionary process common to all animals upon the earth's surface.

To minds schooled in Platonism and in the various kinds of religious and metaphysical idealism which are supposed to represent classical tradition in philosophy such evolutionary views are represented as not only materialist but undignified. Man so far from being a little lower than the angels is discovered to be a little higher than the ape. This is a prejudiced judgment. It is equally possible to say with Lucretius that man has at last been put in possession of his proper inheritance, for he is freed from a burden of anxiety imposed by his own uncertainty regarding the powers and possibilities of his own brain. The Hesiodic rejection of intellect is cancelled. The road is at last open for a generous humanism which is not guilt-ridden. This is precisely the kind of vision to which, within perhaps twenty years, Sophocles gives supreme expression in his *Antigone*. For the first stasimon of that play provides a second main source for both the character and influence of Greek anthropological science in the mid-fifth century:

The world has marvels exceeding strong
But the miracle thing these marvels among
Is the creature man.
The sea is his grey domain
He ranges its farthest coasts
Gale-sped through the trough of the wave.
The earth is his eldest god –
Ancient imperishable –
His scars are on her face.
Summer and winter his furrows turn on the hill
    As he drives the team that he bred and trained to do his will.
                           [*Antig.* 332-341]

Quick speech and the wind-swift thought,
The usage and moods of the town, strong walls that are warm in
   the night,
The builded roof, retreat from the driving rain,
These, these are his self-taught arts
The total resource of man.
Disease may baffle but never defy his intelligent plan
Nor ever resourceless the hazard to come does he face
Death alone shall always master his masterful race.

The skill of the technical hand
Is an intellectual thing
As it guides him on his journey –
This talent astonishing.
And he finds both good and evil
And the solemn oath once sworn
As right of gods he cherishes,
Weaving the lawful usages
Of the land where he was born.
High rise the walls of his city,
But that man must stay outside
Whose companion is incivility,
Whose action is uncontrolled.
My heart with his can never share
His thoughts and mine unequal are.

[*Antig.* 353-375]

Even by the keenest critics the full prosaic import of this
magnificent ode has never been fully appreciated. It is sufficient,
now that the schema of the *Prometheus* is already before us, to set
down the items of the historical analysis which Sophocles has put
into poetry. (The stanza containing items four to eight in the
following was, however, omitted in the translation):

1. Navigation
2. Agriculture
3. Domestication of draught animals
4. Trapping of birds
5. Trapping of other game
6. Sea fishing
7. Domestication of oxen

8. Domestication of the horse
. 9. Language
10. Consciousness
11. Town-temper-and-usage
12. Architecture
13. Medicine
14. Regional custom law
15. Security of compact and contract
16. The city-state society
17. The sanctions of society against its enemies

The figure of Prometheus has disappeared. Man is now truly self-taught. But the historical conception is similar and though much has been made by the critics of differences between the two accounts, omissions and additions may be due to nothing more than artistic accident. Sophocles adds hunting and agriculture and omits divination and metallurgy. Both accounts include language and consciousness; and it is interesting that Sophocles seems to connect (i) language, and (ii) the townsman's temper, and (iii) the actual material construction of houses. This supports our previous guess that Prometheus had also intended to suggest that language, social order and domestic architecture had emerged together. If so, anthropological science was already prepared to see man's intellectual and linguistic powers as socially conditioned, a response to his need to communicate in society; and to see his power to form society as in turn technically conditioned by his material mastery of architecture.

It is the last stanza which has tempted critics to perceive a supposedly more advanced version of anthropological theory. Indeed, some have punctuated and emended the text so as to sever the sense of the stanza from its anthropological context altogether, and represent it as the poet's pietistic correction of man's own presumption and reliance on technique. But in fact the stanza views his technological powers as leading into the creation of civil society and usage, and hence into those sanctions which support morality and perhaps create it. The poet achieves this impression by juxtaposing the factors of technique on the one hand and law on the other. First comes the affirmation of man's almost miraculous mentality, done in language which recalls that 'skill and science' with which Prometheus had been taunted. This is still the mentality of the tool-user, the mechanical contriver. Knowledge is being given no metaphysical status. The gift accompanies him as he 'takes his journey' – the verb perhaps symbolizing the long historical process. The journey, in terms of weal and woe, is still a mixed one – the poet does not forget to include previous commonplaces on this theme. Proceeding, however, still in possession of his talent, man reaches two further achievements: he learns to keep his pledged word, and he learns to 'weave-in' a set of lawful usages by which to organize civil life. Platonizers can read into the context a metaphysic which is not there, by translating 'man cherishes the solemn justice of the gods', but the Greek only means 'the rightful way which consists in keeping oaths under the gods' watchful eye'. In other words, the human and social importance of maintaining pledged agreement is so great that divine sanctions are used to back it up. Religious usage itself therefore marks a step in man's progress towards the building of civil order. Prometheus had hinted that communication with the gods by a sacrifice was a 'dark and intricate technique' which man had learned. In the present passage the same rationalization of theology is implicit in an even more advanced stage. The conclusion of the stanza confirms this interpretation. For after celebrating the Greek city as perhaps the supreme society, the poem identifies the 'unrighteous' man as essentially the 'antisocial' man, upon whom society exercises the sanction of outlawry. It is his acts that have to be measured and these fail to conform to the common pattern of custom law. And perhaps the ode concludes with a hint that a true civil society can be known by the fact that its members have an equality or identity of temper and interest.

The body of the poem, then, celebrates with unmistakable fervour a kind of vision of man as truly *homo sapiens*, in control of his own history and moulding his own environment. The accent on his 'resource' is repeated, viewed either as a capacity within himself to devise and control, or as the tools and materials which become resources as he lays hold of them. And he is a miraculous creature, himself part of that cosmic order which contains other miracles. Flamboyant optimism, the affirmation of progress, the implicit independence of divine jealousy or sanction, stand in starkest contrast to the regressive pessimism of Hesiod and the metaphysical standards of Platonism.

The historical analysis which supports the vision was not that of Sophocles. Is the vision itself his own? Or has he just put into poetry an announcement which Hellas has already heard from her intellectual leadership, that 'Man is himself the measure of all things'?

The conclusion of the chorus carries us beyond the confines of anthropology to the borders of a liberal theory of morals and politics. Some of the terminology used will find its echo in later chapters. Indeed, these lines furnish apt text for the thesis that the moral and political philosophies of Democritus and Protagoras were founded on a social theory derived from the naturalism of historical science.

Some twenty more years go by and the anthropological schematism emerges once more, this time in a drama of Euripides where however its intrusion wears almost the appearance of an accident. The *Suppliants* is a puzzling and unsatisfactory play, and not the least of its problems is presented by the oddly doctrinaire temper of its principal character, Theseus: to whom, for whatever reason, is assigned at one place in the play a speech which begins with a lecture on the role of providence in human life. It runs as follows:

1.   Mankind, it has been said,
2. Encounter bad far more than they find good.
3. My own opinion is the opposite:
4. Life's better things are greater than the bad.
5. If not, how could we live and see the light?
6. That god who took our planless brutish life
7. And regulated it – 'tis him I praise –
8. Put comprehension in us, gave the tongue
9. As messenger to mark the sounds of speech,
10. And sustenance of fruit and herb sustained
11. By skyey rain, that he might raise the crops
12. And water nature's bosom. And he gave
13. Weather defence to keep god's sky at bay
14. And navigation mutually to supply
15. By cross exchange the earth's deficiencies.
16. When signs are doubtful and things hard to read
17. The prophet looks in fire, or on the folds
18. Of entrails, or at birds and gives his sign.

19. What luxury for us if God has given
20. This life's resource when we had none of it!
21. Yet man's intelligence would seek a power
22. Higher than God's. We get verve in our hearts,
23. And think our skill surpasses the divine.

[*Suppl.* 196-218]

Most of the items of this list are easily recognizable despite the moralizing phraseology in which they are presented:

> The initial survival of man(line 5)
> Originally an animal (6)
> Growth of consciousness and intelligence (8)
> And language (9)
> Houses (13)
> Navigation (14)
> Commerce (15)
> Divination (16 – 20)

One item is a new-comer: the concept of commercial exchange transacted over distances by sea and conditioned by the need to exchange products which vary in supply in different parts of the earth's surface. We have already had reason to infer that the anthropologists included in their purview the evolution of man in civil society and the growth of law and order. At this social level, it would now appear that their interests were not confined to issues of justice and virtue: they were prepared also to come to terms with economics, and to consider the growth of an exchange economy, perhaps as a further extension of the historical evolutionary process. They were in fact descriptive historians, not moralists.

It is also possible that the optimism which in the mouth of 'Theseus' is made to serve as text (lines 1–5) for his homily reflects the temper of these anthropologists. For their evolutionary perspective would encourage the conclusion, first that man could master his fate, and second, that his mastery became more complete as history advanced. This progressivism would be offered as a direct corrective to that Hesiodic pessimism which had accompanied the traditional regressive picture of history. Yet, essentially speaking, the philosophy of man and of history present in the scientific original is in Euripides cancelled by the theistic use to which it is put. The original, in fact, is turned upside down; these evidences of man's own development and his powers are converted to testimony of the existence of a providential God; man's brain and invention cease to be historical growths, and become instead donations put into man or given to him by a power external to him and to history (lines 6, 7, 8, 12, 19). To accomplish this feat, the pietistic mind, as it edits the original, adds an irrelevant item, by celebrating nature's own power to produce food from a soil watered by heaven's fertilizing rain (lines 10-12). Heaven, however, though benign in one aspect is harsh in another: man has to build himself house walls to repel the arrows of the storm (line 13). The author's insistent theism involves him in unconscious paradox. This notion of nature's divine beneficence is of course traditional and religious, linked as it is with the spring and harvest cults. Equally traditional is the view that divination, so far from being a human technology mastered by human brain as it had been in the *Prometheus*, is a mystery dependent on God's grace which makes the priest the most valuable member of the community (lines 19 and 20). Such a conclusion, so repellent to a genuine pre-Socratic scientist, is here necessary to prepare for the grand terminus of Theseus' sermon: man's intelligence, he says in effect, by this historical progression seeks to master his fate. Such had been precisely the language of the Sophocles version. But Sophocles, true to the integrity of the vision of his original, left man's intelligence on its pedestal:

> The world has marvels exceeding strong
> But the miracle thing these marvels among
> Is the creature man.

[*Antig.* 332-3]

And again:

> The skill of the technical hand
> Is an intellectual thing
> As it guides him on his journey –
> That talent astonishing.

[*Antig.* 365-7]

Euripides in the person of Theseus proceeds to knock it off the pedestal by blandly foisting upon this description of *homo sapiens* a context designed to discredit him in favour of the supernatural and providential wisdom.

72

Euripides' version therefore is not in fact a report, but a skilful rewrite. It is instructive in that it illustrates the fact that the attempt to stand anthropology on its head and derive from it a regressive philosophy of history in the Hesiodic manner did not begin with Plato. It was the way in which average orthodoxy as early as the last half of the fifth century tried to come to terms with the new teaching. The parallel with more recent times is obvious. Darwinian evolution was a bitter brew for the pietistic temper. But the discovery was made that it could be swallowed if sweetened by being placed under providential control. The evolutionary process is converted into a series of miraculous acts or gifts, and this, as we saw already in Platonism, has the effect of leaving an *a priori* intelligence – the divine one – in the driver's seat, while reducing the operational and pragmatic intelligence of man to secondary status.

The three Greek dramatists have for the historian of Greek science the obvious disadvantage that they were poets and artists, not reporters. Their testimony on the subject of Greek anthropology is only indirect. This drawback is counter-balanced by their contemporary quality. They actually lived in that intellectual atmosphere of the fifth century which produced such speculations; they knew personally the men who were so speculating.

The historian Diodorus Siculus is in the reverse position. His report of Greek anthropology is direct and deliberate; he has his own specific professional reasons for putting it on record. It is all the more aggravating that he comes so late. The space of nearly four centuries which separates him from Euripides is a very long time. How can he be considered a serious authority on this or any aspect of pre-Socratic science? There is one good reason for so considering him. Early Greek anthropology, after finding its inception as a branch of cosmology, came during the late fifth and early fourth centuries to have some direct influence on politics. But its long-term effect on Greek literature was felt most directly in the writing of history. Indeed, it contributed not a little to the creation of a school of historical writers who, unlike the two classical historians Herodotus and Thucydides, conceived their theme not as circumscribed by the course of a single war or by the fortunes of a single nation; but as co-terminous with the career of the whole human race. In short, they were the first writers to

propose the narrative of human culture and institutions on something like an encyclopedic scale. Of this school, properly speaking,
only Diodorus has survived and even he not completely. No doubt,
as stylists and compositors, they were inferior to the classic
historians. It is an understandable paradox of their position that
the scientific importance of their idea of history was in inverse
ratio to their mastery of literary form. It is so much easier to
comprehend the triumph and tragedy of your own people than
to grasp successfully the historical experiences of the inhabited
earth – the *oikumene*; and the source material required is more
within the compass of a single human being. Indeed, in history
viewed as world history, triumph and tragedy as felt experiences
tend to lose relevance, and thus the historian's tale is robbed of
strong thematic structure. Diodorus at his best was no genius;
he seizes upon a conception too great perhaps for his pen, and
produces a farrago compiled from the writings of other men. But
the perspective he attempts, *qua* perspective, far outstrips in
scientific clarity and comprehensiveness the localism and the
heroic prejudices which inspired the other surviving Greek
historians.

The source of this perspective is quite simply the concept of
the human race conceived biologically as a single universal genus
differentiated into a variety of species known as nations (*ethne*)
with specific linguistic and cultural patterns. These are found
dispersed over a given 'ecumenical' area of the earth's surface.
Diodorus thus proposes at the outset that the historian's proper
task is to bring into one historical schematization (*syntaxis*) 'all
human beings, sharing as they do in a common mutual kinship,
but occupying disjunct localities and living in disjunct periods
of time'. [*Diod.* 1.1.3] Thus his subject is really 'the common
history of the inhabited earth' which however, he adds, can be
presented synoptically as though it were the story of a 'single
city' [1.1.4: cf. 1.3.6]. This last phrase, unnecessary and indeed
untrue, is a concession to the political philosophy of Plato and
Aristotle and the school of city-state historians in which that
philosophy is reflected. In fact, as Diodorus proceeds to an en-
comium of the historian's profession, he recalls among other
things the illustrious honour-roll of inventors and inventions
devised 'for the service of the race of human beings' [1.2.1].
Here, while still in his preface, he reveals the universality of his

subject, which he proceeds to make explicit as he plunges into his history proper: 'My subject accurately set forth to the extent allowable in dealing with matters so ancient is the race of all human beings and their history in known parts of the inhabited earth. I shall begin with prehistory' [1.6.2].

A consideration of prehistory involves the possible hypothesis that the world and men were and are eternal; this he states only to ignore it. On the counter-hypothesis that man like the cosmos 'had definite origins in time' [1.6.3], it falls to the historian to describe these origins. But these can be set forth as part of a more general phenomenon – the original appearance of all living things on the earth's primeval surface. Since that surface in turn was capable of producing spontaneously the first forms of life (*phyta* and *zoa*), a complete cosmology is called for which will explain how the earth, not to mention the firmament, originated [1.7.1-2], and what was that original physical condition which produced organic life [1.7.3-7]. This scientific perspective completed, the universal historian is in a position to discuss 'early man' himself and his anthropological development [1.8.1ff.]. In short, cosmogony must be followed by zoogony and anthropogony, and these in turn by anthropology, before Diodorus feels himself in a position to start describing 'the actual recorded history (*praxeis*) of men in the known places of the inhabited earth [1.9.1].

This over-all schematization is compendious and impressive. Lucretius, a near-contemporary, also exploited it in the fifth book of his *De Rerum Natura*. Nearly all its elements go back to pre-Socratic speculations. Whether they had all been drawn together into such a neat package as early as the fifth century must remain uncertain. But at least it is beyond doubt that the epitome reports accurately a key conception of pre-Socratic anthropology: man began his career as an animal, not as a separate and divine or even superior creation. He is simply one among a thousand forms of life, and his career, like that of other forms, is primarily governed by his biological relation to the elements out of which the cosmos is formed. All his civilization obeys this law. His history, therefore, is viewed as in the first instance the management of a relationship between himself and his physical environment.

It is of equal importance that as an animal he must originally have lived like the other animals; that the factors which presently distinguish him from them must have been somehow acquired. In this way it is scientific naturalism which inspires the progressive and developmental view of history as opposed to the traditionally regressive or cyclical notion. Once you derive man from those origins which he shares with all life, primitive Utopias on the Hesiodic-Platonic pattern disappear.

This brings us to Diodorus' anthropology proper. Like the rest of his science it reads like an epitome of previous writings, thinly disguised as a connected narration. Even a fairly faithful translation can easily break it down and render it as a series of the following items:

1. Man's earliest condition was disorganized
2. And animal-like
3. and dispersed
4. As he proceeded to 'pastures'
5. Helping himself to the most suitable fodder available
6. and to the fruits available spontaneously on trees [1.8.1].
7. Under pressure of war waged by the animals on them
8. men undertook mutual assistance,
9. natural expediency (*sympheron*) being their instructor.
10. From aggregates thus formed through fear
11. they came to recognize their mutual characteristics (*typoi*)
12. by a process of gradualism [1.8.2].
13. Speech sounds were originally meaningless and confused
14. till they articulated statements (*lexeis*)
15. by a process of gradualism.
16. By assigning equivalent symbols in mutual intercourse
17. covering the items of the 'substantive data' (*hypokeimena*)
18. they rendered intelligible their mutual communication on all matters [1.8.3].
19. Social nexuses (*systemata*) of this sort grew up all over the inhabited earth
20. with different languages
21. since the common convention of each language was accidental
22. in fact languages became of all kinds
23. and the initial social nexuses became the 'first parents' of all nations (*ethne*) [1.8.4].

24. In the absence of inventions
25. and of any of life's utilities
26. early conditions of life were painful
27. without clothing
28. unused (*aethes*) to houses
29. or to fire
30. and without a concept of domesticated sustenance [1.8.5].
31. In ignorance of how to stockpile wild sustenance they made no storage of products
32. to meet their necessities
33. Hence starvation in winter through cold and food shortage [1.8.6].
34. However, experience being their instructor
35. by a process of gradualism
36. they took refuge in caves in winter
37. and laid up in storage such products as would keep [1.8.7].
38. Then fire became known
39. and the rest of the utilities
40. and by a gradual process
41. the techniques
42. were invented
43. together with everything capable of conferring utility
44. in common social life [1.8.8].
45. Following a general rule
46. sheer need-and-use
47. became instructor of human beings
48. supplying appropriate suggestions
49. of how to learn each thing
50. to an animal (man) with a natural capacity,
51. an animal moreover who had hands
52. and rational speech (*logos*)
53. and mental readiness
54. as his cooperators in all things [1.8.9].

In all epitomes of this sort earlier sources may lie in stratifications superimposed on each other. Some of the layers present
here were deposited as late as the fourth and third centuries. Thus
for example the words 'substantive data', signifying the objects

named by language, reflect Peripatetic terminology, and so must the reference to 'rational speech' (52) as man's special possession, contradicting as it does the earlier naturalistic account of the origins of language (11-18). Or again the achievement by man of the 'concept' of domestication of crops (30) is probably an Epicurean touch. The division of the *oikumene* into linguistic areas or ethnic divisions (19-23) may reflect the science of the fourth century or later. In fact, this epitome is not simply a report of fifth-century sources, convenient though it would be to treat it as such. Taken as a whole, it plays down the applied technologies which get only cursory mention. This, as we shall see, undoubtedly reflects Diodorus' own historical plan, not that of his source; he is going to reserve the technologies for later treatment in a different context.

But, all in all, the compilation is a monumental addition to our knowledge of pre-Socratic anthropology, precisely because it spells out in prosaic detail so many anthropological doctrines which have already been hinted at, barely but definitely, in our fifth-century poetic sources.

For one thing it shows with what complete seriousness the earliest scientists had taken the proposition that man is an animal. That, in fact, is his scientific classification, an animal, but with a special adaptability (50). We now see what lay behind the obscure statement in the *Prometheus Bound* that:

> Seeing they did not see nor hearing grasp
> That which they heard. Like shapes of dreams they lived
> The random planless years all ignorant . . .

And the reference in *The Suppliants*:
> . . . our planless brutish life. . . .

For here the originally savage condition is defined as indeed an ape-like existence. Food is devoured in the manner of other animals and obtained in the same way. *Per contra* it is recognized that the present condition of man rests upon the domestication of plant-life (item 30). This truth had been felt intuitively in the myths of the olive, the grape and the grain as gifts of the gods. That was the version of it to which Euripides had reverted and which Plato had always preferred. But in the *Antigone*, the doctrine of agriculture as a man-discovered art is already explicit.

78

Moreover the 'humanizing' (*hemerosis*) of plants and animals betrays the fact that those laws of adaptation traceable in man's history are also applicable to other forms of life.

The epitome, in short, spells out without flinching the pre-human origins from which humanity emerged. It is less an account of the development of man civilized than an attempt to isolate the growth of those basic skills without which any further attempt at civilization would have been incredible. It is the study of the growth of the human intelligence from pre-human conditions, an intelligence now shared by all present men in all degrees of their culture. Man did not arrive equipped upon the earth with a brain which he proceeded to exploit in order to build ships and cities and so forth. The scientific thinking here is much more fundamental than that. Thus the man-animal here described had originally neither language nor society. It is difficult to imagine a doctrinal position more antipathetic to that of Plato and Aristotle. Since the *Prometheus* also hints at the primitive absence of these, and Sophocles and Euripides refer to the achievement of them, it is a safe inference that fifth-century science sought to trace the development of both speech and sociality something after the fashion described by Diodorus.

Closer inspection of the account given of them reveals a complex developmental pattern in which a sort of animal instinct first serves to create a group: the existence of the group then evokes a sort of primitive social consciousness in its members: this leads to the desire to communicate among themselves: the system of communication develops into a language: common linguistic behaviour then reacts upon the group, making it into a more coherent and cohesive nexus, a tribe nation or people (items 7-20). Thus the chain of development is kept unbroken, from man the brute operating by instinct, to *homo sapiens* operating by calculation. For man begins as an animal, warring after his kind against other animals, and being warred upon by them. Like them he feels fear, and like them, or some of them, he is inspired by this fear to form aggregates of packs or herds for better self-protection (item 10). But simultaneously fear of those outside the group is balanced by aid given within the group (item 8). It is only as the group is formed and persists that its members begin to recognize mutual characteristics (item 11). This apparently means the dawn of some faculty of social awareness which is also a form of self-awareness.

There are two different quotations from the *Prometheus* which may reflect this nascent doctrine of self-consciousness:

> Let me rather
> Relate to you the travailing of man:
> How from the silly creature that he was
> I made him conscious and intelligent . . .
>
> Did you go even further than you said? –
> I made men cease their doom to anticipate –
> To lift this curse what cure did you invent? –
> I made their hearts blind citadels of hope, –
> A brave utility on man conferred!

Then and only then comes the beginning of a system of inter-communication to express this awareness (items 16-18). With the growth of language the language group (item 19) comes into existence. Since this development occurred in parallel in different areas of the earth's surface the automatic result was the gradual formation of many language groups (items 20-22).

In this order of priorities, two axioms of the classic school of Greek philosophy have lost their metaphysical validity. Neither man's reason expressed in the power of rational speech, nor his political virtue, exist *a priori*. The city-state in fact (not mentioned in this epitome though it will find a place elsewhere in Diodorus) whether or not it was regarded by the anthropologists as the present stage of historical development, could not have been for them the one essential form toward which all society tends. The typical social nexus would for them be linguistic and secondarily topographical and economic. And we can infer that the morality of law and of justice, which for the classic thinkers was grounded in the absolute character of the city-state, was for the anthropologists simply a variable pattern of convenient and conventional usage by which any social aggregate sought to maintain inner cohesion and external protection against its enemies. In short, man's capacity not only for language but for ethics is traceable to the need of this animal to protect himself in the war against other animals.

That this kind of thinking goes back to the fifth century is an inference supported by some things said in the *Antigone* and the way they are said. We recall that both the *Prometheus* and the

Antigone seem to link together the phenomenon of society and the skill of architecture. But the *Antigone* also links together language, consciousness, and social usage and temper:

> Quick speech and the wind-swift thought
> The usage and moods of the town, strong walls that are
> warm in the night
> The builded roof, retreat from the driving rain –
> These, these are his self-taught arts. . . .

This could be a chance juxtaposition of the poet's choice; but a comparison with Diodorus suggests that it is not accident. Sophocles, to be sure, is no reporter, and his coverage of the material is properly impressionistic. He omits that initial and crucial stage of society – the group formed in sheer self-defence. But his collocation of 'speech', 'thought', and 'mood' of town usage (*phthegma, noema, orgai*) seems to recognize the same interwoven and interacting relationship between socialization and consciousness and language which is spelled out in Diodorus, and to suggest that it is Diodorus who may be deficient at this point, in not inserting the growth of custom-law (*nomos*) as a development parallel with that of language and consciousness, a development reported by Sophocles in the term 'usage-of-town' (*astunomos*).

The source of man's advance and the forces that mould his history lie either within himself or in the historical process of which he is a part. They are not derivable from divine inspiration or gift, or from metaphysical realities outside time and space. Accident may play a role, as in the formation of the different languages (item 21) but it is a limited role. Accordingly Diodorus' epitome three times refers to the 'instruction' which in effect man continually gives himself (items 9, 34, 47), a self-instruction which is hinted at in the *Prometheus* and explicitly stated in the *Antigone*. However, the process of instruction is further analysed and with considerable sophistication. It occurs empirically in the course of 'experience' (item 34) or as a response to 'need-and-use' (item 46). Even the 'mental readiness' stated in the conclusion of the epitome (item 53) to be a leading characteristic of the human animal points in the same direction. Here is a theory of knowledge which is progressive pragmatic and empirical and behaviouristic. We learn by trying to do and we then do better as we learn. The Platonic notion of human knowledge as wholly dependent upon the control exercised by fixed and eternal verities or forms or categories is wholly rejected. And this empirical terminology may throw light on that idea which is already expressed in the fifth-century versions by the term 'resource' (*poros*). While Aeschylus views the Promethean fire and technology as themselves 'mighty resources', in Sophocles it is man himself who is 'all resourceful', never 'lacking resource' for any problem confronting him. The term is dynamic and not static; it suggests that casting round for ways and means which itself becomes the means of man's ascent. Even Diodorus' statement that need and use itself 'supplied the suggestion' (item 48) finds an echo in a statement of Prometheus:

> By smoke of sacrifice of loin and thigh
> Wrapped in the fat I did initiate
> Man in a dark and intricate technique.

According to Diodorus' report, this empiricism employed by the human being as he 'tries things out' or turns his knacks to account is not by any means directionless. It obeys certain norms which are stated with an emphasis that suggests that they are almost dynamic drives. For men found themselves engaged in 'mutual assistance' in which their instructor was 'natural expediency'. (items 8, 9). This is the terminology of utilitarianism and it is later picked up in the references to 'life's utilities' (25, 39). Civilization as it gathers momentum is marked by the invention of 'everything capable of conferring utility in common social life' (43). This kind of language cannot but recall the figure of Prometheus himself:

> Thou great utility of social man,
> His brightest light since history began,

as well as the description of the metals that he discovered:

> Those great utilities beneath the earth,
> Silver and iron, copper and yellow gold

The dramatist, we suggest, was here using evocative language. He was faithful to that element in his sources which chose to define and describe the direction of human progress and its motive as controlled by the principle of the expedient and the useful. If so, the scientific anthropologists were on the way to offering social utility and personal satisfaction as the proper criteria by which to judge all historical achievement and social institutions. And the case for arguing that Prometheus himself, 'that great utility', was intended by the dramatist as a symbol of the historical process and its direction is considerably strengthened.

One last element in this epitome still remains to be noticed. Four times, no less, it is emphasized that the historical evolution of man from an animal to a civilized human being advances 'by a process of gradualism' (items 12, 15, 35, 40). This emphasis, we shall argue, is again a reflection of the emphasis in the early sources. Why it is so important philosophically can best be seen by continuing on for a while in Diodorus beyond the point where his scientific epitome stops. Now, he says, that we have laid our historical foundation in the description of the origin and early existence of man [1.8.10] let us come to recorded histories of men in known areas of the world [1.9.1]. And let us start with Egypt where it is claimed not only did the gods arise [1.9.1] but the human species also, along with other forms of life in the swamps of the Nile delta [1.10.1]. He then narrates a conflated and rather confused account of the mythical history of early Egypt to the point where Osiris (equals Dionysus) marries Isis (equals Demeter) and sets about organizing the kingdom of Egypt and its inhabitants [1.13.5]. These two together with lesser deities proceed to bestow a whole series of blessings 'for the good service of the common life of man'. The list of these, if we may accept it from Diodorus' ill-written account, is instructive:

Discovery of grain (by Isis)
Invention of way to prepare it (by Osiris)
Substitution of grain-eating for cannibalism (by Osiris)
'because of the pleasure inherent in the nature of the new discoveries
and because there was evident natural interest inherent in the abstention from mutual savagery' [1.14.1]
Present harvest rituals are a memorial [1.14.2]
'to the technical discoveries of the god' [1.14.3]
Then the founding of 'custom-law' (*nomos*)
in obedience to which human beings
render right-redress mutually
and have ceased the lawless life of aggression (*hybris*)

because of fear of punishment [1.14.3]
Then a city (Thebes), founded by Osiris [1.15.1]
and temples [1.15.3]
and honours paid to discoverers of techniques
and those who suggested methods of achieving 'utilities'
[1.15.4]
for example, copper and gold mines,
weapons and tools,
hunting,
agriculture,
and 'humanizing' (domestication) (*exhemerosai*)
of the land
through competitive effort [1.15.5]
The vine was discovered (by Osiris)
and its manufacture into wine
and instruction of mankind generally in its 'use' [1.15.8]
Hermes then came into prominence
in virtue of his capacity to confer utility on the common
life [1.15.9]
He articulated the common language
and discovered writing
and established the cults of the gods ('their honours and
sacrifices')
and he discovered a series of technologies . . . [1.16.1]
Osiris then conducted a campaign across the inhabited earth
to spread these blessings of civilization beyond Egypt's
borders [1.17.1]
Posterity has duly honoured him as a god for his services
as indeed all who invented and introduced means of sustenance [1.17.2]

There are obvious duplications between this historical romance
and the previous scientific epitome. Language already articulated
by man in his savage state is articulated all over again by Hermes
in Egypt. The domestication of given forms of plant life is repeated
and the general humanizing of human existence proceeds in the
same direction. On the hypothesis that in fact this Egyptian fairy
tale is both a sort of parody of and also a supplement to his
scientific sources, it is interesting to note several items omitted in
Diodorus' previous account and present here. These are:

1. The suggestion that man in his original animal state behaved like other animals by preying on his own kind [cf. Plato: *Polit.* 271e2].

2. The suggestion that one principle of his development from savage to civilized habits was the response to an increase in physical pleasure as well as to natural expediency.

3. The suggestion that a pattern of custom law came into existence to regularize the process by which members of the group rendered right-redress to each other. (Hence social justice has developed in accordance with behaviouristic principles.)

4. One of its motives being fear of punishment (supplementing the fear of enemies which in the epitome inspired the first social combinations).

5. The founding of the city-state (symbolized in Thebes).

6. The various tools and technologies (here fairly exhaustively itemized, as in the accounts of the three dramatists),

7. including writing (compare Prometheus).

8. The factor of emulative competition as a motive force for social progress,

9. and the establishment of religion as social cult.

These nine had, in fact, already appeared in the fifth-century scientific anthropologies, as can be proved in later chapters. Diodorus has simply reserved them for insertion in his Egyptian romance rather than in his original epitome. His reasons for doing so and the effect that he thus achieves must, before we leave him, be properly estimated. For they throw fresh and instructive light on the whole question of why in antiquity it was so difficult for these anthropologies to survive in their own stark scientific honesty. Aside from the story-teller's advantage of localizing early man in given surroundings and giving him the local colour of Egypt, Diodorus' Egyptian account has the drastic effect of replacing the gradual imperceptible material process by a series of miraculous inventions and inventors, who do the work for man and on whom man in gratitude comes to confer religious honours. This is precisely the effect already at work in Euripides' version, and applied in Plato's two accounts. The essential quality of man's own pragmatic, empirical, and searching

THE LIBERAL TEMPER IN GREEK POLITICS

power is destroyed, and the historical process replaced by a series of miracles. Traces of the original scientific and naturalist approach inhere even in Diodorus' parody of it. Thus physical pleasure assists Osiris in commending grain-eating to man in place of cannibalism, and natural interest inspires man's development away from savagery. Law, though represented as a divine foundation, turns out to be a pattern regulative of mutual adjustments carried out within the group, enforced not by divine retribution but by the man-made machinery of legal punishment. The divine discoverers, for all their power to donate their inventions, in fact 'suggested methods of achieving utilities' [1.15.4] – this is simply man's own power of finding his own methods as described in the epitome. It is pictured even here as accelerated by competitive effort rather than mediated by divine inspirational leadership [1.15.7]. In short, the descriptive science of fifth-century anthropology, with its basic tenets structurated in a terminology carefully chosen and analytically applied, has been garbled and corrupted by inclusion in that kind of mythical context so dear to the concrete mind – the context of the 'First Inventors' and 'the great heroes' and 'the demi-gods of culture'.

CHAPTER IV

HISTORY AS A COMPROMISE:

THE *PROTAGORAS*, *REPUBLIC* II, *POLITICS* I

THE second chapter ('History as Regress'), in order to introduce the evolutionary pattern of thought characteristic of scientific anthropology, began by presenting its converse in Hesiod and Plato. This order was deliberate. It presented what was traditional and deeply rooted in Greek thinking, by way of illustrating by contrast the radical and even offensive character of the naturalist postion. It is a measure of the danger which Plato felt he saw in this position that he took such pains in the *Statesman* and the *Laws* to subvert it, not by contradicting it in open fight but by turning it upside down, so that man's technological achievement might with safety be admitted, provided it would be represented as occurring in a period of moral regression.

There are, however, two more contexts in Plato's work where, returning to the same theme of man's history on this earth, he still tries to keep it under the control of metaphysics but uses a different method and one which by modern standards is more effective. Rather than attempting to convert evolution wholesale into devolution, he reproduces a copy of the scientific schematism but inserts Platonic additions and corrections in order to bring it into line with his own presuppositions. He edits rather than inverts his source. He produces two speciously progressive accounts of man and of society, which however really leave a final impression that progress is illusory and that it is vain to look for the source of morality in history. Since both versions draw directly upon the same sources epitomized by Diodorus, they form part of the documentation of early Greek anthropology but their testimony needs critical evaluation of the nicest sort.

The first version is placed in the mouth of the sophist-scientist Protagoras in the dialogue called after him. Scholars eager to grasp any available testimony to the teaching of the Sophists have sometimes assumed that Protagoras' speech reproduces Protagoras' teaching. Plato's methods elsewhere in his writings are not those of a reporter. Why should he report when he himself has so much to say? Why in particular should such a genius take the trouble to advertise in his own writings a system already in circulation and put out by a representative of a school of thought which he distrusted? To ask the absurd question is to suggest the right answer. Taking such trouble, he could have had only one purpose – to replace the original by his own version and to destroy so far as possible the effect of the original by dramatizing his own as though it were the original. This, indeed, is a general law of composition applicable to others of Plato's dialogues, and it is to be noted that it proved effective. Later antiquity, as it treasured the dialogues which pretended to memorialize the leading Sophists, ceased to take the trouble to read or to preserve the originals of these Sophists' works.

The story of man told by 'Protagoras' is best given in full:

There was once a time when the gods were, but the mortal species were not. For these in their turn came the appointed time of generation. The gods shaped them inside the earth, from a mixture of earth and fire and all that is commingled with earth and fire. When at the point of bringing them up to the light, they assigned to Prometheus (forethinker) and to Epimetheus (afterthinker) the task of ordering and distributing their appropriate capacities to each species. Epimetheus besought Prometheus: 'Let me do the distribution and you inspect my work'. Prometheus agreed, and he did [*Protag.* 320c8ff.].

His distribution meant attaching to some species strength without speed, and organizing others to have speed without strength. To some he gave armoured equipment, while to others he gave a natural condition which was unarmoured, but provided for their security by contriving some other capacity for them. Did he clothe some in tiny magnitude, his distribution gave them winged flight or subterranean dwelling. Did he magnify the magnitude of others, he used their very magnitude to give them security. Generally his distribution in this way evened things out [320d8ff.]. His contrivance was governed by the care he took to prevent any species from being eliminated [321a1].

Having supplied them with sufficient resource to evade destruction mutually inflicted, he also contrived easement for them against the seasons of Zeus, arraying them in thick hair and tough hides, an adequate defence against wintry cold and a capable defence against summer heat; so that when they went to bed they had their own covering with them in their natural condition [321a3ff.]. Their feet he shod with armour or with hard bloodless bone. Then he made provision for their varieties of sustenance, giving to some the herb of the earth and to others the fruit of trees and to others roots. To some he gave the eating of other animals as their sustenance. To some he gave the property of slow reproduction while others, which were preyed upon by these, he compensated with rapid reproduction. His provision was of security for the species [321b1ff.].

However, the skill of Epimetheus fell short of perfection and he failed to notice that he had used up the available capacities upon the witless creatures [321b7ff.]. He still had on his hands the human species unequipped and he did not know what to do with it. In his dilemma he was approached by Prometheus who came to inspect the distribution and noticed that while all the other animals were set up beautifully, the human being was naked, unshod, uncovered and unarmed. The appointed day for human beings had now come: it was their turn to come up from earth to the light of day. Prometheus, caught in this dilemma and asking himself 'What security shall I devise for human beings?' [321c1ff.], steals from Hephaestus and Athena technological skill along with fire – fire being essential to make it available and usable and useful. This was the endowment he bestowed on human beings [321d1ff.].

In this way they came into possession of the skill of livelihood but not 'the city skill' (*politike sophia*), which rested with Zeus. Prometheus no longer had permission to enter the Acropolis where Zeus had his mansion, and besides Zeus had formidable watchmen [321d4ff.]. However, he did secretly enter the building shared by Athena and Hephaestus in which the two of them pursued their technical calling. He stole the fiery technology of Hephaestus and the rest of technology belonging to Athena and gave them to human beings. This meant that human beings gained easy provision of livelihood [321e1ff.]. Prometheus however, so the story goes, because of Epimetheus was subsequently pursued by penalty for his thefts [322a1].

Since human beings have partaken in divine dispensation, firstly, their kinship with the gods gives them alone among animals a habitual custom of recognizing the gods, and they put their hands to erect altars and images of them [322a3]. Secondly, they quickly used technique to articulate speech and words and to invent houses and clothes and footgear and coverings and agricultural sustenance [322a6]. Equipped with these resources, human beings in the original condition lived dispersed in households and there were no cities.

Well, they kept being destroyed by wild beasts because in every respect they were weaker. Their craftsman technology was adequate as an auxiliary to sustenance, but not enough to deal with war against beasts. They did not yet have the 'city technique' of which one part is 'war technique'. Of course they strove to gather in groups and find security by founding cities. And then, whenever they gathered they did wrong to each other, inevitably so, as not having the 'city technique'. So they were shaken apart again and kept being destroyed [322b1ff.].

So Zeus with fear for our species lest it be wiped out sends Hermes to bring to human beings Restraint and Right, that they might be 'orders of cities' and 'combining bonds of amity'. Hermes asked Zeus: 'On what lines shall I give Right and Restraint to human beings? Shall I distribute them the way the technologies have been distributed? For instance: a single individual possesses medical technique and is adequate to serve several laymen; the same holds for the other craftsmen. Then shall I assign Right and Restraint to human beings on similar lines? Or shall I distribute them universally?' [322c1ff.].

'Universally', replied Zeus. 'All men must partake in them. For if they were like the other technologies, to be shared in by only a few, you could not have cities [322d1ff.]. Yes, indeed, and ordain a custom-law, as originating with me, that:

'if a man is unable to partake in reverence and right he must be treated as a disease of the body politic (city) and killed.' [d4]

The clue to this ingenious and attractive tale lies in the fact that under the guise of a narrative it really dramatizes a series of Socratic classifications. The various animal species are first distinguished in terms of those physical characteristics which look like essential properties. Then man is introduced and identified in sharp distinction from the animals as a technician and tool-user. But his nature is itself then subdivided into two distinct elements separated by intervals in the narrative: his intellectual power is distinguished qualitatively from his social and moral sense.

There can surely be little doubt whose powerful mind is behind this method of presentation. It was precisely Socraticism and Platonism which brought the discipline of definition by class to supplement and indeed transform previous Greek science. But, applied to historical process, it is vital to observe what it does to the process. It breaks it up into a series of leaps and jumps; or, altering the metaphor, it creates a condition of stratification which in effect removes the process altogether. True historical 'motion', to which the historian applies the formula 'little by little', is dissolved as a mere appearance, an illusion. Platonism prefers relationships between formal categories which must retain finality in order to be serviceable to knowledge. Thus two radical alterations are effected in the anthropological material which Plato is borrowing. Firstly, man ceases to be an animal. He is a separate creation; as against the other 'witless ones', he starts his career already equipped with technical intelligence. Secondly, his achievement of society and moral sense ceases to be a part of his continuous development from the savage towards the civilized condition, and on the contrary is converted into a special dispensation. The continuity between his growing technique and his growing power to form aggregates and so learn by experience the way of right and law is completely broken.

The machinery of the story gives fundamental support to these distinctions by using the divine apparatus. Although a concession is made to the view that all living things emerge from the material elements, the pre-Socratic picture of spontaneous generation of animals upon the earth's surface is carefully avoided by supplying the gods as the original artificers, who simply work up the material into appropriate shapes. By their agency *homo sapiens* can avoid the necessity of submitting to a genuinely primitive origin. He can emerge upon the earth already equipped, no eater of grass or roots nor even speechless; only the other animals are '*aloga*'. His special endowment is guaranteed by the care given to it by a special demigod. Prometheus *versus* Epimetheus is intended to dramatize the essential gulf between the 'lord of creation', the forethinker, and the subordinate species. And the later intervention of Zeus which forms the story's climax underscores the divine origin and eternal character of man's social and moral sense, whether viewed as conscience or as justice.

Yet, withal, the tale contains so much that carries the stamp of genuine anthropology. There is the obvious emphasis upon skill and technology, together with language, architecture, and the like; and on empirical 'resource' both animal and human. There is the interesting historical assumption repeated several times that the properties of animals and men are designed for survival and protection (*soteria*). There is the naturalist account of how man came to form primitive social aggregates in the course of war against other species. (But here Plato falsifies the original by identifying all society as automatically civic and political, as though there were no intervening stages between the scattered isolated life of savages and the city-state). There is the definition, expressed as a rescript of Zeus, of the wrong-doer and the criminal as essentially the antisocial human being against whom society takes sanctions.

For these naturalist conceptions Plato, then, has designed a metaphysical setting. But his editorial skill cannot always conceal the seams in the structure, and there are two resultant inconsistencies in his account. The first thing we are told that man did after his creation was to found religion, and the reason given for this is that he has kinship with the gods. But when "Protagoras" began his tale, did he say that men were the sons of gods any more than were the animals? It would seem that Plato had originally omitted this Hesiodic notion, in deference to his naturalist source, and then revived it illogically in order to give a theological explanation of the rise of cult practice; whereas his source, we suspect (see Diodorus), gave a purely historical and institutional account of the matter. To the pre-Socratics, cult was man's way of acknowledging the seasonal benefits of the weather and the earth.

A far more subtle but in the long run more important element in Platonism is revealed by the inconsistency with which technical capacity is treated. As man's initial equipment it results in language and architecture and agriculture. These are essentially non-specialized activities. Language is in fact a universal, yet it is given as the primary expression of man's gift of technical intelligence. Previous sources, from Aeschylus to Diodorus, leave no doubt that here Plato reports his originals faithfully. But when Zeus intervenes with Reverence and Right we are suddenly told that, while these moral qualities are universals, technology is not; it is highly specialized and uneven in its presence in the human species.

This view of technique and skill is a Platonic commitment, nowhere argued or defended, but always assumed and perhaps derived from Socrates. It is significant that Hermes refers here for proof of natural specialization to that typical Socratic example, medicine. The thesis is essential to Platonism if it is to build its political theory on the aristocratic hypothesis that most men are nitwits. But it is equally clear that the anthropologists viewed language and architecture and social organization and the like as essentially achievements of man universal, even if gifted individuals helped to accelerate the pace. The principle of gradualism so emphasized in Diodorus was antipathetic to heroes, inventors, demigods, or naturally superior members of the human race.

The assumption that technique is specialized is to lead in Platonism to the completely non-anthropological notion that the technique of government is also specialized. This brings us finally to consider briefly the role, if any, that Protagoras personally played in this type of speculation. It can be assumed that he used anthropology whether or not he was an original anthropologist. It affords him a theoretic basis from which to defend democracy, and the use he made of it will be examined in a later chapter. But on two grounds he can be personally exempted from any responsibility for the metaphysical structure of this so-called myth. We know that in matters of religion he was a complete agnostic. He is on record to this effect in the most explicit terms. Firstly, is it credible that an agnostic in giving his account of man would have utilized the divine apparatus in quite so structural a sense as the under-pinning of a religious or metaphysical view of the origin and validity of morality and as the efficient cause of man's existence? Secondly, when in this same dialogue he is later allowed to examine the character of human morality, he explicitly states that it is like a 'second language' which, of course, everybody has. This not only reveals his own view of it but exposes the seams in Plato's mythical construction. If man's humanity and his spiritual powers are as natural and as historical and as pragmatic as the development of his powers of communication, then the gulf between the gifts of Prometheus and the gifts of Zeus disappears.

By the time Plato came to write the *Republic* he was prepared to show his hand. The ten books of this mighty work are devoted to the majestic proposition that morality, personal and social, is a system of natural law written upon the heavens, informing the pattern of the universe, and built into the structure of the human soul. It is, therefore, essentially independent of time, place, and circumstance. Yet precisely as he begins in the second book to undertake the opening theme of his argument, he feels compelled to mobilize the resources of the anthropological method in order to get it started. Let us, he says, first observe righteousness as it emerges 'in history'; and therefore let us observe the historical emergence of that institution we call the city-state [*Repub.* 369]. What follows is a view not of the primitive origins of man, it is true, but of his developed civilization. The tale would appear to be taken up where the *Protagoras* left off; the method is descriptive and genetic, as follows:

PART I

1. An individual's (economic) needs are multiple
2. and he cannot meet them all himself [*Repub.* 369b]
3. This forces men to form groups to co-operate in supplying mutual needs
4. We posit that this *synoikia* (conjunction of households) is a city-state
5. The mutual exchange that then occurs serves the individual interests
6. In short the state is created by (economic) need-and-use [369c]

7. of sustenance, housing, clothing [369d]

8. The needs are met by division of labour [369e-370a]

9. which obeys our (Socratic) principle that the natures of men are disparate and specialized

10. and in any case, full time specialization yields more efficient results [370b]

11. Technicians and craftsmen, makers of tools and equipment, and likewise animal husbandmen will have to multiply and form part of the city's complement [370d]

12. As the city enlarges, its limited territory will require the aid of imports

13. which can be purchased only by exports; thus cities like individuals supply mutual needs via commerce [370e]

14. This requires not only an enlargement of the existing labour force

15. but a new class of specialist – the merchants and the sea-farers for sea-borne commerce [371a]

16. Similarly for internal exchange the state will require a marketplace, currency, and a class to operate them – the traders and bankers corresponding to the merchants [371b]

17. This function, in properly conducted cities, is relegated to inferior persons [371c]

18. Nor must we forget the unskilled labour forming part of the city's complement

19. though strictly speaking unworthy to be admitted to community

20. The city-state has now developed to the point of completion [371e]

21. As to righteousness – does it perhaps inhere somewhere in the mutual needs and dealings conducted between its members? [372a]

PART 2

22. Now we come to define the regimen (*diaita*) of such a community

23. It will be very simple and economical in food, drink, and dress [372a]

24. diet will be vegetarian,

25. amusement will be sober, festal merriment,

26. with religious piety,

27. and birth control to prevent poverty,

28. and pleasurable social intercourse [372b-c]

29. and pacifist attitudes

30. healthy and long-lived

31. As men pass away they bequeath an equally idyllic existence to their children [372d]

32. This is the true or ideal state – the healthy state [372e]

PART 3

33. Let us now consider the state at a higher level of material luxury

34. which means the state that has passed into a stage of fever

35. a state which may likewise throw light on the development of righteousness in society [372e]

36. All the material equipment is now multiplied beyond the (natural) minimum; and we get superfluity

37. All the applied arts and crafts are set in motion [373a]

38. the sheer size of the state becomes excessive

39. the fine arts, drama, poetry, etc., are likewise added [373b]

40. plus the arts of woman's dress and adornment

41. plus all kinds of domestic servants from cooks to tutors

42. plus piggeries and other meat suppliers [373c]

43. plus doctors

44. Growth of population and increasing demand

45. and the unlimited pursuit of wealth

46. will lead to aggression and conquest of neighbouring territories [373d]

47. Thus warfare is instituted

48. As to its actual effect for good or evil we say nothing now

49. only asserting that genetically speaking it derives from the worst factors that develop in a state [373e]

50. War requires a professional army (on the principle of division of labour) [374a]

51. and hence the institution of state guardians [374e]

As we have seen, the *Suppliants* of Euripides afforded a hint that anthropological theory, when Plato was still a child, had been stretched to cover the growth and structure of a commercial exchange economy. Plato furnishes the first extensive documentation of this aspect of the Greek science of society. His analysis is governed by those naturalist-materialist principles already exposed. The driving force behind the formation of society is material and economic need for primary sustenance, and those secondary resources which clothe and protect man. That this is, indeed, the governing principle is explicitly stated (item 6). Human motivations and objectives are viewed pragmatically and empirically. The process by which products are exchanged is linked with the specialization of labour (item 8). The economic analysis seems surprisingly sophisticated, and rather off the beaten track of classic Greek philosophical speculation. International commerce between states is recognized as an essential condition for the existence of any one fully developed state (items 12, 13); and no less importance is accorded to the marketplace with its apparatus of commerce and banking and its trading specialists who deal only in monetary values (items 15, 16). Finally and most radically the suggestion is ventured that morality itself is in fact definable in terms of the system which regulates men's relationships in such a society (item 21). The naturalist-historical approach to ethics can in principle hardly go further than this.

Plato at once drops this last suggestion, and in this form it is never resumed. It could be said that he backs away from it with some haste. Why then did he mention it unless it occurred in his source and he has cited it almost by inadvertence? And then, in the same spirit of retreat, he proceeds in the next two parts of his story to carry out a manipulation which carefully undoes the historical science of his first part.

But first it is to be observed that even the doctrine of Part 1 carries within itself certain Platonic elements which collide with the premises of a genuinely historical science. In the *Protagoras* story, the Platonic thesis was already in evidence that men differ fundamentally from birth in mental capacity and aptitude. This could be regarded as a truism of common sense, but the point is to ask whether historically speaking the differences between individuals have been as important as their similarities. Since Greek scientific anthropology began with the hypothesis that man is an animal, but of a given species, it could not be a respecter of persons within the species. Platonism, in discarding the hypothesis, also discards the assumption that what men have in common is essential, and what they differ in is incidental. The present context makes this thesis of the *Protagoras* more explicit. Men differ qualitatively. For the division of labour is founded not only on the fact that the crafts in practice call for specialization (item 10) but that this corresponds axiomatically to human differentiations (item 9); a cobbler is a cobbler from birth and will never make a potter. Plato is building on the social practice by which the crafts were maintained in family guilds and transmitted by hereditary mechanism. This is what a liberal naturalist thinker would call a merely 'conventional' arrangement – a *nomos* – but Plato draws other inferences from it. As it later turns out, he is in fact willing to admit that craftsmen can exchange techniques without disaster; but his axiom of the natural dissimilitude of men is needed to justify the gulf which will later open between the wisdom of his governing class and the mere obedience of the governed.

As the gulf opens, an intellectual difference turns into a moral one; the qualitative distinction becomes total. And this, too, is forecast in the present passage. For, having been compelled by the logic of the descriptive method he is following to admit that the marketplace and its specialists and the unskilled labourer must play an essential role in the economy of the developed state, he proceeds to denigrate the persons concerned. He speaks here of a 'correctly conducted city' (item 17) – the qualification in the context is incongruous. The crude manpower element, after being admitted in response to historical logic, then have the doors of community slammed in their faces (item 19). These addenda are judgmental not descriptive; they are rooted in Platonic notions of what aristocratic virtue is. And they were transmitted to Aristotle in whose *Politics* they reappear as a preference in favour of an agrarian state and the doctrine of the natural slave.

Aside altogether from these prejudices, the account in Part 1, as Plato gives it, is placed under the control of an axiomatic belief, which, whether or not he first fathered it, was certainly solidified by his philosophy to a point where it became an integral part of classic political theory. This is simply that the historical evolutionary process ends with the city-state: the *polis* as he here says is complete and perfect (item 20). And that is why Plato's appearance of using the historical method here is really specious.

Having set human history in motion, he stops it by fiat at the Greek city-state. And indeed he begins it there; that first society which men combined to form is already in his language a *polis*. The social theory of the Greek anthropologists, as we have seen, was not committed in this total fashion to the priority of the *polis*. They were prepared, for instance, to view the linguistic group or nation as a significant phenomenon. In the fifth century they may have tended to think in city-state terms and to regard the city-state as perhaps the most developed condition of society so far attained. But this is not at all the same thing as giving it an ideal and even metaphysical status in history. Democritus, for example, as we shall see, though his imagination was captured by the spectacle of democratic Athens and her institutions, was not committed to seeing the *polis* everywhere and in all stages of social growth. Nor can the view that the *polis* is the final crystallization of society be reconciled with the realistic appreciation of the vital importance of international commerce. If the latter is a development with its own logic and rooted in the historical process, then it points to the conclusion that in the course of historical development larger units than the city-state may at least theoretically be conceivable. These would be regional alliances or federations or nation-states or empires. It will be ascertained from an examination of Aristotle's *Politics* that in fact such social integrations were being visualized by political theorists in the fourth century, men whose views must have had a considerable influence on Isocrates. It must remain an open question as to whether pre-Socratic anthropology was prepared to go as far; but it is at least certain that it accepted the existence of both the market-place and the international exchange economy as a normal and acceptable factor of social growth and integration, without making virtuous reservations about it in the interests of preserving for the isolated *polis* some fancied purity.

Once Plato's adulterations of his source in Part 1 are appreciated, it is almost possible to forecast what he will do with scientific history in Parts 2 and 3. Part 2 simply attempts the impossible by trying to argue that a developed technical and commercial society is really a rustic Utopia committed to vegetarianism and the simple life. Only the spell of Plato's genius can have so long concealed from his readers this patent absurdity. Why does he attempt it? The answer is to be sought in those reconstructions of man's history which he later put into the *Statesman* and the *Laws* and which were reviewed in the second chapter. In them was revealed Plato's real mind – the fundamentally regressive character of his pseudo-history. Here in the *Republic*, where accommodation to the views of scientific history is much more in evidence, the same regressiveness nevertheless has the last word. As he looks at the estate of man his guiding principle is nostalgic. His imagination still lives in the Hesiodic perspectives of history. There must have been a Utopia once, in which men were peaceful and good, and its outlines are derived in reverse by condemning and rejecting the apparent complications, the competition and the licence and luxury and variety, of developed culture. Hence this little Utopian sketch is not 'playful' (a term convenient to critics who have not understood Plato's mind) but a serious expression of his deepest feeling about man.

He proceeds in Part 3 to pass even more drastic judgment. We discover that he is prepared to envisage a leisured society only as a fevered patient. And why? Because essentially the arts of leisure – they are all there, including sculpture, painting, poetry, music as well as gastronomy and women's fashions – are ethically superfluous; he could add that they are biologically superfluous, too. One can live without them and one therefore should. But one cannot live without figs and honey. Where this takes us in Plato's mind we need not further explore. But it is relevant to note that, rejecting the fundamental doctrine of his source, he places the origin of warfare only at this civilized stage of development (items 44-47). Anthropological science, as we have seen, saw war as part of man's original condition in his brutish state and conceived perhaps of his growth away from war towards peace as his technology and social sense improved. Plato, on the contrary, concludes his account of the development of social man with the institution of war, once more revealing his deeply regressive conception of history.

In analysing these few pages of Plato we have spoken of his source or sources. The case for their existence turns upon two factors: there is first the cross-comparison that can be made between the items of his historical analysis and those present in the reports of the dramatists and of Diodorus; second, there are the inner contradictions discoverable in these pages. Plato's systematic mind was, to say the least, not prone to contradiction;

its presence here is most easily explicable on the hypothesis that he is using and adapting material which is intractable.

It follows that the account of the genesis of the state in *Republic* 2 is in effect a supplement to the account of the genesis of society given in the myth of the *Protagoras*. It can perhaps be inferred that in the anthropological sources on which Plato is drawing the two formed two parts of a single continuous account. In each case Plato's purpose in giving the report is identical. He desired to edit it within a framework determined by premisses which are not historical but idealist; and in each case this purpose betrays him into inconsistencies.

His pupil Aristotle was not backward in learning the propagandist lesson. This may seem rather a harsh adjective to use of serious philosophers, but the truth should never be lost sight of that a moral philosopher's task is not only to describe but to persuade, and that the ingenuity of his persuasive art is in direct proportion to his genius as a philosopher. The introduction to Aristotle's *Politics* consummates, so to speak, the act of mastication and digestion which is evident in these two reports of Plato's. Though not regressive and Utopian as are the accounts in the *Politicus* and the *Laws*, and though clothed in the garments of a method which appears genetic and historical, Aristotle's introduction is neither genetic nor historical in any real sense of these words. It affords the crowning example of how scientific naturalism was defeated and absorbed into a teleological system. The briefest summary will suffice to expose this [*Polit.* 1.1ff.]:

Every city-state is a form of community.
All communities are formed to aim at some good.
The most valid form comprehending all others must therefore aim at the most valid good.
This most valid form is what we call the city-state.
Our speculative method shall be that of reducing a composite to its component elements [1.1.3];
That is, a genetic examination of origins, as follows [1.2.1.].
First the mating pair, man and woman;
Second the ruler and ruled, master and slave [1.2.2];
Third the household composed of these two associations [1.2.5];
Fourth the union of households in the village [1.2.6];

Fifth, the association of households in that complete and perfect unit, the city-state,
Comprising the all sufficient limit
which comes into existence to serve living
but actually exists to serve good living [1.2.8.].
Hence every city-state exists by nature,
it being the end aimed at by the original communities,
for the real nature of a thing is its end . . .
Hence the human being is by nature a city-state animal
and if a man is not naturally such
he is a different specimen of humanity, either savage or superhuman [1.2.9].
Man is a city-state animal
to an extent that any bee or herd animal is not.
Proof: Nature makes nothing in vain;
Man alone of the animals has (rational) language [1.2.10];
Animals have speech-sounds merely to signify pleasure and pain.
Rational language however is designed to symbolize and communicate the expedient and harmful
and the right and wrong [1.2.11].
Man's peculiar property vis-à-vis the animals
is to have a sense of good and bad,
right and wrong etc.
It is the association of such elements (or beings?)
that makes the household and city-state [1.2.12].
Finally, righteousness is a city-state thing
For the right-of-redress is the 'system' (*taxis*)
of a city-state community
and this right involves a just determination of the righteous [1.2.16].

Plato treated the city-state as the perfection of the historical process: Aristotle spells this out systematically as the axiom of all social theory. The *polis* is the *telos* towards which all possible historical development must move. It comprehends all other possible forms of community.

So much is patent, and there is no mystery about the rigid teleological control thus exercised by the city-state over the classic school of Greek theory. But Aristotle, besides thus riveting

the axiom upon his treatise, does something else in this introduction which only emerges into the daylight after the previous
contribution of scientific anthropology has been fully appreciated.
To begin with, the proper concessions are made to it: first, man
is an animal; second, adds Aristotle, in order to understand
society let us follow a genetic developmental method; third, he
adduces those analogies to human society found in the swarming
bees and the animals that run in herds; fourth, he notes that even
animals have speech-sounds to symbolize pleasure and pain; fifth,
he recognizes that our notion of righteousness derives from the
pattern of our social practices and is in fact a reflection of the
primitive legal structure, the right of redress (*dike*) which holds
any group together.

These five insights, of fundamental importance, are all borrowed from the descriptive anthropologists. And then with great
skill he subverts them and renders each one of them innocuous.
For man's species as an animal is defined as 'city-state species',
as though in his savage condition he already carried an acropolis
tattooed on his chest. Second, the genetic historical method turns
out to be spurious; it is really an analytical logical device which
takes some existing composite and divides it into its ideal
elements and then starts with the supposed elements and builds
up the composite again. Third, the swarming and herding animals
offered in his sources as a prototype of society are carefully
severed by him from any connection with human beings, that is
from any society of the *polis* variety. Fourth, the bridge between
the animal speech-sounds and human language, as set forth in his
sources, is demolished. Man alone has *logos* – the ambiguity here
in the Greek between reason and language serves him well. And
so man is safely severed from any animal origins whatever. He is
not an animal at all, except in Aristotelian double-talk. It remains
only for the critic to admire this superb process of mastication
and digestion, by which classic political theory not only overcame
its opponents, but concealed from posterity their very existence.

CHAPTER V

THE FRAGMENTS OF THE GREEK
ANTHROPOLOGISTS

ANAXIMANDER (circa 550 B.C.)

1. (From Aetius) [Diels-Kranz *FVS*[6] 12A30]
   Anaximander's opinion was that
   the first animals were generated in the moist:
   they were covered in prickly husk.
   Then as the time of life advanced
   they came out upon the drier part,
   the husk ruptured and peeled off
   and they lived a short time after that.

2. (from Censorinus) [12A30]
   Anaximander's opinion was that
   from water and earth in a warm condition
   there arose either fish or animals very like fish.
   Inside these, human beings took shape,
   the fetuses being retained inside until the period of puberty,
   at which time they ruptured and there emerged men and
   women by this time capable of self-support.

3. (from a scholium on Dionysius Thrax [12c]
   It is alleged . . .
   that the inventor of the alphabet was Cadmus
   or else that he was the conductor of the Phoenician invention
   to us or else . . . that . . . Danaus transmitted it.
   Supporting testimony is given by the Milesian historian
   Anaximander (and by Dionysius and Hecataeus).

Even this meagre report shows how fundamental was the
detachment of the Greek scientific mind towards our own species.
Man for Anaximander at the dawn of Greek speculation is
primarily an animal like other animals. All animal species are to
be viewed in turn as included in those forms of organic life which
grow upon the earth's surface. And all organic life in turn is

viewed as derived from the inorganic; or more correctly the line of development from elemental chaos to plants and animals and men is continuous (item 1). Sea and swamp were the first nursery of life; that is, the marine forms of life are regarded as essentially earlier than the mammals. The latter, including man, evolve from the former (by mutation of some sort). *Homo sapiens* was not always what he is now. Modern science would prefer to derive him from a previous mammalian stage, whereas Anaximander envisages his species as emerging direct from a non-mammalian existence. But the method of reasoning is identical and it is reproduced in the epitome of Diodorus five centuries later. Did Anaximander's original (a poem perhaps?) trace the subsequent development of man as he found his feet on the earth's surface, foraged for food like the animals, and subsequently – with what miraculous invention – devised language and technology and society for himself? We suspect it did, and that from this lost anthropology one precious echo survives: the report that Anaximander discussed the invention of the alphabet. This would be included in a series of ascending inventions in the manner of the *Prometheus Bound.*

XENOPHANES (c. 565-470 B.C.)

4. (quoted by Simplicius) [21B29]
   'Everything that is born and grows consists of earth and water.'

5. (quoted by Sextus) [21B33. cf. B27]
   'From earth and water all of us derive.'

6. (quoted by Stobaeus) [21B18]
   'Men did not originally receive from gods a demonstration of all matters;
   'It is by research carried out in the course of time that they come to improve their invention.'

7. (from Pollux) [21A4]
   . . . or perhaps it was the Lydians who first struck coined money, as Xenophanes asserts.

8. (quoted by Clement) [21B14]
   'Men form the opinion that gods were born
   and have men's clothes and language and appearance.'

9. (quoted by Clement) [21 B15]
   'If oxen, horses or lions had hands
   to draw with their hands or fashion the works that men do,
   horses would be drawing the shapes of gods in the likeness of
   horses, oxen in the likeness of oxen,
   and would be making the bodies similar in appearance to
   their own,
   each according to their kind.'

10. (from Clement) [FVS 1.133.p6-7]
   The several groups make life portraits of the shapes of the
   gods in the likeness of themselves: the Ethiopians, as Xenophanes says, make them black and snub-nosed; the Thracians
   make them red-haired and blue-eyed.

Though Xenophanes' detailed description of the genesis of
plant and animal life has not survived, he seems to have based it
on principles identical with those of his predecessor. 'We', that
is human beings (item 5), as well as all things 'born and grown',
that is animals and plants (item 4), have for ancestry the water
and earth of the primeval slime. His account of man's savage
existence is not extant. Did he attempt one? It is hard to avoid
the conclusion that he did when one considers the emphasis that
he placed not only upon invention (items 6 and 7) but upon the
process of gradualness, of human trial and error by which it is
achieved, and his explicit denial that it owed anything to the gifts
or guidance of superior beings (item 6). His notice of the invention
of coinage (item 7) duplicates the interest of Anaximander in the
genesis of the alphabet. Here then are seven scraps of testimony
relating to these two thinkers which furnish good illustration of the
kind of wreckage which carries the stamp of a specific style of
architecture. They hint at the presence in both of a scheme of
cosmology which found perhaps its climax in the history of life
and of man upon the earth (zoogony and anthropogony).
These can be fitted into the grand design which authorities as
widely separated as Aeschylus and Diodorus make visible to us in
part or in whole. And the tentative conclusion can be drawn that
before the end of the sixth century Greek speculative science had
already begun, after some fashion, to attempt the main outline of
this design; that, if the record of Anaximander guarantees the
biological naturalism of Greek anthropology, that of Xenophanes

does the same for its empirical pragmatic conception of the sources of human knowledge.

Against these tentative conclusions should be set what we know of Xenophanes' 'theology'. It has become famous as the first recorded critical attack on Greek polytheism. But is it not plausible that, structurally speaking, it also, like his views on coinage, was a part of his reconstruction of the history of human institutions, among which he included religious cult? This would require for religion a genetic and historical explanation. Some of the terms used in the few verses of his on this subject that have survived help to support this conclusion. The gods are supposed to have men's clothes and language he says (item 8). Clothes and language, as we have seen, tend to recur in the anthropological pattern of human 'inventions'. Again, when he uses the analogy of what animals would do to make gods if they could, he seems plainly to be thinking in a context in which men and animals are regarded as comparable. Man in fact is only a special sort of animal, who even when he draws and sculpts represents animals, whether intended as gods or men. He is an animal who does this with his hands (item 9). Is it implied that it is the possession of this physical equipment which explains some of man's superior abilities? The suggestion recurs in the Diodorus epitome as also in Anaxagoras below. And does the touch of comparative ethnology in the reference to 'the several groups' of men (Ethiopians versus Thracians) (item 10), who construct cult statues 'each according to their kind' (item 9), when linked with the previous reference to the languages which gods are supposed to speak, suggest that perhaps Xenophanes had already conceived of the development of human culture in terms of linguistic groups (which he saw as also cult groups)? This must remain a guess. But it is no guesswork to detect in him and in his predecessor the outline of the design which inspired that conception of man dramatized in the *Prometheus Bound* of Aeschylus.

ANAXAGORAS (c. 500-430 B.C.)

11. (from Aetius) [59A112]
   Animals are parts of the cosmos according to Anaxagoras
   [and to Euripides]

12. (from Theophrastus) [59A117]
... The assertion of Anaxagoras that ...
the atmosphere (*aer*) contains the seeds of all things,
and that these when precipitated in rain generated plants ...

13. (from Irenaeus) [59A113]
Anaxagoras, styled the atheist, propounded the doctrine
that animals rose out of seeds which fell from the sky to the
earth's surface.

14. (from Plutarch) [59A116]
A plant is an animal rooted in the earth according to the
view of Plato, Anaxagoras and Democritus and their schools.

15. (from ps-Aristotle) [59A117]
Anaxagoras ... asserts that
plants are moved by desire, have sensation, and feel pain and
pleasure ...
and that plants are in fact animals feeling pleasure and pain,
an inference he made from the agitation of their leaves ...
and that they have mind and intelligence.

16. (from Aetius) [59A101]
Anaxagoras' view:
all animals have the activist type of intelligence but not
necessarily the learning type ...

17. (from Aristotle) [59A102]
Anaxagoras says
the human being is the most intelligent of the animals
because he has hands
[but it would be more logical to say that he has hands because he is
the most intelligent]

18. (from a scholium to Aristides) [59A66]
Anaxagoras said that
there was not altogether any providence of the gods exercised
upon human beings;
human history proceeded under the aegis of [chance?]

19. (quoted in Plutarch) [59B21b]
'We make use of our own experience and memory and skill
and technique

and get honey and milk from the animals
and grow things and herd things and stockpile.'

20. (quoted by Simplicius) [59 B4]
'My system being such, the conclusion must follow that
(a) in all these selective compounds there inhere many all-
various properties with seeds of all things and all-various
shapes and hues and savours [2.34.5-7]
(b) in the process human beings have been put together and
all the animals – everything that has life [2.34.8-9]
(c) the human beings have cities formed by combined
settlement and resources which they have fashioned
(just as you can see with us)
(d) and have their sun and moon and so on
(just as you see with us) [2.34.10-12]
(e) and have the earth growing for them many all-various
products
(f) of which those with most utility they stockpile in their
dwellings and make use of [2.34.13]
(g) such is my thesis about the separating out as stated,
namely that it would have occurred not only in our case but
also in other cases.' [2.34.14]

While the first six of these citations (items 11-16) report
Anaxagoras' theories of plant and animal physiology they are cited
here only to establish the chain of reasoning in his mind which led
up to his initial statement on man (item 17). Man is an animal
himself; we therefore infer that, like all animal and plants, he
shares a common descent from the cosmic elements. This would
be in line with Anaxagoras' cosmic principles, but the sense of it,
we suggest, is more concrete and cuts deeper. With his explanation
of vital seeds falling from the sky, Anaxagoras offered a refinement
on the earlier theory that the earth's surface spontaneously
generated life. We suggest that he took the plant rather than the
insect as the prototype of organic life. Animal species were a
cosmic variant so to speak upon plants and were compacted either
simultaneously with plants by a similar process of precipitation or
by some plants becoming mobile and then turning and eating
other plants. The reference to the agitation of foliage in item 15
may be an echo of some such theory of plant mobility. It follows
that man himself at the upper end of the scale of evolution

(though this scale is not spelled out in the extant record) is not merely just an animal but ultimately a variant on a plant. To support this inference that for Anaxagoras all organic life from its vegetable to its human manifestations forms a continuous phenomenon, it can be argued that just as he would regard a man as a plant he had the corresponding imagination to regard a plant as a man. Item 15 bears this out. True, he says only that plants are animals. But the joint partnership of both in sensation, pleasure and pain argues that they belong in man's company, for these are humanistic terms transferred backwards. And accordingly Item 16 goes on to argue that, in fact, even the intelligence characteristic of man pervades all the organic world, though man possesses a variant of it which can 'learn'; that is, in man it reaches technological levels; man can 'instruct himself' (as in the anthropology used by Aeschylus and Sophocles). But this does not make him a special creation.

Against this background it becomes possible to give proper weight to the interpretation of Item 17 and to the correction which Aristotle hastily adds. In the eyes of the naturalist and the evolutionist the human intelligence is a phenomenon like any other with its concrete externals amenable to description. He does not, like Plato and Aristotle, raise problems of metaphysical priority. He is historically minded and as he looks at man and compares him with parallel forms of plant and animal life he concludes that his physical organs are the primary datum with which description must deal. These have developed like everything else out of the elements of the cosmos. Man then, historically, is that animal which has developed hands, and therefore has learnt to walk upright. From this new feature and the capacities for tool-using thus released, as the forefeet become specialized as hands, there follows also the pattern of behaviour which is associated with 'intelligence'. Not the prior direction of an ideal intelligence or a divine mind, but the protean capacity of an elemental nature to evolve all-various forms of life, from the sunflower to the scientist, is the archetypal axiom from which an Anaxagorean philosophy is derived. It can be inferred that when in *Politics* I Aristotle classifies the animals as sentient and pleasure-feeling but man as rational he is both reporting and also correcting this kind of anthropological thinking.

When, therefore, in Item 19 Anaxagoras comes to consider

what man accomplishes with his hands, he gives priority to the capacity to exploit other species. But the intention is not to break the previous continuity and to represent man as the lord of creation. Rather it is to argue that man repeats the pattern found in all the animals of preying upon fellow species. But he now does it by substituting in place of the crude device of slaughter the more sophisticated one of subtracting the sustenance that they secrete or collect. We put the bees and the goats to work for us. Basically this also demonstrates what human 'wisdom' is: it is simply a technical skill (*sophia* and *techne*) which has been built up gradually by storing and repeating experience ('memory') and by following the guidance of trial and error (the Greek *empeiria*) which uses stored experience, that is memory, to suggest fresh invention. (For example, man might obtain from the remembered experience of being nursed at the breast the suggestion that a goat's udder might well do as a substitute). This establishes for Anaxagoras that principle of gradualism in the development of man's mental capacity which, as we saw, was so stressed in the epitome of Diodorus.

Item 20, though a quotation from a book by Anaxagoras – perhaps still available in the Academy library when it was quoted – and though couched in language characteristic of its author, must be an excerpt from his own epitome of his own teaching; for it covers the span of cosmic history from chaos to human civilization in a single sweep. It is obvious that continuity of development is assumed; equally so the view that man is an animal. But sub-sections (c) to (g), which suddenly open up the perspective of human institutions and of a developed technology, can be interpreted in different ways. The passage puzzled Simplicius, who quotes it, but we can exclude his neo-Platonist suggestion that it describes an ideal order of reality prior to the perceptible. It certainly establishes as the doctrine of Anaxagoras the naturalist and genetic conception of civilization and its institutions, including the city-state, as part of the continuous cosmic development. But where is he locating those cultures which occurred 'elsewhere' or 'in other cases'? Possibly he is assuming that there are other solar systems and, if so, that life in them exhibits the same order of development as in ours; or he is affirming that human cultures have developed in parallel in various parts of the earth's surface besides the Aegean coasts; or he is thinking not in spatial but in temporal terms and referring to previous cultures which in past history have formed the basis of the present one. His kind of mind might not necessarily make a sharp distinction between the last two alternatives, between spatial and temporal dimensions. And if so, is his conception not of a piece with that theory of the development of 'systems' of linguistic and ethnic groups in various parts of the inhabited earth (*oikumene*) which we have already had reason to suppose was part of pre-Socratic anthropology?

ARCHELAUS (a disciple of Anaxagoras)

21. (from Hippolytus) [60A4]

   Archelaus' doctrine . . .

   under the head of animals is as follows:

   the earth originally felt the influence of heat in the part beneath where the hot and the cold commingled.

   Here there emerged all the varieties of animals including human beings;

   all had the same regimen (*diaita*)

   as deriving sustenance from the slime

   and were short-lived.

   Subsequently the method of sexual propagation came to be organized.

   Mind grows inherently in all animals alike;

   in fact every one of the animals as well [as the human being] makes use of mind in varying degrees of mobility [2.46.17-20].

   Human beings were separated out from the others

   and then organized (leadership and) leaders and lawful usages and techniques

   and cities and so on. [2.46.21]

22. (from Diogenes Laertius) [60A1]

   It would appear that

   Archelaus as well as Socrates tackled ethical philosophy

   in that he philosophized about custom law

   and what is honourable (*kalon*) and right (*dikaion*) . . .

   his doctrine was that . . . [2.45.2-4]

   the animals were generated from slime;

   right and dishonourable (*aischron*) existed not by nature but by lawful usage [2.45.5-7]

23. (from the Lexicon of Suidas) [60A2; 2.45.21]
Archelaus' opinion:
right and dishonourable exist not by nature but by custom
law.

Archelaus was associated with both Anaxagoras and Socrates
and perhaps mediated the doctrine of the one to the other. But
later antiquity, no doubt under Platonic influence, seems to have
refused to take him or his writings very seriously, and our knowledge of his doctrine very largely depends on the authority cited
in Item 21. Cursory as this report is, it reveals the existence of an
anthropology built essentially on the same premises as the
previous ones, and with details which recall Anaxagoras. First,
there is generation of all life spontaneously from the earth in its
original swampy condition; second, the human species is included
in this primitive genesis; third, its community with all other forms
of life is stressed: their sustenance and regimen is identical; fourth,
primitive existence was, if not nasty, at least brief; fifth, all species
including the human one have subsequently assumed an independent (sexual) means of propagation (and we can add, therefore,
independent identities); and sixth, mind or intelligence is something shared by all living things, but it varies in degree according
to their mobility.

Though Archelaus may not have repeated Anaxagoras' theory
of life originating in seeds sown by the atmosphere, his reference
to degrees of mobility confirms our previous inference that for
Anaxagoras, as now for his disciple, plant, animal and human life
demonstrate intelligence in the various methods by which they seize
upon the environment and move in on it; the plant's leaves and
the human hands are two diverse examples of the same naturalist
law of development. The difference is in degree, not in kind.

Man then begins as an animal, develops a separate identity as
a species, and proceeds to evolve by degrees towards the most
advanced social condition known to the Greeks – the city state
(conclusion of Item 21). So pitifully meagre is the epitomized
record that we merely learn of 'leaders', 'usages', 'techniques and
cities, and so on'. But even this bare list, when placed alongside
what we can learn of these anthropologists in other authors,
becomes evocative. It betrays the loss of what must have been a
fascinating piece of historical and moral science. First, the verb

'organized' (*synistanai*) recalls the term 'social organization', applied in Plato's *Laws* and in Diodorus to describe the first linguistic and ethnic aggregates which were the initial societies. Second, the order 'leaders – usages – techniques – cities' recalls the patriarchal household followed by the codification of household usage followed by the formation of cities of the plain as we find them in Plato's romanticized version in the *Laws*. In short, to compose his regressive versions of human history Plato drew on the evolutionary social science of the pre-Socratic anthropologists no less than he did in those semi-progressive versions given in the *Protagoras* and the *Republic*. The leadership principle was recognized by his predecessors as a stage of development historically prior to the more collectivist and democratic pattern of city-state community (see the next chapter). Admittedly it did not take much to infer this line of development. One needed only to compare Homeric kings and princes with the assembly and the courts of Periclean Athens. But to generalize it as a law of historical development and to perceive that the pattern of Greek custom law crystallized in the tribe and household before the city-state was formed represents a genuine achievement of social insight. Items 22 and 23 indicate that in the later tradition Archelaus was labelled as the first 'moral philosopher', grappling with the validity of personal and political norms of conduct, the good and the right and the honourable. This classification of him is probably artificial, as is the assumption that thinkers of his day had already entered the lists in a formal contest between the claims of 'law' and those of 'nature'. More likely it was the anthropology of which Archelaus was a declared exponent which suggested to the next generation of thinkers the possibility of the collision. What his own generation was prepared to assert was that usage and custom law evolved as part of the historical process and therefore so, also, have right and wrong as formulated by society for its own protection. A similar position is already implicit in the *Antigone*, as we saw, and its echo persists even in Aristotle's *Politics*, as we have also seen. But the historical process is also a natural growing process and hence no conflict between law and nature was theoretically possible. It arose in acute form only when Antiphon later rejected society and its conventions as an impediment to the free pleasurable life; while Plato at the other extreme sought to give to society's law a metaphysical status.

DEMOCRITUS (last half of 5th century B.C.)

24. (from Aetius) [68A139]
   Democritus' doctrine:
   animals were originally generated by an organization [of shapes?]
   as the moist became spontaneously generative of animals.

25. (from Lactantius) [68A139]
   a. The stoic doctrine:
   The world and all therein has been created to serve human beings.
   b. The erroneous doctrine of Democritus:
   Human beings swarmed out of the earth in the manner of worms without benefit of [divine] originator or design.

26. (from Censorinus) [68A139]
   The doctrine of Democritus:
   Human beings were originally generated from water and mud.

27. (quoted in Stobaeus) [68B278]
   a. 'Human beings think it to be one of their [historical] necessities that they get themselves children.
   b. The cause lies in nature and a given condition established in primitive times.
   c. The analogy of the other animals makes this evident:
   d. they all get themselves offspring in accordance with nature without serving any utility [of their own] [2.203.1];
   e. once an offspring is begotten, [the parent] endures hardship for it and nourishes it as far as possible and experiences anxiety on its behalf as long as it is little; and feels pain if anything happens to it;
   f. such is nature as it applies to everything that has life.
   g. The human being, however, has reached a stage where a custom-usage has been created [2.203.5]
   the effect of which is for the offspring also to yield some enjoyment to the parent.'

28. (quoted by Sextus) [68B164]
   'Animals herd with animals of the same species,
   pigeons with pigeons and cranes with cranes ...'

29. (paraphrased by Proclus) [68 B26; 2.148.14ff.]
Democritus' doctrine:
Words are formed by [human] adoption.
He had three [?] grounds of proof for this which he labelled as
1. The 'ambiguous' [several meanings to one word];
2. The 'synonymous' [several words with one meaning];
3. The 'anonymous' [no word for a required meaning].

30. (quoted by Plutarch) [68 B154]
'The animals in very important respects have been the
instructors of human beings . . . the spider in weaving, the
swallow in house-building, the song birds, swan and nightingale, in melodic composition by imitation'

31. (quoted in Stobaeus) [68 B198]
[An animal] when in need knows the extent of its need; but
[man] when in need does not realize [its extent].

32. (quoted by Aelian) [68A151; 2.125.15ff.]
'My view is that in the course of chance, an ass happened to
rape a mare and the mare happened to conceive. Human
beings accepted the instruction offered by this rape; so they
took the successive steps which have led to the established
habit (*synetheia*) of generating [mules]'

33. (quoted by Philodemus) [68 B144]
'Music is a deferred technique; it is not [historical] necessity
that separates it out. It arises at the point where the [condition
of] surplus obtains.'

34. (from Poseidonius via Cicero) [68A138]
Democritus' view:
Men of an earlier period showed technical skill in establishing
the practice of inspecting the entrails of victims, [their condition and colour affording signs of health or pestilence and often of
probable crop failure or fertility].

35. (paraphrased by Sextus) [68A75]
as Democritus says:
Human beings of an early period observed the phenomena
above them, thunder, lightning and bolts, conjunctions of
stars, and eclipses of sun and moon, and felt fear under the
impression that gods were the cause of these.

36. (quoted by Clement) [68 B30]
'Of human beings with power of expression a few extended
their hands to what we Greeks now call "air" [saying]
"All things Zeus declares,
All things does he know and give and take away,
King is he of all".'

37. (quoted by Plutarch) [68 B146]
'. . . [the human being] . . . nourished within and growing his
own inner roots and being habituated within himself to
acquire pleasurable experiences . . .'

Although Democritus has earned ambiguous fame for his
atomic principles and his materialist metaphysic, his anthropological thinking, while not inconsistent with these fundamentals,
seems to exhibit a flexibility and an independence of its own.
Items 24, 25, 26 report that general theory of the origin of all
organic life with which we have now grown familiar. It thus is
perceived to extend from Anaximander at the beginning to
Democritus near the end of the pre-Socratic story. Man therefore
genetically is an animal like any other. The polemical tone of
item 25 though reflecting Christian opinion could not unfairly
be taken also as a reflection of Platonic reasons for rejecting such
naturalism. The original derivation of man from the earth's
surface is clearly presupposed, and may furnish interpretation
for the second sentence of item 27. This interesting paragraph
of direct quotation contains several points which can be deferred
for later elucidation. But when it traces the urge to have children
to a 'condition which was established in primitive times', he
presumably refers to the establishment of sexual reproduction
in place of spontaneous generation. This condition, says Democritus, has since become equivalent to 'nature' though at one
time nature was otherwise; which throws light on the dynamic
and flexible meaning of 'nature' in these thinkers. It means in
fact 'natural evolving process', not the fixed quantity into which
Platonism sought to convert it. The first sentence of the same
item then refers to the procedure of the human species ever since
sexual reproduction became the rule. This procedure looks as
though it had long historical logic behind it – it is one of the
'necessities'. This word defines any aspect of biological process
which seems to be essential to the process. Such 'necessities' can

be immediately painful, if they subserve remoter ends. The logic of history, of the survival of the species, can make impersonal demands. What these are in terms of parenthood is pointed out in sentences c, d, e, and f. But these vicarious pains and anxieties are not specifically or uniquely human. A mother's tender care is only the reflection of her animal status. We carry out the law of nature which applies to all living things. Thus the normal pattern of family relationship is referred to animal analogy for explanation. The gulf between this kind of sociology and the teleology which Aristotle imposes upon the family relationships is in spirit impassable, whatever temporary concessions Aristotle may make to naturalism.

But Democritus at this point only says of this supposed historical necessity: 'that is what we think'. His own thought becomes more complex; he is prepared to pass beyond the confines of merely historical logic. How far afield he goes and in what direction will emerge a little later.

The authority who quotes the sentence about herding in item 28 reports it as though it was intended to illustrate the aggregation of like atoms. It seems more plausible that it was anthropological, and gave the animal analogy either for man's general tendency to be gregarious and hence to form civil society, or – since the cranes and pigeons are different species of the same single genus bird – for the formation of different ethnic groups – for example Scythians and Greeks – within the same genus man. This would bring Democritus' theory into line not only with the epitome of Diodorus but with the thinking of his predecessors. What he may have added as his specific contribution was a more detailed description of the processes by which human beings in linguistic groups formed words. Item 29 seeks to entangle his views on this subject in the controversy over whether names have an *a priori* status or are a flexible human convention. But this may be an anachronism. What he clearly did do was to notice some of the odd and illogical ways in which language behaved, and to argue that its development had depended to some extent on a human direction which was erratic. The concepts of chance and of spontaneity, of usage and of convention, played a role in his anthropological thinking which can be reviewed a little later.

Items 30 to 34 all deal with the development of technological skills. That divination is included (item 34) shows that his list had correspondence with that of the *Prometheus*. He must have recognized it as a skill historically developed by human society, though he need not be held personally responsible for the further assumption made by Cicero that it was effective. But in general it would seem that his theories about technology as the vehicle of human civilization have a special analytic keenness. He did not content himself with mere lists of inventions, or indulge in sentiment over the miraculous quality of man's achievement. He asked himself: By what actual steps, precise and subtle, can invention actually have taken place? And he answers: There must always have been a prompting suggestion, an intervening link which closes any gap and prevents the possibility of sheer miracle. Man is an animal: first then he goes to the animals for his primary exemplars, and with his hands and tools he copies what they do (item 30); thus the possibility of any hero or master inventor or demi-god as having historical importance is decisively removed. 'Instruction' in the language of Democritus carries quite a different sense from that which the Socratics would give it. But man, unlike the animals, has an 'open future', only in part predictable (31). Here, what would be a defect in the eyes of Platonism (i.e. lack of knowledge) is for Democritus a human asset. How it works in practice is seen in the example of item 32. In the animal world, besides regular and rhythmic operations (nest-building and web-spinning), you have the occasional intervention of chance, and of what we might call a chance mutation, which has produced an occasional mule. But man has mental equipment to seize on this chance, and turn it into an instructive example. Some men – a very few at first – do this, but the idea 'catches on' gradually. So human beings take the successive steps; that is, the device of mating asses and horses is increasingly adopted. Mule-breeding becomes an established practice or social habit. In this way Democritus spells out that doctrine of historical gradualism so emphasized in the epitome of Diodorus. His perspective is progressive and his phraseology often shows it. Compare 'took the successive steps' (item 32) with 'we have reached the stage where . . .' (item 27g) and 'music arises at the point where . . .' (item 33).

The Greek originally drew no formal distinction between the sciences of use and those of leisure, between technology and the fine arts. Music ('musical technique' in Greek) accordingly finds its place in the invention lists along with navigation and agriculture. But Democritus thinks he perceives a distinction (item 33). Although already long developed, music is historically speaking a new-comer, and it escapes those impersonal formulas set by biological necessity. It is an art of leisure. Whether his language involves a notion of economic surplus is doubtful. But theoretically he accepts music in this way as a 'fine art'; and the gulf once more between anthropology's descriptive approach to man's culture and Plato's judgmental evaluation is evident. For Plato in the pseudo-anthropology of the *Republic*, after accepting the Democritean classification of music as a leisure or surplus art, converts this into a moral reproach against the fine arts as instruments of luxury and decadence.

A good many of Democritus' insights are inspired by a growing interest in the processes of applied psychology. This becomes conspicuous in his treatment of the origin of religion (items 35 and 36). Presumably he dealt with cult, as with language and society, as characteristic of the human historical development. The ability to view cult with this objectivity was at least as old as Xenophanes, who, as we saw, had defined the mechanisms of self-imitation which men followed when they fashioned cult images. Democritus goes further and asks what is the psychological necessity which prompts men to want such images in the first place. And he finds it in a displacement of emotion, of fear and of gratitude, evoked by the physical phenomena of the sky. In thunder or eclipse it terrifies us; in benign weather it nourishes us. We construct the figure of Zeus to represent the projection of these contending emotions. The 'few with power of expression' may refer to the mythic poets and to Hesiod in particular, whose *Theogony* as Herodotus remarks had given the Greeks their theology, and whose *Works and Days* opens with a proem to Zeus the all-powerful, at whose pleasure 'all prosper or wither'. Democritus, that is, is not only giving a general theory to explain the origin of religious myth, but a specific historic account of the origins of the theology adopted by the Greeks. It was formulated by the bards. Now this theology, he says, has specific linguistic characteristics: 'Zeus' is a Greek name and it was originally applied to what in Greek is called 'air' (item 36). Did his anthropology view the development of language and of religion in parallel as both equally ethnic in their configuration?

We cannot be sure, but a cross-comparison with Xenophanes, who evidently already deduced the ethnic character of the cults from the appearance of cult statues, makes it plausible that in the subtler theory of Democritus this conclusion was linked organically with the whole anthropological process.

Item 37 is included here only with hesitation, for it is quoted by Plutarch to illustrate the method of inner virtue found through personal temperance. This is in the Platonic mood and manner. But was the formula applied by Democritus historically to describe how, out of an instinctual animal, biologically and blindly controlled by 'necessity', there emerged a creature capable of self-direction and of pleasurable experience in the humane sense? The formula sounds organic – a human being is a plant that has growing roots; he is also a domesticated animal that is broken in by habituation. The language describes him ambivalently as finding his development within himself and yet as interacting with his environment. Only such an ambiguity can do justice to the total historical process. And as he grows he develops a specific capacity for a pleasure self-sought and self-realized.

Whether or not this particular saying will stand such full weight of interpretation, it helps to uncover the fact that the mind of Democritus as it confronts the problem of man is able to operate at more than one level. It is capable of envisaging and of seeking to describe not only humanity in the raw but humanism in its civilized form. His theory of the psyche and its true pleasures and its need of moral self-expression seems to have contributed not a little to that discovery of the individual which is usually associated with Socraticism. This aspect of his thought, though not impertinent to the problem of political theory, can in this place be conveniently neglected – but with the following exception: When he described how men in mule breeding seize on a material accident and convert it to a human use, when he described the psychological-linguistic process which creates religious practices, when he noted the presence of a 'surplus' (in contra-distinction to the 'necessary') as characteristic of the stage of the fine arts, he was observing that man, though controlled by the historical biological process which brought him from the primeval slime, is capable of imposing patterns of his own upon that process. There comes a stage when man contributes to his own development; he uses his own past experience to complicate his future.

It is at this level of self-invented experience, we suggest, that Democritus saw operating the specifically human forms of pleasure (*terpsis*) even though pleasure is shared at all levels by the whole organic kingdom. He may even have argued for its presence at the atomic level of the inorganic.

But in reference to political theory, which as we shall see is to flower in his mind as the crowning commentary upon his anthropology, it is more significant to notice how he connects the operations of humane pleasure with those of custom law. Item 27 to which we now return describes the historical-biological necessity which governs the self-perpetuation of the species and in which the pleasure interests of the individual tend to be ignored. Being nothing if not a realist, he is aware that sexual gratification is only a device of Aphrodite to seduce us into the perils and pains of parenthood. But at this point he argues that man has now reached a stage where 'a custom-usage has been created the effect of which is for the offspring to yield some enjoyment to the parent'. He is commenting in fact upon the growth of that familial pattern of *mores* in which children have duties to parents as opposed to the reverse relation of parental duty to children which alone obtains in the animal world. Etymologically, the root of his participle describing the growth of 'custom-usage' (*nomizon*) is identical with that *nomos* which later hardened into the idea of 'law', and which furnished one term of the later controversy between 'law' and 'nature'. But it is fairly clear that for Democritus the two are not antithetic. He speaks in sentence (f) of 'nature' (that is the process of exploitation of parents by offspring) as applying to all living things, and in sentence (g) of custom-usage as an invention of man superimposed on nature, without appearing to feel that there is any inherent conflict. Similarly it might be added that the breeding of mules is an artificial habit conditioned by biological chance and integrated with man's technical historical progress.

But this is not quite all. In a group of statements which we have not recorded [68 B 275-278], Democritus takes a long look at the problem of parenthood and concludes that to secure a happy home in which your children as you educate them do not disappoint you it is better to adopt offspring of known character (presumably therefore not infants) rather than beget them, since inheritance is so uncertain. His radicalism rather takes our breath away, especially if our notions of Greek family *mores* are patterned upon Aristotle. The point, however, is that man is capable, once he reaches the level of usage and custom which is man-made, of introducing further modifications to suit his inner needs without, we suggest, breaking his continuity with nature. This flexibility will prove to be an important clue to the political theory of Democritus, which likewise operated at more than one level.

The insights of Democritus on the subject of man's origin and growth have approached that borderline where anthropology passes into political and moral philosophy. A backward glance over the territory now traversed can reveal as in an aerial photograph the contours of a science of anthropology in the pre-Socratic period. While it follows a perceptible development from Anaximander to Democritus, the surviving scraps are too tenuous to encourage the scholar to draw elaborate lines of classification between different schools of thought in this common area. Much of the substance and of the terminology employed has to be filled in from those Greek secondary sources from Aeschylus to Diodorus who furnished us with our archetype. And it is hazardous to make any final distribution between different thinkers. Indeed, any attempt at such discrimination can distract the scholar from perceiving the point of over-riding significance. There was a common area of speculation which by, say, 440 B.C. had established a pattern of thinking common to many minds and strong enough to inspire and control a whole school of political thought which we have agreed to call 'liberal', in contradistinction to the formal, the teleological, and the authoritarian theories of Plato and Aristotle. For the liberals man is to be taken as you find him and therefore his present political institutions are to be taken as given also. For practical purposes, in 440 B.C., this meant the Athenian democracy; and Democritus and Protagoras and Gorgias, who constitute the first generation of political theorists, accordingly concentrate empirically and descriptively on this kind of political mechanism. But their empiricism under the influence of anthropology has historical depth. So they expect to understand the system by relating it to man's whole previous historical development. Since, moreover, in the eyes of descriptive science, it is the generic man, not the hero, and the piece-meal historical process rather than the miraculous leadership, which is the secret of history, the liberals were drawn to explore the social and political processes whereby this generic man formed society and institutions and controlled them by decisions, the effective criterion of which was that they must be common decisions embodying a common interest of the human group. Hence anthropological theory continues to underlie the political pragmatism of the sophists in their reliance on the formation of human opinion to guide society.

Sharp disillusionment in Antiphon brings a break with the forms of the city-state as such: but this only reinforces the underlying axiom of naturalism: that history deals with the destiny of the human being as a member of a biological species. Man's self-expression and his own pleasure and happiness must be the goal sought by all forms of law; these are the only true natural justice. Antiphon's naturalism is strident but it paves the way in the fourth century for a reformulation of liberal social theory on more universalist lines.

In both its earlier and its later phases, liberalism lay outside that thought-world common to Plato and Aristotle. These two philosophical geniuses had their own practical preoccupations: how to furnish that authoritarian support in morals and in epistemology necessary to found and to enforce a Greek system of higher education; and how to devise political means of ensuring executive efficiency in government. In the image furnished by these preoccupations they drew their own pictures of the ideal state. It could never be a popular democratic or universalist community in the liberal sense. Their version has persisted in Western Europe as the archetype of Greek political thinking. To begin the task of correcting the distortion and of restoring the Greek liberal theory to its proper historical dignity we now return to the pragmatic, sympathetic and subtle intellect of Democritus.

CHAPTER VI

THE POLITICAL THEORY OF
DEMOCRITUS

THE political theory of Democritus has been preserved by antiquity in the form of some twenty-three aphorisms, or programmatic statements, attributed to his name. These are contained in a large 'chrestomathy' or anthology of useful statements compiled perhaps in the early fifth century of our era by John of Stobi [4.1 On Polity; 4.2 On Laws; 4.5 On Government]. The reader whose conception of Greek philosophy follows traditional lines will, when he looks at this allegedly Democritean material, be tempted to say to himself: 'Democritus was famous in antiquity for a materialist metaphysic. He taught the doctrine of a mechanical universe in which infinite atoms moving through infinite space perpetually collided to form combinations essentially fortuitous. Whatever be the precise meaning of these statements about man in society, their doctrine must derive from the general theory of his system. Let us, therefore, in attempting to interpret the political theory of Democritus, first assume that it depends on his atomic principles and reflects the same mechanism and determinism.'

But when we consider the problem of how to connect his atomism with his politics, the testimonies fail us. Democritus clearly had precise views about many matters affecting society and the city state and law and justice. But no writer of antiquity reports where Democritus the atomist stood in relation to Democritus the political scientist. There were writers after him who claimed the Democritean tradition, and who did make the connection for themselves. One thinks, for example, of Lucretius, but this is not the same thing as reporting for Democritus, the man of Abdera. This adopted son of Athens was an intellectual of the Periclean Age. That a connection existed between his politics and his cosmology is virtually certain. Quotation from Democritus conveys the impression of a keen and a coherent mind, thinking structurally. The impression is reinforced by what tradition says of his metaphysics. If we say he was coherent and cogent rather than systematic, it is because the term systematic is better reserved to describe that mastery of the technique of exposition which was achieved in the ideologies of Plato and Aristotle. The style of Democritus is essentially pre-Platonic. It reflects those methods of organizing ideas which were characteristic of the age. We perceive in him an intuitive coherence which we can, if we choose, reformulate and reproduce as a system. But in the absence of any explicit report which defines the connection between his politics and his metaphysics, let us postpone this question. Let us first estimate his statements about man and society in their own right and determine whether they exhibit an inner direction. If they do, then a just estimate of their logic may put us on a road of connection between metaphysics and politics more reliable than any that might suggest itself if we used traditional assumptions about materialism and mechanism.

It is difficult to describe the sayings of Democritus as either aphorisms or proverbs or axioms or maxims. They overlap these categories. To understand them, one has to understand the role of the gnomic method in antiquity. Here it is pertinent to note a historical distinction. The rounded sentence began its career in the preliterate days of oral communication, when indoctrination depended on word of mouth and retention of doctrine depended on the memory. Democritus himself was a writer, but he wrote in a period when readers were still outnumbered by listeners. It is therefore not surprising that he compressed his ideas into gnomic formulations, for he can be pictured, like the poets who were his contemporaries, as composing under what we may call a form of audience-control. Collections of *gnomae*, therefore, stamped with the hallmark of individual thinkers were characteristic of the first stage of Greek prose writing. But the anthologies of such which were accumulated systematically in the Hellenistic Age and later, and which dominated so much thinking and writing in later antiquity and the Middle Ages, were devoted to the special task of preserving in an epoch of books and readers that kind of material which was still suitable for oral memorization. Fresh thinking was now done on paper in continuous exposition. Thus the province of the *gnome* (Latin *sententia*) ceased to be the creative and became the commonplace.

This tended subtly to alter the vocabulary, temper and tone of the ancient gnomic statements as they were preserved. It was as though the chemical thinking of pre-Platonic antiquity, a dynamic creative process, had now been precipitated in crystallized form at the bottom of the glass; and one collected, arranged and packaged the crystals in commonplace books. The historian, therefore, who examines the preserved statements of any pre-Platonic thinker has to fortify himself against two quite different sources of error, the one in the text, the other in himself. On the one hand, there are the ancient compiler and the compiler from whom he may have compiled; they may have edited the material subtly but inescapably out of its archaic and awkward originality, by changes in vocabulary or syntax, by omissions or eclectic additions of commonplaces of other thinkers. The historian, therefore, is all the more thankful when he deals with a philosopher who adhered to metre. But on the other hand, even when an original survives in its archaic stiffness and angularity, the modern mind approaches it half expecting that it will be, indeed, a commonplace, a proverb or maxim with recognizable relation to the accumulated truisms of Western culture. What is specific and original in terminology, what is surprising and significant in syntax, will tend to be glossed over and ignored. The sayings of Heraclitus are notorious for their concentration and obscurity, but are only an extreme example of a method of exposition which is still discernible in Anaxagoras. The sayings of Democritus are stylistically intermediate between these two thinkers. They are little universes in themselves, and yet also they can be said to be flung like the feathered phrases of the epic minstrel from a mind comprehensive in vision, yet intensely particular in formulation. In short, the political sayings of Democritus present themselves both as self-contained units and yet as items in a 'system'. They can be marshalled and deployed one by one in a sequence which gradually exposes the coherence of their inner logic. They are, so to speak, electrically charged, but the messages they deliver can be monitored because they are transmitting over a consistent wavelength.

1 [*FVS*⁶ 68 B257]

As to animals in given cases
of killing and not killing the rule is as follows:

if an animal does wrong
or desires to do wrong
and if a man kill it
he shall be counted exempt from penalties.
To perform this promotes well-being
rather than the reverse.

2 [B259a]

According as has been written concerning wild things and
creeping things,
if they are 'enemy',
so also [such is my doctrine] is it needful to do in the case of
human beings.

3 [B258]

If a thing does injury contrary to right
it is needful to kill it.
This covers all cases.
If a man do so
he shall increase the portion in which he partakes of right
and security
in any [social] order.

4 [B259b]

According to the custom laws of the fathers
you kill the 'enemy' in every [social] order
where custom-law in that order does not prohibit;
for the several groups there are prohibitions
of local religious sanctions
of solemnized contracts
of oaths

5 [B256]

Right is to perform what is needful
and wrong is to fail to perform what is needful
and to decline to do so.

6 [B261]

If men have wrong done to them
there is need to avenge them so far as is feasible.
This should not be passed over.
This kind of thing is right and also good
and the other kind of thing is wrong and also bad.

This group of formulations has a long ancestry. In its curiously stiff archaic simplicity and its participial constructions, it recalls both the syntax and the subject-matter of the Code of Hammurabi, that cuneiform original of the legal systems of the Near East and the West. But the Greek thinker has cast his legalisms in a typically Hellenic and rational context. He is looking at the behaviour of man in a cosmic and historical setting. Why concentrate on such a trivial matter as the ethics of disposing of dangerous animals, the goring ox, the vicious dog? In primitive communities, such issues provoked disputes between neighbours over valuable property, and it is easy to see how their disposition required the aid of regularity in a code. But Democritus is not interested in the custom-laws of a rural economy, not, that is, for their own sake. He is looking at the usage of men toward animals in order to extract a criterion for the usage of men toward other men. He says so explicitly (No. 2). We might expect the reverse line of reasoning. Surely the disposition of hostile animals is an application of the laws of property among men. But this is not the historical genetic approach of Democritus. He is searching less for the principles than for the methods by which human communities have been able to found themselves. He finds the method in law enforcement. This in turn depends for its effectiveness on the application of sanctions, and the essential sanction is the right to kill, legally that is. The power to execute is primary, if societies are to exist at all. He finds the prototype of this power in the right to kill animals. Why? The only answer can be that his conception of human society is based upon an anthropology in which man, himself an animal species, proceeded to organize himself in social orders (*cosmoi*) in order to protect himself against other species. When Democritus first states the rule of killing and not killing, he speaks of animals as 'living things' (*zoa*). This word could include men; in the 'zoogonies', the origin of the animal and human species was described without distinction of kind. In the anthropologies constructed on this foundation, organized war against the animals had been recognized as a necessary stage in man's social advance. Such had been the *mythos*, the drama in which his early departure from primitivism had been imaginatively conceived. Democritus takes this drama and uses it genetically to establish basic criteria for right and wrong. In the same genetic spirit he cites ancestral usage, not to support some specific party programme in the present, as was often done by practical politicians, but in its most general sense as that pattern of behaviour historically devised and normatively sanctioned in the remote past.

What then do we mean by 'Right' and 'Unright' (*dike* and *adikia*)? This is the question he asks. And his mind (we can see the naturalist, the materialist at work here) argues that to understand them we have to understand the minimum parts, so to speak, out of which they are constructed. In a civilized society they may be symbols for complicated value-judgments or applications of value-judgments; but they had an historical origin. This was essentially simple; nor will they ever lose the quality of their origin. The origin lay in the sanction of protection to achieve security. The sanction itself in its simplest form was negative – the right to kill the 'enemy'. To forget this is to betray society (as he later argues). It is not verbal looseness on his part when he speaks of animals 'doing wrong'. He deliberately reduces wrong, and therefore right, to bare essentials by viewing animal as man and man as animal. To make this quite clear, he reformulates the rule in the most general terms possible:

'If a thing does injury contrary to right it is needful to kill it.'(3).

By 'contrary to right' he indicates the violation of another's security, and to make clear that this minimum condition of right and wrong is meant seriously as a definition of their essence, he makes the definition explicit –

'To do right is to do what you have to do,
to do what there is *need* of . . .' (item 5)

– in the most simple and concrete sense.

If we have defined the repulse of injury as self-protection, however, we can begin to mistranslate the direction of his thought, which would seem an apology for modified anarchy, with atomized individuals repelling wrong but otherwise minding their own business. Strictly speaking, Democritus has no word for individual, that is, for individual self-subsistent personality, and he is incapable of thinking of the concept. His terminology baffles us because while viewing groups or aggregates as made up of simple parts he never seems to visualize the laws of behaviour of the parts without automatically visualizing that behaviour as social. He certainly considered the savage condition of man as pre-civic; but he almost certainly never imagined it as wholly atomized into individuals. Just as in the early anthropologies, the killing of 'enemies' was rationalized as that condition necessary for protecting organized society, so in Democritus as he warms to his theme and further defines the action taken against 'the enemy' the action is discovered to be social (item 4), sanctioned by the social order (*cosmos*) in which you are living. If you kill, you kill in the name of social security, and your act is sanctioned by this 'need'. Nay more, in those human groups which constitute social orders, the definition of 'right' (*dike*) now advances to a more complex level: the sanction of killing is regulated. It is qualified by religious provisions and exceptions. These, he observes keenly, are local (item 4). His empiricism here reinforces his historical method. The right of asylum, for example, the protection afforded by temples to wrong-doers, depends upon the validity of local cults. There is no standard pattern for these. But solemnized agreements accompanied by libations (his next example) reflect practices widespread and accepted, and so do the oaths by which host swears to protect guest, or friend defends friend, or tribes and cities ratify their agreements. These also cut down the freedom to kill the 'enemy'. Democritus in effect argues that no social group ever applies the simple law of self-protection in its total sense. There is a possibility of mitigation, of truce, of agreement in the unending effort to establish security. Is he in effect pointing to the regulation of intergroup relations as requiring a set of rules more complicated than mere outlawry? Is he hinting that societies, as they progress, learn other usages beside that of right and unright? He has not yet reached the *polis* but he is getting nearer to it.

Thus far, unright and right, respectively, could be described as symbols of aggression on the one hand and repulse or correction of aggression on the other. The first premisses of moral man, if such these be, are disappointingly negative. But when Democritus sums up the rule of the right to kill and states it as a general principle 'covering all cases', he significantly describes the wrong-doer not merely as the 'enemy' but as the 'injurer' (No. 3). He uses the participle of an epic verb. His style still falls short of the prosaic in the technical sense of that term. But, stylistic considerations apart, he adopts a word which in Homer indicated injury, damage, disaster, done in hostile relations between enemies (for example, by Greeks or Trojans). Injured feelings are not in question. He is advancing by implication a definition of unright as the infliction of material damage. This supplies a hint of the direction of his thought, a hint confirmed by his defence (No. 1) of killing the animal who is 'enemy'.

> 'To perform this promotes well-being
> rather than the reverse.'

Injury or damage on the one hand, well-being or prosperity on the other, are placed in antithesis. You have to prevent or decrease the former, and to assist or increase the latter. He is thinking perhaps in terms of some calculus, for he says:

> 'contribute to well-being rather than the reverse'

and it is also symptomatic that when he formulates the right to kill as a necessary law (items 2, 3), his verb of compulsion (*chre*) symbolizes the need arising out of the inherent situation, rather than that impersonal compulsion (*ananke*) imposed from some source external to the situation.

This calculus suggests that he is looking for an operational definition of right and unright. Across the intervening centuries we hear an echo of this, of course unpremeditated, in the accents of Jeremy Bentham. But the comparison with English Utilitarianism is no sooner made than it should be withdrawn. The greatest good of the greatest number is a formula built on the conception of units of personality which can be added up to form arithmetic aggregates. No fresh values enter in at the group level which are not present in its atomized parts. Democritus, to repeat what has already been said, shares with his age an inability to reach such a concept of the human ethos. He would have rejected it as an illusion, we suspect, had it been stated to him. His utilitarianism, then, if it be fair to use the term – and it probably is, for the symbols of utility, profit and interest had already been advanced by thinkers of the naturalist school before Plato united them strategically with the form of the good – his utilitarianism conceives of well-being versus ill-being, of profit versus damage, as indicating alternative conditions which affect the person and his community simultaneously, for a person's 'way of life' is life in a community. The group and its component parts have a double-acting relationship. The group is a dynamic context. This is not spelled out for us in Democritus' statements. It is reflected, however, in the ambiguity of his terminology. For example, when he surrounds the right to kill with qualifications (No. 4), he says:

'For the several groups there are prohibitions.'

Here the phrase 'several groups' seeks to translate an untranslatable ambivalence. More strikingly, he says of the man who carries out the need for killing the injurer (No. 3):

'He shall increase the portion in which he partakes of right and security
in any society.'

Democritus means that such a man in the first instance increases the security of the community. But to this security he has himself contributed by his act. He therefore feels good because of his service and also deserves well of the community which he has served. His 'portion' is not a fraction of the whole, but amounts to a degree of participation.

So far the Democritean theory of right has presented itself in these legalisms as resting on narrow and negative premisses. To argue that human society could only start its ascent toward civilization by strict enforcement of the most primitive laws of security is no doubt true and valuable; but it does not express the hallmark of civilization itself. Seized as he was of the value of security as a positive thing, Democritus was bound to enlarge and advance his conception until it could comprehend action not only narrowly defensive but also helpful and co-operative. This he begins to do by propounding axiom No. 6; that if you repulse injury and punish it, you do not do this for yourself alone. In a community, you do this in the interests of others who are wronged.

'If men have wrong done to them there is need to avenge them so far as is feasible.
This kind of thing is right and also good.'

This carries us beyond narrowly selfish considerations. Such action is therefore always in danger of being ignored or 'passed over.' But (if we may fill in his thought for him) a community comes into existence not as a mere sum of private interests, each protecting their own security, but as a complex in which the need of avenging all who are wronged becomes a matter of 'principle', we would say. It has to be recognized, regardless of whether or not the particular victims are strong enough to protect themselves without help. He uses the verb 'avenge' perhaps to locate the rule far back in primitive society as he has already located the right of self-preservation. It is the prototype of those methods of legal redress which an advanced society makes available as a substitute for direct succour. But the point is that at least some vengeance must always be taken, whoever is wronged, in order to guarantee that a collective system of mutual security will work for all members. If he asks for it 'so far as is feasible', he may mean to hint that group protection by members for other members has always had limited efficacy as contrasted with direct action. But when he vigorously defends this vicarious rule as 'right and also good', and the opposite as 'wrong and also bad', the second adjective in each pair points up the utility and strength which accrue to the community as a whole.

Two-thirds of Democritus' social and political axioms still remain to be considered. They deal with matters of increasing complexity – law and custom, faction and consensus, the *polis*, its ethos and administration. His thinking in politics seems to have proceeded along organic lines, viewing the human group as founded on a very few simple principles but discovering and then solving more complicated issues in later stages of development. This kind of progress means that the problems formulated for solution cease to be negative and become positive. They advance from mere security to the creative values and enjoyments of a *polis* type of community.

7 [B249]

Faction within the clan is a bad thing for both sides.
Those who win and those who lose share impartially in common disaster.

8 [B245b]

Envious malice between men constitutes the genesis of faction.

9 [B245a]

The custom laws would not prevent each of us from living his life in accordance with those powers and opportunities

which are his own
if it were not true that A inflicted injury on B.

10 [B248]

It is the desire of custom law to do good to the way of life
of men
but it is able to do this only when men also desire to have
good done to them.
If men hearken to it
the custom law demonstrates to them that excellence which
is its own.

To establish the basis of sociality, human beings must initially
recognize sanctions which protect the group from without. This
is a simpler matter than maintaining its cohesion within. If right
is a value-symbol to be placed on action taken against the anti-
social 'enemy', then the objective of reconciling tensions within
will call into play other terms and different formulae.

These four political axioms focus their attention on the pro-
venance of custom-law. In Greek tradition, Greek law (*nomos*)
came to be viewed as the specific creation of the city-state. The
virtual identification of nomos and polis was already implicit in
the theory (or the myth) of law-givers who had established
'polities', that is, civic institutions. The idealism of Plato and the
teleology of Aristotle only confirmed the identification and made
it an article of faith. But Democritus true to his genetic method
sees law generated as a solution to problems which were already
crystallizing in pre-civic conditions. The factional quarrel which
threatens to split the civic group and end its existence can be seen
already at work in the clan of blood-kindred. Long before
Democritus, Solon had phrased it in this way, and his successor in
the democratic experiment, Cleisthenes, had set out to solve the
problem practically, by breaking up the ancient clans and distributing their members among *demes*. Perhaps both men confronted an ancient inheritance, handed down from more primitive
days, in the form of blood-feud, which dividing a clan of kindred
families can decimate its members. Herodotus saw the same
danger in a Pan-Hellenic setting: the quarrel over the command
of the united forces against Persia at Salamis; and he applied the
same phrase to describe it. These examples show that the clan
(*phyle*) did not describe a kin-group of any defined size. Depending

on context, it might refer to the consanguinity of a kin-group within a *polis*, or to all members of a *polis* as for example Athenians, or to all Greeks as a 'race'. Democritus, then, in presenting the factions of the clan as a problem in politics, takes advantage of the ambiguity. He wants a term as general as possible in order to view faction historically as a process endemic in the social order at all stages of its evolution. Upon this perennial and now proverbial danger he places a reflective interpretation. Historically, the way of settling a feud had been a conflict which ended in victory and subjugation. This solution is illusory, says Democritus. The victors and vanquished have suffered a common destruction. Of what, we may ask? In any immediate sense, the vanquished lose definite things like life or status or property; and the victors gain corresponding and equally definite benefits. Democritus cannot be defining loss in these terms. Something has been destroyed which was the common property of the two factions before the fighting began.

That common property could be defined as the group's over-all security, or its law. But Democritus does not at once jump, as a more traditional and superficial thinker might, to the necessity of supporting law at all costs – *eunomia*, the Greeks called it – as a preventive of faction. The enemy from without the group had been simply 'the enemy', externally viewed. You do not have to deal with his ethos or motives. You establish the rule of right (*dike*) on purely positivist lines. Punishment by expulsion or elimination or execution is the first law of group survival. But it is only the first law. For an in-group problem, you are forced to consider the inner ethos and motives of human beings. Thus, still looking at the cause of feud genetically, you discover it in the propensity of the human animal to compete and to conceive and nurse a grudge against his competitor, to make envious comparisons. These connotations are all packed into the Greek noun *phthonos* and its more ancient verb *phthoneo*. Competition, primarily envious, secondarily emulative, between fellow-craftsmen had become a proverb before Hesiod. Envious malice describes an emotion not self-generated in isolation but one which *ab initio* exists between two or more people. The curse of Adam is the way Adam handles his primary relationships with other Adams. Adam the single man never existed. The 'grudge' is almost the condition of being a human being so far as our manhood depends on some relationship to other men. Hence Democritus, viewing the growth of morals and politics from an anthropological standpoint, at least implies that within this growth are comprehended two warring principles: an inherent grudge of man against man; and a compulsion nevertheless to live in groups which can cooperate because the grudge is somehow controlled or sublimated. Hebraic analogies even when helpful can often mislead. Did 'malice' express the Greek equivalent for original sin? Or was it not more characteristic of Greek realism combined with Greek rationalism to assume that if two men or groups could advance in prosperity at mathematically equal rates, grudge and envy would not arise; but that chance and fortune see to it that they almost never do; and so the envy on one side and the fear on the other that result are reactions of the human material to an emotional strain imposed upon it by the non-mathematical operation of circumstances. This might have been Democritus' complete doctrine. We cannot be sure. In what we have of him, we start with the fact of the competitive grudge as an originating force (*arche*) which sets in motion divisive and destructive faction.

For this endemic danger the remedy is law, and the initial operation of law has to be viewed negatively as a restraint on the use of one's own elbow-room (no. 9). Up to this point, the mind and method of Democritus have sought to understand and to solve political problems simply by describing them. Is he here, at the introduction of law, at last forced to take refuge in a solution conceived *a priori*: a *deus ex machina*, some force, moral or theological, exercising a power over the historical process which is independent of that process? In making law the personal subject of verbs like 'prevent' and 'do good,' it might almost seem that he does, indeed, resort to that kind of syntax in which the structures of idealists are built. But the Greek *nomos*, when he used the word, had not yet acquired the *a priori* or 'geometric' significance with which Plato's later thinking endowed it and which passed over into the natural law of the Stoics, of St. Thomas, and of the rationalists of the seventeenth century. *Nomos* is not translatable by a single word. It had an ambivalence in the Greek mind, and yet the shape of this ambivalence was incisive and powerful. When Pindar sang that 'custom-law was lord of all men', Herodotus in effect added, 'Yes indeed: the lawful customs of the races of men are various; but each evokes its own fierce loyalty from its own devotees'. These two citations give the polarity of the Greek term better than anything else that could be said about it. It is un-translatable because it comprehends two concepts later split apart in the Western tradition: custom, usage or habit on the one hand, created by man locally and fortuitously, but also controlling man in attitude and act; law on the other hand, passionless, wise, universal, above and beyond men, but requiring their obedience and reverence as to a god. *Nomos* in fact in the fifth century was 'usage-which-is-solemn'.

Thus Democritus in effect is arguing that one positive and inherent force in men, that of competitive suspicion, can be balanced or controlled by another and often is: the preference for conformity to collective habits which we might call a sort of force of inertia. *Nomos* gathers momentum in society and controls its acts and relations by virtue, perhaps, of an inherent laziness, a conservatism in the human raw material which while aggressive and envious is also prone to prefer the familiar and the consistent. The 'right way' of behaving in a thousand matters of daily decision is just the accepted way. All this Democritus does not say: but his term *nomos* speaks for itself if we keep it in the context of the vocabulary of the fifth century and do not transfer it to the late fourth. There is a theoretic capacity plus opportunity (*exousia*) at the disposal of every man personally (item 9), but it is only theoretical. Man is normally too given to familiar standard-ized usages to exercise it outside of or against the group, except he have the support of a group within the group. Hence it is factionalism (*stasis*) of group within group that is really dangerous (item 7) much more so than the anarchism of the lawless man. With him society can and does deal. He does not have any *nomos*-support whatever. But in a sense every member of a faction or a class does have support: he has that minimum portion of law which can be used as group loyalty, though it is not the fully formed law of a society.

'Envy' and 'custom', then, have always been competing forces, genetically speaking. But Democritus makes a value-judgment here: he expresses a preference, the Hellenic preference. Custom law is good and useful. It can indeed be viewed as having a desire or purpose to 'do good to man's way of life' (No 10). Democritus is still speaking historically. The way of life is not mine or yours personally. It is the life lived in a society, as the anthropologists had spoken of it. The restraint of common custom is not merely negative, then: it paves the way for a more positive possibility. Wherever Democritus speaks of 'good', he is looking to the future, to the further utility of man in society. What benefits of custom law he has in mind will appear in due course. But in the present stated axiom, what preoccupies him is the paradox that while custom-law has a power to benefit this power is not automatic. It depends for its validity upon the equally valid acquiescence given by the members of society. The reasoning is in a closed circle. It has to be, to accord with the complete facts of life. Perhaps he means too that custom-law is a total thing. It either works, is accepted and loved and finds its own justification in the smooth functioning of harmony between men, men's obedience and their sense of benefit: or it disintegrates wholly, collapses into lawlessness (*anomia*); the group ceases to function as a group. And automatically the members thereof are deprived of their power to understand or imagine the virtue of that condition which is now not theirs. For their very anarchy controls their judgment. *Nomos* is not like a piece of property which you could abandon or pick up again at will. It is painfully acquired; it makes total sense when you have it; but when you lose it, it becomes indeed a lost cause.

What else Democritus has to say about politics -- and there is a good deal – moves us into more familiar ground, familiar, that is, from the point of view of Plato and Aristotle. The city-state, its character and peculiar problems, come into plain view. Hitherto they have not been in the foreground. Whether Democritus was prepared to construct a series of ascending social integrations from savagery to the city and, if so, what these were, is uncertain. It would seem that Aristotle's simple and elegant sequence of household, village and city is in that form the creation of his own teleological needs, rather than a faithful reproduction of the Greek anthropological view. Demo-critus certainly conceived of society before the city-state. But the evidence for this lies mainly in the kind of terminology he uses, rather than in explicit historical statements. He must have refused to posit the *polis* as the one definitive social order. For example, he uses the two words 'order' and 'shape' (*cosmos* and *rhuthmos*) to describe a given stage or type of social organization. But his method is not typological, nor is his approach constitutional, in the manner of the idealists who followed him. His mind moves in genetic relations, not in *a priori* forms. Thus he speaks (in a statement still to be presented) of the Athenian democracy as the 'presently constituted shape of things'. This is not quite the same thing as saying 'under this political constitution'; and the temporal qualification suggests that there have been and will be other shapes. Indeed, both *cosmos* and *rhuthmos* are dynamic terms describing an animated order and a moving shape. They were so used also in his atomic metaphysics.

A citation of Plutarch's reports a reference in Democritus to

'governments or polities and friendships of kings'

as the source of

'great and glorious benefits for our way of life'.

This sounds like a recollection of some genetic account of the rise of government with authority to organize society, a stage which Democritus may have superimposed upon his validation of right and custom-law. That is, he may first have looked at those fundamental sanctions which support the existence of any society, primitive or advanced, and then proceeded to consider the problems of constitutional authority and to indicate some of the solutions achieved historically in tribal oligarchy or in monarchy or in democracy alike. But this reconstruction of his thought is speculative. That his premisses were historical is revealed in the preserved vocabulary of his axiomatic statements about the city-state. A group of three of these can now be presented.

11 [B260]

If a man kill any highwayman or pirate
he shall be counted exempt from penalty
whether [he kill] by direct action
or by orders
or by vote.

12 [B262a]

In the case of those who commit acts that deserve expulsion
or imprisonment
and in the case of [all] who deserve penalty
the vote must condemn them
and not absolve them.

13 [B262b]
If a man in violation of custom law
absolve [another]
using [motives of] gain or pleasure to formulate [the issue]
he does wrong
and inevitably this will be on his heart.

On the face of it, these three axioms repeat the primary proposition already fully covered that the very existence of any society depends in the first instance upon the enforcement of sanctions against the social 'enemy'. Justice, genetically validated by the measures taken by the human species against other species, originates at this elementary and negative level. But in axiom No. 11, which heads this group of three, Democritus classifies three kinds of sanctions, and the distinctions are significant. In the first, penalty is imposed by direct action; this identifies the condition of primitive society. In the second, it is done by orders given; this, we suggest, identifies a more organized community in which responsibility for social security is wielded by a king; in this authority the original right of direct action, always close to anarchy, is now vested. Any seventeenth-century believer in the divine right of kings would have understood at once what Democritus meant here. But there is a third possibility: action can be taken through vote. Democritus would not limit this procedure to what would be styled in a technical sense democracy. He could have in mind any society in which legal sanctions can be taken by collective decision. Under certain circumstances this could be true even of Homeric society and certainly of any city-state unless governed by a despot. But the order of precedence in these alternatives is not accidental; it suggests the thought that organs of collective responsibility tend to displace earlier and simpler devices of government. The anthropological method of Democritus, proceeding from savage to civilized condition, has reached the voting society, as we might call it. The language of No. 12, the next axiom, is the language of Athenian democracy. The area of application for sanctions which protect society is no longer confined within the simplicities of robbery or piracy, and the penalty of liquidation through killing is also far too simple for use in such a complex organism as a city-state. But the principle remains that sanctions must be implemented: that is our first duty to the society in which we live, for only this can guarantee the initial stability and authority of what is becoming (Democritus does not say so) a legal system responsible to popular control. Statement No. 13 makes it even clearer that Democritus is now addressing himself to the Athenian judge and jury (no distinction was drawn between them) whose primary function is not mercy or leniency but the decision to convict where conviction is deserved. In this way is the stern logic maintained by which a society stands or falls. The citizen in a voting society will be tempted to deviate from this, because in a voting society the voter's immediate interest and the long-range social interest can come into conflict. So political theory has at this point to take note of gain and pleasure (item 13) as twin motivations which complicate the process of judicial decision. Democritus did not oppose either provided they coincided with public utility, or at least did not conflict with it. But the latter must predominate, and this requires a correct 'formulation' of the issue in the voter's mind. Democritus has here involved his political with his psychological theory, which no complete account of his philosophy can afford to ignore. However, the political thread of his thinking is separable and the final unwinding of it is near at hand.

14 [B255]

At that time when the powerful [classes] confronting the have-nots take it on themselves to pay toll to them and to do things for them and to please them:
This is the [situation] in which you get [the phenomenon of] compassion and the end of isolation and the creation of comradeship and mutual defence
and then civic consensus
and then other goods beyond the capacity of anyone to catalogue in full.

15 [B250]

It is consensus that makes possible for cities the [execution of] mighty works
enabling them to execute and carry through wars.

16 [B252b]

A city managed prosperously means complete stability-and-success for everybody.
In this [condition] is comprehended all.

If this [condition] is secured, this means general security; if this [condition] is dissolved, this means general demoralization.

17 [B252a]

It is needful that greater importance be placed upon the [area of] the civic than on any other,
and upon its good management:
avoiding any competition
that goes beyond reason
and any access of private power
that may cut across the utility of the common [wealth].

18 [B251]

Poverty under a democracy is as much to be preferred above
what men of power call prosperity
as is liberty above bondage.

The first of this group of statements constitutes the most remarkable single utterance of a political theorist of Hellas. Considering its epoch, it is as remarkable as anything in the whole history of political theory. Neither in content nor in temper has it a parallel in the better-known classic thinkers. Ethically speaking, it seems to carry the colour of certain values which are defined in the New Testament; politically, with its stress on what looks like a social conscience, it reads like a formula suitable to the liberalism of the age of Mill or T. H. Green. It is true that the objective towards which the statement is directed was becoming a commonplace: unanimity of the citizen body had been viewed as a political ideal long before Plato cemented the conception into an almost mathematical unity of the state. It is equally true that this condition of consensus adds little to Democritus' previous principle that the cohesion and the stability of the group are the first objective of politics. It does however describe this as a mood, so to speak, of a citizen body which is facing up to this condition consciously and deliberately.

But what is the originating cause of such a mood? A less subtle thinker would reply: obedience to the laws; an idealist would substantiate this answer by the proposition that the laws represent eternal forms of Good and Right which give them independent validity and influence over the minds of men. For Democritus causes are always genetic not teleological. He looks to processes rather than to patterns for the explanation of politics. Law, as we have seen, is for him the sum of a system of habits, which places a brake on human wilfulness. But this can never of itself evoke the co-operation of a harmonious community. So Democritus is forced once more to get behind custom to ethos, that complex of behaviour patterns out of which standardized practice grows. Is there some element here which historically becomes the means of calling social consensus into being? He finds it in a human propensity, under given conditions, to altruism and compassion.

It is often said that Greek rationalism could not find room for pity as such, and might even deplore it as a sentimental violation of a good man's integrity. This does not misrepresent the main tradition as defined by the classic writers and thinkers, to the end of the fourth century. There were however exceptions. Even in the fifth century, Aeschylus in his portrayal of Prometheus chose to dramatize not only the hero's gifts of technology to man but his compassion for man, and in the same spirit the Chorus are invited to have compassion on him. The tragedy conveys to its audience the strong impression that somehow, in the unfolding history of civilization, the cause of technology and the cause of compassion are bound up together. The remarkable thing about compassion in Democritus is that it is presented in conjunction with altruism as a political principle of the first importance, a kind of human energy comparable to other energies of the human ethos, and one which can have structural effect upon the condition of the body politic. In this respect, the thought of Democritus is tougher and more systematic than that of Rousseau. Compassion is not to be viewed as an intuitive recoil from suffering in others, a vague but powerful sentiment rooted in the untutored primitive. It is a phenomenon which presents itself at an advanced stage of human culture, and it is the specific property of the stronger and more successful elements in that culture.

But why should it arise at all? Democritus, without breaking the sequence of his genetic method, could have argued that the necessary concessions which may be made by the strong toward the weak, by the rich towards the poor, are simply exacted from them by the demand for over-all group security. Instead of that, he proposes an addition to the ethos of human beings, a fresh ingredient in their make-up. Does he here then take leave of his method, abandoning history in favour of an unsupported aspiration? Does his picture of altruism mean that he is tempted into the fantasy of wish-fulfilment?

A Marxist, schooled in the doctrine of class-struggle as fundamental, would say he did. Democritus, be it noted, goes half-way towards such realism. He does not pretend like Plato that class divisions in the city-state can be treated by the theorist as abnormalities. They, as much as right and law, are part of the historical process of politics. But where does his discovery of altruism – which at this point mitigates the class division so decisively – come from?

The riddle can be read and the method of Democritus placed in consistent perspective once it is assumed that he is looking at a famous crisis in the history of the city-state. His working model is the Athens of Solon, when a programme of political reform was adopted by consent. The crisis was in its overt aspects economic, and was alleviated by a famous financial arrangement later known as the Great Disburdening. But the underlying problems were those of political conciliation and they were solved in some body of legislation in which the competing interests of rich and poor, hill, plain and coast, landowner, merchant and craftsman were reconciled. The most conspicuous of these reforms made office-holders responsible to audit, political and pecuniary, after their terms of office; and the right of audit was vested in the commons. This feature had impressed itself upon the mind of Democritus, as we shall see.

Tradition in retrospect always likes to dramatize political policies as personal at the expense of the social forces which made policy possible. But Democritus goes behind the sanctification of Solon and asks what made possible his choice as umpire and what made his solutions acceptable. He finds the only possible answer to lie in some ethos of consent on the part of the privileged classes of that period. For change was effected by voluntary reform, not enforced by revolution. Nor, presumably, in the philosopher's view, could any revolution have been successful; or rather, if it were, the community as Democritus viewed it would have been destroyed. Had he not said that in a collision of factions victors and vanquished suffer a common destruction (axiom 7)? At any rate, discord in Solonian Athens did not come to the breaking point: it proved negotiable. He might have pointed to simple fear as the ethos causative of prudence; however, knowing some of the recorded facts perhaps better than we do, he discerned as the causative factor some mood of altruism and compassion latent in the governing classes, a mood which he describes as self-generated. For 'they took it on themselves'.

This historical frame of reference suggests a vivid context for the succeeding statements. Solon led to Cleisthenes, and to the formal establishment through further constitutional reform of 'The Democracy'. Cleisthenes was followed by Marathon and Salamis. Victory over the Persians was followed by the Delian League and the rise of the Athenian empire, culminating in the Age of Pericles with its supreme confidence and its brilliant achievements. Democritus views the entire story and frames an explanation for it. It is a single political process set in motion when liberal political principles were originally applied. Once those precious ingredients were released, the vital dynamic consensus of a city came into being, not as a single mood but as a continuing and evolving energy. So were made possible the 'mighty works', 'the execution and carrying through of great wars' (item 15). The mechanism of civic strength and achievement lay not in individual leadership but in a happy race of men: when the city-state is managed prosperously, this means stability and success for all its members (item 16). He is looking now at the Periclean age in which he lived.

However, Democritus does not allow these historical glories to carry him over into some Hegelian vision of the corporate community. His analysis remains complex: consensus had been achieved in a competitive situation by the addition of non-competitive forces. Once achieved, it therefore cannot be viewed as becoming a static condition or even an ideal formula into which individual energies become absorbed. Itself produced by process, it releases further process; thus competition between individuals and groups continues, but now it does not go 'beyond reason' (item 17): men continue to seek power for themselves but within a formula set, not by custom law so much as the 'utility of the commonwealth'. This is a rational criterion of civic good. Presumably therefore men had a capacity to envisage it and calculate it and in his psychology Democritus elsewhere explains that they have.

What is the total character of such a society? Has it a name? He names it himself in his summing up. 'Poverty under democracy is better than any prosperity among the powerful (item 18). This reads like the sentiment of some man of Athens, say between 440 and 420. He was not a native son but he had come to Athens to live there. And like Herodotus in the same period he fell under Athens' spell. May this not help to illuminate the obscure chronology of his life? He was surely a spiritual son of the age of Pericles. It is also hard to avoid the conclusion that when Thucydides penned the Funeral Speech of Pericles he was expressing an intellectual debt to Democritus.

If the philosopher turns to the age of Solon and after to explain the origin and behaviour of a liberal society, can his methodology as a theorist be defended as genetic and as consistent? To a modern mind, equipped with distinctions between sciences to which he was a stranger, it might seem that while he laid his foundations in anthropology and argued then deductively from a few principles, his superstructure is empirically derived from a quite recent and limited historical experience. This would recall a similar split in the thinking of Hobbes, where a deductive psychology is allied with Hobbes's present sense of the need to support absolute monarchy under given historical conditions. But for a thinker of the mid-fifth century B.C., the distinction between anthropology and history scarcely existed. The ancient times were in perspective foreshortened and their vast story of previous social development was telescoped into traditions of recent memory. Had not human history for Hesiod begun with the heroes of the Trojan war? Thus it is reasonable to assume that when Democritus says of compassion and the end of isolation that these arose 'at that time when the powerful took upon themselves to pay toll', etc., he is fitting the phenomena of the Solonic epoch into their genetic place in the anthropological story: here was a crucial stage in the advance from primitivism towards civilization. A science of man better equipped than his can afford to smile at the naïvety of such a foreshortening, but can it afford to dismiss his premiss that altruism has a historical basis?

19 [B254]

If inferior [citizens] proceed to the prerogatives of office
the more unfit they are when they proceed
the more negligible they become
and are filled with witlessness and overconfidence.

20 [B267]

The exercise of authority is by nature proper to the superior.

21 [B265a]

Men have better memories for errors than for successful performance.

22 [B265b]

If [a trustee] restores a deposit
he need not expect to be [morally] approved.
If he default,
he can expect to have bad things said about him and done to him.
It is just [to treat] anyone in authority in the same manner.

23 [B265c]

A man in authority is expected to perform well and not badly.
This is the [formal] assumption on which he was elected.

The political vision of Democritus is complex – more complex, as far as we know, than that of any of his successors. Perhaps it was because he kept his eye closer than any other did to all the factors of the historical process which had generated politics, and not just to some of them. Having recognized the quality of the Athenian democracy and the Athenian democratic process from Solon to Pericles as a supreme achievement, he raises at once the problem of effective authority in such a society, and gives an explicit answer: it can be solved only by recognizing the aristocratic principle: society divides itself into the superior and inferior; to entrust government to the latter is folly (items 19, 20).

The first thing to realize is what he means by superior. In this word, *kreitton*, the meanings of stronger and better crossed each other. The ambivalence produced a great deal of semantic confusion in Democritus' successors, a confusion compounded by Plato's polemics against them. What Democritus means by superior is sufficiently indicated by the terms in which he describes the behaviour of its opposite number, the inferior: negligence, stupidity, overconfidence. If the last is a partly moral defect, the first two are certainly intellectual. The first criterion of distinction is brains. So far, then, Democritus seems to anticipate the principle of Plato, that men are disparate in terms of intellectual ability. Therefore his argument for natural superiority comes to no more than the proposition that democracy must somehow get men of quality and ability to assume authority, and that, if it does not, the common estate suffers. He calls such types the 'effective citizens' (in No. 24 below). Yet he assumes that they are 'elected' and not self-appointed (No. 23). It is perhaps symptomatic of his position as a social theorist that he seems to suggest that the defects of the inferior are compounded by inappropriate responsibilities (item 19). That is, the social context available to a man's ethos can determine what becomes of the potentialities of that ethos. Plato after him made a similar point when, in insisting on specialization of function appropriate to each type, he argued that round pegs in square holes exhibit dangerous effects which would otherwise not arise.

Government, then, as distinct from society, is by nature proper to the superior. Does Democritus see the problem of reconciling this with the presuppositions of democracy? It is to his lasting credit that he does. The dilemma is very real: if political responsibility is to be distributed widely over society, this implies a degree of popular control over the state apparatus. Yet if office should be restricted to the superior, how can you have popular control of the superior, and how justify it? The answer given, with striking originality, anticipates the theory of government propounded by Hobbes, yet in a version subtler than Hobbes's political circumstances allowed him to envisage. Authority is a deposit which the community is capable of vesting in the holder of authority as in a trustee (item 22): that is, a virtual contract is entered into whereby we surrender the right to rule to those best able to exercise it. But when Democritus says a deposit, which the trustee is expected to return and get no thanks for it, he envisages a contract with a time-limit. He is obviously inspired here by the audit system instituted by Solon and further developed in the Cleisthenic constitution. Office-holders are elected for a term. Then they surrender their deposit and are examined on the use they have made of it. Conceivably the metaphor, borrowed from elementary commercial practice, was used in Solon's day to justify the arrangement; or perhaps Democritus invented it. At any rate, it reconciles Hobbes's perception that for effective government you have to assume the existence of some kind of contract with the requirement of an Athenian democrat that sovereignty be never absolute – a requirement which for historical reasons did not trouble Hobbes. The theory, or more correctly the analogy in which the theory is implicit, also has the effect of viewing political power (*arche*) as executive authority rather than as legislative sovereignty. It would have been better for Plato's political theory had he more plainly seen the distinction himself. Democritus, still keeping the audit system in view, argues that no form of political authority can ever be explained as privilege or prerogative. It comes into existence by definition only as a vehicle of good government (item 23). Plato would agree in the abstract, but Democritus applies this to the actual man who governs, not an ideal philosopher, but a fallible official subject to recall.

The contract theory thus stated had in various versions a long history after Democritus' day. It may be doubted whether it was ever stated so succinctly or with such satisfaction to the competing claims of authority and liberty. Positing as it does an arrangement between citizens and their rulers, it is to be distinguished from a parallel but different concept of compact (*syntheke*), an agreement between the citizens themselves. This was advanced in the generation after Democritus to justify the existence of custom-law within the body politic, as against the executive authority that rules over it. In Democritus' own day, the urgent need was to devise a theory supporting the practice of annual elections which could command intellectual respect. He earned the eternal credit of supplying it.

24 [B253a]
For the effective [citizens] expediency does not lie in omitting their own business
in order to handle affairs.
Their own business gets into a bad way.

25 [B253b]
However if there is some error or omission in public business
the cry of disapproval goes up
even though no dishonest or wrongful act is involved.

26 [B253c]
Omission and wrong-doing alike incur the peril of criticism and indeed punishment as well.

27 [B253d]

Error is inevitable,
but for men to sympathize with it does not come easy.

28 [B266a]

The shape [of society] presently prevailing has no device
against wrong being done to men in authority
even though they be perfect . . .

29 [B266c]

Somehow, the [shape of] things should be so ordered
as to cover the following problem also:
if a man does no wrong himself,
no matter how thoroughly he censure wrong-doers,
he should never find himself in their power.
If his acts are right,
some defence, of ordinance or otherwise,
should be there to protect him.

For Democritus, there were some problems that remained
unresolved. As his rationale of man in society nears its conclusion,
he casts his eye upon a stubborn fact: a democratic society cannot
yet be a just society in any Platonic sense of that word. Better the
Solonian democracy than any other polity, far better. But a
question remains. He is still looking at the audit of office-holders
and the way it is carried out. It is an operation of the multitude,
relying not on judicial precision, not even on their collective will
to achieve a common good. It may be doubted whether Democritus could ever have accepted the conception of such a will had
it been proposed to him. No, the audit relies on certain factors in
the human ethos: here again he turns to his psychology of that
motivation in men which, as we have seen, is for him so complicated:

Men have better memories for errors than for successful
performance (No. 21).

This is what creates the possibility of the audit system and makes
it effective. Men can always summon zeal for it. But, equally,
the audit can therefore be undiscriminating. There are forms of
error which are pardonable, as distinguished from crimes which
are punishable. But the human ethos, with its proclivity to

remember vice and forget virtue, can alter the focus of the facts; forgetting the virtues that mitigate errors, it can convert errors into crimes. How then do you combine the audit with complete justice to the executive? He notes that in Athenian democracy at its best, the effective citizen who had his own business to manage makes sacrifices if he takes on governmental responsibility (item 24). He does not actually say he should be paid, compensated by a salary for it: yet his intent may be to justify this Periclean policy. It also follows, because of the motivations upon which the machinery of the audit relies, that in addition to the sacrifice the citizen exposes himself to a genuine risk: honest administration need not be perfect; a man can err and yet be guiltless of crime or peculation (item 25). The end result for him is, however, the same as if he had committed crimes (item 26). He

'has wrong done to him' (item 28).

This violates the rule of moral logic. The just should not be exposed to injustice. There should be some mechanism or device, legal or otherwise, both to prevent an irrationality and to defend the security of the just (item 28). Thus at the end Democritus returns to the problem of security against wrong with which his story of civilization had begun. But it is now viewed at an advanced level of culture in a context of great complexity.

It would be interesting to reflect upon later solutions to this question thus posed by Democritus for western society. In effect, no absolute solution has been found. After Aristotle, political theory was for a long time formulated in mainly teleological or authoritarian terms. Since the problem is specific to the democratic process, it could not agitate the attention of thinkers very closely until after Cromwell. Since the eighteenth century, western democracy in effect has formulated a double solution. On the one hand, it has distinguished judicial and executive functions from legislative, and on the whole (with exceptions, to be sure) has made the former a matter of 'civil service' not subject to audit and reprisal. The acts of the legislative power, on the other hand, are in fact subject to audit through the party system, by which a government is 'voted down' and 'thrown out of office' for what are judged to be errors or crimes according to the voter's prejudices, and very often for errors which it did not commit. The solution, in fact, has been to separate the concepts of criminal guilt and political error, and to assume that guilt, under normal circumstances, does not arise in the processes of government. As to error, it is penalized unfairly, but the penalty consists merely in the deprivation of opportunity for the further exercise of power. A thinker of ancient Athens would be no more capable of drawing these distinctions achieved by modern democracy than he would be of rationalizing and accepting the party system as a genuine method of government.

This takes us far afield from Democritus. But that the problem he posed had to await the long passage of time for even partial solution is a tribute to the greatness of the man who could face and state the problem; who could realize that the triumphant democratic polity of Athens was not the last word in politics, without making that an excuse for rejecting it in the lofty manner of Plato. It may be said: did not Plato face the question? He did, but he solved it only by erasing it, for the problem turned on the complexities of the relationship between democracy and authority; and he would not admit that the relationship had any right to exist. Having educated the superior to be superior, he proposed to put them in power and give them machinery for self-perpetuation. So far as the issue of sovereignty was concerned, this was a simple regression to the mythical centuries before Solon. Part of Plato's weakness, as of Aristotle's, was the conviction that in politics all problems, as they may be soluble theoretically, must therefore be solved now.

Democritus was content to leave something unsolved, and his readiness in this respect reveals the measure of his stature as a political thinker, for it grows from his conception of politics as a continuing process which, as it began far back in the past, in the savage, will still continue beyond the present. That is why the words *cosmos* and *rhuthmos* recur in these axiomatic statements. The anthropological story is one of the invention of successive tools and devices which in politics are addressed to solving political problems. We are waiting just now, he says, for a fresh addition to these devices. For the presently constituted society, no such device yet exists.

The same anthropological story describes how human beings have become successively shaped into societies none of which have teleological finality. The present shaping now asks for a piece of ordering, a new addition to the accumulating patterns of human relations.

This conclusion to his politics makes it feasible to suggest the basic relationship of his political theory to his physics or metaphysics. It would have been dangerous to suggest it at the beginning of our study. Do not all historians repeat the tale of his neat mechanical universe of oscillating or rotating atoms blindly throwing themselves through a limitless void and blindly engaging, among other things, in the accidental creation of the human species, which with equal accident is then moved by mechanical impulsion of pleasure and pain upon its amoral course?

This nightmare is a figment of text-books, even if the text-books go back as far as antiquity. What we do perceive is a naturalism, rather than a materialism, which insists (1) that the world is a physical 'order', as its Greek label *cosmos* implies, successively integrated out of chaos and successively replacing simple patterns by more complex ones, though without benefit of an ordering mind, since the tendency to organization is inherent in atomic behaviour; (2) that human society equally forms itself from the dust into increasingly complex patterns describable in terms not of mechanical but of political behaviour, patterns not produced in response to eternal verities nor directed by an all-powerful providence, but rather themselves producing for solution a series of problems with which atomic man has to wrestle, for they are problems of pleasure and pain, profit and loss, right and wrong, good and bad; and these have always been of major importance to the human species since it was first formed.

CHAPTER VII

IN DEFENCE OF DEMOCRACY

THERE is something about Democritus for all his antiquity that seems to anticipate those intellectual and rational energies characteristic of the seventeenth century, as they were put forth by Grotius, Hobbes, Newton and Leibnitz. The comparison would be more obvious if extended to include atomic physics and psychology. But Democritus' political and social theory sufficiently establishes his conviction that even as all physical processes exhibit a configuration which is amenable to rational description, so also does the historical process which has generated human institutions. It need not be a simple process; it need not even be benign, though it may gather some momentum of benignity as it proceeds. But it is reasonable, and there is no aspect of political behaviour however violent or untidy which is not amenable to rational description and explanation; no unsolved difficulty for which a theoretic solution cannot be sometime expected, even if no actual solution is yet in sight. Democritus and Hobbes and Grotius were all driven to over-simplify in different ways the nature of man and to condense and to telescope the variety of historical process. But they unite in signalizing an age of reason, Greek on the one hand, European on the other, which shall extend the claims of the rational to cover the political behaviour and institutional patterns of human beings. A case could be made for arguing that in this field it was the vision of Democritus which was the most complex.

The next chapter in Greek political theory has less of the clarity of Hobbes, and more of the compromise and ambiguities of Locke. It is a chapter written not by one man but by a group of men whom we shall call the Elder Sophists. And their social doctrines, however unsatisfactory to idealists and logicians, share with those of Locke the surpassing merit of dealing with an actual situation and a working apparatus of government which was itself confused, untidy, contradictory but operative. This was the

Athenian democratic process as it functioned under Pericles and as it continued to function, after suppression and restoration, in the fourth Century. They sought to describe and in some sense to defend and in some sense to improve what actually went on in assembly and law court of self-governing municipalities.

The comparison with Locke therefore as against Locke's predecessor must not be pressed too far. The systems of Hobbes and Locke were formed as responses to different political conditions, albeit they overlapped, and to competing political claims – that of the absolute sovereignty of the crown so rudely destroyed by Cromwell and that of the Act of Settlement of 1688 by which claims of crown and parliament were reconciled and compromised. But Protagoras, Prodicus, Thrasymachus, Hippias and Gorgias dealt with the same democracy which had gripped the imagination of Democritus, the historical roots of which he had sought to determine. He and they are all men of the Periclean culture who, strange as it may seem, were all aliens in Athens, yet dedicated to the city's political concepts and method. The difference between himself and them lay basically in this: that the Elder Sophists were not scientists primarily interested in laws of historical growth and patterns of structure. They all use anthropology – they accept its fundamental naturalism – but what they specifically attend to is the process of verbal communication between men and between groups of men which made the democracy workable; and that fierce play of ideas and emotions of which words were media. This they made their business. If Democritus kept his eye on *cosmos*, that is the physical and social pattern, for these men the word was *logos*, the flexible discourse of human beings. Chronologically Protagoras in the tradition is usually regarded as the oldest of the Sophists and as a little older than Democritus. The difference in years must have been trivial. It is at least clear that, while Democritus even in his politics still represents the scientific objectivity and severity of the physicist, Protagoras is the father of the communications-men.

The Elder Sophists sought to rationalize the process by which opinion is formed and then effectively expressed, and by which leadership is imposed and followed, sentiment is crystallized, and common decisions reached. The activity of the group filled the last half of the fifth century before Christ though one or two may have remained active and influential into the opening years of the fourth. In a sense they can be thought of as a 'Socratic' group, for their careers coincide with that of Plato's master and to some extent competed with his (as Old Comedy makes plain). Plato did not like them very much, and he devoted a considerable portion of his literary energies to criticizing them and discrediting them. As a philosopher, and considering the firmness of his own intellectual position, he was perfectly entitled to do this; and the fact that he did it makes them 'Socratics' in another and para-doxical sense, for it has become impossible to think of them historically without thinking of Socrates and Plato also. And this guarantees that we think of them negatively rather than positively. The fact that to this day in western society the practical politician with his eye on public opinion, the negotiator, the dealer in compromises, without whom liberty would not survive a week, is still a person on whose account we feel obliged to feel embarrassed, bears witness to the effectiveness with which Plato performed his task of undermining the moral status of the Elder Sophists.

The mention of Plato's denigration of Protagoras, Prodicus, Gorgias, Thrasymachus and Hippias brings up the whole question of how to document and determine the precise content of their doctrine. The historian who essays to include them in any serious account of Greek political theory needs to be candid about his sources. For these are imperfect and imprecise and the task of piecing them together to make a coherent picture requires philological discipline, a good deal of finesse, and also an exercise of over-all judgment which must be content to leave some things unsettled. We can never pretend to know the precise form in which Protagoras cast his thought. We can only define that anti-Platonic position which in Plato's pages Protagoras is used to represent. This is only one example of the reservations which must be made. The available testimonies are very diverse. This is true even when, as in these chapters, the perspective is limited to what pertains to Greek political theory. They include two precious portions of actual works written by Thrasymachus and Gorgias; one or two sayings of Protagoras which though not political can be used to control some of the other testimony which is political. This exhausts the stock of *ipsissima verba*. There are two brief Platonic parodies of certain political ideas put into the mouth of Prodicus and Hippias; there is a rather extensive Platonic exposition of certain social and political theories put into the mouth of Protagoras and a Platonic critique of these which begins in the *Protagoras* and is supplemented in a few paragraphs of the *Theaetetus*. There are finally two polemics against Thrasymachus and Gorgias respectively, both of them too intense, too fiercely saturated with Platonic conviction, to be of much use as documentation for the thinkers represented. Xenophon and Aristotle add a little – but entirely from a Platonic standpoint. Isocrates has an unimportant word to say. The authors of later antiquity preserve scattered notices, sometimes illuminating when not dependent on Plato, as they too often are.

All this is not an imposing foundation on which to build an edifice of democratic political theory. And yet it is there; the complex farrago will yield unexpected and even dramatic sense. But it calls for a critical method for which the historian needs to take his reader into his confidence, exposing in outline step by step what it will be.

During the century between say 450 and 350 the Greek title *sophistes*, which Pindar had been proud to appropriate as the sobriquet proper to a poet [*Isth.* 5.28; cf. *sophos* in Pindar *passim*], was used in the speech of the cultivated to describe any man of science or learning. Its closest English analogy would be 'intellectual' or 'thinker'. Thus Herodotus calls Pythagoras and Solon 'sophists'. Diogenes of Apollonia addresses his fellow physicists as 'sophists'. Isocrates attached the title to Anaxagoras, Parmenides, Melissus and Gorgias as a group. The orators refer to Socrates and Plato as sophists. But early in the same period the same word began to acquire an equivocal ring. *Sophistes* could when pronounced sound respectful or contemptuous according to the prejudice and social status of the speaker. The title began to behave like our word 'intellectual' and for the same reasons. The whole mental history of an age is symbolized in this growing ambiguity. Intellectualism always invites anti-intellectualism. The playwrights of Old Comedy played upon the prejudice with telling effect, if they indeed did not create it, and when Plato uses the word *sophistes* it has lost its dignity. He cannot forget, perhaps, the burlesques staged in his youth which he had either read or seen. For himself, and for his master Socrates, and for his future disciple Aristotle, there was needed a new professional title which should shake off the odium of *sophistes*. This was found in *philosophos*, the 'philosopher'. The 'intellectual' was replaced by the 'lover of intelligence'. *Sophistes*, now thrust into the margins of intellectual respectability, is next narrowed down by Plato and used to identify the names of five men already mentioned. He does this most effectively by creating dramatis personae for his dialogues and naming them after the five. This is the safest way to put it, rather than saying that he took historical characters and put them into dialogues. Identity between original and portrait cannot be taken for granted. Historians in search of actual information covering the 'sophists' are always eager to credit Plato with their own motives and their own standards of reporting. Plato was a philosopher, not an historian, and the standards governing the literary composition of his day gave wide latitude to the dramatic manipulation of historical figures.

The reconstruction of political theory attempted in the following chapters, so far as it uses Plato, does not rely on the assumption that the personal portraits and the originals closely correspond. His *Protagoras* features a thinker of that name as its protagonist, and includes brief portraits and parodies of two other named figures, Prodicus and Hippias. His *Gorgias* includes a character of that name who, however, yields the centre of the stage to others before a fifth of the dialogue has been covered. The first book of his *Republic* is devoted mainly to a verbal duel between Socrates and a character called Thrasymachus. Two shorter dialogues both called *Hippias* feature a character of that name who is treated with some levity. Finally Plato wrote a dialogue with the general title *Sophist* which more than anything else was responsible for fixing the sophist as a type in the later tradition and thus encouraging the assumption that the big five represented this type. It is fixed in the following terms:

The sophist we have determined to be
(a) a paid hunter of young men who are well-to-do
(b) a sort of trader in the intellectual disciplines of the soul
(c) in fact a dealer at retail in these commodities
(d) standing in person behind the counter
(e) he also has turned out to be a veritable gymnast in competitive discourse creating and establishing the technique of eristic
(f) rather doubtfully we also agree to credit him with the function of dissolving those mental attitudes which block the learning process in the soul [*Soph.* 231d-e].

Plato's prejudices are repeated in Xenophon, and his definition was transmitted to Aristotle. Between them the three completed the polarization between sophist and philosopher and crystallized the latter as the symbol of the Socratic ideal. But if we now return to the label sophist, as it was employed by cultivated persons who either preceded Plato or in his lifetime stood aloof from the controversies in which his own convictions engaged him, their usage may have more to say about the reality behind the label than Plato's denigrations would suggest. In brief, if the pre-Socratics and Socrates and Plato himself no less than Protagoras and Gorgias were, in the eyes of the dispassionate, all regarded as sophists, this argues that all of them enjoyed in those same eyes a roughly similar intellectual status and prestige. All were thinkers with divergent opinions, but taken seriously as thinkers by the cultivated of the age. If, then, in Plato's pages there happen to be five such thinkers prominently featured who none the less enjoy in these same pages only an equivocal status as semi-intellectuals confused or dishonest, pompous, superficial, or dangerous, it is probable that this reflects not their historical status and importance but Plato's personal and judgmental relationship to them. The theories they taught and believed may or may not be possible of reconstruction, but they were at least serious theories, intellectually respectable, culturally dynamic, with their own specific integrity. They must be treated seriously or not at all. This is the first step to take in the difficult task of reconstructing their position.

Plato is a philosopher of the soul, a dramatist of the inner life of man. His touch is so sensitive, his imagination so sympathetic to this drama, that Platonists have great difficulty in accepting the fact that he could be unfair to anybody. How could the prophet of personal sincerity and scientific clarity be himself a propagandist muddying the waters of history? The answer would seem to lie in the very strength of his conviction that the inner psychic life self-motivated is the only real life, and that the eternal verities which lie outside time and space are the only verities: only as the inner life lays hold on these does it become really 'alive'. For one obsessed with this conviction and fighting for it against all the opposition offered by the unconscious pragmatism and materialism of the common man, any group of thinkers which actually sought to defend and to rationalize this pragmatism could only be 'The Enemy', in a sense in which rival metaphysicians could never be. The collision seen in historical perspective was intellectual; but for Plato it was moral. This amounts to saying that the basis of Platonism lies in a kind of religious experience, and religion, however humane, is always intolerant of purely secular thinking and of pragmatic discourse. For it believes that secular anthropology and historical causation and the social sciences perpetrate an act of robbery upon the soul. Hence it is part of Plato's own sincerity that he should be unable to conceive of sophistic pragmatism as sincere at all; that he should be unable to visualize the problems faced by the sophists as being real problems; they are irrelevant to the autonomous soul and its destiny and therefore their authors were not thinkers.

But the historian, even as he discounts Plato's judgmental evaluation of sophistic, can find in Plato's hostility a valuable guide, a signpost, to what precisely sophistic doctrine was. It was everything that Platonism was not. Somehow it looked at men from the outside; it was non-psychic. Perhaps it was historical; certainly it must also have been relativist and anti-metaphysical; and we can pursue the matter further, still using Plato as our guide before letting him go. When he framed that formal definition of the sophist already quoted, the terms of his bitter hostility addressed themselves in the first instance to the sophist's function as teacher, educator, instructor – '. . . a paid hunter of the young . . . a sort of trader in intellectual disciplines of the soul . . . a dealer at retail in these . . . standing behind the counter in person. . . .' This was Plato's consistent conception; the *Protagoras* which is a much earlier dialogue than the *Sophist* anticipated it with precision as follows:

> Hippocrates, don't you think a sophist is really a sort of trader or dealer at retail in those imports which nourish the soul . . . that is, in intellectual disciplines. . . ? Then mind, my friend, in case the sophist in advertising his wares should delude us . . . as the trader and dealer in foodstuffs do . . . Do not the sophists hawk their disciplines around the cities of Greece selling them across the counter, advertising to would-be buyers? [*Protag.* 313c-d]

This is the warning addressed by 'Socrates' to a potential disciple of the great Protagoras later to be introduced. It sufficiently declares Plato's consistent and fundamental hostility to the profession even of one whom, it is often alleged, he handled otherwise with respect.

The objective historian confronting this kind of attack is required to ask two different questions: first, was it any offence on the sophist's part to take fees? What is the morality of this procedure? The answer from any modern standpoint would be that certainly they should take fees; a professor or lecturer or writer has got to live by his trade like anybody else. Was it an offence by Greek standards? We know from Middle Comedy that Plato's Academy charged fees and high ones at that. We are compelled to reply that by Platonic standards the sophists committed no offence. There remains the condition of public opinion at the time; but here the reported financial success of the sophists speaks for itself. Public opinion must at least have tolerated and perhaps approved their ability to earn high incomes.

The second question cuts deeper. Did such fee-taking condition the doctrines taught? Only those who could afford it would pay; clients were therefore the well-to-do. Did this mean a form of pressure under which sophistic doctrine was framed to flatter the taste of the rich and to rationalize their desire for privilege and power? It is often alleged that this was so and that sophistic political theory was a thinly disguised apologia for oligarchy. The only real evidence for this lies in the kind of Platonic innuendo already quoted. And these innuendos do not really point in this direction. The stress on trading in ideas across the counter, semantically speaking, aligns sophistic with the trading class (the *demiourgoi*), not with the wealthy aristocracy who despised trade. It is even possible that in this kind of language Plato turns against the sophists a theory of their own according to which an exchange economy required the services of a class of professors and theorists who, like the traders of the marketplace, are not producers but middlemen dealing in human relations. This is speculative, but it has indirect support elsewhere in Plato and Aristotle. In any case, the same kind of argument would automatically discredit any historian or thinker who ever relied on a patron.

But the vehemence of the invective points steadily to the conclusion that in Plato's eyes the pretension to educate was somehow central to the sophistic profession – at least to the profession of the five whom we call Elder Sophists – and that the claim cut Plato to the quick. We say in Plato's eyes; for it is again possible that he selected for frontal attack an item which in their programmes was incidental. That is, it was Plato who was professionally obsessed with problems of education and instruction, which he made his own. At least we are fairly entitled to discern between his words the pressure of professional competition. Plato was not only an educator; he gave most of his life to founding and developing an educational institution. He had good reasons for thinking that in this device he had solved certain problems of curriculum and discipline with which his predecessors and his contemporaries failed to grapple. This failure was viewed by him as one of basic educational logic and it justified for him at least the picture of such indoctrination as they gave as a piecemeal and superficial process; the same picture had of course the indirect effect of commending by contrast his own more organized, elaborate and rigorous solution.

There would be nothing discreditable even to a genius in this kind of motivation behind his polemic. But in fact, as we have suggested, Plato's deeper aversion was inspired less by sophistic method than by sophistic content. The professional targets of his criticism whom he actually names did not live on far into the fourth century. They were not personally taking away his own pupils. But their ideas certainly did live on, and it was these that Plato feared, and to these that, after discrediting the method, he meant to address himself. If we have given a little space to noticing the fact that Plato picks a quarrel with the sophists over educational method, it is only so that the issue can be dismissed and the ground cleared for an estimate of his testimony as to what precisely they taught – what was the area or field of their instruction.

The dialogue which comes nearest to any kind of report on this matter is Plato's *Protagoras*. Aside from some items of dramatic verisimilitude on which we will not rely, the dramatic theme of the dialogue is the desire of a young man to attend on Protagoras and acquire instruction from him. Socratic dialectic is brought to bear upon the why and wherefore of this situation and elicits the information that Protagoras is a 'sophist'; this is his formal title; and he teaches a *sophia* or intellectual skill defined as 'effectiveness in discourse'. But to the question: 'Discourse about what?' no answer is available. This provides the occasion for that Socratic homily already quoted upon the dangers of entrusting the soul to the sophistic trader in intellectual disciplines. Thus, before ever Protagoras and his peers are brought on the stage, the introduction centres attention on the word 'sophist' – it is used some thirteen times – and on the theme of sophistic. And when the great professor is then encountered in the house of Callias he is represented as formally and fully claiming the title of 'sophist' and the pretensions that go with it. Plato's intention to treat him for dramatic purposes as the embodiment of the type is unmistakable. Thus, for instance, the terms in which Protagoras is made to describe his own professional activity in the cities of Greece have a close verbal resemblance to the same description given in Plato's *Apology* by Socrates of the activity of Gorgias, Prodicus and Hippias. This should warn us that throughout the dialogue the dramatis personae are conceived less biographically than typically, as dramatizations of theories which for Plato were grouped under the heading of 'sophistic'.

Moreover, rather a point is made of the fact that Protagoras intends to come into the open and speak frankly and fearlessly in his character as 'sophist'. Plato, we suggest, thus indicates to his readers that while sophists and sophistic reappear in other dialogues, the *Protagoras* is dedicated formally to a Platonic presentation and critique of the main substance, the leading ideas, the central doctrines of sophistic.

What this substance is has been a question already asked by Socrates of the young disciple – with no answer forthcoming. It is now in effect repeated to Protagoras whose first reply is simply that his instruction 'makes a man daily better and more effective'. As Socrates responds with the further question: Better in what? the reader is propelled towards the crucial definition:

(a) I have indeed an intellectual discipline (*mathema*) (says Protagoras)
(b) which consists in the 'formation of correct decision' (*euboulia*)
(c) covering the most effective management of the household
(d) and the most capable administration of civic business
(e) and expression (in discourse)
(f) You mean (says Socrates), the political (civic) technique?
(g) Precisely (replies Protagoras). This is my professional competence [*Protag.* 318e-319a]

It is not Protagoras but Plato who is writing these programmatic sentences. The real Protagoras was already dead. His doctrines belong to a previous epoch; they had been conceived and promulgated before Plato was born, in a different Athens prosperous and powerful that Plato never knew. Can they ever be resurrected from such a source as this dialogue?

Argument has been given above for supposing that the *Protagoras* is committed as no other dialogue is committed to giving a report on sophistic. A similar commitment would not apply for example to the use made of Gorgias in the *Gorgias* or of Thrasymachus in the first book of the *Republic*. It has also been argued that the *Protagoras* is not written in such a way as to encourage the reader to think it is a report on Protagoras personally. If it is indeed a report on a school of thinking, let that school for present convenience in this chapter be labelled 'Protagoreanism'.

The five items (a) to (e) in the quotation just given have the air of being spelled out as an intellectual position. Do they in any sense contain the germ of an actual report on this school? The hypothesis is going to be attempted that they do; that certain doctrinal clues are here supplied, the consequences of which can be traced and amplified through the subsequent pages of the dialogue, revealing by degrees the outline of a coherent and formidable body of political and moral theory; formidable that is from the standpoint of Platonism.

No philosopher in his senses will take the trouble to report with historical fidelity views which intellectually he cannot accept. What he is committed to is a critical examination of them, which passes judgment by the light of his own system, and the judgment becomes part of the report. What conceivable criterion then can guide the critic who would attempt to disentangle genuine Protagoreanism from the context in which it is estimated and judged?

The task would probably be hopeless unless he could begin by bringing to bear upon the Platonic evidence some external controls which did not depend on Plato. These he can find in that portrait of 'liberalism' (as we have agreed to call it) which has already begun to emerge from the remains of the Greek anthropologies and of Democritus; provided, that is, that the critic assumes that the doctrines of Protagoreanism were conceived in essentially the same context. Plato's dialogue, in fact, itself supplies some evidence that they were by inserting in Protagoras' mouth a 'Platonic' anthropology which has been already submitted to analysis in an earlier chapter. Democritus, as is well known, is never mentioned in Plato. But his own remains guarantee that he was committed to the anthropological method and, if Protagoreanism was too, then the critic who is willing to assume some continuity between Democritean and Protagorean politics has ground under his feet without having to rely on the common origin of the two men (Abdera) or the biographical gossip which connected their careers.

The five short items already exposed on a tentative basis as a sample of Protagoreanism may be programmatic but at first sight they do not seem to be particularly profound. They seem pragmatic and practical – a formula offered for worldly success, social, financial and political. Such a judgment of them should be checked very quickly by the reflection that it is, after all, Platonism itself which influences us in forming such a judgment. The contrast between the practical politician and the true statesman is always there at the back of our minds, and it is Plato's work. As we have seen, the dialogue no sooner introduced sophistic than it also included some subtle denigration of sophistic; the reader is already being softened up; his will to believe in the integrity of sophistic as an intellectual system is already partly sapped. But suppose he re-asserts his own independence of judgment and allows himself to ask: how do these five items read if they are placed in the context of those conceptions of man and society fathered by the anthropologists and by Democritus?

They at once take on a new look. The previous chapter has already shown Democritus grappling with the problem of 'capable administration of civic business'; and he had, as a matter of fact, things to say also about 'the effective management of the household' which that chapter did not include. His political doctrine was controlled by a pragmatism and an empiricism which however did not concern themselves with vulgar success but with a serious rationale of the existing institutions of democratic Athens. A comparison with the anthropologists further established that a political theory pragmatic in method and favourable to democracy was grounded on a sociology derived from historical principles. And it was shown that for Democritus some problems of democratic government remained unsolved. Why should the pragmatism of the Protagorean programme not have rested on similar historical foundations? And could not the specific questions to which it is here represented as addressing itself be regarded as a supplement to the Democritean position? For these are the 'formation of correct decision' and the problem of 'effective expression'. Now for Platonism and all idealist systems of political theory the formation of political decision relies on the guidance afforded to superior persons by *a priori* and eternal verities. But for the liberal statesman political decision can rest only on a common denominator discoverable through communication between members of that community which is served by the decisions; or, if formulated by superior persons, then formulated in response to community need and pressure and offered for the community to approve or reject. In short, the simple Greek terms *logos* and *legein* – effectiveness of speech – if placed in the theoretic context proper to them at this time might imply a serious theory of social communication; and the Greek *euboulia* – 'reaching correct decision' – might include an equally serious theory of how in a democratic community opinion is formed and decisions are made.

If these suggestions are entertained, then a critique of the text of the dialogue is established which will follow along a groove of thinking alien to Platonism and to the literary spirit in which the dialogue is composed – admittedly a hazardous procedure. The critique will be committed to looking for concealed clues leading to unexpected revelations, which the art of the dialogue itself is intended to disguise. For it must be remembered that Plato's chief philosophical method in dealing with intellectual positions other than his own is not so very different from Aristotle's. He is less interested in polemics than in a process of digestion and absorption. If he can redirect the mistaken insight of others into new forms which fit his own preoccupations and his own metaphysic, he has accomplished what to him is the task of dialectic. The critic in search of the originals that have passed through this warping process certainly needs the lantern of intuition for his guide, no less than the apparatus of philology. In particular, what he must watch for is the way in which the problems set by Plato in his dialogues for the sophists to solve, or to fail at solving, are Platonic questions to which sophistic was not equipped to give an answer; and quite properly so, because it did not ask them. If therefore sophistic is, so to speak, put in the witness box and allowed only a yes or no to the questions selected by the prosecuting counsel, it is likely to stutter and stumble. It is not being allowed the privilege of speaking its own language, nor of addressing itself to those specific questions which sophistic considered important, though Plato did not.

Thus the text of the present dialogue, after allowing these five items of Protagoreanism to be stated, at once transfers them into a non-political context. Can this civic excellence be made a subject of instruction? asks Socrates. It is to this problem, instruction, its content and method, that nearly the whole dialogue is addressed. In fact: 'is virtue teachable?' It was a very proper preoccupation for an author who intended to found such an educational institution as the Academy.

But to suggest that sophistic should have seen this problem as Plato saw it, and should have been prepared with the epistemology which he saw as necessary, is to suggest an anachronism. It foists an alien context – the educational – upon an original system of ideas which was sociological.

Is this civic excellence of yours teachable? asks Socrates [319aff.], and proceeds at once to give ironic reasons why it is not. His irony is at the expense of Athenian democratic practice, and his reasons, it turns out, for inferring the negative are precisely those which Protagoras later will convert into the positive.

Protagoras is then allowed to speak [320cff.] and as the first part of his answer there is assigned to him that pseudo-anthropology in which are buried some elements of the genuine article; that is, elements of an original which viewed the rise of society, civilization and law from a purely naturalist and historical perspective. This, as edited by Plato, turns into a divine myth which is put into Protagoras' mouth. It was argued in an earlier chapter that the features of it, if any, which were peculiar to Protagoras personally cannot now be identified. Nor perhaps does it greatly matter what they were. The content of the anthropology, like that of the rest of the dialogue, is typical rather than personal.

The myth being concluded, Protagoras is allowed the privilege of continuous and fairly systematic exposition of his theories of man and of man's society, his morals, politics and education. The continuity with the myth is tenuous, simply because the myth is a myth, whereas the exposition is pragmatic and descriptive of society as one actually finds it. The continuity with that short programme of five items of Protagoreanism already examined is, however, fairly close; indeed it is obvious from the opening sentence. And as the exposition continues and enlarges it becomes increasingly evident that it has a basic structure which is rooted in the whole liberal scientific view of man and society.

(a) . . . mankind, Athenians included . . . when they reach the stage of forming joint decisions in the field of civic excellence – a process which wholly involves righteousness and temperance – with good reason tolerate any man's voice

(b) it being axiomatic that every man properly partakes in this excellence

(c) as a condition of cities existing. This is the basis for the practice [*Protag.* 322d5-323a3].

(d) There is no illusion here; the impression that all human beings really do assume every man to partake in civic excellence and specifically in righteousness is quite correct. Here is further proof of it:

(e) (In the case of other excellences, as you say, should a man claim to be as good at flute-playing or any other technique which he has not got, he is ridiculed or objected to. The members of his household go and see him to put sense into him, thinking he is insane.)

(f) But now take civic excellence and specifically righteousness. Suppose a man recognized by others to be a doer of wrong personally declares the fact at his own expense in the presence of witnesses. An attitude which in the former case would be taken for proper sobriety is in his taken for insanity. We hold that all men properly say they are righteous whether or not they really are. Or else if they do not lay claim to righteousness they must be insane

(g) it being axiomatic that all men without exception necessarily partake in it to some degree

(h) as a condition of existing among human beings [323a5-c1].

(i) To repeat then: with good reason we tolerate any man's voice in forming collective decisions in the field of this excellence

(j) because we assume that every man partakes in it. That is what I have been saying [323c3-5].

These are memorable words, less for their style than their content. Here is a reasoned defence of democratic process as it obtained in the mother of all democracies. Classical literature, Greek or Latin, is not replete with such utterances. Herodotus supplies the first, the funeral speech put into Pericles' mouth is perhaps the second; this is the third and, though the least readable of the three, in a theoretical sense it cuts deeper. Item (a) establishes the fact that for Protagoreanism the problem of forming correct decisions was conceived as occurring in a social and political context. The decisions are collective. By what precise processes of group psychology this occurs is not here spelled out (it will be later), but the governing principle is stated flatly. The mind of every human being in the assembly that is debating policy can have a contribution to make. The fact is stated not in terms of any rights he may have – this is a modern conception – but in terms of his inherent capacity. This is the way it is put in item (b) and repeated three more times in items (d), (g), and (j). We all partake in this excellence. What precisely does he mean? What is this shared thing? The clue is supplied in items (c) and (h), though it is not stated as explicitly as it should be (Plato, be it remembered, is here allowing some grudging exposition of a theory he disliked). The political capacity in each man is not his personal property; it is something he shares with others; it is that in him which enables societies to come into being and exist at all. Reversing this relationship, it is equally true that it is only the kind of excellence evoked by societies and required by them of their members which allows the members to become and remain human beings. The moral-political individual both creates society and yet is created by it.

Such a theory exactly fits the conditions presupposed by descriptive anthropology. The human being never begins as a political animal; he only becomes such in the course of his social evolution from the savage to the civilized condition. And his excellence correspondingly has never been a fixed and permanent quantity, but an evolving pattern of habit and response and value. It is precisely this picture of its mobility and flexibility which Socrates subsequently selects for attack.

In fact, righteousness itself is simply a kind of index to man's sociability; or more correctly, if we fill in an argument which Plato found distasteful, it is the rules of the game which hold society together, the formula which regulates and adjusts relationships between its members. This is the logical consequence for which item (d) provides the bare hint. In Plato's report, characteristically, the 'excellence' of an individual and his 'righteousness' are treated as identical. There was in the original theory some operational difference.

Items (e) and (f) report, though again in a disguised and innocuous form, a further refinement. One of the indicators of our common sociality is our common language, and above all the tendency to use agreed evaluative terms, whether pejorative or the reverse. Even philosophers, let alone ordinary mortals, may argue eristically the precise meaning of good and right till they are out of breath. But as human beings they somehow exhibit the curious and ingrained habit of never wishing to admit that they are themselves bad or wilfully wrong. If a man does this (unless, it is surely implied, in temporary repentance), if he avows his own immorality, he is by common agreement crazy. Hence on the one hand linguistic usage, and on the other the psychological reflexes of human beings as betrayed in their language, presume their common partnership in a social nexus. And our morality derives from this fact.

The statement then concludes by reaffirming the democratic process as the only satisfactory expression of the social and historical principles defined above. Be it noted that democracy is not defended (as it was in Herodotus) as an egalitarian society, but as a participating society, in which the opinion-forming capacities of all men are involved. There is no theoretic room for a class division between leaders and led, or between the political science of the statesman and the passive demotic virtue which is trained only to obey.

Critical intuition has been used to elucidate the intellectual structure behind this passage. It can be supported by a comparison with Democritus and with the historical formulation on which he had built. There is a common preoccupation with the problems of decision-formation in a society as an instrument of government; and a common conviction that the norms by which society operates are not to be sought outside the processes which have formed society but are in effect the device invented by society for its own protection. The pragmatism and the historical spirit are there in both, and so also the tendency to look for clues in the behaviour of language and in unconscious human psychology. For all we know, Protagoreanism may have exhibited no difference in principle from the teaching of Democritus. But a difference in flavour is perhaps perceptible. The more severe thinker had sought a science by which institutions could be described; the more pragmatic had sought the rationale of communication by which they actually worked.

Such a theory does not really distinguish between a man's morality and his 'civility' and between his personal ethics and his political sense. These constitute his 'humanity' and they must have developed historically as society has developed, for when society did not exist they did not either. But the process though historical is not mechanical or even automatic. The theory is subtler than that. In any given society, the correct behaviour-patterns do not maintain themselves without effort and without enlisting the aid of human energies. To each generation is given the task of transmitting the *mores* to its successor. The fact that the commitment is historical does not mean that it is performed as in sleep-walking; on the contrary, we bring deliberate and collective pressure upon each other and upon the young to develop and practise that sociality which is our human excellence. In each individual, therefore, the same excellence, though describable in terms of biological growth (in the sense that all society from its origins to the present is a growth), is nevertheless also a personal acquisition. For we all once were savages and theoretically might still be. The inherited and remembered experience of the past which has built cities and laws still relies on a kind of group indoctrination for its perpetuation. So Protagoras continues:

We all then suppose that every man shares in this excellence. Naturally therefore we all expect every man to share in forming decisions which involve it.

We do not however assume that the excellence exists by nature automatically. We assume it is instructible and accrues to its possessor as the result of concentration. This is the next thing I must demonstrate to you.

There are evils which can come upon men by nature or chance. No one gets angry over these or re-educates or instructs or punishes the victims to stop them being what they are. We just pity them. I mean for example the ugly, the dwarfed, the physically feeble. Is anyone so insane as to attempt any correction of such? The fact is, we realize that it is nature or chance that sends these things on human beings – I mean either what is fair and fortunate or the reverse [323c3-d5].

But if you take the things that we think accrue to the benefit of human beings as the result of concentration and practice and instruction and find a person who does not have them, but the opposite of them, does not such a person invite our anger, our punishment, and our re-education? What he exhibits is immorality and impiety and in a word all that is the opposite of city excellence. It is these that make one man angry with another and provoke him to re-educate him. Clearly on the assumption that city excellence is made ours as a result of concentration and instruction [323d6-324a3].

This paragraph combines two social propositions which are separable. The first is a paradox according to which our virtue as human beings, though historically conditioned, does not come naturally to us. This will be spelled out more fully at a later stage. Civility in men may be viewed as a necessary human condition for forming societies, yet it is the pressure of the social group as it is formed which historically produces the civility. And this pressure takes concrete form in the educational activities of the members of the group at any given moment. The forms of our group goodness are hammered into us. The liberal sociology in fact did not deal in primary causes and secondary effects. It rather saw the historical process as containing within itself its own propulsive mechanisms which descriptively speaking interact on each other.

But secondly the paragraph raises the question: What is the mechanism by which group pressure exerts itself? It imposes penalties for deviation. So Protagoras, to support the argument that social morality is in fact inculcated and not inborn or accidental, appeals to the universal social habit of punishing. Once more the voice of Democritus is heard describing the primary sanctions whereby society is created and supported. The individual who punishes or feels he should punish only expresses the group pressure of which he is the (unwitting) instrument. That this, and not private revenge, is, descriptively speaking, the spring of his action is a thesis that Protagoras proceeds to defend:

> Consider the concept of punishment, Socrates, and what it actually means to punish wrongdoers. The facts will show you that human beings must think that excellence is a procurable thing. No one punishes wrongdoers just because wrong has been done. It is not on this that he directs his attention. Nor is this his reason unless he is taking vengeance irrationally like a wild animal.
>
> If a man sets about punishment rationally, he does not exact vengeance for crime in the past – he cannot make undone what has been done – his purpose deals with crime in the future, to prevent the wrongdoer from doing wrong again and to prevent anyone else also by the force of example. If this is the kind of conception that animates a man, he must conceive of excellence as being educatable. So he punishes in order to deter. This then is the idea all men have when they exact penalty whether in personal or public relations. Anyone believed to be a wrongdoer is always penalized and punished by people and not least by your fellow citizens of Athens. My argument then amounts to saying that Athenians like everyone else must be numbered among the men who hold that excellence is procurable and instructible [324a3-18].

What centuries of angry superstition are rolled back in this statement! One would think that Greek tragedy must have been played out in some other city than the Athens which is supposed to be the scene of these enlightened sentiments. To assert that in the scheme of human punishment there is no room for retribution; that the past is the past, and that to attempt to compensate for it on the eye-for-an-eye principle is irrational, is to fling the doctrine of divine nemesis out of the window and with it the whole tragic scheme of inherited guilt and sins visited on the children by jealous gods or capricious fortune.

In human terms it excluded the desire for revenge from the normal scheme of values. This, in the realm of ideas, was a revolution indeed, and if sophistic fathered it, as there is evidence it did, then it fully deserves the credit for giving leadership to what is sometimes called the Greek enlightenment. Credit, however, should be shared by Solon and his successors and by the men of

Athens themselves, responsible as they were for the tolerant temper of social custom and legal administration which had made the city famous.

What had been an unconscious tendency is here converted into a theory and rationalized as a norm of all human conduct. The naïvety of the argument with which the theory of corrective punishment is supported seems at first sight hopelessly unrealistic. Men are not in fact rational in the sophistic sense. The general or unconscious opinion to which appeal is made, that punishment only makes sense as a corrective or as a deterrent, seems to be an invention of Protagoreanism. Retribution as a public or ritual conception, and revenge as a private right, were surely rooted deep in the Athenian *mores*, as they still seem to be in the *mores* of the twentieth century. Yet it is plausible that the original version advanced by the liberals was more serious than it is made to appear in Plato's text.

Its appeal to the standards set by reason was not made in Platonic or Stoic terms, as though they were the standards of an ideal wise man or of a Platonic philosopher. The assumption made is that punishment like any other facet of human behaviour has arisen in order to serve social use. This is true of the origins of all personal and public morality, and punishment is no exception. What is it that sets the criterion of usefulness? Clearly on Democritean principles this was in the first instance the security of the group and its members. This required the primary sanction of death imposed on society's enemies. But as society grows secure, complex and peaceful, and emerges into the democratic Solonian formula, punishment no longer needs to be Draconian. It is still directed toward protecting the group organization. Primarily, therefore, it is deterrent. But secondarily it can now afford to be corrective. It becomes a form of instruction, which is the thesis to which the present passage is addressed. We observed in Democritus himself a recognition of the growth of compassion and consensus as a political principle superimposed upon the original law of sanctions applied to aggressors. The sophistic formula for punishment is an amplification of this social development.

We suggest that when Protagoras names 'all men' as his court of appeal, he is thinking historically and genetically of any society of men and its structural principles. The phrase 'all men' is too loose to express his meaning. The logic to which he appeals is not personal but historical. It may be significant in this connection that the act of retribution is classified as not only irrational but also as characteristic of animals. We suggest that Plato here reproduces a genuine echo of his source which argued on anthropological lines that as society developed out of savagery, patterns of retaliation tended to be replaced by those of correction.

Protagoreanism thus rationalizes the spirit of what seemed an age of social progress. Like Democritus, it looked on the Athens created by Solon and governed by Pericles and found in it the optimum of social values. Disillusionment was soon to follow in Antiphon. But these pages of the *Protagoras* are dedicated on the whole to the pragmatic confidence of the Periclean enlightenment:

This brings us to the next problem which you raised about persons who are (socially) effective. Why is it they can give their sons instruction in those subjects that instruction can handle, and can make them skilled, but cannot give them any superiority in that excellence which has conferred on the parents their own effectiveness? I will not use a story, Socrates, to cover this problem but a discourse and I shall ask you to entertain a concept on the following lines: Ask yourself: is there or is there not some one thing in which all citizens must inevitably partake if you are going to have a city at all. Here if anywhere is contained the solution to the problem which you raised. Suppose there is such a thing, suppose this one thing is not carpentering or metallurgy or making pots, but righteousness and discipline and being pious and in a word suppose I name it the excellence of man; suppose this is the thing which all men are expected to share in, and that this is what every man must already have when he wants to be taught anything else or do any other business, and that without it he cannot take any other step; suppose that anyone who fails to partake in it, whether child or man or woman, has to be instructed and punished until such time as punishment improves him; suppose that a man incapable of responding to punishment or instruction must be treated as irredeemable, and outlawed or killed –

suppose all this; suppose this is the natural condition of the matter, and then imagine if you can that effective men have their sons instructed in everything else except this one thing –

ask yourself what miracle would in that case be required to raise up successive generations of effective men [324d2-325b4].

I have demonstrated that the thing is regarded as a subject of instruction, both at the private and public level. If it is instructible and educatable, are men going to have their own sons taught everything else – where there is no penalty of death if they fail to learn the lesson – but when it comes to matters where the penalties for children who have not been instructed or educated in excellence are death, exile, confiscation of property, and in a word, practically speaking, the smash-up of their home – are we to believe that instruction in these matters is not given and careful concentration is not attempted? Far from it, Socrates [325b4-14].

Plato's report becomes a little repetitive. There is a colour of over-emphasis – perhaps in reminiscence of Protagoras' style, perhaps reflecting Plato's own feeling that such ideas only stated the obvious. Protagoras however continues the sophistic task of rationalizing the procedures of society as he finds it. Since from Plato's point of view this society of the Periclean age has failed, there is no point in rationalizing it, except to memorialize a superficial sociology which his own political theory is intended to destroy and supplant. But though Protagoras is repeating himself under the guise of replying to a fresh difficulty which is not really fresh, his social methodology becomes clearer with every repetition.

For the third or fourth time he returns to that condition or property in human beings which makes society as such possible. For Plato any society to be significant must be a city. He may have edited the original here, if the original spoke in Democritean terms of 'social shape' or 'order' or 'system'. This property is now isolated as 'that one thing necessary' aside from other human skills. Protagoras is made to call it righteousness and discipline. This again may reflect Platonic editing, for he is laying the ground for a damaging logical attack by Socrates on Protagoras' conception of the unity of virtue later. And as we watch the ground being laid we must remember we are reading the artful composition of a purposeful dialectician.

Plato, however, we know, did not himself invent the term 'righteousness' and sophistic theory may well have coined it to identify the combination of social instinct and civic responsibility in human beings. The primary point to be made here is that this one thing has a double nature or can be described from two different perspectives which supplement each other. On the one hand it is an identical property possessed by all human beings, the universal hallmark of humanity; on the other it is a creation of persistent social relationships, and its presence is guaranteed historically by social sanctions. The absence of it is visited by exile, execution, or social disaster. The echo of Democritus is unmistakable. 'This one excellence' is not only the product of group loyalty; it *is* that loyalty. Having drawn men together for security, it becomes their capacity for co-operation, not as a spiritual aspiration of individuals, but as an instinctive reverence for and obedience to a pattern of existing law. Protagoras' argument is not quite as circular as it sounds.

It amounts to saying 'since our common humanity is simultaneously the source of and the response to the process of socialization and civilization, and since we find this essential to living, is it credible that the older generation should fail to transmit it to the younger? Of course not; its transmission is inevitable though not altogether automatic.' (The next paragraph is to describe the semi-automatic mechanism of the transmission.) Thus in sophistic theory excellence or virtue is used to symbolize that condition of *mores* which makes any society stable and politically effective and its members likewise. By definition therefore it is popular, not aristocratic, and by definition transmissible.

On the other hand, behind the original Socratic question: Is it instructible, had been a much more intellectual and aristocratic conception of virtue. The question meant: Is there an independent scientific procedure for formulating and communicating this (Platonic) excellence of man? To this kind of problem Protagoras never addresses himself. For him, human excellence is not a conscious science but a conditioning. The Platonic problem would be meaningless to him. That is why his answers are made to seem so ineffective.

The Socratic question is already forecasting the split between ideal theory of what a human being should be if all his powers were realized and the actual levels achieved in existing societies. But Protagoras' descriptive sociology cannot envisage this split. The dialogue progressively dramatizes his failure to come to grips with the Socratic problem and the reader is meant to feel the failure. But the historian can afford to separate out the report of a sociology, at once positivist and egalitarian, which by indirection has thus been preserved.

What is the actual mechanism by which the basic social sense of how to behave socially is transmitted between the generations? The descriptive account continues by reviewing the institutions of transmission available to Periclean Athens. They need here be only summarized:

> Beginning when they are little children, and continuing as long as they are alive, instruction and indoctrination persist. Directly a child understands what is said to it, nurse and mother and tutor and finally father exert themselves to perfect him . . . [325c5ff.].
>
> explaining this is right and that is wrong, etc. [325d3].
>
> . . . if he is refractory they bend and straighten him out with threats and blows like a piece of wood . . . [325d5].
>
> then they send him to school and tell the schoolmaster to concentrate on the child's discipline before letters and music . . . [325d7].
>
> the schoolmaster compels him to read and memorize poems which are full of indoctrination . . . [325e5].
>
> the music master concentrates on discipline no less . . . [326a4].
>
> and compels his psyche to become familiar with rhythms and harmonies to make him more gentle, a more rhythmic and harmonized personality, who thus becomes a useful citizen when it comes to speaking and doing . . . [326b1ff.].
>
> furthermore he is sent to the gymnast to improve his body and put it under the control of his mind and so avoid flinching . . . in war and in life generally . . . [326b6ff.].

Plato has made education so much his own subject, in the *Republic* and elsewhere, that the above reads like his own description of how it was conducted. But even here he is drawing in all probability upon sophistic models. If the sophists, according to his frequent testimony, strove to define their own status as educational, this may well have provoked them to ask the question: What in fact is education? – a question which, put formally as a problem requiring a systematic answer, may have been no older than they were. Educational procedures before their day are likely to have accumulated slowly by unconscious social adaptation. Sophistic sociology would then perform the historical service of discovering that there was such a thing as 'education', which as handled within the family became an identifiable process though only part of the over-all mechanism by which society conserved itself, a pressure-process consciously and purposively applied by the old to the young.

As the rationale of educational practice continues, it returns almost imperceptibly to social and political theory:

> This system is practised most of all by those most capable of doing so. These are the wealthiest group, whose sons after starting to attend instruction at an age earlier than others, are the last to finish with it. After they do finish with it, the city in its turn makes it compulsory for them to be instructed in the custom laws and to live by these as their prototype to prevent random (political) action taken on their own initiative. Compare how copymasters use the stylus to draw strokes in outline for the children who have not yet mastered writing, and then hand the tablet over to them and make them write by following the guidance of the strokes. Exactly so does the city draft in outline the custom-laws, which have been the invention of excellent lawgivers of old, and compels men to rule and be ruled under their direction. If a man goes outside their limits, the city punishes him. 'Corrective audit' is the term you give to this punishment, in Athens as also elsewhere. The assumption being that the application of right [in judicial process] acts as a corrective and straightener [326c3-e1].

This is a compressed passage into which Plato has telescoped two separable theses of sophistic sociology. The first deals with the character and function of civic law in the interest of group security and stability. Law, or rather lawful usage, continues that process of social conditioning which was begun in the household. The laws are described as the outlines drafted like letters for the citizens to copy. Democritus, we know, was fascinated by the alphabet as an illustration of the workings of his cosmic atomism. It could be in keeping to suggest that he inspired the present analogy. The suggestion is strengthened in the fact that the outlines are also described as 'prototypes'; that is, civic custom-law composes the formal 'atomic' structure out of which patterns of daily living are compacted. This is speculative, but it is not speculative to observe that the identification of the Solonian political mechanisms as prototypes and the consequent idealization of the Periclean democracy is quite anti-Platonic (Editors accordingly would like to excise the reference to a prototype, but Plato is reporting).

The gulf between sophistic politics, which pragmatically identified its model with an existing society, and the Platonic politics founded on the Forms discoverable only by *a priori* methods, is unmistakable. The gulf is equally wide between this kind of social optimism, which we shall ascribe to the group called the Elder Sophists, and the disillusioned attack upon custom-law which in Antiphon draws battle-lines between law and nature. When Plato expends ink on this issue, he is not attacking the elder Periclean sophists but the postwar disillusioned sophists. It must be emphasized – and Democritus provides explicit confirmation – that for the men of Protagoras' generation nature and law did in effect coincide, whether historically as for Democritus or pragmatically as for the sophists.

But it is probable also that in conceptualizing the custom-laws as outlines or as models, Protagoreanism prepared the ground for abstracting them in analytic isolation from the human behaviour which they controlled. Sophistic did the same thing for 'law' as a normative concept (*nomos*) as it did for 'education' (*paideusis*). Nor does this exhaust the possibilities of legal theory which they opened up. If sophistic was to give some attention to the process of taking counsel and forming group decision (see the next chapter) which goes on in a democracy, it was on the edge of visualizing law not as an invention of 'men of old' (the formula is a tribute to Solon) but as a positivist programme of continuous and adapted regulation implemented by votes (*psephismata*). Conceivably they saw this, and argued that the process was in effect only filling in the outline of the original law-givers. All this, if indeed it was proposed as a theory of popular legislation, Plato omits. He naturally might, since it proposes a conception of law so alien to his own thinking.

The transition from the topic of education to that of law has been bridged by mention of a specific class in the community –

the sons of the wealthy. And it is their role which also prompts the transition, though this is not at once apparent. For they have an accepted part to play in liberal political theory at least as that theory was conceived by the Elder Sophists. This is the second of two theses which Plato has telescoped into each other. It would seem that the sophists accepted the pragmatic fact which any member of a liberal democracy is forced to accept: that educational opportunity tends to be available in proportion to family means. On the one hand a doctrine which made social virtue generic and universal had to be egalitarian; any man was as adequate a judge of political morality and interest as any other. On the other hand, in practice, any society requires some leadership, which by definition accrues to the more powerful and effective and 'better' citizens. How did the Solonian formula treat this paradox? It met it with a solution approved, as we saw, and rationalized by Democritus. The office holder held office 'on deposit'; his decisions are subject to popular audit. This is precisely the formula here put into Protagoras' mouth, with the difference that the audit is identified more generally as the whole power of law to impose a criterion on men's political acts, and also as the judicial process which the city sets in motion to do this. The *plethos* or people in assembly or law court are presumed to be the voice of law: *vox populi vox legis*. Only such a theory could support the Solonian arrangement, which sought to respect the force of law and the freedom of democracy simultaneously.

Now, where do leaders and office holders come from? One replies, from the people themselves, who take their turn at 'ruling and being ruled'. This formula is used here, and is later copied in Aristotle's *Politics*, where a theory of political power democratic in character is uneasily wedded to a quite different and patriarchal conception of society – and a compromise evolved from the two. But, pragmatically speaking, did not leadership tend to fall into the hands of the privileged, of whom Pericles was a conspicuous example? Yes, reply the sophists readily, we accept the fact in a pragmatic spirit; it does not violate the ethos of democracy, provided you keep the public audit and continue to limit office to yearly periods, even if they are renewable.

Nor, they could add, does it violate the premises of our sociology. Although the political-social sense of man is universal yet (a) it depends for its existence on continuous group training and (b) as a trained faculty it can therefore admit of degrees of improvement achieved by superior education. And men themselves in their social-political capacities differ in degree, though none are dunces. In this way, native endowment and instruction combine in varying proportions with opportunity to form the end product. This suggests a rational and acceptable solution to the problem of leadership, because in fact the wealthy have better access to education, and hence are better trained for the job, even though they may not always have the superior capacity. This, we suggest, was the sophistic reasoning. It is an accommodation to the Democritean and indeed traditional principle that 'office belongs to the superior', while reconciling this with legal equality (*isonomia*). At the same time, it neatly rationalized the sophists' professional role in society, for they, so they argued, had merely arrived on the scene to perfect the existing educational arrangement and bring it into focus by supplementing the guidance of the household and the pressure of environment with their own teaching.

The telescoping of this formula with the rationale of law's general control over all men results in a grammatical ambiguity in Plato's text. Who are the 'men' who on leaving school are forced to live according to law's prototype, or are kept in line by audit? In one sense, all citizens, so far as the audit could be conceived not as confined to a specific institution, but as a general checking up from day to day imposed by lawful usage upon ordinary men. But Plato's language calls attention to the technical sense also, and thus tends to identify the objects of audit as office-holders, and the previous context helps to suggest that these are the wealthier and better educated men. We do not suggest the ambiguity is altogether Plato's. The Elder Sophists, in their adherence to democracy on the one hand and their acceptance of a measure of plutocracy on the other, may have been just as ambiguous themselves, and, if so, they have legions of imitators in modern times. Marx and Disraeli had sufficient cynicism to insist on a formal distinction between plutocracy and democracy; but this capacity in political theorists is rare. In fact, pragmatically speaking, it seems doubtful if theory can ever formalize the distinction into two mutually exclusive systems. The sophistic ambiguity, though exposed to all sorts of attack for courting the rich, had the advantage of conceiving of politics in terms of compromises which had worked.

The exposition as it draws towards its peroration, though on the surface still addressed to the problem of instruction, returns in fact to the fundamental theories of social anthropology:

Why is it, you ask, that many of the sons of effective fathers are themselves indifferent persons? Here is the explanation: if what I have said hitherto is true, it is to be expected that if you are to have a city at all, then in application of [political] excellence no man can enjoy non-professional status. To repeat then; if the situation is as I say it is – and it certainly is – I want you to imagine how it would be if you took any other of the professions and intellectual disciplines – take anyone you like; suppose you could not have a city unless we were all flute-players, to the capacity of each individual; suppose everybody was instructed by everybody in flute-playing at all personal and public levels, and everybody harassed everybody else who could not play well, and we all unflaggingly kept it up, just as under present conditions we all unflaggingly keep up the cause of the right and the lawful, and make no professional secret of it as we do of the other technologies . . . [326e6-327b1].

Even before the apodosis is reached, enough has been said to disclose what might be called the operational or instrumental view of social morality held by Protagoreanism – a view consistent with the historical role assigned to technology. This morality is a developed faculty of man the tool-user:

'A tear is an intellectual thing'.

It is developed and maintained by a discipline which the whole of society 'keeps up' as members of a profession keep up their skill; only, now, the profession coincides with society itself. We have returned to that assumption which, as was argued in an earlier chapter, underlay the fable of Prometheus, had the fable been told without benefit of Platonic editing: namely, that technology viewed historically contains the whole clue to man's specific quality as a species: his social organization, justice and law are themselves developments of that same kind of faculty which lit the first fire or lifted the first wooden club to substitute for the purely defensive equipment which Afterthought had used up on the animals. Indeed it is only in social organization that the

effective exellence of man's endowment of forethinking is completely felt. For social invention, unlike the club, soon ceases to be
a mere apparatus of reaction to danger and takes charge of man's
way of life, infusing into it an increasing degree of political complexity.

Before the apodosis to this 'suppose' clause in Plato's text is
reached the exposition interrupts itself. And one of the axioms of
liberal sociology is allowed by Plato to emerge almost accidentally:

> As a matter of fact our righteousness and excellence in mutual
> relations serve our own interest. If everyone is so zealous in
> the cause of the right and the lawful, ready to speak and give
> instruction to everyone else about them, that must be the
> reason [327b1-4].

The fable as it was told had omitted this cardinal principle of
liberalism: morality, social and personal, does not form against
the grain; it is pleasant, or should be, if its rules are not distorted.
For it is a great human invention which, like agriculture or
metallurgy, fills the concrete need of human beings and so yields
them profit. That need is for group security and then for a
civilized way of life. Even the technologies cannot become fully
effective without the co-operation that the presence of the social
sense guarantees. In short, human morality is also human utility.
A religious or inspirational source for it is ruled out. The naturalists were not afraid of the criterion of self and social interest as a
foundation of morality. It has appeared already in Democritus
and will re-appear. Nor in his own special sense was Plato afraid
of it either. He has a streak of utilitarianism which he shares with
his pragmatic opponents and it was inspired like theirs by the
great role assigned to technological process in the scheme of
values. Only, for them technology was an historical force, whereas
for him it was a model of epistemology.

The long 'suppose' clause in Plato's text now reaches its
apodosis:

> Suppose then, as I say, Socrates, that we all gave each other
> mutual instruction in flute-playing and were as zealous and
> unsparing in keeping it up. Would you think that the good
> flute-players always favoured parents who were good at it
> too? I think not. If a father had a son who became great and

famous at flute-playing, it would be because the son happened to have been born with a specially favourable capacity for flute-playing and if he were insignificant as a flute-player, his innate capacity must have corresponded. Frequently you would get a son of a good player turning out poorly and vice versa. All the same, everyone would be (normatively speaking) a flute-player, adequate enough in comparison with anyone without professional status at all and with no training in flute-playing. What you must realize is that this analogy applies to things as they actually are. True, you may visualize a man, Mr. X, a human being reared in the midst of laws and of other human beings, as excessively unrighteous. But suppose you evaluate him in comparison with a Mr. Y, who has enjoyed neither an educational system nor law courts nor laws nor any compulsion continually forcing him to concentrate on excellence – a human being who would be in some sort a savage like the chorus of the play put on by Pherecrates last year at the Lenaeum. It would be quite right to conclude that your (apparently) very unrighteous Mr. X, by comparison with Mr. Y, was actually a qualified craftsman in the performance of the thing we are talking about. Yes indeed, put yourself in such company as those disgruntled, cynical characters found themselves in, when surrounded by the chorus in that play – it would be a great relief to you to meet a couple of our normal scoundrels. Human beings in our world may be bad, but you would sigh for the company of their badness [327b4-e1]. The fact is, you are spoiled, Socrates, and don't know it. Every man of us is an instructor in excellence to the limit of his personal capacity; and you think nobody is [327e1-3].

This rather vivid passage returns to the conception of social morality as itself not only one of the technologies of civilization, but the universal technology. Otherwise there could be no point to the emphatic analogy. As a technology, it is maintained by organized communication and instruction, father to son, citizen to citizen. For a universal technology requires a universal and accepted system of communication. In other words, social morality is envisaged as both a skill and yet also as a vast and unconscious conspiracy in which we all engage to keep the skill up.

It must never be lost: it is too precious. It is identical with the basic sense of belonging to and sharing in the group *mores*. You get it just by being raised among human beings and among laws and – it is added – among law courts. The model of Periclean Athens is there as the sophistic prototype of what a complete society really is. But it is only a model of conditions which apply wherever civilization is found. The term 'human being' is reiterated because human beings as such constitute their own environment and create their own mutual conditioning.

Protagoras is even made to say that a normally immoral man – judged by ideal standards – is nevertheless a 'qualified cratfsman' of political virtue. This is an extreme statement, though perhaps logically consistent with the sociological premisses. Does it reflect a liberal sophistic opinion that the craftsman class – the *demiourgoi* who are the *demos* and yet serve the *demos* – are the typical citizens, the political animals par excellence in the historically mature and therefore technological society? The suggestion jibes with the form in which the original Socratic problem had been framed: the problem which provoked the sociological defence. The standards used in estimating the behaviour in the assembly are those of the craftsmen; not only so, but we get the feeling that, aside from the few wealthy, the assembly *is* the craftsmen; who abandon their professional exclusiveness when they debate political issues. The Protagorean exposition reads like a defence of a craftsman democracy, rather than as an apologia for the interests of the wealthy with whom the sophists are too often identified.

The passage documents the hopefulness, the pragmatic satisfaction with the present shape of things, characteristic of Periclean liberals. And it does something else. It illuminates that effort of historical imagination which had gone into the construction of their anthropology. Civilization has been a prize dearly bought; too precious to be gambled with. Although the savages referred to are those portrayed in a stage production, they come out of the pages of the anthropologists who for their model of the primitive society probably drew on the Homeric example of the Cyclops – a savage race without right or law living in isolated households. Thus here again the peroration returns to the theme of the fable told at the beginning which described how men lived in this first household till they invented (or 'received' says Plato) Right and

Reverence. The evaluation placed upon the historical progress by the Elder Sophists was as important in its way as the history itself. They refused to tolerate the notion that primitive men were preferable to their descendants. Savages were not noble. Such a notion would have collided head-on with their own claims that education is vital. Athenian democracy had its cynics, its tired men, nostalgic for an imaginary past – like the cynical heroes in the lost play here referred to; or else they surrendered to some fantasy of present escape like the dreamers of Aristophanes' *Birds*. But liberalism was affirmative; it said 'Whatever the defects or compromises of this kind of state in which you live, you have never had conditions so good. It is because you are so leisured and secure and safe that you have licence to groan.' The reflection almost reads like a piece of Plato's own self-criticism. He was to reject the democracy and the Periclean past, and in so doing was to spend a good deal of his life proving that this social sense, this conspiracy to maintain a civilized way of life, was not enough – was worse than useless. But here he lets the liberals have their say undiluted.

To demonstrate still more emphatically the universal character of social morality, a fresh analogy is pressed into service. But this time the example chosen strikes closer to the genetic and historical character of morality itself:

> It is as if, Socrates, you were raising the question: Where are the instructors who teach us to speak our own language? You could not point to anyone. Or again if you raise the question: Where shall we find the instructors who give the craftsmen's sons their technique? In fact, of course, they get it from their fathers as far as the fathers are able, or from their father's connections in the same craft. Where then are their formal instructors? Do they exist? It will be difficult, will it not, to find them? But you could always point to instruction available for the uninitiated. The case with excellence and so on is exactly parallel [327e3-328a8].

In telling the fable of Prometheus, Plato, so it was suggested, had inserted the special gifts of Zeus to amend an original version in which human technological capacity had been treated genetically as a universal of the species man, itself adequate to explain the development alike of language and of social morality. The suggestion is supported here, by this concluding and clinching argument of Protagoreanism. Political virtue is a sort of second language, a skill it is true, but communicated by processes and pressures in which all men partake. Again we catch the note of a vast social conspiracy in which human beings become involved. Then, rather interestingly, the same kind of transmission is inferred for the handicrafts themselves. This is a fresh facet of the descriptive sociology; it grasps the role of the family guild in a pre-literate society. Skills are transmitted empirically within the kin group who live together and allow the force of daily intimate example to operate. The argument infers a distinction between this kind of schooling and the procedure of formal instruction. By implication it limits the scope of the problem raised by Socrates to indoctrination of a more professional sort given in text-books. This would be the kind of instruction available to the uninitiated, that is, to those without benefit of family connection to unlock the gates of a skill for them; it envisages a mechanics institute or trade-school instead of a household system of apprenticeship.

The distinction thus drawn gives warning of a coming revolution in educational theory and practice according to which the technique or science of a liberal education is going to be taken out of family group control and made available as a university training to any who have the capacity and leisure for it. But the present passage does not pursue this avenue and it is uncertain how far the Elder Sophists foresaw the institutional consequences of their own activities. The structure of their thought – it is to be repeated – was sociological rather than educational. And it is on the note of sociology that the last paragraph of the exposition has ended.

'Protagoras' is made to add only a brief codicil stating his own professional claims to 'accelerate' that process of social education achieved via the group ethos which he has been at such pains to describe [328b1-c2].

But Socrates as always is allowed to have the last word. The irony that creeps into his tone is consistent with Plato's purpose, which is to bring in a report on the philosophy of his opponents, but to do it in such a way as to seem to rob the original of its validity:

(Socrates speaking) This was the lengthy lecture delivered by Protagoras. After he had stopped, for several moments I remained under the spell still looking at him and waiting for him to say something else. Finally I collected myself . . . and said: I am extremely grateful to have heard from Protagoras the lecture he has given. Hitherto I had been under the impression that a discipline which made effective citizens what they are did not exist among men. Now I am convinced . . . except for one small thing that I still find a block. Obviously Protagoras will proceed easily to clear up the difficulty for me, considering how many things he has cleared up already. I should however explain that one has only to join the company of any of the public men to hear discourses similar to this one and in the same field delivered by Pericles or anyone else with adequate powers of expression. It is when you ask one of them something – even a small point in what they have said – they echo back like a brass gong that goes on booming till you stop it . . . [328d3-329a7].

In this way Socratic control is now asserted over the dialogue to steer it towards the dialectical method, with consequences which we reserve for the next chapter. The denigration is subtle and effective. Protagoras' discourse has been shorter than many Socratic ones, but a few phrases have deflated it for us and reduced its sociology, already partly disguised, to a thing of minor relevance to philosophy. But, as he denigrates, Socrates identifies the period of these sophistic doctrines and confirms our estimate that they rationalize the social structure and democratic achievements of the age of Pericles. The statesman himself is cited as a mouthpiece of this kind of liberalism.

It was a philosophy of man, of history, of society, of morals which had crystallized about or just before the time when Plato was born, before the age of anxiety had set in. His report on it, we should remember, is written forty to fifty years later, as he looks back to a land that he felt he had lost. Tides of disaster had swept over that far shore and receding had left it looking bleak and barren as it had never looked to the men of that earlier time. We can forgive him if his report of how they thought and felt fails of objectivity and completeness. Is he not already preoccupied with a different and more difficult doctrine which alone, he feels, can build a breakwater against a renewal of that disaster for which they were unequipped?

CHAPTER VIII

HUMAN OPINION, PRAGMATIC JUDGMENT, AND THE PARLIAMENTARY PROCESS

A RATIONALE of civilization on historical lines, and of the city-state as the great social institution to which that civilizing process had led – these are twin achievements of sophistic. But something is still missing. We have a sociology but not a politics. We have stopped short of being told how the present social apparatus functions: what makes it tick administratively, and what patterns of behaviour human beings do in fact practise to keep the group system vital and effective. Moreover, since the sophistic rationale was in purpose didactic and claimed to make men more 'effective', did it not have suggestions for training in these behaviour-patterns so as to maximize their effectiveness? The historical process has culminated in the Periclean model of society. So the question becomes: what are the rules of behaviour and administration in a Periclean democracy?

That sophistic theory sought to come to terms with this kind of problem has been indicated already. The first clue occurs in that statement of professional pretensions attributed to 'Protagoras' and already quoted:

I have an intellectual discipline
which consists in the formation of correct decision covering
(a) the most effective management of the household
(b) the most capable administration of civic business
(c) and the most effective exposition thereof in discourse, in fact the political or civic technique.

The course of the dialogue, by pressing Protagoras to prove that such a technique can be a topic of instruction, has forced him to prove that such a technique could and did exist. He could do this only by falling back on fundamentals. Hence this sophistic rationale of history and society. This furnished a theoretic foundation on which to build what might be called a methodology of social judgment, the process we have translated as 'forming correct decisions'. The Greek term signifies 'sound counselling' and 'correct deliberation'. This is not a single act of intuition or will but a process of ratiocination leading to practical conclusions. Since its field of reference is household management and civic administration, the judgments in question when they are formed are economic and political and pragmatic, not scientific or abstract. When 'Protagoras' returns to the topic of pragmatic judgment, after the conclusion of the myth, it is to defend the process of joint participation by all members of the assembly in forming those decisions required in all matters of 'civic excellence'.

The conclusion to be drawn is that sophistic did not aim at an epistemology of private judgment any more than at one of scientific method. Its attention, both speculative and practical, was fastened upon what went on in the assembly and in the law court, and also in the conduct of what we would call business and commercial matters. It watched the process of debate and of talking things over, of committee work and of business deliberation and calculation. It observed the crystallization of a single political policy by persuasion and by vote. What kind of process is this? It concerns all the men involved but, since their decision depends a good deal on leadership in debate, it concerns in particular the abilities of leaders to realize in themselves what the group wants and to formulate it.

Sophistic associates this technique of counselling with that of 'verbal expression' – the Greek noun *logos* and the verb *legein*. At this point in the development of the Greek language the advance of theory has outstripped the capacity of vocabulary. A dawning realization of how complex were the varieties of communication required an enlargement of the terms used to describe them. *Logos* and *legein* were called on to carry an impossible burden. Suffice it to say that for sophistic the term *logos* implies in the first instance a communication between human beings about their joint affairs, and in the second instance an improved variety of communication which becomes organized discourse presenting ideas and channelling emotions in more effective form, but still bearing on common affairs. The methodology marches with the fundamental sociology: technique is generic to the human race and the use of language is a prime example. The linguistic faculty is acquired by social practice, and reacts in turn as a form of social pressure, and admits of different degrees of proficiency though we all share it. Discourse as a technique and political judgment as an operation of psyche go hand in hand. Each reflects our social conditioning and also helps to create it. Political judgment, indeed, is hardly distinguishable from communication. The effectiveness of one is also the effectiveness of the other.

We have anticipated here the general course that this chapter will take in order once more to clarify at the beginning the degree to which in these matters and at this level sophistic and Platonism were antithetical. Since our sources are partly Platonic, this is pertinent. In the eyes of sophistic, man's morals are his *mores*; justice and law are inherent in the historical process and yet help to create it. They are formal names identifying patterns of act or attitude which may be still undergoing historical development. As names, they are modes in which man articulates his speech. As this articulation develops into increasing communication, so does the effectiveness of social organization and hence of moral and political judgment. Therefore there cannot be any question of going outside current discourse to discover the language of justice, nor of transcending current opinion in order to define its sources, any more than we can go outside the present city to discover an ideal state. Sophistic 'rhetoric' so-called should really be translated as the technique of linguistic expression. Sophistic argued that as this was studied and clarified and made more effective the norms of justice and social order became clearer. Moreover, discourse is social or it is nothing; its topics and problems are by definition common ones, group notions; the words of men act on other men and vice versa. There is exchange of opinion, alteration of opinion, discovery of common opinion, consensus and decision. It is not a discourse carried on in the private soul.

Platonism collided head on with this whole philosophy at every point. The laws of discourse, it said, are not historical but mathematical; the criterion of its effectiveness is not political utility but logical integrity. Its proper content, if practised at the educated level, is always scientific not pragmatic. It is carried on fully in the private soul, when that soul is properly disciplined and brought into contact with the formal laws, cosmic and moral, which lie outside historical process though they may control it. This kind of self-dialogue is exact and scientific – it is *episteme*. Whenever discourse becomes a vehicle of group or collective opinion and decision, it becomes debased. The contrast between the two systems can be prolonged further, but this will serve.

It is to be noted, however, that Aristotle modified his master's teaching in the field of moral and political epistemology and in so doing returned to the pragmatic point of view of sophistic which he endeavours not very completely to rationalize. This occurs in several passages in his *Ethics* where he insists on the difference between exact and approximate judgment and between abstract and pragmatic sciences. In the latter, your axioms like all axioms are self-evident, but not in any analytic sense. They derive from that social consensus which refuses to argue about whether it is right or wrong to murder or steal. Their source – we may interpret – lies in the civilizing process now historically achieved. Their validation is provided by that social 'necessity' which has formed such rules and made them essentially human and unanimous. In this pragmatism and flexibility and this kind of historical epistemology Aristotle shows his debt to sophistic. And when he tries to analyse the process by which men morally choose and decide – his doctrine of purposeful choice – he pays another debt by giving a large role to the process of practical deliberation. Perhaps also his willingness to recognize the factor of emotional drive or 'desire' behind any moral decision is due to sophistic influence. However, he remains almost wholly indifferent to those kinds of choice which are collective or 'democratic'. This area sophistic had to itself. It is plain that neither Plato nor Aristotle had much faith in votes or show of hands.

As for Plato's epistemological objectives, they were urgent but totally different. He was rightly preoccupied with providing a rationale of scientific procedure – that precious set of mental habits which require such elaborate training and protection. Political and practical judgment of affairs as they are run in this world of compromise he left to look after itself.

We now return to the sophistic story. But it will have to unfold not in the order of its own inner logic but in the order prescribed by the sources. First there is what is still to come in the *Protagoras*, as attributed therein to Protagoras, to Prodicus and to Hippias. Then there are a few pregnant statements – not many – which

Plato allows 'Protagoras' to make in his dialogue the *Theaetetus*
Then there is a little – a very little – that he lets Gorgias say in
the *Gorgias*. Then there are a few relevant items – and alas very
few that are independent of Plato – which survive in the tradition
of later antiquity and bear upon Protagoras and Gorgias. There
is a precious fragment of a political discussion by Thrasymachus
and a single complete theoretical exercise by Gorgias. As these
are deployed and interpreted, perhaps the original pattern as its
authors would have wished to give it to us will slowly emerge.

The discourse put into Protagoras' mouth being concluded, the
Socratic method is allowed to take over control of the dialogue.
The reader henceforth moves through its pages carefully conducted within the framework of ideas and problems postulated
not by sophistic but by Socratic logic:

Soc.: You were saying that Zeus had sent righteousness and
reverence to human beings and furthermore repeated several
times that righteousness, discipline, holiness, and so on were
in a word, taken together, equivalent to one thing, namely
excellence. Could you please answer the following question
methodically and precisely? Is excellence one single thing, of
which righteousness and discipline and holiness are parts,
or are these as I name them all just expressions identifying
the same one thing all the time? [329c2-d2].
Prot.: Your question is not difficult to answer, Socrates;
they are parts of the one excellence.
S.: Are they parts in the sense that mouth, nose, eyes, ears
are parts of the face, or in the sense that particles of gold
belong to a piece of gold, with no difference between each
particle and the next or between any of them and the whole
lump, except in magnitude?
P.: I think they are to excellence as parts of the face are to the
whole face [329d3-e2].
S.: Do human beings when they partake in any one of these
parts inevitably possess all of them or do they variously possess
them separately?
P.: The latter is the case. For many men are courageous but
unrighteous, and righteous but not intelligent.
S.: Then intelligence and courage are also parts of excellence?
[329e2-330a1].

P.: Very much so, don't you think? Intelligence indeed is the greatest of all the parts.

S.: Every one of them is different?

P.: Yes [330a1-2].

S.: And has every one of them a faculty or function? Take the parts of the face for instance: the eye is different from the ear and has a different function. Every one of them is quite different from every other in function and everything else. Similarly the parts of virtue must be quite unlike each other as parts, and in their respective functions. This is inevitable, is it not, if the analogy is to apply?

P.: Yes, that is so [330a4-b3].

Having manœuvred Protagoras into taking this position, the Socratic elenchus proceeds to argue that in fact it is an impossible one: the virtues cannot be wholly unique parts. To begin with, righteousness and holiness must correspond. The logical weapon used is fallacious – that if B is different from A it is opposite to A – but the objective is perfectly serious and is reached when Socrates takes his own position on the problem of the virtues:

S.: Speaking for myself, I would answer that righteousness is holy and that holiness is righteous and I would make it your answer too, if you would let me. If righteousness is not in fact identical with holiness, then at least it has the closest possible resemblance to it. Surely righteousness and holiness are *par excellence* like each other. Do you still think you cannot say yes to this? [331b1-8].

P.: I think that to agree that righteousness is holy and holiness righteous is to over-simplify the problem. No, I still feel there is some factor of differentiation here . . . [331b8-d1]. However, it is also true that righteousness has a resemblance to holiness. In a sense you can say that X always has an element of resemblance to Y. There is a sense in which white has some resemblance to black and hard to soft and so also in other cases where the antithesis seems complete. Take the parts of a face: we said of them that each had a different function and was different from any other part. Yet there is a sense in which they do resemble each other so that one part is similar to another [331a1-e2]. But because X and Y share some similarity, it is not right to say that they are similars, nor, if they have dissimilarities, is it right to say that they are necessarily dissimilar even though the similarity they have in common be quite insignificant [331e2-4].

S.: This argument astonished me. I replied: Do you really think the relationship between holiness and righteousness depends on the fact that they share some insignificant similarity?

P.: No, that isn't quite it. But the way you think is not quite true either.

S.: Well, anyway, I notice you feel difficulty in handling this problem, so let's abandon it [331e4-332a4].

The structure and direction of this guided thinking is, to repeat, wholly Socratic. Sophistic is allowed to present itself only as it fails to meet Socratic requirements. To disentangle the sophistic position as it would be focused and formulated in its own medium and on its own ground it is necessary to be clear as to what that Socratic position is toward which the dialectic seems to move but from which the dialectic also has taken its point of departure:

Excellence in human beings is derived from their degree of contact with its Form. This Form is a structure with the self-contained completeness of a geometric theorem. It is systematic and final. Hence it is vital to perceive that excellence is a unity. Its oneness is a simple way of affirming its property of being systematic and complete. Therefore like any other complete system it cannot allow approximation or variety or shift, or be partly one thing and again partly another, without ceasing to be a system altogether. If it loses the finality of its definition the whole 'Idea' collapses. The nature of this Form cannot be sought inside history or time or 'facts'; it is strictly a timeless conception. Equally it must be sought outside of any existing social arrangement thrown up by history. How then does it get into history and into social arrangement? Men have the ability to copy the Form in varying degrees; they produce approximations to it. History and society as we know them do partake in or imitate excellence at several removes from its real source and quality, or they may fail to imitate it altogether. From the ideal point of view, copies are all bad or at least inferior, though they can be improved as men are trained to understand abstract forms and to alter the patterns of their actions to correspond. Finally this moral Form can and does reside in the soul of man. There, if anywhere, is its location on the edge of space and time. The soul is itself capable of being as wholly organic and unified a thing as the Form of its excellence. The one unity, that of the psyche, is akin to that of the other, namely of righteousness. Thus the unity of excellence has its psychological foundations as well as its formal and metaphysical ones. The Socratic psychology is not exploited in the present context, but it is there latent in the argument, and its presence makes intelligible the force of the collision between Socraticism and sophistic.

On this showing and from a Platonic standpoint the really significant thing – perhaps the only significant thing – in the sophistic sociology was the stress on the 'one thing' which all men must have to make a society. This is at once seized on and lifted from its historical and sociological context and treated formally and analytically. Either holiness, righteousness, courage and the rest are names of aspects of a single structure of excellence, or else they exist themselves formally in their own right and the structure of excellence is broken up. Linguistically, Socrates argues, this leads to impossible conclusions. So, of course, excellence remains a unity. Even though some logical fallacy is employed to press home the axiom of formal unity, the necessity of the axiom from an ideal standpoint remains unaffected. And the desire of Protagoras to preserve ambiguity and flexibility and the like is made to appear as a failure of mental precision. Denigration is added further to discredit his position. He is represented as ill at ease; that is as feeling inferior to the Socratic elenchus – as well he might if in real life he had ever allowed himself to be led by the nose as he is here.

Protagoras is by Socrates offered the proposition that each feature of the face has its own function. He agrees and is then drawn on to concede that this implies a complete uniqueness and isolation of each feature. This is the concession which on his own ground he never should have made. It is true in Socratic terms; it is quite untrue in his own. What had the original sophistic notion of a 'one thing shared in by all men' exactly meant? The question can be correctly answered only by asking in what way, by what methodology, had the notion been formed in the first place? The answer is not by formal and abstract methods. 'This one thing' is a descriptive hypothesis formed to account for the actual fact that societies had come into existence and do exist in stable form. It is a symbol of a process, not a formal identity, and it is intended descriptively and not analytically. It is a convenience of language, but not a Socratic definition. It follows that it is essentially an approximation to the truth, in the sense that it over-simplifies in order to bring out the vital importance of social direction as exhibited in man's growth into a civilized animal, and what we called earlier a single social conspiracy maintained to support a civilized society. Thus it is not in any Platonic sense a self-subsistent condition of the soul. It describes a set of attitudes, induced by group pressures and needs, and responsive to them. It cannot have the unity and integrity which to a Platonist would be characteristic of the complete excellence of a private and perfect personality.

The semantics of the two schools, sophistic and Socratic, are in fact completely different, because they are attending to quite different orders of experience. The sophistic view, therefore, of human excellence as expressing a historical direction and a social loyalty is not incompatible with the view that it varies a good deal in its types and qualities, because men themselves vary in their moral capacities, and still more do those relations vary in which they find themselves. Thus Protagoras is ready to admit that excellence has parts like the features of a face. Whether or not this was in fact a sophistic analogy does not matter. There is, after all, the whole face. The sophist would think of it as symbolizing not one single form of excellence but a very complex pattern of group *mores*, the custom-laws of a society. No two faces are ever quite the same, and perhaps they argued that no two cities are alike either. However that may be, they certainly postulated that within the framework of any single social consciousness you found a great variety of citizens, and of civic virtues and vices. This was their pragmatic acceptance of men as they are. It was not incompatible with emphasizing the fact that men as they are all embody a basic social consciousness which they express in various ways and with varying success, and that virtues can never be hypostatized in the absolute apart from the people who have them. In fact they are only descriptions of people and their behaviour. There are the blood and bone of the structure of the face – of any face. But a face only exists as it is articulated into a variety of features. The expressions of excellence will be uneven just because men are like that. So the righteous but stupid, and the courageous but irreligious, continue to jostle each other in any social complex without breaking up the whole pattern of the face. Indeed (sophistic may have argued) it is from the very variety of comparative vices and virtues that the whole social organism derives its vitality. Whether they exploited this notion is speculative.

Epistemologically speaking, the important deduction for sophistic is that, if it is the total social picture you want to talk about, language is only an approximate medium for describing it. This is the justification for Protagoras' qualifications in the text. He protests against over-simplification; he argues in effect that moral vice and virtue are not entities but over-lapping attitudes, and shifting ones at that. This is why in a sense they show similitude and in another sense they do not. The parts of a face have a certain similitude – he does not say what it is but he must mean the fact that they are parts of any face and hence composed of common tissue and perhaps united in a single facial composition. Similarly the basic common denominator in human excellence is humanity – the socially induced capacity to be civilized. The specific examples of human character cannot be simplified and defined in this abstract way. You cannot make formal entities out of operative and fluid relationships.

All these qualifications look pretty lame and muddled when they are made to strike their heads against the unyielding structure of Socratic logic. But there is warning here that we should not define in the field of human behaviour what escapes definition. To describe – yes that is the task; human attitudes and relations are not mathematical; their measure (we are coming to this later) or yardstick is the human being himself, a dynamic, flexible and varying quantity, but not for that reason wholly incalculable.

From all this it follows that the method of political judgment, since it involves the estimate of given human beings and their actions, is two-fold; the operation is conducted at two levels. You begin by viewing a human being as sharing in a common humanity with all others. This consists in his social sense and basic capacity to be a citizen at all. This itself is no light matter but a highly developed technique of living, though we would call it an unconscious set of skills. Presumably it is proper to go further and formulate the outline of this common humanity or common morality; it would have a content. Certain types of behaviour are fundamental as being sociologically necessary. If a man showed aberration at this level, he would be a serious case indeed. Superimposed on this level is a great variety of moral capacity and incapacity labelled as the virtues and vices. The over-all operation of political and moral judgment takes in these two levels simultaneously. At bottom, then, all social judgment of human beings is tolerant. There is no absolute standard by which to weigh them and find them sinners or saints. But also and equally – though here we anticipate a step in sophistic theory which our sources have not yet taken – despite the clashing and competing varieties of excellence and non-excellence, there is always in a community of human beings the possibility of joint common judgment and of agreed group decision. This follows from the fact of one and all having the 'one same thing' – the sense of a minimum right and reverence which cements the society together. Such common judgment is not likely to be formed automatically. The varieties and degrees of political excellence are bound to produce varieties of opinion – at the surface. It will need some process or method as yet unexplained to achieve a 'common mind'. But the foundation of the common mind is there. The premiss of common humanity as defined sociologically provides epistemological basis for common decisions. In sum, the sophistic political methodology had to be complex and very flexible, pragmatic and not mathematical. This is not to say that it was confused until made to appear so by the use of formal logic. It had its own foundations. As can readily be seen, it stands the Platonic convictions on their head.

The dialectic which would formalize the unity of holiness and righteousness has now, in the text of the dialogue, been broken off, but the excuse for doing so is the inserted suggestion that Protagoras feels 'difficulty in handling this problem'. The argument is suspended but Plato's polemical purposes are pursued without interruption. Socrates returns to dialectic and next pursues the objective of unifying temperance and intelligence into a single excellence. He is allowed to formalize this conclusion, with Protagoras acting as lay figure to supply the necessary yes and no where required, though with reluctance. Then the dialectic proceeds to the task of formalizing the unity of temperance and righteousness. It is handled so as to allow one more facet of the Protagorean position to be exposed, and then again broken off in such a way as to discredit it.

Soc.: Do you feel that when a human being does wrong he can show temperance in the act of doing wrong?

Prot.: It is true many human beings say yes. But I would gravely hesitate to admit it.

S.: Shall I then address my discourse to this group or to yourself?

P.: If you please, I would rather your dialectic engaged with the formula as it is held by the many.

S.: It makes no difference to me, provided you give the answers, whether you agree or not. It is primarily the formula that I am examining though it can turn out that both the questioner, meaning myself, and the respondent get examined too [333b8-c9]. To this, at first, Protagoras was for retiring upon his dignity, complaining that the discourse as formulated was difficult to handle. But afterwards he came around and said he would give answers [333d1-3].

S.: To resume from the beginning, do you think men can do wrong and be temperate when they do it?

P.: Let us grant they can.

S.: By temperance you mean 'good thinking'?

P.: Yes, and good thinking means the formation of effective decisions about the wrong that they are doing.

S.: Let us grant it so. Would this mean that as wrongdoers they do well or do badly?

P.: They would be doing well [333d3-8].

S.: Now do you posit the existence of certain goods?

P.: Yes.

S.: In that case do you agree that the goods are those things which for human beings are also useful?

P.: I certainly do . . . [333d8-e].

The short explanation of the dialectical method offered near the beginning of this passage is unwittingly frank. Protagoras' own opinion becomes irrelevant; the task is to sustain the logical thread of the Socratic refutation. This is directed against the latent opinion, always and easily present in men, that unrighteous people are nevertheless effective people. Plato's sense of the importance of this moral issue is very acute. He knows we can all become immoralists because of our secret or grudging admiration of the smart people who so often get ahead while sacrificing some inner integrity. But Protagoras, it must be emphasized, is not an immoralist. Plato here virtually admits that sophistic was not cynical in the sense in which 'Thrasymachus' and 'Callicles' are cynical in those dialogues where they are made to appear.

The Socratic elenchus, however, must be allowed an open channel; the respondent must be available to allow its course to proceed. For it is to come at once to the edge of that moral position where the logic of Platonism, so Plato felt, collided head-on with that of sophistic. The process of giving correct decisions implies the achievement of effective or 'good' results. Protagoras fully agrees; this is his position. And a 'good' result means a useful one; goodness and utility must coincide. So far again Platonism and sophistic agree. But Platonism would go on to assume that this goodness and utility (which can be treated as one) are criteria derived from a Form of cosmic proportions, always self-consistent, a system of value which holds true for the universe including the human society in the universe and the individual men in the society. The task of the philosopher who would hew true to this kind of principle is to uphold the criterion of the consistent good, which is also the consistently useful, applicable as a uniform measuring rod to every kind of relationship in the universe. The really useful can never cease to be useful; a thing really good must never cease to be good. Hence goodness and usefulness are timeless abstract values, not concrete specific evaluations.

Once more the quarrel is irreconcilable because it is so rooted in semantics. A pragmatic view of morals and politics was interested in identifying various relationships which 'work' and in which, operatively, the effects are 'good'. The material or means employed will for the purpose of that operation be good too. But equally we must be prepared to reject the same means and material when dealing with other relationships and uses. For they may be inappropriate and therefore 'bad' or not useful. In the whole scheme of things, if you had the mind of God, you might see an over-all Usefulness and Goodness operating (in capital letters), but, instrumentally speaking, this is too vague and abstract to assist the day-to-day intelligence, which must continually make correct decisions, and learn how to do it by collecting a fund of empirical evidence as to what works in given cases.

It is exactly this kind of practical epistemology which Protagoras at this point is allowed to divulge.

Soc.: Do you agree that goods are things which human beings also find useful?

Prot.: I certainly do, and there are also things which even though useless to human beings I would still posit as goods ... [333d8-e2].

S.: Do you mean, just when useless to human beings, or do you mean that there are goods which could be in an absolute sense useless? [333e5-334a2].

P.: No, no. What I rather mean is that I know of a thousand things injurious to human beings, eatables or drinkables, medicinal potions and the like, which would be useful in other connections and vice versa also. Again there are things which are quite indifferent so far as human beings are concerned that do have utility or injury for horses. The same is true of cattle or dogs. Other things are useful or otherwise not to men or animals at all but to trees. Things that are good for the roots of a tree are bad for the shoots; manure for instance, when spread, is good for the roots of all growing things, but should you propose to throw it on top of the shoots and buds, it destroys everything. Take, for instance, olive oil – very bad for all growing plants and very antipathetic to the hair of all animals except human beings but beneficial to a human being's hair and the rest of his body too [334a3-b6]. The fact is that good is a variable, complex and complicated. Take the last instance again. A thing physically good for human beings externally can actually be very bad internally. That is why doctors always forbid the sick to use olive oil when it is intended to be taken internally except in the smallest possible quantity, enough to counter the nausea excited by grain and meat foods and communicated to the senses by the nostrils [334b6-c6].

Aside from the pragmatic epistemology of this passage, it is of interest in several ways as an illustration of the actual content of sophistic education.

1. The problems touched on concern animal husbandry and agriculture with some veterinary and medical lore. Plato is not interested in picturing these as departments of knowledge, so they emerge only incidentally, but they are there.

2. They may well be a clue to the content of an important item

of the sophistic curriculum. That curriculum, as it had been staked out by 'Protagoras' at the beginning of this dialogue, had included along with politics 'the formation of correct decision concerning the most effective management of the household'. Our word – and indeed the Greek word – for this is 'economy'. Animal husbandry and agriculture were the basic economy of Greece and were conducted in household units. In fact, the household at this date was still the main instrument of all economic activity, banking, manufacture and agriculture. The dialogue has also referred all the mechanisms of apprenticeship in the trades and skills to the household unit. Household management therefore meant not just handling servants, spring cleaning, marketing, and petty cash transactions as it would today, but the processes of agriculture, manufacture, commerce and banking. There are relevant passages in Aristotle's *Politics* which illustrate the point effectively – and which will be treated in a later chapter. (It is possible that much of the original schematism of Aristotle's economics came from the sophistic technical treatises.) Once again the testimony bearing on Democritus is relevant. The reported titles of his treatises show that he had felt it proper to organize such subjects himself and give them systematic treatment.

3. In dealing with these topics the present excerpt, brief though it is, uses a method of classification which determines respectively what benefits and what injures. That is, the classification is of acts and performances of things done by men in given situations, and the criterion of distinction is the pragmatic effect of a given act. It is not a classification of things in themselves in their genera and species. It therefore is an arrangement which clarifies existing empirical knowledge. It does not set about the construction of a body of scientific principles.

4. But this pragmatic classification is intended to assist the formation of correct decision at the point of immediate application where something has to be done. It is doubtful whether the Platonic division and classification, useful as it was for exact science, could ever have accomplished this end. In other words, it may not be unfair to ascribe to the sophistic technique of correct decision some credit for providing the basis for Aristotle's 'practical wisdom' as it is developed in his *Ethics*. But Aristotle's Platonism was strong enough partly to denature the influence he here received. He has his eyes always on the soul of a gentleman

detached from economic action rather than on the entrepreneur with daily responsibilities whom the sophists sought to assist and to educate.

The Socratic context, however (to repeat), is designed to make the reader immune to the force of such a pragmatic programme by inducing him to view it from the vantage point of Socratic scientific epistemology. So he virtually concludes 'Here is mere relativism, in goodness, as elsewhere in truth', and he dismisses the item as another example of sophistic opportunism.

To make quite sure he does, Plato next resorts to an artifice as unfair as anything anywhere in his dialogues. Socrates figuratively throws up his hands exclaiming: 'I cannot deal with long speeches; they confuse me; I can't remember the drift. Protagoras cannot play the game according to my rules, so I must go home' [334c8ff.]. Thus any effect that the paragraph of sophistic economics might have had is cancelled by being represented as a lapse into rhetoric. Rhetoric, indeed, and fee-taking are the two characteristics of sophistic which Plato continually exploits as though they were the essentials. This is his own pejorative technique. In the present instance the accusation of long-windedness is grotesque. The dialogues are peppered with dozens of Socratic harangues of far greater length. One would think that here, if anywhere, Plato's readers would get a little out of hand, and protest the propriety of his hero's attitude. But Plato is skilful – he must be, to judge by the procession of professors who have obediently followed the lead of this preposterous propaganda.

The statement by 'Protagoras', illustrating the sense in which he would use the words good and useful, provokes what appears to be a dramatic interlude. There is some applause, followed by the protest from Socrates already cited against the statement's length. Protagoras defends his own style of discourse; Socrates concludes that it is useless to continue the dialogue and gets up to go [335c7]. Callias the host – the *mise en scène* is laid in the courtyard of his house – puts his hand on his arm to detain him, begging him to compromise with Protagoras and continue the dialogue which is giving such pleasure to all. Socrates repeats and underlines the inability of his dialectic to compromise with Protagorean 'oratory' [335c8-336b6]. Alcibiades interposes to side with Socrates, and converts the situation into a competitive challenge flung at Protagoras: is the sophist afraid to match his skill at dialogue against Socrates? [336b7-d5] This does not solve the impasse, but Critias speaks up and turning to the sophists Prodicus and Hippias, two other members of the group who have been listening, appeals to them as neutrals to use their good offices to bring the two parties together [336d6-e4]. Prodicus rises to the occasion promptly with a little address designed to this end, and Hippias follows on equally promptly with his contribution; the net result being that dialogue is resumed under an agreement that Socrates and Protagoras exchange roles, so that Protagoras becomes the questioner and Socrates the respondent [337a1-338e5].

It should be said at once that in terms of the doctrinal objectives of the dialogue, this interruption is more apparent than real. For a brief moment Plato allows the scene itself, the personalities, and some of their gestures to come alive, and the arid dialectic is replaced by what reads like a piece of genuine conversation. But the content of what is said both by Socrates and other parties continues the task of formulating the antithesis between Platonism and sophistic, at the expense of the latter. It is as carefully contrived for this purpose as anything else in the dialogue. The protests of Socrates on the one hand are designed to suggest that Platonism has a logical structure inseparable from its conclusions and exercising supreme authority over them. The statements of all three sophists on the other hand are designed to expose still further the concentration of sophistic upon purely human opinion and attitude and behaviour; its preoccupation with a variety of ways in which attitudes and opinions find actual expression, especially in democratic assemblies; its facile (to Plato) assumption that in human opinion itself, for all its variety, there resides a common denominator on which rules of rational and effective action can be built. Though the interlude ends in apparent reconciliation, this is dramatic persiflage. The collision between Platonism and sophistic continues to be total, and in particular the brief speeches attributed to Prodicus and Hippias are as effective an example of Plato's satirical polemics as anything in his works.

This then is one more example of those Platonic contexts where a show is made of dramatizing something which sophistic has to say, but where in fact the purpose is to dramatize something that Platonism has to say. The former is reported through the medium of the latter and suffers refraction in the process. It is proper first to isolate the control before seeking to determine the report. What is it that Platonism is saying here on behalf of itself? The answer is discoverable if the non-Socratic contributions to this conversational interlude are for the moment ignored. This allows concentration upon the four Socratic statements that are offered, three by Socrates and one by his admirer Alcibiades, as follows:

1 (Socrates to Protagoras). I am one of those people who have rather poor memories and if I listen to a lengthy statement I forget the subject of discourse. Imagine for example that I was a little deaf; then if you proposed to hold dialogue with me, you would feel you had to raise your voice. In this case, since it is my memory that is the trouble, please cut down and shorten your answers to let me follow you [334c8ff.]

2 (Socrates to Protagoras). I have no more inclination than you to carry on our converse in a way which violates what you must do. If ever you consent to hold dialogue in such a way that I can follow you, then I will hold dialogue with you [335b3ff.].

3 (Socrates to Callias). If you want to be able to listen to myself and Protagoras, ask him to give me answers in the way in which he gave them to me originally. I mean, making them brief, and restricting them only to the actual questions asked. For there is no other possible methodology for these dialogues [336a5ff.].

4 (Alcibiades to Callias). No one can tell me that Socrates takes second place to any man in his ability to hold dialogue, and in his mastery over the technique of rendering and receiving discourse. If Protagoras is willing to admit that he is the inferior of Socrates in holding dialogue, Socrates wins [336b9-c4]. But if he wants to contest the claim, he should hold dialogue by asking and answering questions. When the question is put, he should not stretch the reply into a lengthy discourse delivering ringing statements like knockout blows and refusing to render discourse properly and prolonging matters until most of the audience have forgotten the point to which the question was addressed [336c4-d2].

These four statements pretend to address themselves to the conduct of genuine dialogue, an impression reinforced by the use of Socratic irony to suggest that he can manage a relaxed conversation but not a formal speech. But they really address themselves to something quite different:

(1) the requirements laid down are restricted to the conduct of an interrogation, not that of a dialogue;
(2) the rules prescribed are restricted in purpose, being designed to control the respondent, not the questioner;
(3) replies must be confined strictly to the point raised by the previous question;
(4) they must be as brief as is humanly possible;
(5) the purpose of numbers 3 and 4 being to maintain the strict continuity of the questions asked.

It does not take any great degree of objectivity to realize that this amounts to a demand that the discourse be placed under the complete control of the questioner. The answers will have to be very largely restricted to 'yes' and 'no' or 'please explain', as in practice they are in Plato's dialogues. This is not a conversational method, nor a genuine exchange of ideas. Nor is it intended that such an exchange should take place. There are quite a few set speeches, long and short, in Plato's dialogues, but over the length and breadth of them a genuine conversational handling of serious ideas between equal minds is not to be found. The only possible kind of thinking which they allow to take place is dogmatic thinking. That is, the questioner knows where he is going, and is going to direct his questions in that direction, and already possesses in his mind the main framework of ideas which the process is to expose bit by bit.

Why then cultivate the method at all and make such a point of it? It has one purpose, which is achieved at the expense of the respondent, and it can be called an apologetic purpose. In the so-called aporetic dialogues various opinions elicited from the respondent can be reduced to apparent self-contradiction by the device of getting each of them reworded in terms of the questioner's own principles. The systematic and *a priori* character of these principles is quietly and steadily strengthened by implicit contrast with current confusions of human opinion. The catch may be that, from a pragmatic standpoint, the confusion is itself not essential but is created by Plato's own type of evaluation.

But a more important purpose by far, and the one foreshadowed in the present description with its emphasis on the necessary continuity of the questions and the restriction and brevity of the replies, is to allow the Platonic system of ideas to be broken up and developed step by step in logical series. That is to say, the questions could just as well be statements, so far as content is concerned, but by requiring answers the questioner provokes a series of interruptions to indicate the rungs in the ladder which he is climbing. The respondent is a foil whose answer is used as brief confirmation of the correctness of the step just taken. His replies are so many intervals marking the steps in an endless series of syllogisms. The rules of logic controlling the analytic consistency of human thought were in an embryonic condition when Plato wrote, and the simple device of this dialectic as he perfected it was an invention of the highest genius exercising incalculable sway over the conduct of human thinking processes. To what extent in its disciplined and dogmatic form it had already become a Socratic device before Plato put it to use in his writings is an open question.

Our business is with Plato's sophistic opponents and with the record of their own positions, so far as it can be recovered. To disguise the dogmatic and one-sided character of his own dialectic, Plato follows the device of pretending that the same method is understood and practised by Protagoras – if he will only consent to follow it in the present instance. This has the propagandist effect of winning all readers to Socrates' side – he seems so fair – but Plato, while he re-interprets, never wholly invents the views he ascribes to the opposition and, in fact, the present passage says a good deal at least implicitly about sophistic discourse and its methods and objectives. The first relevant statement on the subject was made by Socrates earlier, at the conclusion of Protagoras' main exposition. Its gist is here in this interlude repeated twice, and then supplemented by other statements put into the mouth of Protagoras and Callias, as follows:

(1) (Socrates' original statement, to Hippocrates). The competency of our friend Protagoras is two-fold: he can deliver a lengthy discourse of admirable quality as we have just seen or he can submit to questions and give answers in short style and also pose a question and then wait while the answer is given and take it in – a talent few people have [329b1ff.].

(2) Prot.: Make my answers short you say? Well, should I shorten them below the requirement?

Soc.: No I don't mean that.

P.: They should correspond to the requirement?

S.: Yes.

P.: Who is to decide the requirement for my answer, you or I?

S.: Look here, I have been told that you, yes you, Protagoras, can give instruction in a topic either with a lengthy and indeed inexhaustible discourse or with short statements that out-do anyone else in their brevity. If you want to hold dialogue with me, please use the latter style of yours, that short style [334d6ff.].

(3) (Prot. to Soc.) Many is the time I have made my entry against other men in discourse-competition. If I did what you tell me to do and held dialogue according to the rules set for me by the speaker of the opposition, my superiority would have no chance of being demonstrated nor would Protagoras have become a name to conjure with in Hellas [335a4ff.].

(4) (Soc. to Prot.). Both by reputation and your own claim you are capable of using either the long style or the short style in the conduct of group converse. You are an intellectual master. I am incapable of using the lengthy statement. I wish I could [335b7ff.].

(5) (Callias to Soc.). We can't let you go. If you do leave, the dialogues we enjoy won't be the same. I beg you to stay. There is no one holding dialogue to whom I'd rather listen than to you and Protagoras [335d2ff.].

(6) (Soc. to Callias). I always thought that holding dialogue mutually in a private gathering, and an address given by public men, were two different categories [336b1ff.].

(7) (Callias to Soc.). But look, Socrates, Protagoras feels he has a right to expect that he can be free to hold a dialogue in the way he wants just as you do in the way you want [336b4ff.].

Three of these passages (3, 5, and 7) imply that there was a dialogue type of discourse recognized as such in intellectual circles which did not necessarily correspond with Socratic require-ments. Characteristically it is Callias the host, whose patronage of sophists had become traditional, who supplies what may be called the neutral testimony here. His words imply that holding dialogue was an expected feature of the sophistic gathering with or without Socrates. He pleads to let the Protagorean style of dialogue have equal honours with the Socratic. Protagoras himself refers to dialogue as a familiar feature of his own activity.

This brings up the question of what the verb 'hold dialogue' (*dialegesthai*) meant in Greek parlance before the Platonic method took hold of it. Literally the symbol of 'cross-talk', it is applied, with the subject in the singular, to uttering speech which invites exchange, or, in the plural, to actual exchange of speech. The former sense may slip into the meaning of just 'talking' to somebody. But it does not apply to one man who simply addresses another. Twice in Thucydides the verb is used to describe conversations held between the respective delegates of two opposing sides leading to an arrangement which arrests a conflict. These are interesting examples, for the context is political and the exchange of opinion leads to a negotiation of issues and policies.

The gulf between the style of sophistic cross-talk and the Socratic dialectic is patent. But, according to Plato himself, sophistic must have sought a refinement of the procedure by exploiting the relationship of questioner and respondent. Passage number one is quite explicit on this point. Its testimony, properly interpreted, sharply distinguishes the sophistic from the Socratic technique of dialectic, revealing two fundamental differences of procedure which Plato is rather anxious to conceal. First, sophistic did not seek to place the pupil at an intellectual disadvantage as compared with the teacher. One can speak here of actual procedure followed, regardless of whether or not personal vanity in the teacher might intrude (as it often does). Procedurally, then, either side can ask questions and expect answers. The reader of any Socratic dialogue does not need to be told that in Plato this impartiality is not practised or even considered. Second, in the role of interrogation the sophist 'waited to take in the answer' (item 1). This is conspicuously what Socrates has just refused to do in the case of Protagoras' analysis of goods and utilities. In fact, this serious acceptance of an answer as perhaps supplying a new factor in the discussion which the interrogator has not thought of is absent in Socratic dialectic. It has to be, or else the logical continuity of the purely Socratic vein of thinking is interrupted. On the other hand, any leader of a discussion group knows how vital his own patience is to the successful conduct of the discussion; and how important it is for other members of the group to follow his example. Questions must be taken seriously; even the most foolish may contain a germ of constructive truth, the beginning of an idea which when rephrased in other words becomes fruitful and so on. In the light of this contrast we suggest that the phrase 'to render and to receive discourse', which seems to have been a standard description of philosophical dialogue at the end of the fifth century B.C., must have described not the Socratic but the sophistic practice of the art. Platonism here borrows the formula of its rivals and seeks to make it its own.

Three times reference is made to the sophistic 'short style' as against 'long style' (items 1, 2, 4). These formulas appear to be technical, and perhaps were coined by the sophists themselves – they are also attributed to Gorgias in the *Gorgias*. They seem to make a theoretically important distinction between two types of discourse. Was this the distinction between the dialogue method and the expository method, the discussion group *versus* the lecture? Passage number one suggests that it was, and if so we may ask why should Protagoras object to using the short style in dialogue with Socrates. The answer is that he does not object. His short style, however, would be a genuine discussion-group style; we suggest that a specimen of it has been already provided in his explanation of goods and utilities. This was not a long speech, but an explanation of the speaker's meaning, addressed to a point already made by another speaker.

Plato, we suggest, is once more guilty of philosophical propaganda. What he really wants to suggest and get his readers to believe is that even this short style is not only not dialectical – it obviously is not – but that it can never yield anything except mere verbiage – that is from Plato's standpoint. Why is this? Why is his antagonism to this loose but perhaps creative technique of discourse so fundamental? The answer is one which has already been uncovered in viewing his antagonism to sophistic sociology. The material of discursive discussion is contributed by giving voice to the common opinions, attitudes and prejudices of men. Any creative results achieved, or any formalization of conclusions or decisions, are still a consensus of that kind of opinion. Plato will have none of it. Truth for him is scientific, and is sought in other quarters and by other methods altogether.

So far the application of such methodology to politics and public questions has not been touched on; but passage number three has still to be accounted for. While Protagoras is here still speaking of 'holding dialogue', he is made to give this a competitive colour as of a performance by a performer which wins him crowns and applause in all Greece.

A modern reader might ask could the self-advertisement of any professional man be so naïve as it is made to appear in this concluding boast? Yes, it could, in Greece at this epoch, and for good historical reasons. Professional men faced the problem shared by all artificers of the spoken and written word including poets and dramatists. They had to publish; and, whether or not they were writers, publication could be only by oral methods of communication. This meant in practice that a writer had to be a performer as well as a writer, and usually a competitive one also. For the established tradition was for the poet to publish by competition with his fellow poets at the festivals. Thus even the masterpieces of Greek drama were themselves all conceived as potential prize winners. It was characteristic of sophistic to make explicit and to rationalize any social custom, not least one that applied to itself. Hesiod or Pindar might clothe their competitive motives with grandeur; sophistic with its flair for applied sociology simply exposed the essential social situation in which any composer of words found himself, and made a virtue of it. The result was to encourage the cultivation of a certain virtuosity. The Sophists were new men after all, demanding an attention which their audiences had previously given to poets. Protagoras was even on record as the 'knockout' artist (see Alcibiades' description of his style above) whose discourses could 'bowl over' an opponent. None of these considerations could invalidate the fact that a great deal of vigorous new thinking was going on in the midst of these fireworks, even when the bangs were loudest.

All this was happening in a period of technical transition in the process of verbal and social communication. Plato completed the transition by founding an institution in which pupils were enrolled to hear lectures for which they paid fees to the institution. Educational methodology had now been revolutionized. It no longer relied upon attention solicited on a casual basis in the salon or at the street corner. This gave Plato a professional advantage over the sophistic method and explains the present quality of his report on Protagoras. For, when he writes it, he already envisages the logic of the new method, whether or not he had yet purchased the site of the Academy. He has chosen here, as so often, to select an incidental – the competitive colour of the style – and use it to suppress the essential – the pragmatic aim and content of sophistic discourse. By doing this, he can put into Protagoras' mouth a purely superficial reason for declining Socratic terms for dialogue – namely that he can't afford to be beaten – when the real reason is that Protagoras requires the condition of a genuine discussion conducted on a fifty-fifty basis. This is partly disclosed earlier when he says to Socrates (item 2) 'Must I shorten my answers below the requirement?' Socrates of course says, 'No.' Now, by the term 'requirement' Protagoras intends to indicate that length which is sufficient to make the respondent's meaning clear; but, by adroitly making him shift ground and talk competitively, Plato induces the reader to interpret the 'requirement' as 'long enough to let me win'.

The English word 'competition' like the Greek *agon*, can cover contests either military and athletic, or artistic, oratorical and the like. But it would be felt inappropriate if used today to describe parliamentary procedure. The Greeks of this period felt no such inhibition; a debate in the assembly for them was also an *agon*, a competition. This was not because a good debate was peculiarly contentious. The usage rather reflects the fact that for new political habits and institutions a traditional terminology was still the readiest means of description. This factor of vocabulary, and the way it lagged behind the increasing cultural demand of the Periclean Age, goes far to explain more than one apparent paradox in the literature of the period between 450 and 350 B.C. Accordingly, the satirical attack on Protagoreanism at this point has a double target: not only the oral conditions under which the sophists published their literature, but also those processes of public debate in the legislative assembly of a democracy, upon which they had turned their theoretic attention. This inference is confirmed by the fact that in the same general context Protagoras uses the expression 'holding dialogue according to the rules set for me by the speaker of the opposition'; and Socrates (passage number 6) describes the antithesis between himself and Protagoras in terms of 'holding dialogue mutually in a private gathering' versus 'address given by public men'; where the latter phrase translates a Greek verb which literally means 'speaking among the people', a process which included both debate and formation of policy. The reference to Pericles has already been noted. There is a political undertone to the conversations which occupy this interlude. The English phrase 'hold dialogue' is scarcely more appropriate to parliamentary procedure than is the term 'competition'. Yet here again the Greek equivalent has a wider application and can describe a discourse carried on in public situations. In short, the sophistic theory and practice of communication covered:

a. formal expository style whether lecture or text-book;
b. the verbal exchange of a small informal discussion group which could generate new opinions and perhaps might lead to common conclusions;
c. the antithetical formulation of public positions and the setting of party lines which took place in any parliament or assembly where power was at stake and public policy was made.

The fact that, as aliens, sophists could not enter the assembly and join in its debates left them free to visualize in some detachment the theories needed to explain the legislative and judicial processes that went on there and for which they as ghost writers supplied speeches for others to deliver. In Plato's present dramatization, these three applications of their theory of *logos* are partly confused and partly disguised in order to cast over all of them a colour of irresponsibility, shallowness and irrelevance to Socratic aims and principles. But it is the parliamentary procedure in particular on which Plato now has his eye and as the conversation further develops and draws in the by-standers, so does his attack develop also:

> CRITIAS (turning to Prodicus and Hippias): It seems to me that Callias is on Protagoras' side. As for Alcibiades, he is always a fervent partisan. But as for ourselves, instead of showing partisanship for either Socrates or Protagoras, we ought to make a common appeal to both sides not to break up the present association [336d7-e4].
>
> PRODICUS: You are quite right, Critias. In discourses of this kind there is need that the hearing given by those in attendance should be common [impartial] on the one hand, but not equal on the other. For these two are not the same thing [337a1-4].

It is necessary that the hearing accorded to both sides be common on the one hand, but the proportion of distribution be unequal on the other.

The more intelligent side should on the one hand get more, and the less intelligent on the other hand should get less [337a4-6]. I therefore in my own person addressing both of you, Protagoras and Socrates, request and expect you to find common meeting ground.

You may over these discussions engage in mutual debate on the one hand, but not in mutual contention on the other [337a6-b1].

Debate on the one hand is characteristic of amicable relationships involving good will; contention on the other is of mutually irreconcilable relations between enemies. If these principles are followed, the present association is likely to be extremely successful [337b1-3].

For they would mean that in the case of yourselves who hold discourse you would in the judgment of ourselves the audience gain good opinion and avoid glorification [337b4-5].

One can win good opinion on the one hand in the judgment of the souls of the audience without deception.

One can also win glorification on the other in discourse by deceiving the audience against opinion [337b5-7].

As to the case of ourselves the audience, these rules mean that we would gain the maximum satisfaction of mind without relish to the body.

Satisfaction of mind on the one hand involves [acceptance of] instruction and participation in thinking with commitment of consciousness.

Bodily relish, on the other, means eating something or undergoing some other physical experience which is relishable [337c1-4].

Plato's parody is so broad as to verge on farce. Pomposity of demeanour and a laboured artificiality of style could scarcely go further. These are those attributes of his victim that he desires to impress upon his readers, and he succeeds. With this success he also wins a second objective, that of half convincing the reader that the content of what is said must be as trivial as the way in which it is put. This indeed is his philosophical purpose. But few passages of reporting in his dialogues pack in more of significance than this one. It is as though, confronting a system of concepts comprising the whole theory of human communication which he is determined to destroy, he decided to make it up into a distilled concentrate of his own manufacture and put it in a bottle and then smash the bottle.

Beginning with Critias' remark, the impasse which the dialogue has reached is treated as a parody of a situation in the *ecclesia*. Two factions are engaged in a violent and partisan debate. The neutral influence of a speaker or chairman or presiding authority is needed to restore harmony and produce that measure of agreement which will allow the proceedings to function. The committee chairman speaks up with a chairman's formality. He represents the main body of those in attendance, the audience, and keeps reminding the two factions that he does. This is a debate not a free fight; it is on the judgment of the audience that the issue depends (a view irreconcilable with Platonism); to that judgment, therefore, the speakers should address themselves; avoiding meretricious appeals and preserving sincerity in what they say; both sides must expect a fair hearing but both sides cannot win; the issue will be settled by an inclination of opinion in one direction rather than the other.

The style of the parody being parliamentary, one is entitled to ask what prompted Plato to treat the situation between Protagoras and Socrates as a parliamentary one. The parallel is not obvious; in fact it is rather strained. The connecting link, however, has already emerged while Protagoras still held the centre of the stage. The kinship of his method of discourse and perhaps of its theory with parliamentary procedure has already been suggested. This indeed is a significant link. The portraits of the three sophists, Protagoras, Prodicus and Hippias, do form part of a pattern. But if Plato is merely emphasizing the rhetorical temptations which beset sophistic he is surely labouring the point.

It is more plausible to suppose that sophistic, represented by the three indifferently, was widely known for its achievement in rationalizing the rules of parliamentary procedure, and that Plato here derides this achievement and seeks to reduce it to insignificance. As the fifth century wore on, the power and responsibility of the Athenian assembly gathered momentum; it became the legislative instrument of government and of an empire. What more inevitable than that procedures for its conduct had continually to be improvised and improved? And what more natural than that the theorists who professed popular discourse as their province should seek to assist by rationalizing these procedures and teaching them as part of their curriculum? The elements of such a rationale are implicit in the present passage: a parliament in practice must consist of a majority who listen and vote and a minority who do the speaking; their speeches have the function of crystallizing opinions antithetically, an operation the suggestion of which has already been put into Protagoras' mouth; but there must be rules to control this process so that it retains the character of a debate and does not degenerate into open faction, that bane of politics, Greek or modern; this is where the function of the chairman who heads the presiding committee of the senate comes in; he can and should intervene to restore order and calm passions; aside from factional perils, the process is open to a second danger; it inevitably tempts the speaker to misconstrue the facts in order to get support he might otherwise lose; but he must discipline himself in this matter.

There are rules for the audience also. They have to vote but they cannot vote intelligently without giving both sides an equal hearing. They have therefore two functions to perform: an assimilation of what is said on both sides of the debate – this is in effect a learning process to which they must give their full attention – ; then they have a decision to make which is bound to favour one side rather than the other. This requires a commitment on their part. In short, the voters as well as the speakers must have an intellectual conscience.

The modern reader may feel that such rules as these could be discovered and applied by common sense and constituted no great philosophical invention. To which reply should be made that, if they and their like can be accepted as common sense today, that acceptance has a long history of painful experiment behind it. We are watching here not perhaps the infancy of European democracy but (shall we say?) its early adolescence. It still has to learn some techniques not foreseen by the sophists before it will function as a vigorous adult. If sophistic saw the kind of primary skills needed, and sought to accelerate the process of learning them by formalizing them and perhaps putting them into text-books, it was an achievement of no small historical importance.

Besides rules of procedure, the passage retains some significant echoes of a serious theory: what might be called an epistemology of public opinion. This shows up in some of the technicalities used. The passage has to be re-read before it is realized that the focus of attention is not primarily on the speakers but upon the reaction of the audience and upon the process by which they form group judgment. Prodicus is represented as contrasting the hearing, which is accorded 'in common', with the 'proportion of distribution' made, which is 'unequal'. Distribution of what? The object is not explicitly stated; we are just told that the more intelligent side is accorded more and the less less. Does he simply mean approval or applause or votes? Or is the object more complicated and hence not stated? The context has a good deal to say about opinions and states of mind. These are themes which recur. We suggest that the object, unstated, of distribution is two-fold: it is from one point of view the vote cast; from another it is that mental event which takes place when the vote is cast, an event which leads to, and is indeed itself, the act of formation of judgment.

Now for the Platonist this would have to be a self-governing operation of the soul, organizing its experience under the control of formal and *a priori* categories. And the Platonist, viewing the mass or mob mind at work, would say on the other hand that any formation of opinion that goes on here is either not scientific or not a genuinely psychic operation; it is a passive emotional reception of, and obedience to, external persuasion.

The actual sophistic theory of popular cognition and decision seems to have lain between these extremes. First, the audience is not passively receptive; it has to make its own 'distribution'. Second, its distribution is not mechanically allotted wholly to one side or the other in the debate; it gives 'more' to one and 'less' to the other; that is, some point of decision is reached which is not an exact representation of either of the two speeches which have been offered, though it may be more like one than the other. The voter makes, in other words, a fairly complex calculation.

Does this theory envisage opinion (*doxa*) as essentially a collective thing, a kind of electric field of thought made up of a thousand components? the two sides which have been evoked by debate are the two poles; the pointer on the dial which represents the common decision which has to be taken, after oscillating between the two poles, comes to rest at some point between them usually nearer to one than to the other. Whatever the propriety of this analogy, it is fairly clear that the language of Prodicus implies that there is a valid state of mind in the audience which is independent of the speeches but yet uses the speeches to guide itself. This is compatible with the stress that he also places upon personal involvement in the decision when the vote is given, on 'participation in thinking with commitment of consciousness'. It must be given with sincerity and after hard thinking. He therefore envisages a process going on in the audience which is more complete than anything which occurs in the speakers. All this is leagues away from that popular impression of the sophists created by Plato which would represent them as concentrating on the speakers at the expense of the audience.

Finally, does not such a theory imply the premiss that there is some common denominator in all human beings which provides the foundation on which a possible agreement is built? If sophistic demanded sincerity and total involvement by the audience personally, how does it get over the danger expressed in the aphorism: *quot homines tot sententiae*? Prodicus speaks of deception practised 'against opinion'. Does this hint at the existence of a basic *doxa* or frame of mind in people which can only be fooled in the short run but never in the long? The phrase is ambiguous, and could mean merely that insincerity which violates the speaker's own opinion. It is more significant that, in warning against partisanship, stress is laid on 'amicable relations involving good will' as that condition necessary to fruitful debate. The phraseology, though innocuous at first reading, recalls the fact that amity and good will played some role as historical principles in the anthropological account of the rise of civil society. They recall also the emphasis of Democritus on the historical import-ance of social compassion and consensus. They will recur in the address of Hippias which immediately follows that of Prodicus. And the last chapter of this book will indicate that the theorists of the fourth century came to accept philanthropy as a political principle of first importance. In short, the language of the present passage, though worded by Plato as though it were a mere appeal for friendship between two parties, may echo a theoretic tenet which was much more fundamental; one which posited in any social unit the existence of a common mind, itself the reflex of a natural amity, to which the legislative leader could appeal and on which he could build.

Such a state of mind might be normally dormant or unconscious, and would be activated only if need arose to make common decisions involving some concrete common interest. Why then at the point of application should debate and division arise at all? Why do human beings who confront concrete problems which require action not automatically agree? There was a Utopian wing of liberalism perhaps not earlier than the fourth century which argued that they would agree if convention and custom-law had not intervened to corrupt their true notion of interest. But the main stream of liberal theory always recognized that custom and law were inevitable and as much part of the natural human arrangement as was the basic identity of interest among human beings.

The phenomenon of contention – of diversity of opinion – was probably explained as due to the tremendous variety of ways in which the general notion of utility worked out in practice. For the complexity of deciding 'what is good for what', taking into account the particular circumstances, objectives, people, place, materials involved, would demand the activation of thought and reflection, and produce an initial stage of uncertainty and confusion in which many wrong formulas would be suggested until the process of debate and consideration worked through to the right one. This would link up with the previous exposition by Protagoras of the pragmatic relativity of 'goods', given as a sample analysis of these complexities, which men should bear in mind when they come to make pragmatic decisions. A training in such pragmatism would be of direct benefit to a democracy. The sample given was related to economic decisions; but it is easy to imagine that the same method of organizing examples in contrasted series could be applied to political problems and used to instruct would-be members of parliament in the correct kind of thinking process required for political decisions.

There is still one more connection that can be traced between Protagoras and Prodicus, that is, between the two documentations of sophistic theory represented by these two lay figures. It was suggested earlier that the technique of 'holding dialogue', as sophistic understood it and practised it, included the negotiation of opinion, the meeting of minds in discussion and the finding of common ground. The procedure would be private in the sense that 'cross-talk' (*dialegesthai*) unlike 'counter-talk' (*antilegein*) cannot easily be organized on a parliamentary basis. But there was nothing to prevent members of the assembly from cross-talking among themselves, and presumably they did. Whether or not sophistic thought of dialogue-technique itself as extending into the assembly, the important point is that the theory of the possibility of human communication implied in 'dialogue' was equally implicit in the group-mind theory which underlay the assembly's practice. We spoke earlier of a magnetic field of group opinion. This can be imagined as latent and homogeneous in quality or wave-length. But a concrete issue arises – the surface layer of this field becomes agitated and the agitation becomes polarized between two extremes – the two sides in the debate. But meanwhile a multiple series of cross-currents are also operating within the field and between the two poles and a whole series of dialogues takes place in which negotiation of opinion finally produces a common product, which, to repeat, is nearer one pole than the other, but is not likely to be identical with either. Presumably we have now mixed up our scientific metaphor sufficiently to offend any physicist. But may it be at least accorded the tolerance granted to a Platonic myth, even though it is a myth which to Plato would have seemed like a nightmare?

The appeal of Prodicus is next supported by Hippias in the following speech:

Oh, all of you present here, I hold and do proclaim
that you are of the same kin, the same household, the same city –
all of you
but only in nature not in custom-law
for like to like is by nature kin
but custom-law, being tyrant over men, employs many violent pressures which violate nature [337c7-d3].
We therefore do incur dishonour
in that we know the nature of affairs on the one hand
but on the other being the most intelligent men of Greece
and in terms of this very intelligence being now assembled
at the very presidential house of intelligence of Greece
and in the greatest and happiest house of this very city

we do not illustrate our lustre by any honourable achievement
but rather fall to mutual contention as though we were the
lowest
of human kind [337d3-e2].
It is therefore my request and also my counsel to you,
Protagoras
and Socrates,
that you come to an accommodation, with us as your
arbitrators
to bring you to the mean of accommodation [337e2-338a1].
and that you [pointing to Socrates] do not over-zealously pursue
that form of discourse which is the 'short form', if this be not
likeable to Protagoras,
but rather relax and give rein to your discourses that they
may make
a greater show of magnificence and propriety before us,
and that Protagoras in his turn should not shake out every
reef and
let go before the wind vanishing on to the high seas of
discourse
with the land left far behind [338a1-6].
No, let both parties cleave a middle course;
thus indeed you will do, and hearken, I say to me
and elect a marshal, a presiding officer, a president
whose superintendence shall preserve the measured mean of
discourses
held by either party [338a6-b1].

The strokes of Plato's satire are growing broader; he is laying
it on with a thick brush. It is clear from other contexts besides
this that he had difficulty in taking Hippias seriously. There is
something slightly hilarious about the figure of a man who elsewhere is made to display his virtuosity by explaining how he
once attended a race meeting wholly attired in an outfit of his
own patent manufacture. Nevertheless, the address he makes here
is another piece of interesting documentation.

Prodicus could convert a small gathering in the courtyard of
Callias' house into the amphitheatre of the Pnyx; but even these
limits are too narrow for Hippias' bounding imagination. He has
already transported himself and his audience to an assembly of

pan-Hellenic proportions – he himself hailed from Elis near Olympia – and mounts an imaginary platform to address an international gathering of spectators. Where Prodicus' voice boomed along the rows of seats, Hippias shouts across the crowded plain.

Not all that he is made to say is consistent with this setting but his exordium fits it exactly. His audience is drawn from the cities of Greece, all of them separate states with exclusive citizenship. He appeals to them to recognize their common kinship – their citizenship in a hypothetical city-state – the community of the Hellenes. The custom-law against which he protests as a violation of nature is very concretely the citizenship laws of the several states. This is pertinent to his own status and that of all the sophists. As itinerants, they were usually in the position of visiting aliens with temporary residence permits; they could not vote or speak in the assembly to which so much of their theory was addressed. Nor could they plead in person in the courts. Their profession needed a doctrine of pan-Hellenic citizenship to be fully realized. The price of exclusive sovereignty for the states themselves was a condition of endemic war between them. So Hippias attacks the mutual contention of his imaginary listeners. The little dispute over method between Socrates and Protagoras has become in his mind's eye the kind of division into hostile camps (*diaphora*) which Thucydides notes as characteristic of the inter-Hellenic conflict which he described in his history.

Again, in appealing to the parties to use the assistance of arbitration in order to find an accommodation between themselves, he exploits two terms which in Greek usage were applied to international negotiation. Herodotus for example describes how Athens and Mitylene at one time used the 'arbitration' of Periander to reach a mutual understanding; and Thucydides describes an 'accommodation' brought about by Athens and Thrace and Macedon.

But it is part of that laughable quality which is intentionally placed upon this version of Hippias' style that he is allowed to mix his metaphors so thoroughly. He launches his appeal for arbitration upon a Socrates and a Protagoras whom he visualizes as (shall we say?) commanders in the field. Then Socrates (in his vision at least) doffs his general's uniform and jumps into a chariot where he is discovered urging on his steeds of discourse at a gallop, with Hippias cheering him on from the sidelines with cries of 'illustrate your lustre: demonstrate your equipage'. This at least keeps one of the protagonists on the plains of Olympia, but a kind of incipient surrealism now takes over. For where is Protagoras? He is at the helm of a ship racing Socrates' chariot, all set for an Odyssey upon the high seas where his words carrying before a full gale are in danger of vanishing over the horizon. The portmanteau of Hippias' imagination – if we may now be allowed to complicate things by one more metaphor of our own – does indeed contain many good things, even to the bursting of its seams. For one item in its contents has still to be mentioned: if the plain of Olympia can become a stormy sea, why should it not also become a town hall, the presidential meeting house? Indeed it should, for by this device the orator, dangerously suspended and in need of assistance, can establish brief contact with reality. From the town hall he descends to the house of his host and lets his eye rest for a moment on the objects at which he is actually looking before imagination once more takes over.

It is this metaphor of the town hall which suggests the continuity that connects these Platonic parodies of sophistic political theory. As Hippias abandons internationalism and conducts himself and his companions to Athens as to the 'Prytaneum' of Greece, he is using a parliamentary symbol. The Athenian assembly was chaired by a rotating committee of presiding officers whose expense accounts during their term of office were met by the expedient of housing and feeding them 'in Prytaneum', the hall of the Prytaneis or presidents. When Hippias winds up his address he compresses his metaphors into one last flourish: elect he says a marshal (for the international games), a presiding official (a term used of the games and of the assembly), and a president (a term restricted to the assembly). In this last touch Plato briefly satirizes the institution of chairmanship which had been devised to assist assembly procedure. We have previously entertained the suggestion that Prodicus had spoken in the role of a parliamentary chairman and that his address is meant as a satire upon sophistic rules of parliamentary procedure. Here the suggestion is confirmed and the office of chairman actually named, as Plato crowns his satire.

In fact, while Prodicus' admonitions are intended, it may be said, to govern the general tone of the debate, Hippias speaks as though his job were to control the actual length of the speeches, according to some mean or measure not otherwise explained. This would be consistent with the supposition that sophistic theory, noting the need for better regulation of debating and of voting, argued in effect for the creation of the office and authority of Speaker – a suggestion far ahead of its time.

In the middle of his address Hippias had gone so far as to visualize Athens herself as the town hall of Greece. Is this an echo of a serious metaphor employed by the sophists for theoretic purposes? Was the Athenian parliament, with its chairman presiding over and composing factions, taken as a model or standard for the way in which a pan-Hellenic assembly should be organized, and of the objectives it could achieve? That is, a leading city presides, but all cities debate and vote. We happen to know that this was for a time the kind of policy advocated by Isocrates in the interests of pan-Hellenism. The theoretical interest of the suggestion, however, lies in the fact, if true, that in looking for a technique of pan-Hellenic accommodation sophistic referred to the procedure and theory of democratic communication, by which an assembly of factions within a single community can be converted into a legislative instrument.

The kind of mind which could deliver this sort of address we have likened to a portmanteau. It contains a medley of miscellaneous materials all of them interesting in themselves but exhibiting no discernible principle of choice or organization unless it be the fantastic inspiration of metaphor. It is as though Hippias had gone shopping to the stores of other thinkers and had come home with a mixed bag of very good stuff. If this was the kind of man he was, he would make an easy target, but he would always be liable to have something interesting to exhibit.

There is one item of interest in the present collection which might easily escape notice. The term 'nature' is used twice in different contexts. After saying 'you are all akin in nature', Hippias adds 'we therefore do incur dishonour in that we know the nature of affairs but do not illustrate our lustre by any honourable achievement'. The lapse into athletic metaphor casts a cloak of absurdity over what he is saying and disguises what may be the philosophical importance of the phrase he has used. On the surface he is simply paying a tactful compliment to Protagoras and Socrates. He appeals to their undoubted intelligence which

227

can prevent meaningless quarrels. But the notion that men who are themselves akin in nature should also possess a knowledge of the nature of things and in that knowledge find agreement perhaps points to that kind of epistemology of group communication on which Prodicus had relied in his own discourse. The hypothesis would be that human beings, precisely because of their partnership in 'that one thing' which makes society possible, have potentially a common mind which in given group situations becomes articulate and functions as the sub-stratum at least of group decisions based on common interests. Borrowing perhaps from the physicists, sophistic argued that the minds of human beings exercise this kind of cognition when they apprehend 'nature' and that their conclusions can agree because nature itself is a constant. But here they made a shift. Hippias says 'the nature of affairs' not the 'nature of reality'. The Greek is *pragmata*, 'things that happen or that you do', whereas a physicist (or a Platonist) would be more likely to use the word *onta*, 'things that are'. The common mind knows the nature of all pragmatic situations; and sophistic probably added, it knows their nature intuitively, even as a social human being, created by society, must know the nature of affairs in that society automatically. The problem of a double standard of experience, divided between the senses and the intellect, did not come up.

Finally, if Plato had special provocation for disliking and deriding Hippias, it would lie in that internationalism which is the chief target of his satire here. Over this issue Greek liberalism was to collide head-on with that teleological conception of the city-state which Plato bequeathed to Aristotle. The issue, involving as it does the collision between the local custom-law of self-contained cities and the law of nature which is supposed to unite all human beings in a common partnership of natural needs, is better postponed until Antiphon's polemics have clarified it. The exact chronology of this developing ideology is obscure. The notion of mankind as a universal society is best viewed as a post-war phenomenon born of the experience of the conflict between Athens and Sparta. The political problems of the present chapter are still those set by the Periclean democracy, even though solutions offered already hinted at a more universal conception of politics. Sophistic methodology, based as it was on a universal sociology, could not but open the avenue to internationalism.

Plato correctly interpreted this tendency and in his *Republic*, discussing war between Greek states, made certain concessions to it. But at bottom he had no use for it. The ideas of the historical Hippias may themselves have been transitional or he may have been used here as a lay-figure in whom Plato combines the liberal views held in different generations. It is possible, for instance, that in his remarks on law and nature and the kinship of mankind he really speaks for Antiphon. On the other hand, as we shall see, it was not in Antiphon's character to bother with pragmatic problems of legislative procedure.

But in leaving Hippias it should be said: he has been treated roughly. Whether he personally deserved it, in an intellectual sense, we shall never know. What we do realize is Plato's contempt for politicians and for the jargon, the platitudes, the compromises that form an inevitable part of political negotiation in democratic societies. Since we sympathize, we readily smile. Parliaments, except when they face some mortal peril in open fight, are not generally uplifting spectacles. But the operation of dismemberment performed here by Plato upon the doctrine of man's common nature and brotherhood and world citizenship is not quite forgivable. It has produced the historical illusion that the Greek mind never seriously grappled with an international conception of society until Alexander the Great forced the conception upon it.

This has done something to diminish the moral authority of Hellas by suggesting that the cosmopolitan ideas of Stoicism were a form of weariness and of defeat, the natural concomitant of Greek submission to Macedonian and Roman conquerors. The truth would rather seem to be that the ideology which guided and informed the civilizing policy of the conquerors had already been crystallized by the Greek genius before conquest had occurred.

At the beginning of the previous chapter of this work the question was asked: What did the title sophist represent in Athens in her golden age and what kind of persons were the Elder Sophists? The bare outline of what might be called a group portrait has now begun to emerge from the pages of Plato's *Protagoras*. This seems to confirm the notion that, if we intend to use the term sophist of these people in its modern derogatory sense, the title is a misnomer, and that, even if we rearrange our values sufficiently to grant that they grappled seriously with problems of language, discourse and communication, we still have not made a sufficient historical adjustment. The notion has to be discarded that their primary interests were focused on rhetoric. Of course they taught rhetoric as a technique for the effective formulation of political ideas, but as ancillary to a bigger thing, a larger view of life and man altogether. If there is one quality which identifies them, and yet which is wholly incompatible with their traditional reputation, it is a sense of social and political responsibility. Beginning with the sociology attributed to Protagoras with its rationality, its humanity, its historical depth, continuing with the pragmatism which seeks to understand the common man's virtues and failings and to guide his decisions by a flexible calculus of what is good and useful, and ending with a theory of group discourse as a negotiation of opinion leading to agreed decisions, we are steadily invited to keep our eye not upon the authoritarian leader, but upon the average man as citizen of this society and voter in his parliament. The discourse in question has identified not the practice of unscrupulous persuasion upon the blind emotions of masses of men but those complex processes and subtle currents of judgment which go to the making of the collective mind and the group decision.

The critic may object that so far this portrait has been elicited from about one half of one of Plato's works, and that, even if it is provable that the work in question is a report of sophistic theory, the outlines that have been elicited are very tenuous and are not in fact those that Plato himself intended to draw.

The sophists were speakers but they were also writers who wished to leave their theory on record. The indifference of later antiquity defeated this purpose. The wreckage of their works that survives, taken by itself, is so sparse and miscellaneous that it defies the best efforts of the historian to build any construction upon it which can be coherent and complete. One surviving piece, and only one, happens to be a fragment, not inconsiderable, of a parliamentary discourse. It is precious because it is parliamentary. It is constructed as a contribution to a debate in the Athenian assembly. A writer on text-book rhetoric of Augustan date who happened to want a specimen of a given style quoted the opening paragraphs of this work. But for us, unlike him, the question of style is trivial compared with the question of content. The speech turns out to be an appeal to an assembly split by faction and bitterly divided over fundamentals to come to terms with itself by a negotiation of opinion, which the orator argues is entirely feasible, and for this he rests his case on the assumption that beneath the division and confusion that he sees there exists a common mind waiting to be evoked by the processes of reasoned inquiry and careful debate.

The address must have been composed for somebody other than the author to deliver. We do not know for whom, though he speaks as one of the rising generation who wishes to turn his back on the past and feels he has something different to say. It is not spoken in the confident accents of the Periclean golden age. The phraseology bespeaks a sense of political strain, with perhaps a touch of reflective sadness. Some of the affirmations of Democritus and Protagoras are already abandoned. They had seen city-state society as continually renewing itself by the automatic transmission of its own *mores* through the family. The present speaker has no such confidence. But he clings to a belief in the capacity of a democratic assembly of Athenian citizens to function and to find agreement even on the most perilous issues. One feels, perhaps, a note of desperation in his belief. It is held against the dark prospect of the impending collapse of the Periclean system. But the parliamentary postulates are there, precise testimony to the character of sophistic political theory.

We have postponed naming the author. Had he been identified at once, the reader of Plato, recalling that character labelled 'Thrasymachus' whose supposed political philosophy is dramatized in the first book of Plato's *Republic*, would have prepared himself inevitably for a specimen of unscrupulous pleading in defence of the doctrine that might makes right. No surviving piece of documentation is so damaging to Plato's claims as a reporter than this one. For its author we are told was that same Thrasymachus. But now he speaks without the aid of Plato's ventriloquism, in his own right [*FVS*[6] 85 B1].

Men of Athens, I could have wished to have partaken in that time of old when the younger generation fulfilled their duty by saying nothing. That was when historical events did not make it necessary for us to speak, and the government of our elders over the city was successful. But since we have been reserved by our destiny for a time that has now accumulated to the point where the good fortune of the city is what we are told about, but its disasters are what we personally experience, and of these the greatest are not the product of the gods nor of fortune but of those in charge, then I say it becomes necessary that we speak. A man must surely be insensitive or else have a heart of iron if he can continue to expose himself to the mismanagement of persons prepared to mismanage, and himself assume the burden of blame for the plotting and the malpractice of other parties [2.322.2-14].

Enough surely for us the time that has gone by, that has on the one hand seen us give up peace to live in war, passing through perils to this present time when we are contented for the day that has gone by and our fear is for the day that is coming; and that on the other hand has seen us give up consensus to arrive at enmity and mutual discord. Now, for other men on the one hand the multitude of their good things conduces to arrogance and faction; but as for us on the other, it is in the company of good things that we used to be disciplined, whereas amidst bad things which have the habit of teaching others discipline we have lost our reason. Then tell me, why should a man delay to speak what his mind sees, if on him has fallen affliction at what is before him, and also the thought that he has the kind of thing which will prevent this other kind of thing from continuing any longer [2.322.14-323.11].

In the first place I shall demonstrate that those parties from among the speakers or the rest of you who have fallen to mutual contention have in the process of discourse been affected by a mutual attitude which becomes an inevitable attitude in men whose partisanship is uninfluenced by thought. They think their discourses are mutually antithetical but are not aware that the policies pursued are identical, nor that the discourse of their opponents is inherent in their own. Ask yourselves, going back to the beginning: What is it that both sides are looking for? In the first place, there is the issue of the constitution of the fathers; this, which throws them into confusion, can be grasped mentally with the greatest ease and is supremely something in which citizens have community. Thus (a) as to matters beyond our own cognition we must of necessity depend on the discourse of olden times to tell us about them; and (b) as to anything that came within the purview of the older generation we must ascertain from the men with the information . . . [2.323.11-324.6].

The translation has tried not to spare the style of the piece. However, our division of it into three paragraphs brings out the fact that it is only the middle paragraph that breaks down, its integrity overcome by the devices of assonance, antithesis and attempted symmetry. By contrast, the third paragraph, once the author's exordium is out of the way, becomes business-like and clear. These faults make it easier to sympathize with Plato's compulsion to burlesque sophistic. Morally and politically he feared its philosophy, but the artist in him probably reserved his contempt for sophistic's vastly inferior competence in the art of the written word.

It is noticeable that the author's virtuosity in the middle paragraph gets in the way of what he is trying to say, needlessly complicating the presentation of what he intends. Some of the artificiality is created by the attempt to express pictorially an important idea which required abstract assistance. The notion of time's passage from past to present and into the future is played upon in six different contexts; the actual word 'time' has four occurrences in two paragraphs. And the participle 'gone by' occurs twice in successive clauses. This seems to betray a poverty of vocabulary and it does, but the speaker or rather the author is partly preoccupied with the spectacle of history, the history of Athens in this case, as a process in which men get involved and which has a power of its own to condition men and control their reactions. But we see this power retrospectively as time divides itself into periods. This would be in line with sophistic historical naturalism but it is also the beginning of a new and provocative concept, one in fact which Greek thought had some difficulty in accepting. It is not very explicit even in Thucydides, whose own historical powers derive in part from the way his mind remained anchored in the traditional habit of viewing time in terms of concrete and intense moments. As for Plato, we have already sensed his hostility to the historical way of looking at human beings. If the point is worth mentioning in connection with the present fragment, it is not to suggest that Thrasymachus has in fact achieved a concept of historical process – as to that, we do not know – but to notice one of the reasons for the breakdown of sophistic style. The trouble often was, not that it was trying to say too little, but that it was trying to say too much.

Within the speaker's mind the distant past and the immediate present confront each other in painful antithesis: 'I would have wished to have partaken in that time of old . . .' 'but we have been reserved by our destiny for a time now accumulated . . .' a time, he says, of 'disaster'. In between there has intervened a period of prolonged war, and that has made the difference, for it has brought in its wake acute civil dissension: 'enough surely for us the time that has gone by, that has seen us give up peace and live in war and give up consensus to arrive at enmity and mutual discord'. These sentiments seem appropriate to Athens in those last years of the Peloponnesian War when, under the pressure of increasing hardship and military stalemate, political partisanship became exacerbated. The impression is strengthened by the reference to the constitution of the fathers as the primary issue between parties. This was the rallying cry of the oligarchs who in the days of defeat became democracy's embittered critics.

Is the speech then written for one of their spokesmen? The orator, whoever he is, is one of the younger generation; he attacks the irresponsible mismanagement of those in power, for which other innocent people must pay the price; he wishes to end the state of war; he regrets the passing of social discipline. All this would fit a member of one of the oligarchic class, some young aristocrat of Spartan sympathies, a member of the peace party who would, if he could, do away with popular assembly and courts, and limit the franchise to his own class. But yet this view of the speech, however plausible, won't do. It does not fit in the least with its non-partisan quality, its air of objectivity, its plea for clarity of thinking, its dispassionate search for solutions. Behind its artifices of phraseology there are apparent a serious intellectual position, a rationale of political behaviour and method, if not a theory of politics.

To begin with, he assumes that the purpose of government is to be successful and efficient; this is the criterion by which it should be judged. Success lies not in our stars but in ourselves – 'the greatest of our disasters are the product not of the gods or fortune but of those in charge'. He assumes that prosperity and disaster are not god-given but man-made; and, secondly, that it is the purpose of any government to preserve the one and avoid the other. This is the criterion by which any government is to be judged – 'in time of old the government of our elders over the city was successful', but in the present 'the greatest of our disasters are the product not of gods but of those in charge'. Why then should any man 'continue to expose himself to mismanagement?' This is the voice of rationalism and utilitarianism. Traditional piety, and the archaic fatalism of the Greek temper, seem to be rejected; the impression is strengthened by something he says a little later: 'now for other men the multitude of their good things conduces to arrogance and faction but as for us . . . it was in the company of good things that we used to be disciplined whereas in the midst of bad things which have the habit of teaching other men discipline we have lost our reason'. That is, appraising the actual course of historical events at Athens and matching them against the moral temper of the men involved in them, the speaker discards the traditional and pietistic equation – 'success equals insolence followed by nemesis which teaches prudence'. This formula had accurately reflected the way in which the Greek mind had earlier sought to make moral sense out of historical processes, when these seemed to get beyond human control. The speaker's empiricism forces him to reject it as an explanation of the present condition of Athens; he is not radical enough, at least in this speech, to suggest that it should be rejected universally.

What is the task of government, the performance of which affords the criterion by which its efficiency is to be judged? Plato and Aristotle both reply that one of its functions is to be able to wage war successfully. Presumably, Democritus would have agreed: the protection of the group against fellow groups is a first essential. For our author, security and war are incompatible. The political objective is to achieve external peace on the one hand and internal harmony on the other; each condition, the international and the internal, depends on the other. All forms of tension reduce the area of security, maximizing hatred and minimizing amity: 'enough the day that has gone by that has seen us give up peace to live in war, passing through perils to the present time when we are contented for the day that has gone by and our fear is for the day that is coming . . . that has seen us give up consensus to arrive at enmity and mutual discord'.

Consensus (*homonoia*), as we have seen, had been a traditional ideal of politics, examined by Democritus and found to be dependent historically upon the exercise of altruism on the part of the privileged in favour of the poor. Our author however in the manner of the Elder Sophists is looking more closely at the contemporary process of group discourse, by which in the give-and-take of parliamentary procedure a consensus is actually formulated and made into policy. 'Those parties who have fallen to mutual contention have in the process of discourse been affected by a mutual attitude inevitable for men whose partisanship is uninfluenced by thought. They think their discourses are mutually antithetical, but are not aware that the policies pursued are identical, nor that the discourse of their opponents is inherent in their own'.

The crux of this paragraph lies in the last clause. In a given political situation, those who debate the issues may offer apparently irreconcilable solutions. But, in fact, this dichotomy is an illusion, of which they themselves in the course of the debate have to be perpetually aware. Not only is there only one complete solution. Examine what is said, and you will find that its elements are present in both sides of the controversy. There is always common ground between the parties; some formula or *logos* to which they both give allegiance.

He goes on to describe how one goes behind the apparent conflict to discover what this common ground may be. It seems evident that at the back of his mind there is an epistemology of public opinion and a conviction about the character of the common mind which he shares with the Prodicus whom Plato had parodied. Thrasymachus puts it in terms of policy rather than of psychology. In the minds of the persons composing any deliberative assembly, once a problem or topic is raised, there is discoverable a common objective which debate should serve to clarify. Each side of the debate has its contribution to make to formulating the objective. Some such axiom is essential to democratic political theory. For democracy ultimately presumes consent on the part of all its members. It would follow that the formulation of antithetical positions on party lines is, logically speaking, only a convenient instrument to assist the process of formulation. In any final sense the antithesis is illusory. Thrasymachus therefore implies, as also do Prodicus and Hippias, that when the debate is conducted properly neither side wins an exclusive victory. The common *logos* that emerges in the form of a voted decision has some resemblance to each of the antitheses, but can be equivalent to neither.

Only rationalists convinced that reflection had power to penetrate and control the emotions could have held such a faith. Thus for Thrasymachus the ever-present danger is excessive 'partisanship uninfluenced by thought'. And he then goes on to apply the principle of his parliamentary method to the case in hand. The first thing you do, in the manner of a Socrates, but now collectively as a group, is to apply *skepsis* – investigation and self-questioning: 'Ask yourselves, going back to the beginning, what it is that both sides are looking for'. The issue is expressed in the phrase 'constitution of the fathers'. This is an issue which 'throws us into confusion'. But whereas the Socratic method at this point to solve the confusion turns inward and asks analytically What is the meaning of the term constitution? and seeks to frame an analytic answer, sophistic method turns outward to human experience, to human opinion and to historical facts.

'This [i.e. the constitution of the fathers] can be grasped mentally with the greatest ease and is supremely something in which citizens have community.' He means that issues of political policy derive from our partnership as human beings in a common group organization. This organization *is* us; and any ideas for managing or improving it must reflect our living experience of it as members of it. The source of political knowledge is wholly pragmatic. It is knowledge by acquaintance. The sentence plays on the overtones of the term 'community'. In so far as men are organized by 'intercommunication' within the group, they also form or find the 'common mind' without which no 'community' can exist. To ask: Which then is prior, the common mind or the common social unit? is to ask a Platonic question, to which sophistic was indifferent, as indeed all historical method must be indifferent. But the existence of such a mind also guaranteed that any group of men could collectively form and implement political policy for the government of themselves. This axiom of social community lies, in fact, behind the doctrine of the common discourse and the unanimous policy which Thrasymachus has already used.

The speech breaks off in the middle of a paragraph which reveals a further step in the author's thinking. Once you have accepted the principle of the common mind which is going to discover common policy, you still have the problem of mobilizing those areas of human experience which are relevant to the policy that is needed. You still have to gather information and the data. The constitution of our fathers is in one sense us, but this does not help much until you realize that our unconscious acquaintance with it has to be made articulate and informed. This can be done only by drawing upon relevant sources of information. These can be precisely defined. Part of the information we require is 'beyond our own cognition'. Here 'we must of necessity depend on the discourse of olden times to tell us'. In this fashion Thrasymachus assumes what we would call historical sources and relevant documents even though these might be of a miscellaneous kind, poetic or prosaic; a body of tradition rather than a set of authorities.

Secondly, 'as to anything that came within the purview of the older generation, we must ascertain from the men with the information . . .'. This kind of information is still not that supplied by immediate experience but, so far as it falls within the life span of the older generation, its source can be sought in living men and not in record. It is an eye-witness type of source. Thirdly, perhaps, if the speech had been preserved, we would find the speaker going on to define the direct information available to ourselves out of our experience of what the constitution now is. This is a classi-fication of sources of knowledge required for political judgment, and we suggest it points directly to the historical methods em-ployed by sophistic and to its pragmatic epistemology. Even the foreshortening of perspective, which visualizes on the one hand the whole span of ancient tradition and on the other the life span of men still living as correlative sources of knowledge, is character-istic of the infancy of the historical method, as was demonstrated in the case of Democritus.

In a parliamentary crisis, Thrasymachus is more interested in the possibility of agreement, than in the process of debate which precedes agreement. This urgency is characteristic surely of an age of insecurity; the parliamentary theory of Protagoras and Prodicus has not changed, but the emphasis falls more exclusively on the end product and less on the 'dialogue' that produces it. Consensus, that traditional civic ideal, has now become a critical necessity. Yet once the liberal theorists had turned the light of their intellect upon democratic process, and seen it as a process, they could never envisage consensus as automatic, or as an *a priori* requirement of good citizenship. We can feel Thrasymachus challenging his audience, seeking to arouse those powers of reason and calculation which will make negotiation of opinion possible.

There is a fragment of political theorizing preserved in the anthology of Stobaeus which underlines this dependence of consensus on the process of calculation and on human effort. Whoever was its author, it can be quoted here as a supplement to Thrasymachus [*FVS*⁶ 47 B3]:

> Calculative reasoning is an invention which stops faction and enlarges consensus. Once it is activated, aggrandizement ceases to exist and equivalence begins to exist. For with its help, in the field of our transactions, we enact mutual agreements. Because of its effect, the poor receive from the powerful and the rich give to those in need, both parties believing that through its medium they will achieve equivalence [1.437.7-12].

The echo of Democritus on consensus is unmistakable. The author is prepared to go behind that formal ideal of civic concord to which all right-thinking Greeks gave allegiance, in order to affirm that the political goal depends upon the exercise of intellectual process. Democritus had seen how it depended on altruistic relations between classes. Our author, repeating this part of the social analysis, goes on to urge that calculative reasoning lies behind the exercise of altruism. This is quite in the manner of the Elder Sophists. It fits the proposition that collective decision is a process of 'holding dialogue'. The calculation involved is at once personal and also social; it operates in the realm of human opinion; it is not the Platonic logic engendered within the confines of the soul, and operating with propositions exclusively analytic.

CHAPTER IX

THE METHOD AND VALIDITY
OF POLITICAL DECISION

A RATIONALE of the democratic process in its formative period could not afford to neglect the necessity of leadership over the creation of opinion, exercised in the assembly by effective speakers. Traditional accounts of the sophists, besides concentrating on this professional interest at the expense of others, have encouraged the impression that the training thus given was irresponsible. Professional competence, it is supposed, was narrowed down to the limits of a 'technique of rhetoric', its objective being viewed as 'cleverness at speaking', or a manipulation of language without regard to its content; and directed to gain emotional control over mass opinion without regard to the ends served. 'Speaking on either side of a question', a practice which was in fact encouraged to crystallize issues and assist the formulation of decision, has been represented as a further example of irresponsibility, a facet of those demagogic tactics which continually encouraged a speaker to 'make the worse cause appear the better'.

So runs the familiar indictment. A reader of the previous chapters, who has allowed himself to realize the necessary collision between any theory which takes public opinion seriously and one that does not, will be prepared to see in this indictment a dogmatic judgment pronounced by Platonism upon a rival theory of politics, a theory with which Platonism could not be expected to sympathize.

Yet it is not all the invention of prejudice. A democratic process does indeed involve the engagement of paradoxical forces. On the one hand it must allow a degree of participation on the part of the minds of all individuals in the assembly and make possible the formulation of agreement which is built on some common and communicable factor in these minds. On the other, this effect is not spontaneous nor automatic; it requires energizing by the clarification of issues which have to be presented to the audience so that they can think about them. The issues as formulated must bear some relation to their own half-formed thought, and yet must carry that thought a stage further.

This is the business of group cognition leading to group decision. It is pragmatic and has its own specific epistemological discipline, which does not consist in the objective and complete summation of all the facts and conclusions in the manner of science, but in the initial fragmentation of the issues through affirmative declarations which are partisan, but which then communicate with each other through a process of mutual negotiation. In short, not inquiry in the Platonic sense but debate in the liberal sense is the essential first weapon for setting in motion the processes of opinion formation.

Sophistic sought to come to terms with this process as a whole: it began by affirming the validity of common human opinion in all matters pertaining to political action. It realized however that the means of achieving this in concrete cases were complex and it was perfectly prepared to allow that in this process the leadership of gifted individuals – a trained minority – was important. Any modern democracy makes identical though perhaps unconscious assumptions, and it is hard to see why in classic Athens they should be viewed as improper. But, in order of philosophical priority, the negotiated opinion leading to consensus came first, and to this the actual method of leadership through persuasion was secondary. It is the error of traditional accounts of sophistic that they reverse this order.

It is characteristic of the fragment of Thrasymachus, written for dangerous times when the strains of insecurity increasingly tended to split the state apart, that it reverts with urgency to the factor of common agreement lying behind the tensions of debate. The bold acceptance of the tension itself as the prior operative means by which agreement is finally produced is by tradition assigned to Protagoras. This bespeaks the democratic courage and confidence of his generation, when consensus and effective decision in the assembly could be taken for granted as the normal accompaniment of the speeches. The more pungent the previous debate, the better the machinery of decision worked. Testimony to the Protagorean theory of democratic debate has been already noticed in Plato. It is here repeated with a few additions which later tradition may have preserved independently:

1. (Protagoras speaking)
Many is the time Socrates I have made my entry against other men in discourse-competition. If I did what you tell me to do, and held dialogue according to the rules set for me by the speaker for the opposition, my superiority would have no chance of being demonstrated, nor would Protagoras have become a name to conjure with in Hellas [*Protag.* 335a4ff.].

2. (Prodicus speaking)
You may over these discourses engage in mutual debate on the one hand but not in mutual contention on the other. Debate on the one hand is the characteristic of amicable relationships involving good will, contention on the other is of mutually irreconcilable relations between enemies [*Protag.* 377a8ff.].

3. Eudoxus records that Protagoras . . . taught his pupils to approve and condemn the same proposition [from Stephanus Byz. FVS[6] 80A21].

4. Protagoras was the first to declare that two discourses can be disposed antithetically on every [pragmatic] issue [from Diogenes Laertius. FVS[6] 80A1: 2.253.24].

5. Protagoras says that concerning every issue you can argue on both sides of the question with parity [from Seneca. FVS[6] 80A20].

6. The Greeks say that any discourse can be confronted by its antithesis, Protagoras having initiated this view [from Clement, FVS[6] 80A20].

If these testimonies preserve an almost forgotten contribution to the theory of parliamentary process, they have passed through the prism of a double distortion. For, on the one hand, the antithetical method was often represented as an immoral sub-version of better principles by worse; and, on the other, logicians viewed the two opposing discourses of the debate as two anti-thetical propositions in logic, so that Protagoras was represented as asserting the impossibility of logical contradiction. The first two items, from Plato, correctly define the context in which the antithetical technique was employed. Item 3 describes the train-ing designed for those who would lead debates in the assembly. This is not to deny that the same procedure could not be effec-tively employed on non-parliamentary topics, such as the disputed meaning of a poem. But to evaluate the theory of debate technique correctly, it is vital to identify the specific social situation for which it was designed. If it had been visualized as occurring primarily in the context of private discussion (like the Socratic dialectic) then its aims were indeed logical or verbal and it is from the standpoint of such aims that it is judged in Plato's pages. But if it was conceived in the context of the assembly, even though the sophists themselves never got into the assembly, then is it too much to say that the sophists anticipated the necessity of the party system as a vehicle for conducting a democratic government?

Perhaps, so stated, the proposition goes too far. The Greek mind was always too rational and unambiguous to envisage compromise itself as a final principle. It always felt disagreement should end in agreement, and that parts should be resolved back into wholes. It is indeed fascinating to trace here, in this the adolescence of European democracy, the first outline of an emerging pattern of democratic conduct pragmatically effective for a time during the fourth century (compare the party of Demosthenes versus that of Aeschines) yet never rationalized and formally accepted until the genius of Edmund Burke grappled with the facts and produced the permanent party formula. The seeds of the formula are there in the 'twin discourses' of Protagoras, and it is easy to see how such tendencies could be abhorrent to Plato's notion of a mathematical harmony.

The practice of distributing any political issue into a series of arguments *pro* and *con* naturally stimulated the search for effective expression which at this level could be studied in isolation from the fundamental merits of the case, simply as a method. One can say that at this narrowly technical level the art of communication improved itself by raising itself by its own bootstraps. If those whose skill improved were excited by their own virtuosity, this was no discredit to the general mental labour which went into the formulation of issues *pro* and *con*. Popular taste recognized the 'skill of speech' as the most immediate and thrilling result attainable by pupils of the profession. The conversation between Socrates and the young enthusiast which opens Plato's *Protagoras* will illustrate the point:

(Socrates to the eager and insistent Hippocrates): What does all this mean? Do you have anything against Protagoras?

Of course I do, he replied, laughing. He is the only intellectual there is, but he is doing nothing to make me intelligent too.

Oh, but surely he will if you can induce him and pay him.

Ah, ye gods. If only it depended merely on paying him! . . . [*Protag.* 310d3ff.].

Suppose one were to ask what department of intelligence does the sophist command? What would be the answer? What is the business he controls?

Presumably the answer to that one is that he controls the production of skilful discourse.

True, perhaps, but it does not carry us far enough. Our reply provokes further question: on what subjects does one employ this skilful discourse produced by the sophist? . . . [312d3ff.].

I suppose they must be those in which he transmits intellectual competence to his pupils.

And what are those subjects in which the sophist has intellectual competence and in which he imparts intellectual competence to his pupils?

Now you ask me, really I don't know [312e3ff.].

The items of this piece of dialectic are embedded in separate and successive contexts of the introduction. But taken together they constitute a skilful design which has the effect of isolating 'skill of discourse' from 'competence in subject matter'; and of introducing the suggestion that perhaps for sophistic this competence does not exist. This is an example of distortion which results when positions occupied by one school of thought are reported in terms of the premisses of another. If the sophists assumed the validity of human opinion as forming the raw material of discourse, and that this material became clarified and pragmatically effective in the course of intercommunication, then properly speaking no metaphysical distinction could be drawn between the language and its content, the discourse and its subjects. The science of one is the science of the other. This was anathema to Plato's formal realism and it was perfectly proper for his own philosophy to insist on the separation between the formal content of intellectual competence (*episteme*) and the mere discourse or words in which men voiced their thoughts and feelings.

Pressing the same kind of distinction upon Gorgias, Plato in his dialogue the *Gorgias* succeeds in narrowing down the Gorgian science of communication to the limits of a merely verbal rhetoric:

> Soc. Do you think Gorgias would consent to engage in dialogue with us? I want to find out from him what is the effective force of his technique, and what he professionally claims to give instruction in . . . [*Gorg.* 447b9ff.].
>
> (Socrates to Gorgias) Gorgias, please tell us personally how should one identify your intellectual competence? What technique forms its subject?
>
> GORG.: (The technique of speech or) rhetoric, Socrates.
>
> Soc.: You are to be identified as a (speech expert or) rhetorician?
>
> GORG.: And I may add a good and mighty one, allowing, that is, that I can, Homeric fashion, carry the title I claim for myself.
>
> S.: Certainly you may.
>
> G.: I accept your compliment . . . [449a2ff.].
>
> S.: And what is the reality which forms the subject of that scientific competence which is rhetorical technique?
>
> G.: (Verbal expression or) discourse, Socrates . . . [449d9ff.]. The science of most technologies deals almost wholly with manufacture and similar activities. (Speech technique or) rhetoric has no such manufactured product. Both its material and its accomplishment are (verbal expression or) discourses. Therefore I claim that the subject of (speech technique or) rhetoric is simply 'discourse' [450b6ff.].

The suggestion thus conveyed of a Gorgian rhetoric divorced from responsibility for its content is reinforced in a companion piece of reporting given in Plato's *Meno* by a disciple:

> You will never hear Gorgias committing himself to this proposition [viz. that the instruction he gives is in 'virtue']. Indeed he derides the claim in others, too; what he thinks one ought to do is to produce skill in speech [*Meno* 95cff.].

The antithesis here is framed in terms of the Platonic assumption that the objective in all instruction must be moral education, and that this depends upon intellectual training in first principles.

But the antithesis falsifies the context in which sophistic training was conceived and the purposes it was designed to serve, the context being parliamentary practice, and the purpose being the formulation and execution of political policy.

The stuff or raw material, so to speak, of this operation was discourse or it was nothing. Hence Gorgias correctly says that the 'material' with which rhetoric works is 'discourses'. But that his mind already viewed this material as being deployed in an arena of public policy-making is seen from what Plato allows him to say as the dialogue called *Gorgias* gathers further momentum:

Soc.: Rhetoric then is precisely one of those techniques that transacts and executes everything by means of discourse.
GORG.: Yes.
S.: What then among possible realities is the subject of this discourse employed by rhetoric?
G.: The field covers those transactions of human beings which are supreme and most excellent . . . [*Gorg.* 451d1ff.].
S.: What is this thing which as you allege human beings find most excellent and of which, you say, you are the architect?
G.: As it is in very truth the most excellent thing we have, Socrates, it is also the ground of our freedom as human beings, and equally the ground of the government we exercise as individuals over our fellows in our respective cities.
S.: Meaning what?
G.: The power of persuasion by means of discourse exercised upon judges in a court and on councillors in a council and assembly members in an assembly – in short in every group combination which is civic and responsible . . . [452d3ff.].
S.: You mean that rhetoric is the architect of persuasion; this is its entire business, its sum and substance?
G.: Yes . . . [453a2].
S.: What type of persuasion? What is its subject? . . . [454a8].
G.: The type is that exercised in courts and in other group gatherings, and the subject is always the rights and the wrongs (of any issue) . . . [454b5ff.].
S.: . . . whenever the city holds a meeting to elect doctors or shipwrights . . . [455b2] clearly it is the man with the best

technical equipment who has to be picked. . . . [455b5]. If then anyone associates with you, what capacity for public counsel will he acquire? Will it cover just subjects of right and wrong, or the technical topics as well? . . . [455d2ff].

G.: . . . You know, don't you, that these dockyards and walls and the building of the harbour resulted from the counsel of Themistocles, or else of Pericles, but not of the craftsmen as such?

S.: So they say about Themistocles. As for Pericles, I heard him myself when he took part in our decision about the middle wall.

G.: As to the selection of the technical experts you mentioned, observe how the orators are the ones who give the counsel and are the authors of the opinion that prevails . . . [455d8ff.].

Plato for his own purposes is going to oppose the technique of persuasion, viewed as a manipulation of 'possible beliefs' operating in the field of fluid opinion, to the stringent discipline of scientific instruction which explores formal relationships dependent upon axioms which exist *a priori*. The one, from his standpoint, is immoral and lacking in intellectual integrity; the other provides the sole foundation for an inner integrity of soul in tune with unchanging verities. He has a perfect right on his own premises to view the sophistic technique of public communication in this hostile light. But sophistic's own premises were quite different. And it is false to argue that its technique was in fact politically ineffective or morally irresponsible. It sought to be the means of clarifying great public issues, such as: Shall we build the Piraeus? The problem offers itself pragmatically and historically in a given moment of time. That is precisely Plato's objection. But equally it is precisely the kind of problem that democratic politics is called on to decide. It will be argued *pro* and *con*, and the debaters will frame their views in terms of what is right and proper, wrong and improper.

Gorgias is not given a chance to demonstrate how the pragmatically right thing to do in a given situation could be clarified by debate and executed by common agreement. He would have to postulate the existence of a common denominator, and even of a common mind, resident in the members of the group, which they don't themselves know that they have; but the competing orators then take over and bring the audience to realize their decision. This is the total process, which his example is designed to illustrate, and which was outlined in the speech of Prodicus in the *Protagoras*.

The technique of persuasion, as Plato pursues it to what he conceives to be its logical conclusion, through the mouths of his puppets 'Polus' and 'Callicles', turns into an emotional domination exercised by an unscrupulous mind over the masses. But Gorgias has already been allowed to speak to this point for himself:

> As it is in very truth the most excellent thing we have, Socrates, it is also the ground of our freedom as human beings, and equally the ground of the government that we exercise as individuals over our fellows in our respective cities [*Gorg.* 452d5ff.].

This is a broad hint that sophistic distinguished between power which used sheer force as its instrument, and that power exercised in free assemblies, which has to rely on the effects of communication, and therefore on consent. The abolition of power-relations themselves can never be the issue in politics except in Utopia. It is the methods by which power is held and exercised that make all the difference. The sophists were here not so far behind the nineteenth-century liberalism of Mill. Plato would have substituted a political police enrolled in the service of all wise autocrats. Persuasion, in short, is the art of leadership in a free assembly. Protagoras had admitted, as we saw, that its facilities were likely to be at the service of the more privileged who had had a better education. In fact the sophists, always pragmatical, retained the formula of Democritus and indeed of Solon: 'Only the superior should hold office'. But the whole point is that they have to persuade, and cannot use force, and the act of persuasion to be effective must engage at some level with the minds of those being persuaded, for they do the voting and make the decisions.

Neither leadership in persuasion nor the voting of the common decision was conducted in a vacuum. Aside from the fact that the common mind exists, so to speak, sociologically and generally, what is there that guarantees its specific existence in a given pragmatic situation? What guarantees that it will emerge as a coherent point of view responsive to a given issue? It is the presence in every pragmatic situation of a 'more expedient' and a 'less expedient' line of policy: the factors in any situation calling for decision are complex, but as they are debated the direction of a general utility emerges. This is why, despite the tone of the later parts of the *Gorgias*, sophistic discourse was never conceived as politically irresponsible. It sought to actualize the politically good and socially useful. Here let Protagoras speak again for sophistic as he is allowed to in the *Theaetetus*:

> I am far from denying that intelligence is a real thing, and the intelligent man a real person. But my definition of the intelligent man is as follows: In the judgment of anyone of us, a thing may appear bad and is bad; the intelligent man can change this judgment and make the thing to appear good and to be good [*Theaet*. 166d5ff.].

Good judgment for Plato is based on absolutes resident outside time and place and circumstance. And the term 'is' for Plato indicates the eternal validity of such goodness, which therefore is also eternally 'true'. For sophistic, 'good' is the index of a pragmatic and political solution to a given social need. It is concrete, empirically determined, and 'is' only for as long as the need which evokes it exists also. Thus for sophistic the terms 'good' and 'is' (a) do not have eternal validity and cannot be true in a Platonic sense; but equally (b) they have some political social validity independent of the mere whims of individuals, even though those whims enter into the equation. This intermediate and political validity was for Plato inconceivable. Hence in reporting Protagoras he washes out the political and parliamentary references and the pragmatism, and represents the 'good' and the 'is' of Protagoras in stark opposition to the eternal good and the constant 'is' of Platonism. This forces these terms as used by sophistic to descend abruptly to the level where they are merely indexes of individual whim, capricious relativity, unredeemed flux, which the 'intelligent' man, that is the skilled speaker, can manipulate to and fro, guided only by his own corresponding whims. It is much the same picture as is given of rhetoric in the *Gorgias*.

The character of this misrepresentation is betrayed by the terms in which 'Protagoras' is allowed to develop the defence of his formula as the dialogue *Theaetetus* proceeds:

1. A man may have an inferior psychic condition, and so form opinions which correspond.

2. But a superior condition can influence him to form a second set of opinions corresponding to this superior condition.

3. These latter [impressions] are by some labelled the 'true' ones, but this reflects a lack of empiricism.

4. In my view the second set is 'better' than the first but not 'truer' [*Theaet.* 167b1-4.].

While this paragraph does not yet reveal precisely what is the reference of the terms 'superior' and 'better' as Protagoras uses them, it makes it quite clear that they are not simply labels for whatever a given individual happens to prefer at the moment. They do not simply identify 'my' notion of what is good, for it is presumed that 'I' may have an inferior mental or psychic condition which causes any opinions I have to be inferior or bad. By 'bad', Protagoras means, we suggest, 'not useful in a given context', precisely as he had used the word 'bad' in those pragmatic examples put forward in the *Protagoras*. What Plato wishes to emphasize is that these pragmatic 'goods' cannot be said to be true in any *a priori* sense; and he makes Protagoras admit this. But the admission, while wholly relevant to Platonism, is irrelevant to the pragmatism of Protagorean politics.

That the reference of Protagoras is to political utility emerges as he proceeds:

5. What do I mean by the intelligent man? Dealing with bodies, he is a doctor; dealing with growing things he is an agriculturalist.

6. Yes, even an agriculturalist, when dealing with a growing thing which is unwell, can be said to replace inferior sensations by superior and healthy ones.

7. Similarly the orator deals with a city.

(8. Cities have opinions as to what is right and wrong. They may think the bad is right and the good is wrong.)

9. The superior and intelligent orator is he who can replace an opinion which identifies the right thing with the bad thing by one which identifies the right thing with the good thing [*Theaet.* 167b5-c2].

This very interesting passage invites four observations. Firstly as we have said, 'good' and 'superior', 'bad' and 'inferior' are intended to index judgments of political policy. Reverting to the *Gorgias* and the example given there, we can say it was 'good', that is, politically expedient at the time, to build the Piraeus. But many opinions of individual voters were otherwise. These reflected an 'inferior condition' and 'inferior sensations' (items 1 and 6) on their part; that is (if we may supply a missing item in the theory) a disposition which was not in tune with the need invoked by the circumstances, and the environment human and social. Secondly, the power of the orator is conceived as politically responsible. An intelligent orator is one who is in tune with needs. His task, therefore, is to convert opinion into the same channel as his own. His weapon is verbal persuasion and, if he is not properly equipped with it, his effort may fail. Thus sophistic oratory is intended to be the instrument of a morally responsible statesmanship. The leaders in a democracy have two qualifications, (a) they have a more intelligent understanding of need than their audiences; and (b) they are better able to express their opinions in words. (c) We could add that since these opinions are based on a proper response to environment, the decisions to which they win over their audiences will, when accepted, prove to be what they wanted all the time, hence they will be 'natural' and produce consensus.

Thirdly, items 5 and 6 recall the fact that in the *Protagoras*, when trying to explain his pragmatic conception of good and useful, the same speaker resorted to the practices of medicine and agriculture, not just as analogies, but as instrumental illustrations of how 'the good thing to do' is related to specific cases and to different organic specifications in each case. It would appear that sophistic viewed political problems and decisions as exhibiting the same kind of instrumental diversity, and as calling for a complex and flexible method of estimating the expedient in given cases. Fourthly, in appealing to the agriculturalist method of improving growing things (by substitution of correct soil and fertilizer and other conditions as set forth in the passage in the *Protagoras*) as a proper analogy for politics, Protagoras reverts to that naturalism of the anthropologists which supplied the foundations of sophistic political theory. This viewed men in their cosmic context as a species of growing things that are alive upon the earth's surface. Hence also a 'superior' disposition politically means one which is in tune with the needs of the social environment and responsive to them, as Protagoras envisages a healthy plant responding to soil and sunlight.

'Man is the measure of all', said Protagoras, 'of the things that are, that they are, and the things that are not, that they are not'. It was intended as a controversial statement when he made it and it has remained so, famous or notorious according to one's point of view. The word 'measure' raises issues of epistemology. The sophists were rationalists, not intuitionists, not mystics, nor even sceptics. The human panorama was a process but it had a rationale, it made sense. Human relations have an inherent normality, which is yet flexible and can be continually adjusted. By what standard was that judgment to be formed which carried out the adjustment?

That statement of Protagoras recently quoted from the *Theaetetus* drew a basic distinction between the 'good' thing and the 'right' thing. In practical politics, they are not necessarily identical. The opinions of a citizen of inferior psychic condition will identify as 'right' a thing which is bad. This semantic split between good and right, bad and wrong, Plato found intolerable, and in his pages anyone who defends such a split is tarred with the brush of moral irresponsibility or logical relativism. But sophistic must continue to be evaluated within the terms of its own premises, not those of Plato. The statement made by Protagoras in the *Theaetetus* continues with the following significant sentences:

> 10. The kind of opinions formed about what is right and wrong in any given city do in fact constitute right and wrong for that city, as long as the opinion persists as a custom.
> 11. What intelligence can do is to replace inferior opinions on several appropriate occasions by superior ones, making them exist, and also exist as opinions [167c4ff.].

Item 10 reveals that for Protagoras, as for Democritus, our notion of what is 'right' (the term 'just' had better be excluded here, precisely because the modern word 'justice' is controlled by Plato's absolutes) is formed historically as the response to the needs of the social group. The primary need is for material security, and secondarily for an ordered stable set of relationships. The complex set of sanctions and habits that results is the city's version of what is 'right': its custom-law. There Democritus had left the problem. Sophistic focused attention upon the parliamentary process by which, in effect, continual adjustments in the system of 'right' and custom are carried out. It confronted the question: Why should adjustment occur at all? If it does occur, is there any rationale which can guide or steer the process? That vehicle by definition cannot be itself the 'right' and the 'proper' or the 'customary', for these represent the existing pattern, not the needed adjustment. Some other power, therefore, is operative upon the pattern; if we accept the evidence of the Protagorean statements in the *Theaetetus* and the *Protagoras*, this other power was identified by sophistic as the 'good', the 'useful' or the 'healthy'. These terms as distinct from right or proper (*dikaion* and *kalon*) were made the criteria of political action. Now, these are not symbolic of permanent and unchanging laws, but of pragmatic solutions to temporal and historical needs: a decision to raise taxes, to build a harbour, to declare war or make a peace, and so forth. These involved a flexible and pragmatic skill in determining the 'useful' and the 'good' in given cases and contexts, whether the area was that of economic or political knowledge. What is good for horses is not good for men. But men do need good horses. If we should ask: Is there then any permanent reality within which this flexible operation is conducted? – the answer would be: Yes, the historical process and progress of man, taken as a whole, taken as given, and taken as good. It is inherent in this process and part of it that man himself, at a given stage of cultural development, is called on to control it in part by his own political decisions. The sophists may have avoided giving such a complete philosophical answer.

If what is 'lawful' represents the presently established group opinion as to the way things ought to be; if the 'right' thing to do means merely what accords with this present group opinion in a given case; if the 'good' thing to do represents a response to some fresh pragmatic need; and if the present 'right' has to be brought into line with this need – it is clear that 'man', both in society and as individual, is indeed himself the criterion and the measure of all that is lawful, right and good. For practical purposes the measure is to be found in his half-realized opinions of what he must do, but with the important provision that these may need clarification in relation to new needs, and hence are continually subject to improvement, a process in which superior intelligence and persuasion play a vital role.

On this showing, when Protagoras said: 'Man is the measure', he did not and could not by definition distinguish man generic from man individual, since the individual for him only exists as a social being whose opinions emanate from his group relations. When he went on to say 'measure of the things that are that they are', he refers to the things that are lawful or right or good. The context in which the aphorism is framed is the life and action of man himself.

But Greek thinkers had already begun to view 'what is' in a quite different context, as indicating those concepts or relations or equations which might support the structure of the physical cosmos, a structure external to and independent of human action. This, the pre-Socratic geometric vision of reality, was in effect the vision which captured the allegiance of Plato, who merely transferred the co-ordinates to fit the life and habits of man as well. Thus sophistic, as reported by Platonism, is inevitably judged by the fierce yet cold light of metaphysics. Social custom and right, evolving as an historical growth, were turned into cosmic justice and law; and the famous Protagorean aphorism became interpreted as a relativist attack upon an idealist morals which actually came into existence only after Protagoras was dead.

CHAPTER X

ANTIPHON

O F those thinkers of Greece who in the classical age made contributions to the liberal or democratic school of political theory, only two are documented by their own utterances. Antiphon shares this distinction with Democritus, and even he only because of an accident. Papyrus fragments of his work preserved in Egypt were recovered in this century. Later antiquity was not interested in reporting him, and it is easy to see why. His embittered criticism of the society of the city-state was far too fundamental to be regarded as viable. Those were the centuries in which the spiritual hold of Athens over the imaginations and minds of men grew ever stronger as the memory of her political power receded.

In Greek liberalism, it is only the mental temper which is constant. The vocabulary changes, the ideology shifts direction. To chart its course with precision is a speculative task, impossible but for the twin guide-posts supplied by the *ipsissima verba* of these two men. It is not that the two thinkers are alike; in fact, they represent within the liberal camp diametrically opposed positions. But these positions are determinable, the connection between them is discernible, and the future course of liberalism, once their joint influences have united, becomes predictable.

The chronology of Antiphon's life, nay, his very identity, is in doubt. We may say at once that it is wholly improbable that our Antiphon, the 'Sophist', so-called, was the same man as the orator and politician admired by Thucydides and executed in 411 for his oligarchic leadership. But any attempt to identify the sophist's own generation depends on what seems to be his doctrinal relationship to other thinkers of the time. The attempt is better postponed until his own words have spoken and have been interpreted.

These words do indeed exhibit one trait which links Antiphon with Democritus. They are often phrased in the participial style of ancient case-law. This is not accidental. Both thinkers, pioneers in their subject, attempt to formulate social theory not in the light of principles conceived outside politics, as in the manner of the Socratics, but in the idiom of custom-law itself as it existed in formulas at once traditional and also basic to the corporate life of the actual Greek community. Only, while Democritus sought by rationalizing these formulas to accept them into a body of social theory, Antiphon, by the acid of his criticism, seeks to expose and disintegrate them.

Antiphon is an angry man; and angry men are not given to coherence of argument. If to anger is added wit, satire will render readable what would otherwise not be read. But Antiphon has no wit; he registers his scores against society in a jagged dialectic, a style oddly compounded of pedantry and passion, curiously moving when the phrases are separated and spelled out. But he cannot organize a smooth Socratic discourse. He hurls his principles at the reader before he has made clear their application; he argues his conclusions before he has brought in his evidence for them; he indicts the enemies of mankind before he has identified them. The passage which more than any other has made him notorious opposes the demands of nature to the rule of law so imperatively and cynically that it reads like an open invitation to every kind of immorality. Cynic he certainly was, but behind his cynicism lies the driving force of impassioned principles. It is better to consider his attacks on law in the light of these principles, so far as the mutilated record allows their substance to be recovered and presented.

I

[*FVS*[6] 87 B44; 2.352. B.23ff.]

... but if a man be of lowlier family
we feel no awe for him and show him no veneration.
This is a case where
in our [social] relations with each other
we have 'barbarized' ourselves.
For by nature all of us in all things are constituted alike
both barbarian and Hellene.

There is evidence available
in the [area] of those [resources] which by nature are essential
to all human beings ...

ANTIPHON

... and in this [area] barbarian and Hellene among us are not
definable separately.

For we all use our mouths and nostrils
to draw breath in and out of the atmosphere
and we all . . .

It is useful to begin with this passage, fragmentary though it is,
for the argument by which it is concluded establishes once and
for all the continuity of Antiphon with that naturalism represented in Democritus, which drew from the Greek anthropologies.
Man is an animal, with mouth and nose, and he is an item in that
physical cosmos from which he respires the air by which he lives.
This animal is of a single species, identifiable by common traits.
So far as the species is concerned, these are universals, and they
are biologically determinate. Antiphon's breathless logic tele-
scopes two arguments which support this common identity: first,
the biological identity of the human organs, and second the
physical identity of their common resource, the air. It is therefore
established, as for Democritus, that the foundations for an
analysis of human behaviour must be naturalist, scientific and
biological; the reverse of idealist or teleological. In estimating man
and his behaviour, you begin not with the mind but with the lungs.

But, starting from these 'zoogonic' premisses, shared by his
predecessors, in what a very different direction is Antiphon then
steered! The biological identity of the species is pressed to its
logical conclusion: the division of mankind into castes and races
is a fictional creation. Stated thus, in general terms, the conclusion
might still be theoretically tolerable. But Antiphon is not concerned to spare the susceptibilities of his audience. He takes their
Pindaric pride in heroic inheritance, and their Hellenic sense of
a genius in themselves unique among the Mediterranean peoples,
and with a single squeeze of his logic he punctures them both.
Hellenes, so confidently Hellenic in dealing with barbarians,
suddenly find themselves 'barbarized' in their own racial family,
unable to speak each other's language, yammering and chattering
to each other across the barriers of caste, in all the incompre-
hensibility peculiar to lesser breeds without the law. It is an insight
worthy of Swift, but without Swift's gift of narrative fantasy to spell
it out for the pleasure of the imagination. Antiphon's intentions
are confined to stringent argument. What becomes of those nice

R   257

dialectical definitions of 'natural barbarians' (or 'slaves') versus the 'natural free man' (that is, Greeks)? They dissolve like smoke in the logic of his naturalism.

The positions of the philosophers have governing moods behind them. We know of Hobbes that the discipline of his deductive psychology obeys the political demands of his day, and has to lead to a throned authority of a monarch: of Locke, that his compound of principle and expediency, of rationalism and intuitionism, reflects the common-sense compromises of the Act of Settlement. Premisses to be defended are selected in the light of contemporary experience. What is the contempory mood of Antiphon? He writes as one who has seen through things: he has seen through Solon and civic virtue, and the city-state, and government based on the 'best people'. Wherever he belongs chronologically, he is in spirit not of the era of achievement but of the age of anxiety. He has emulated Democritus in one thing. As that earlier thinker prepared, in astronomy and metaphysics, to pass beyond the confines of the visible cosmos and let his mind range through an illimitable universe, so Antiphon is preparing in social thought to pass beyond the walls of Athens, of Sparta, of Thebes, into some kind of brotherhood of man.

What else he had to say in this area of his thinking is lost. But we can be sure that not for him was there any illusion that the road was easy, or that the values of the city-state were in any way compatible with this wider vision. Programmes of human brotherhood can be notoriously uplifting and also innocuous, provided they are divorced from the day's work and the way the world actually goes. This was not Antiphon's indulgence. He has more principles to argue, unaccommodating and maybe paradoxical, which like levers he prepares to thrust into the foundation stones of Greek society itself.

2a

[*FVS*[6] 2.353.1.1ff.]

. . . . . .

. . . if a man is held by [social] opinion as righteous,
to witness true report
in our [social] relations with each other
is taken as lawful for him . . .
and by the same token as 'useful' for the business of human beings.

But if it is true that
it is righteous to do wrong to no man if you are not wronged
yourself
then, if a man do the above, he cannot be righteous.

For if A give report of B,
even if he witness true report,
it is necessary that in some sense A do wrong to B
and that A in turn be wronged by B for what he said about
B . . .
. . . . . .
B, the object of the adverse report, finds himself 'caught',
and loses possessions or life
because of A, to whom he does no wrong.

This is a case where
A, by making B the object of his adverse report, does wrong
to him
in that A does wrong to a man who has done no wrong to him.

The Jewish Decalogue prohibits men from bearing false witness. The Sermon on the Mount exhorts men not to judge at all,
lest they be judged. Between these two there is a gulf, easily
bridgeable by those accommodators who would like to insist that
all men's moral insights are based on absolutes. But a gulf it is,
both historical and moral. Society for the Decaloguist rests on
legal sanction properly administered. For the New Testament,
society is a shell within which, and in despite of which, the soul
of man must find its own private norms in communion with
another world.

There is a sense in which Antiphon also is obsessed with the
same contrast. Society for him is also only a shell. Being a Greek,
he is not other-worldly; he probably did not even believe in a
soul, as Democritus or Socrates might have done. What he does
perceive, exactly as Democritus before him did, is that society
rests upon a legal apparatus enforced by pains and disabilities.
But then, unlike Democritus, he refuses to recognize that the
machinery is compatible with or grows out of the biological
process. He refuses to allow that law has any genetic roots. On the
contrary, legal procedure violates the material needs of man at
every turn.

He is however a moralist as well as a naturalist. That is, he wants to keep and to use the terms 'right' and 'righteous', and to define them normatively, just as much as Democritus did. But, now, 'right' is no longer the positive right of group preservation, maintained by sanctions against the anti-social 'enemy'. It is the (negative) abstinence from all forms of aggression against a fellow human being.

If it is righteous to do wrong to no man if you are not wronged yourself. . . .

In this clause he exposes a basic premiss of his moral philosophy. It had precedent in the commonplaces of Greek morality. But Antiphon extracts it from such a context, posits it as unique and exclusive and mandatory, a sort of categorical imperative, and in so doing converts a relative truism into an acid criticism of contemporary custom and *mores*. This marks a shift, curious and decisive, in the Greek mood and temper. For Antiphon, virtue lies primarily in abstaining from hurt; he is tender-minded; he has turned inward; he would guard his private world from interference, rather than involve himself in group loyalties which carry with them the duty to participate in group protection.

The hurt to be avoided is in the first instance verbal. This is of course characteristic of a civilized and complex community in which direct action has been replaced by moral sanctions plus legal processes. Antiphon, then, here addresses himself in the first instance to what men say, as the initiating cause of what they subsequently do. Within these limits, we can say that the doctrine of personal non-aggression as the first norm of human behaviour has now made its appearance in Greece.

Using this as his weapon, he proceeds to a criticism and a subversion of the normal processes by which the social group enforces its sanctions and maintains 'justice'. It is not always possible to determine when Antiphon is thinking in terms of group pressures in general – the sanctions of public opinion – and when he is thinking of legal process, enforceable in legal institutions like the courts. It is indeed characteristic of his epoch, and of the vocabulary of his epoch (as we shall see) that he should confuse the two. The 'bearing of witness' he treats as always inimical to genuine righteousness, simply because it involves any two men in a sequence of mutual 'wrongs'. We can complain that he should not use the term 'wrong' so ambiguously. If A gives true testimony of B which happens to be adverse to B, wherein, we ask, can A be said to 'do wrong'? Antiphon's answer rests on a position which is fundamental to his argument, but which is defended or at least explained only later; the terms right and wrong as properly applied should identify only the purely personal effects of personal acts done to other persons. His premises virtually isolate the individual from society. They assume indeed that in terms of the natural realities society does not exist. This shows how far his biological naturalism will carry him. If our mouths and noses and the air we breathe and the feet we walk on are the realities of which we should keep reminding ourselves, this means that the unimpeded exercise of these functions, for each and all of us, is the one objective, and forms the one criterion of what is right and what should be. Fines, imprisonment or execution, social dislike or degradation are all alike violations of our 'natures'. If this makes legal process impossible, so much the worse for legal process.

2b
[*FVS*[6] 2.354.35ff.]

and A, by making B the object of his adverse report, is likewise wronged by him
in that, because of having given true report, he is hated by B,

and in that, aside from this hatred,
A, for the rest of his life, because he gave adverse report against B,
will have to be watchfully intent against him.

Hence A has turned B into an enemy of his,
meaning, B will say and do any harm he can to A.

Though this passage is continuous with the preceding, Anti-phon here weaves a new thread into his argument. He has stated the principle of personal non-aggression mathematically and bloodlessly in a formula characteristic of the Greek rationalist temper. You don't love your neighbour; you simply balance two zeros in two scale-pans; if he has not violated your right, you do not violate his. But if you break this principle by consenting to be an adverse witness, certain consequences follow which though mathematically certain have grave emotional and social bearings. The victim of your report will resent the initiative you have taken against him, and he will feel hatred for you. This hatred then becomes a force let loose with which you have to reckon for all your life, says Antiphon. It is quite concrete in its effects: hatred is not just an attitude; it issues in acts done to you: it means harm will be done to you, if possible at all, either verbally or otherwise.

Now if this is meant to describe the mutual reactions of parties to a legal suit (for the term 'witness' could apply to both plaintiff and defendant as well as third parties), it obviously inflates them out of all proportion to the usual facts. Men involved in legal proceedings need not become mortal enemies. Hence it is surely here that Antiphon's curious logic should be understood as a general logic, deductively applied rather in the Hobbesian manner to describe an over-all social condition, though one of which Antiphon, unlike Hobbes, wholly disapproves. His focus is upon a kind of interacting system of mutual fears and hates which is set going when you violate the strict non-aggression principle. In this system, we are converted from severe guardians of our private bliss into suspicious spies upon each other's moves and motives.

This whole business of social relations in which we artificially acquire enemies and so become enemies ourselves implies, surely, that in a state of nature we are rid of this kind of relationship and that we then feel and employ only spontaneous amity toward each other. Antiphon in the preserved fragments of this discourse does not say so. Was he like Rousseau in his utopian moods committed to the proposition that man in a state of nature is a brotherly and non-aggressive creature, whose friendly instincts get distorted by the corrupt influence of a society which expects him to 'bear witness'? This question seems rather fundamental for determining Antiphon's philosophical position: and yet it can only very cautiously be answered. Our documentation is insufficient. One can say that a good deal of his bitter criticism of law and social custom only makes sense if it depends ultimately on the premiss that man is naturally benign and seeks to express himself in amicable fellowship. But did Antiphon see this himself? Quite obviously he is no Callicles, arguing the right of the strong man to be strong. His social criticism takes a wholly different direction. But it is not quite clear whether he regarded hatred as the main impediment to nature's way of life or only one among others. It is not, indeed, clear that he was a systematic social thinker at all in the sense that Democritus certainly was. His penchant for sheer destructiveness in criticism may have been too much for him. Antiphon's utopianism, then, remains implicit rather than explicit. There are indeed a few more things that can be said about it, but they are best deferred until the present document has been fully reviewed.

2c

[*FVS*[6] 2.355.12ff.]

Now surely here are [resultant] wrongs
evidently of impressive proportions
the wrongs done to A
and the wrongs done by A.

For it cannot be that
(i) these results are right, if
(ii) it is wrong for A to do wrong to B if B has done no wrong
    to A.
No, of necessity
either (ii) is correct and (i) is false
or else (ii) is false and (i) is correct
or else (i) and (ii) are both false.

There is something undeniably Euclidean about this little paragraph. The argument is summed up and clinched in a sort of triumphant geometric demonstration. The use of the logic of exclusion has a Socratic twist to it. Enough of Antiphon's prose has now been presented for its effects to register. They justify the method of breaking it up into these short paragraphs, and resting the analysis on them taken separately. For, despite his thread of continuity, his excessively abstract thought continually polarizes itself around a little series of key words which he organizes repetitively in antithetical pairs. The clues to his over-all system, so far as he has one, occur in those passages where he combines or equates different pairs with each other.

Here the significant thing about this summation is that he makes it turn on an absolute antithesis between the symbols 'right' and 'wrong'. These words had definite and mutually exclusive meanings. His basic contention is that the whole system of reporting against a man, being hated by him, and guarding against him in turn, produces a series of actions and relations

which are 'wrongs', i.e. violations of something, acts of aggression
or interference. If not 'wrongs', they must be 'rights'. But how
can they be right if the original principle of non-aggression still
stands? Of the three alternatives which he then insists on thrusting
at us, only the first is of course to be taken seriously. The other
two are in the nature of *reductiones ad absurdum*, which, by excluding
all other possibilities leave number ii in possession of the moral
and logical field. Semantically, therefore, he wants right versus
wrong to stand. He is no immoralist. But he has his own passionate
definition of what they mean.

2d

[*FVS*[6] 2.355.25ff.]

It is evident that
to hold court, to give decision, to press arbitration to conclusion
are not righteous,
for that which benefits some
damages others.

In this case
if a man is benefited he is not wronged
but if a man is damaged he is wronged. . . .
. . . . . .

The papyrus fragment number 2, as we have called it, breaks
off with these lines in the middle of the argument. They seem to
identify the target of Antiphon's attack as explicitly the courts
and the legal process, but they are not so closely connected with
the preceding as to imply that he is now formally identifying the
main topic of his previous discourse. Rather, the courts in his mind
form that area of civic business in which unnatural behaviour,
elsewhere pervasive, is most conspicuously concentrated.

His onslaught on the legal apparatus is total: his condemnation
absolute. He is not moved by specific inequities nor interested
in possible reforms. By his own rigid standards of right as identical
with non-aggressive behaviour, legal process is simply wrong.
'To hold court' (*dikazein*) in Greek is 'to handle rights' (*dikai*), and
Antiphon may be punning upon the assonance, with that verbal
irony peculiar to early prose writers. 'Courts-of-right' do not
really handle 'rights' at all, he implies. It is interesting that he

includes the process of arbitration in his condemnation, where however his emphasis is on pressing it to conclusion. In another sense one could argue that Antiphon's moral position required in fact that arbitration as a means of settling disputes be substituted for the procedures of 'justice'. But he is not interested enough in social mechanisms to say this, and his utopian tendencies perhaps precluded him from entertaining the thought that disputes in a state of nature need arise at all. The note of philosophical anarchism is unmistakable. Society and its inter-relations and its elaborate machinery for preserving justice in these relations has turned sour.

In the same breath he supports his attack by advancing a new criterion and a fresh antithesis. Right and wrong are identified with 'benefit' and 'damage'. Indeed, it is possible that this passage formed only the beginning of a whole section of his treatise in which legal process was subjected to the criticism that it did not meet the requirements of a utilitarian calculus. This would be, in a manner, anticipating Bentham. The compression of Antiphon's style is evident, for the transition introduces a new chapter in his thinking. The fragments give us no systematic statement or defence of this calculus and its rationale. It will intrude again in other portions of his work, but it can be said at once that 'benefit' and 'interest' and 'pleasure' are used by Antiphon as correlatives, in antithesis to 'damage', 'non-interest' and 'pain'. Thus his utilitarianism has hedonist overtones, but they are a little complicated and can be reserved until we come to them.

The criterion of utility we treat first: justly so, for it is here equated with the criterion of right. Utilitarianism in Greek thought has received only incidental notice from historians. It has been crowded into a corner by Plato's idealism and Aristotle's teleology. Yet even Plato's Form of The Good when applied tends to be the Form of The Useful. As was said in an earlier chapter, the fifth century saw the development of a vocabulary of moral evaluation, a vocabulary which Plato sought to arrange systematically in his writings. The Greek intellect, at once practical and rational, engaged in a quest for what might be called an operational definition of ancient and revered terms. In place of honorific emphasis on what was solemn, proper, lawful or traditional, in the manner of Hesiod and the poets, the intellectualist *avant-garde* sought actually to describe what these might mean as symbols of preferred human behaviour. They came up with a solution that can be described as instrumental. The right thing, at a minimum, is the technically effective thing, the useful thing and the applicable thing. It works. This functionalism was reinforced from two quarters: medicine on the one hand used the terms benefit and damage to identify the conditions which produce health and disease – conditions mainly of environment and diet; anthropology on the other, examining the genesis of technology and society, and looking for a label which would describe their motivation in terms, so to speak, of a lowest common denominator, found it in *need*, and in that utility and serviceableness which satisfy need. If human beings have gathered themselves together, organized governments and fostered various inventions, they have been doing so in response to the promptings of 'interest', and the cosmic resources which they have exploited thus become their 'utilities'. In this way, the terms in which man sought to describe his relation to his environment cease to be religious and mythical and become operative and functional.

Hence all theories of society, on which political theories in turn were built, tended to assume utility and interest as normative concepts by which to describe the goals of technological progress and the values promoted by social institutions.

This digression has relevance for we have now had enough of Antiphon to appreciate his link with the anthropologists – his whole underlying premiss of a state of nature derives from them – and with medical biology. Man is an animal, his physique and the manner of its normal functioning, the very process of breathing, are where you begin before deciding how man or man's society should behave. Yet there is a paradox in Antiphon's use of the utilitarian calculus, and it grows plainer the more his words are explored. Utility, unlike hedonism, is a banner for the socially conscious to wave. Its relevance in Greek thought is primarily addressed to the task of the political management of men in their relations with each other. Democritus, we have seen, introduced a hint of the calculus precisely in this context. But equally, this is precisely the kind of problem to which Antiphon is most indifferent. Indeed, he has already taken a little fling at this kind of utility when he said

To witness true report . . . is taken as . . . useful for the business of human beings,

266

where he may be attacking that school of political theory which
sought to interpret civic institutions or sanctions as social utilities.
This indeed was basically the position of Democritus, who thus
represents the application of utilitarianism to the ethos of a
period of confidence, when society, much as it is, is accepted.
Antiphon's brand, in a period of personal retreat and rejection
of society, draws closer to the narrower and biological frame of
mind which measured utility in terms of a man's private digestive
reactions to the food he eats.

3a
[*FVS*⁶ 2.346.6ff.]

. . . righteousness . . .
to avoid breaking the lawful usages
of the [particular] city where citizenship is operative.

If a human being is to follow that [form of] righteousness
most [compatible] with interest
he should when attended by the testimony of reporters
treat the customs-and-laws as sovereign
and when [he finds himself] isolated from reporters
[substitute] the [rule] of nature.

Two surviving portions of Antiphon's work, each fragmentary,
have now been considered. The third and longest is introduced by
the words quoted above. They have made his philosophy notorious. The first impression they unavoidably create is of a profound
cynicism. Is he inviting the citizen to indulge in malpractice on
the sly while observing a Pecksniffian hypocrisy in public? If so,
Antiphon is not a serious thinker. But we have had before us
evidence that he is, and the sentiments to which he now exposes
us, for all of their crudity, deserve to be read in the light of
principles already expounded. A utopian thinker, devoted to a
kind of Golden Rule of non-aggression, fiercely critical of social
and legal machinery which he thinks artificially makes man the
enemy of man, is not likely without warning to confront us
with the leering visage of an immoralist. He would have to be a
Dr. Jekyll and Mr. Hyde to do so. One could explain this advice
here given as ironic, intended as a satire on current hypocrisies,
not to be taken as a serious statement of Antiphon's own precepts,
were it not for the fact that the rule of nature, as we now well

know, is the rule he thoroughly approves of. He cannot then be describing the secret behaviour of hypocrites of whom he would disapprove. The truth rather seems to be that hypocrisy as measured by stern idealist standards is something for which he has a large measure of sympathy.

The first clue to his philosophical intention lies in his application of the word 'righteous'. We have seen that he takes it seriously; but also that he wishes to substitute for the conventional and honorific use an operative meaning which will relate itself to the biological needs which govern a human being. The syntax of the word righteousness in the first incomplete sentence is unclear. What he proposes of it in the second is that righteousness be the symbol of a flexible behaviour-pattern which involves a double standard. Idealists of all schools would violently object. What Antiphon insists on is that you accept society as a necessity and get on terms with it, even though its rescripts be arbitrary. For society's reporters can be dangerous to you. But reserve a private area of judgment where your behaviour can be natural and can rest on the conscious integrity of a value-system that makes sense and is real. He does not ask the citizen to carry his values into the public domain. The Cynic philosophers who did so could never claim Antiphon as their prophet. He renounced that intellectual rigour in logic, as in life, which Antisthenes shared with all the Socratics and which made him suitable to serve as a Cynic pattern. Antiphon's frame of reference is the biological organism, not the geometric theorem, even though he will on occasion argue geometrically. The organism accommodates contradictions and indeed grows by them.

What his special kind of cynicism, if that be the term for it, does is to validate a way of thinking and living which has become increasingly common in the twentieth century, though it has, to be sure, remained persistent in all epochs. It may be characteristic of ripe civilizations that they tend to nourish a split between private judgment and public observance. He is the first Greek candid enough to see this. In a sense, then, he is not a political theorist at all. For he despairs, it seems, of making the social apparatus conform to those organic intuitions which he insists should guide the actual living human being. His principles, though fiercely held, are those of a purely private integrity. There is a complete antithesis between his law of nature, as we might call it, and that majestic conception of natural law which came into vogue under Rome. We observe that to identify the goal which a sensible but also a sensitive man will pursue he employs the term 'interest', as he has already employed 'utility'. The formula, then, by which a human being fulfils his real interest turns out to be a rather flexible behaviour-pattern. We might object: if your genuine human being requires the law of nature to fulfil himself, how does he avoid compromising his true interest when he makes the necessary public concessions to social convention? Antiphon has no answer for this: he seems to assume that legal or moral collision with society is painful and therefore to be avoided by compliance where necessary. But would not such compliance bring with it a pain, a frustration of its own? Maybe it would, and may be Antiphon would argue that the law and custom of the group is our form of 'necessity', an inherited curse that we must do the best we can with.

This same paragraph in which he resumes the problem of the human being's relation to witnesses who will report on him introduces the term law (*nomos*). We have earlier suggested that though he includes positive law and the legal process that enforces it in his criticism, his philosophical target is wider and comprehends what we would regard as the non-legal effects of social sanctions; that in fact he is attacking the *mores* and conventions of society no less than the courts. He here defines the usages to which we must give lip-service as those

of the particular city where citizenship is operative.

This qualification is very significant. It shows that he is prepared to recognize law explicitly as local custom and therefore as variable. Traditionally, the Greek mind had been prepared to accommodate under the term *nomos* two formal contradictions: local custom on e one hand, and divine law on the other. The distinction had not bothered Herodotus, and Democritus, intent on rationalizing the methods by which the social group subsists and coheres, was quite prepared to accept custom as a social dynamic which 'did good' to man's way of life. Antiphon's hostility, by separating *nomos* from human good, has the effect of defining the laws more precisely and narrowly as mere customs and accepted usages, both various and arbitrary. However, within this narrower conception even he is unable as yet to distinguish sharply between positive written law and unwritten usage. He can switch to and fro between legal process in court on the one hand and trial by neighbours or 'public opinion' on the other. He is not clearly aware of the difference, nor perhaps was any Greek till some time later. Would he have written differently if he had realized the difference? Probably not, for the target of his profound pessimism is, after all, any social system considered as a complex of imperatives which involve the citizen in artificial strains and tensions. This is not to say that the activities of informers in the Athenian courts, a class already obnoxious to Aristophanes, may not have given Antiphon his cue. But he generalizes the sort of thing they represent as though the citizen walked always on a narrow, treacherous path between social perils which might seize on him and devour him at any moment. These are the accents of a society in transition, perhaps defeated in war, insecure and confused; or rather, they are the accents of a civilized human being who feels himself drawing away from such a society. It is symptomatic that Antiphon twice speaks of the 'lawful usages' rather than just 'laws' to describe those social imperatives to which he counsels public conformity. He probably felt that the element of custom in Greek *nomos* was primary, as indeed it was. Hence its translation is best rendered, though clumsily, by the combination custom-and-law.

'Law' has now entered the lists against 'nature'; the antithesis made so familiar by textbooks is now before us; but not in that context in which Plato placed it, a context faithfully imitated by idealist historians of recent periods. Idealism in fact, by interpreting the 'nature' of the liberals as arrogant self-assertion, and its own law as co-operation, harmony and fellowship, reversed Antiphon's meaning, even as it sought to destroy the effect of his criticism. What we are struck by in his own philosophy is how, within the city-state, an area of private resource and judgment has now been defiantly asserted. No wonder patriots and idealists and group-thinkers of all persuasions could not stomach his gospel. He does not say so, but so far as the city-state claimed priority over men's allegiance and was identified with the ideal of the good life, to this extent he declared war on it. The *polis* is no longer the mistress adored, but a necessary incubus, something of a harlot in the demands that she makes on our insincerities.

And her 'law' has therefore its limits. It is a tyrant, but tyrants can be flattered and evaded when they cannot be fought. The estimate of law's irresponsible power is matched by the reservations of judgment which set that power at a spiritual distance from the private man. Any subject of a totalitarian state – and the city-state had its totalitarian aspects – and indeed, citizens of a democracy, in this present age of war and anxiety, know what Antiphon meant.

3b

[*FVS*[6] 2.346.23ff.]

The [prescriptions] of custom-and-law are reached by compact
but those of nature are [scientifically] essential;
and the [prescriptions] of custom-and-law being covenanted
  are not native growths
while those of nature being native growths are not covenanted.

Should a man transgress lawful usage
provided this passes unobserved by the parties to the covenant
he is separated from [social] demerit and [legal] penalty
and if it is observed, he is not [so separated];

but in the case of those [rules] which are nature's native organic growths
if a man applies [artificial] pressure to any of these in defiance of the feasible
the evil is no less, even if unobserved by all men,
nor any greater, though all men see it.

The damage inflicted rests not on [social] opinion
but on [objective] truth.

As a general [proposition]
the evidence so far received is in support of the following [conclusion]:
what is right, as constituted in terms of custom-and-law,
is mostly an enemy to nature.

It was remarked, à propos of Antiphon's attack on distinctions of caste and race, that he probably derived his principles from a genetic view of society which founded itself on anthropology. The present passage substantiates this inference, for it assumes a genetic or anthropological view of the origins of law. So far from having been given by the gods or framed by the wisdom of inspired law-givers, it is simply the embodiment of certain conventions or common agreements achieved by a given group of human beings. It is man-made. Here is that theory of law which views it as resulting from a social compact reached by society's members, a theory which, after being suppressed in classic Greek thought, was to revive and to enjoy a long and varied history in modern times.

Democritus, using a similar naturalism, and viewing the state as an historical growth, had advanced a parallel conception of the social contract by which the group delegates power to its government. But, though parallel, the conceptions are by no means identical. Democritus, accepting society as a supreme device of man's invention, was interested in substantiating the claims of government to exist and to serve the interests of group stability. Hence he focuses his attention on the relation of the state to its rulers as two parties between whom a limited contract is undertaken. Antiphon's whole bias precluded him from considering the basis of government seriously. What he did take seriously was the nexus of habit and custom which lies behind governments and which closes in on the citizen every day of his life. Hence he advances a theory not of contract between two parties, but of compact reached by many parties – a *homologia*, in the Greek, a sort of consensus, not a deposit made on trust. This readiness to get to the bottom of custom-law itself, as against the mere basis of sovereignty in the ruler, might be viewed as an advance on Democritus. Yet in a sense, because of Antiphon's peculiar bias, it is a cause of regression, so far at least as political theory is concerned. For he uncovers the foundations of custom-law only to destroy them, so far as he can. They are for him an artificial intrusion which weighs on the natural life of the individual; and in terms of his 'metaphysic' of the individual they do not represent anything that is real. His reasoning is that to be real they should take effect automatically: their virtue should be inherent. But this is not true. Their sanctions operate accidentally and unreliably, if someone happens to act as reporter of a violation. Later in the treatise he will argue that their positive succour, in defence of those who do not break them, is equally unreliable and accidental.

Thus he is still concerned with operational definitions. For any principle to be valid, it must be shown to work always. But his argument certainly involves him in a philosophical difficulty of his own making. If law is a compact reached historically by human beings, why is it not natural and organic as are other items in man's progress? It would seem that for Antiphon nature and convention are historical forces working against each other. Perhaps it is safe to suppose that though he borrowed from anthropology up to a point, he never accepted the full implications of the historical method which it made available. If he had used it to support the hypothesis that man's early condition was anarchic and that this was an ideal from which society, in the city-state at least, had artificially departed, his dialectic would make sense. But it is possible that his utopianism was never worked out systematically: it is hard to tell. His analogue temperamentally seems to be Rousseau, and certainly Rousseau managed to combine illogical elements, so why not Antiphon? Thus this passage paradoxically adds to political theory an important speculative contribution and yet in the same breath robs it of historical significance and relevance. Indeed, the passage poses acute and perhaps insoluble questions bearing on Antiphon's relationship to other political theorists. We know of two other versions of the social compact, both pre-Aristotle. In one, the formula was advanced positively and so to speak dynamically as both an historical justification of the necessity for law and as a basis for evaluating its provisions in the interests of human beings. Aristotle in one citation associates this theory with the name of Lycophron. The other version, as stated in the second book of Plato's *Republic*, gives a hostile account of the theory. The compact is represented cynically as a device by the weaker to keep the stronger in their place. This version shares with Antiphon the presumption that law is against nature; but the kind of human nature it is against is totally different. Is Antiphon's critique the ancestor, so to speak, of both these others? That is, does Plato seek to get rid of him by misrepresenting him, while Lycophron, seizing upon the valuable insight contained in the idea of compact, expands it to proper proportions? Or is Antiphon replying to a theory of compact already raised, and saying in effect: Yes indeed, law is a social compact, and as such, how frail and irrelevant to human nature! These problems will be canvassed and a solution proposed in the last chapter, but they are mentioned here to illuminate the specific character of Antiphon's rather peculiar position.

As against the compact, which is not operative automatically, the rules of nature operate with the precision of scientific laws like gravity. He calls them 'native organic growths'. Can we determine more precisely what he means? The compression of his thought is too hurried to allow him to illustrate as he should. But he must be thinking of a human being as an organism which, biologically speaking, requires the right food and so forth and needs freedom to develop spontaneous habits, an opportunity which is dependent on peaceful co-operation with the rest of his species; if co-operation is too strong a word, then certainly let us speak of amicable relationships which leave the person free to develop. Later we shall find him attacking the adverse effect of parental influence. He seems to feel that the human organism is like a plant which should be given soil and sunshine but left to itself; then it will grow naturally; if you deny it its natural condition, it will inevitably become distorted or stunted. If this is the line of his reasoning, Plato and Aristotle obviously borrowed from the same school of thought but adapted the requirements of human nature (*physis*) to a teleological setting. It is interesting that Antiphon speaks of the effects of artificial 'pressure' which can damage the human organism. A comparison with certain other sources may indicate that he is thinking of war, or at least of the necessity imposed by group-patriotism to engage in hostile relations with other men. Indeed, if his basic formula for right- eousness is non-aggression, it would follow that all forms of artificial social pressure amount to one result – the forcing of human beings into aggressive poses.

He then clinches his argument by referring the question to the standard of utility: the pressures imposed on nature by law do actual 'damage'. This operative criterion of what right and wrong really mean is, as we have already seen, inherent in his naturalism. And so he is brought to his conclusion with a flourish of denunciation:

> what is right, as constituted in terms of custom-law, is mostly an enemy to nature.

Perhaps his choice here of the very concrete symbol of 'enemy' to describe a logical antithesis is coloured by the conviction that custom-law does indeed sow actual enmity among men, whose unspoiled nature requires spontaneous amity to express itself.

3c

[*FVS*⁶ 2.348.2.30ff.]

It has been by custom-and-law determined
for the eye, what it is supposed to see and not see,
for the ear, what it is supposed to hear and not hear,
for the tongue, what it is supposed to say and not say,
for the hand, what it is supposed to do and not do,
for the foot, whither it is supposed to proceed and not proceed
for the heart, what it is supposed to want and not want.

But verily
in terms of what is more *versus* less amicable, more *versus* less proper to nature
there is no difference between what law averts human beings from
and what it exhorts them to do.

To be alive is a natural [condition]
as also is it to die
and, for human beings, to be alive is numbered among their interests
and to die, among their non-interests.

This assault on the severity of law is so whole-hearted that at first sight it might be interpreted as an attack on the kind of legislation which has been labelled 'Draconian', and of which it was said that the ancient laws of Athens were written in blood. Is Antiphon registering a humane protest against the wide application of the death penalty? His polemic is introduced by that Greek verb which would describe a lawgiver's function; and he seems to be pleading that legislation be framed so as to spare the lives of human beings –

To be alive is a natural condition . . .

This would place him in company with Protagoras as an advocate of at least mildness in the application of legal penalties, and perhaps as an opponent of the principle of retribution. Such a position would accord with his deep feeling for the inviolability of the human organism, in contrast to the legal severity which, in

275

the name of idealism, is exhibited so unpleasantly in Plato's *Laws*.

However, Antiphon's words, here as previously, suggest that his target is wider than the specifically legal aspects of civic life, even though it includes them. If it is true that custom-law for him ambiguously combines the effects both of positive legislation and also of unwritten usage, this suits better the detailed character of that control over eye, ear, tongue, etc., which he seems to be attacking. He speaks of the laws as both averting certain kinds of behaviour and also as exhorting or encouraging others. Positive written law tends increasingly to concentrate on the negative: it devises sanctions to prohibit anti-social acts, as Democritus saw, but leaves to the emerging individual an increasing area of private but positive moral choice. The law that Antiphon is attacking included that body of guidance and instruction which we would in a modern state identify with religious influence, family control and educational training.

The language in which he attacks the regulation of eye, ear, tongue, foot, hand and heart recalls the kind of advice which oral wisdom loves to enshrine in proverbial teachings. Were Antiphon acquainted with Judaic literature, we might suspect the influence of the wording of such a passage as the following from the Book of Proverbs:

> Keep your heart with all vigilance
> > For from it flow the springs of life.
> Put away from you crooked speech,
> > And put devious talk far from you.
> Let your eyes look directly forward
> > And your gaze be straight before you.
> Take heed to the path of your feet
> > Then all your ways will be sure.
> Do not swerve to the right or the left
> > Turn your foot away from evil.

Here indeed is legislation laid upon the heart, tongue, eye and foot, and it would be easy to garner from the same source some other directives laid upon ear and hand. But the idiom of such formulas as these was not the monopoly of any race or nation. The Greeks had their wisdom literature. Parallels can be sought, for example, in that collection which in later antiquity passed as the *Sayings of the Seven Wise* [*FVS*[6] 1.pp.63-66]. Of a total of

128 of these, some eleven counsel caution in the use of tongue and speech, a great variety counsel care, sobriety and so forth in exercising the choices of the heart. One saying actually urges the pursuit of a list of no less than twelve virtuous objectives. Six warn against pleasure or gain, five harp on the theme of deference to parents, two specifically urge obedience to the laws. With the spirit of such inhibiting advice it is easy to see that Antiphon would have little sympathy. Occasionally his teaching may be worded specifically to contradict an ancient saying. On the other hand, there are a few sayings in this collection which, benign in intention and tolerant in temper, seem to echo his teaching rather than contradict it. The truth is that the collection embodies different moral stratifications, ranging from primitive caution and harshness ('speak good of friends and evil of enemies'; 'envy but never pity'; etc.) to civilized relaxation, compassion and co-operation. If a loose corpus of such generalizations, designed in the first instance for instruction in home and school, continued to gather accretions during the fifth and fourth centuries before being frozen in the third, it is possible that the social and moral teaching both of Democritus and Antiphon not only was influenced by it, but exercised influence upon it.

Antiphon has been steadily attacking not particular social or legal abuses, but the very premisses which support the validity and the mechanisms of any lawful society as such. This paragraph on the control of hand and eye and foot helps to make it clear why he feels compelled to such fundamental criticism. He is in the name of man's specific biological nature (it would not have altered his direction if he could have spoken in terms of man's spiritual nature) protesting against the assumption that a tradition in which man is trained and to which he is artificially accustomed is either necessary or proper. The city-state which provokes his criticism had, for all its factionalism, a tenacious group-ethos, which made it, in one sense, and Pericles' Funeral Speech to the contrary, a closed society. This ethos, concretely speaking, embodied itself in a thousand acts and attitudes which custom-law encouraged and gave shape to. The character and typical re-actions of a citizen were literally controlled by a complex system of habituation. Aristotle saw this with perfect clarity and approved the process, and wrote his *Ethics* to describe how it worked. Antiphon before him saw it with equal clarity, and passionately strove to undermine and reject what Aristotle approved. He saw the whole complex system of tradition as first dividing Hellenes from non-Hellenes and then dividing Hellenes into cities, and dividing the cities into castes and families. Between all these socially conditioned divisions there was tension and enmity. 'Right' and 'wrong', not in Antiphon's sense but as currently employed, were labels used to evaluate the kind of behaviour which cordially responded to this system. That is, 'right' identified compliance with it and 'wrong' the reverse. The laws supplied the formulas by which deviation was punished and civic warfare arbitrated. They also were those precepts which drilled the youth in an ethos of obedience to the system and in specific habits of parental reverence, submission, discipline, oath-keeping, truth-telling; not to mention proper pride and hatred and courage and retaliation, when one's place in society requires them to be shown.

Thus Antiphon's over-all target is the grip of the group and its traditions, and its power to suppress individual human nature. It is ironic but understandable that he speaks here as though he were attacking the influence of Solon the Legislator, whose political liberalism had been well grasped by Democritus. There is epigraphical evidence that even written law included moral precept as well as legal enactment. Antiphon has his eyes fastened not on Solon's political and constitutional programme but on what he regards as the dead hand of that tradition which equally went by the name of 'the laws'.

Once more it is necessary to save him from an undeserved reputation as an immoralist. Bearing in mind that his frame of reference is drawn from anthropology, it is just to conclude that the kind of attack he directs on Greek *nomos* anticipates the sort of historical scholarship which has been able to trace the gradual emancipation of the individual from the group, and which has seen the right of private judgment as something won only lately and slowly against the claims of a value-system which are essentially primitive and cautionary. This constitutes Antiphon's claim to be included in the history of moral and political theory, even though he was long before his time. The right of the individual human being to act as judge over the very traditions that have nursed him was, indeed, in the air during his epoch. Otherwise he could never have written as he did. But it is equally true that the city-state had been and remained a closed corporation, with a strongly traditional culture, and that Antiphon confronting this fact had reason for his anger and frustration. Plato and Aristotle as they rejected the validity of public opinion upheld by the Elder Sophists rejected also the more extreme individualism of Antiphon. Plato indeed would have moved back the hands of the clock to where they had stood before even the hour of democratic reform had struck in the days of Solon.

Antiphon's critique of traditionalism rests itself on two arguments. The first is scientific, or at least logical. The law's effects are arbitrary: he has said this already: here he repeats the point. If nature is your criterion, it becomes impossible to make sense of custom, for its prescriptions may work for or against nature's needs. Hence Antiphon anticipates that conclusion which comparative anthropology tends to support, that group-custom whatever its origin may survive in the group less for its functional usefulness than just because it is custom, something familiar to which the sluggish mind of man clings as dear; it saves us the trouble of new, self-made adjustments. Hence, strictly speaking, Antiphon's gospel for all that it offers of hedonism is a call to independence, to risky isolation. This he probably did not see.

His second objective cuts deeper and can be more clearly inferred from the statement which continues and concludes the present passage.

3d
[*FVS*[6] 2.348.3.25]

To be alive is a natural [condition]
as also is it to die

and for human beings, to be alive is numbered among their interests
and to die, among their non [-interests].

Interests as constituted by law are bonds laid upon nature
but those constituted by nature are liberating.

If correct calculation is used
the things which give pain cannot benefit nature
more than the things which give pleasure;

hence the things which give pain cannot be to our interest
either
rather than the things that give pleasure.

For things truly to our interest are not supposed to do damage
but to benefit.

The first four lines formed the conclusion of the previous
excerpt, and are here repeated as the beginning of the present one.
There is something briefly poignant about them, as though Antiphon, viewing some young soldier going to battle, were saying
softly of him, 'There is so little time'. Or, it might be, holding some newspaper in his hand with a photograph of a
condemned man tied blindfold to a pillar before the firing squad,
or walking to the chamber of electrocution, he would murmur,
'But to remain alive, for a human being, is numbered among his
interests'. There are other interests, but sometimes only this one
is relevant. What some have called reverence for life emerges here
fairly clearly from the crabbed text. The Homeric mood and the
heroic ideal are now left leagues away.

This reverence, however, would be misunderstood if it were
merely equated with a dislike of capital punishment. There are
more ways than one in which you can kill. For all of us, the
prescriptions of custom and public opinion are laid upon hand
and foot, and ear and tongue, in our goings out and comings in.
These dam up the native springs of our pleasure and clog our
spontaneous feelings by an oppressive weight of overdirection.
For the organism that is overdirected pays the price by becoming
inhibited. His perspective is fastened upon the whole human
organism, its thirst for self-expression and satisfaction, its need for
unhampered growth, which in total opposition to Aristotle he
sees as obeying spontaneous rules. This spontaneity is a living
process: death is the name for its stoppage; but he seems to mean
that a half-death is possible too. He has spoken earlier of the
artificial pressure which custom-law can impose on the tender
plant of man. Here he speaks of bondage and liberty to make the
point over again.

What is new in the present passage is the hint of a psychology,
a view of personality as essentially spontaneous in its natural
condition, but as damaged by inhibitions formed in response to
pressures from the group, its man-made environment. This seems

a large structure to build upon a monosyllable, that short Greek verb 'to be alive' (*zen*). It can perhaps be supported by a notice in Aristotle, even though Aristotle does not mention Antiphon's name:

> If just to be alive is good and pleasant . . .
> and if the man who sees is conscious that he sees
> and the man who hears is conscious that he hears
> and the man who walks is aware he is walking . . .
> and if to be conscious that one is alive is one of the essential pleasures –
> for life is by nature a good,
> and to be aware of a good inherent in oneself is pleasant –
> then to be alive is one of man's preferred objectives . . .
>   [*E.N.* 9.9.9; cf. *Polit.* 3.6.4-5].

This curiously biological evaluation of self-consciousness is by Aristotle woven into a teleological context, where he wants to argue that friendship between morally good or superior men is a sort of heightening of self-consciousness. If the form in which he casts his theory has some kind of spell in it, this is due less to the idealistic requirements which he makes for friendship than to the purely naturalist conception of the functioning human organism which he here incorporates in his non-natural context. The language is close enough to Antiphon's protest in defence of the natural functions of eye and ear and foot to suggest that the two passages may supplement each other. Aristotle, then, would be thinking of a theory which defended free, unfettered and full enjoyment of the human faculties as itself the goal of the good life: the sense, in fact, of being 'fully alive'. Such a doctrine of uninhibited self-consciousness may lie behind Antiphon's defence of nature against law.

This gives perspective to the hedonistic calculus which concludes the present passage. Antiphon, so far as we can tell from his remains, ignores those complications of hedonistic terminology on which Aristotle spent some pains. Nor did he attend to those qualifications with which later theorists, Cyrenaic and Epicurean, variously surrounded the calculus. Hedonism is a slippery word which can cast an aura of irresponsibility and even immorality over a variety of quite serious and often conflicting theories of the good life. So far as such labels are permissible, Antiphon was a hedonist. It follows from his biological materialism, his plea for spontaneous experience. But it is to be noted that here, where the calculus is introduced, it is subordinated to the criteria of benefit and interest. You define pleasure as that which benefits the organism. There is no irresponsibility about this view. Both Democritus and Antiphon are hedonists, but their perspectives on pleasure were differently slanted, and the difference was matched in the opposition between their views on politics. For Democritus, society is good, acceptable, normal, even if man-made. Hence the rules of the political life occupy him a good deal, and he shows no impulse to defend the claim of pleasure as against convention. Hence he prefers to speak of the good life as a whole, a condition of well-being, with its specific moments of delight. His political theory is built not so much on personal psychology as on group security, even though it finds room for a personal psychology separable from group security. For Antiphon, society is not friend but enemy; it is so evaluated because of his estimate of what the biological personality is and requires. Hence his psychology does control his social theory as that of Democritus does not. Correspondingly, his view of the good life is more fanatically concentrated on its biological savour than is that of Democritus. So he equates pleasure and interest and benefit without qualification, as he has earlier equated interest and benefit with righteousness. They are synonymous or at least coeval criteria in judging what is good.

3e
[*FVS*⁶ 2.349.4.32ff.]

. . . . . .

. . . the case of a man who
adopts self-defence when he is the object of act
but does not himself initiate act,
the case of a man who
does good to his parents
even when they do bad to him,
the case of a man who
allows another to make sworn deposition adverse to himself
but does not himself do this –

in the stated [cases] investigation will discover
many [factors] enemy to nature

they contain the [factor of] being pained more
                        rather than less
                        and of being pleased less
                        rather than more
                        and of being the object of act
                        instead of avoiding the act.
Now,
if a man who adopted such [a course of behaviour]
found his support increased from the side of the laws,
whereas a man who did not, but rather acted contrary to this
course,
found his support diminished,
obedience to the laws would not be irrational.

But as it is we find that
if a man adopt such a course
the [power of] right [emanating] from law
is not adequate to support him,

For
(i) it does nothing to prevent the object of act from being the
object, and the subject from acting as subject.
It does not stop this at the time and

(ii) when [the case] is referred [to court] for vengeance
the object of act has no specific advantage over the subject
who did it.
For he has to convince the court that he has been the object
and he pleads for the power to get right-redress.
But the subject has the same privilege;
he can repudiate. . . .

The beginning and end of this passage are both mutilated, yet
it pursues a single theme with more consistency and a coherence
more prolonged than is elsewhere characteristic of his style. It
was attached to the previous section by a transition now lost, and
it repeats the hedonistic calculus of that section, stressing here
that it is indeed a calculus of more and less. But he has shifted his
focus, from the defence of the uninhibited life of natural man to
a renewed and very bitter attack on the *mores* of that society in
which the natural man is condemned to live. The cynicism here,

as in an earlier example, can easily be misunderstood. Is he inviting the citizen to adopt the initiative in aggression against his neighbours, so that he can take them at a disadvantage? Would that be the situation of more pleasure and less pain which his philosophy approves? If so, he has flatly contradicted his own earlier thesis that nature does not seek to create enemies. The fact is that Antiphon's inverted argument stems from a sort of myopia. Despite his own inner convictions, his vision is filled with the spectacle of how men actually do behave towards each other. The actual relationships cast a spell over his mind, so that he presents them continually as though they were the real thing, and he describes the ways in which these rules are accepted and played out as though he were accepting them himself. Yet through his description there runs a fundamental rejection of that whole social order which makes things so.

The present argument could be called a protest against the Vulnerability of Innocence in the world as we find it. It is a deeply pessimistic passage; morally speaking as pessimistic as anything in Greek literature. It begins by subsuming a man – the case-law style here recurs – who sticks to Antiphon's rule of nature, the rule of non-aggression: he does not initiate: he merely takes measures of self-defence when he has to. 'Preventive war' is not in his code. But Antiphon is now prepared to visualize the problem he has so far ignored. This ideal man cannot in practice isolate himself or always be sure of company equally ideal. Put him up against other men who are aggressive, whose behaviour though presumably dictated by convention is none the less actual. What happens now?

He subsumes this unpleasant situation at three levels: first, he puts it generally, as it can occur in every type of social relationship; simply stating the basic contrast between victim and aggressor, between mere self-defence and offence, between the innocent and the offender; a contrast which implies a basic inequality and unfairness. Second, he cites what from his point of view is a recurrent instance of this kind of relationship; the child versus his parents. This is shocking, of course, and is meant to shock; nor does he annotate his example sufficiently to show what he means. We have to refer back to his attack on the closed character of Greek society and tradition to realize that in positing parents who, in his words, 'do bad', he is deliberately attacking a Greek institution – the family – in which the grip of the conventional tradition on human nature was preserved and reinforced. The laws, written and unwritten, unanimously inculcated an uncritical respect for the family, and placed in the hands of the elders a large means of control over the ethos of the city-state. Antiphon's meaning is that this relationship in fact makes the children 'victims' of their parents; he is attacking less the particular case of bad parents than the institution and powers of parenthood, as still understood in Greek society, which gave to all parents power over the organic spontaneity of their offspring, and in the case of bad parents made this power even more hostile to their needs.

From the family the bitter polemic turns to the courts. Antiphon had previously attacked the 'lawful convention' by which witnesses were expected to make enemies for themselves by the effect of their testimony. Here he turns his eye on the other party, the object of the testimony. He is however a special case, the kind who would never use initiative to involve himself in such a situation. Following Antiphon's rule of nature, he avoids recourse to legal process until he is forced to it. One might, using standards of modern jurisprudence, object that if A has in fact impaired the true interests of B and B has taken legal redress, he is justified in taking it, and A has no justification for complaint. Antiphon, replying in the terms of the society in which he lived, might say: 'Legal process as understood in Athens in my day does not rest on an accepted body of criminal and civil jurisprudence, nor on the mechanism of law-enforcement agencies. It is a kind of arena in which competing gladiators fight out their respective claims, with victory going to the strongest fighter.' He might go on to say: 'Does not your modern legal process in practice often involve a similar trial by combat, in which victory goes to the man with the most money, influence and aggressive force?' This is the kind of cynical social criticism which preoccupied him. In Athens, he views a party cited against his will in the courts not as guilty but as inherently innocent, just because he had obeyed nature's rule of non-aggression and avoided involvement in the social combat.

It is this involvement which brings with it the increase of pain and decrease of pleasure. Non-involvement – call it social quietism, if you will – increases pleasure and decreases pain. He is clearly thinking of the psychological tensions which are set up by the very necessity of taking defensive measures. This spontaneous happiness – the inner peace, if you will – of nature is cancelled artificially by the requirements of social convention.

He then proceeds to ask: Will the structure of law at least give to nature's innocent some protection? That function is surely law's excuse, as understood by the anthropologists themselves. But Antiphon says No. He might reply to Democritus: 'Law's assistance is available to defend the group as a group and the group *mores*; it fails the innocent individual who asks only to be left alone.' Thus, in effect, just as he earlier accepted the liberal explanation of law as a social compact, but derided the quality of this compact, so here he takes note of the liberal deduction that law as a compact is a means of guaranteeing security for the partners to the compact, and he rejects the claim.

He supports his rejection by two reasons, and the first of them shows in a flash what Antiphon means by law. He says: It does not prevent or anticipate the act itself, the initial situation in which the aggressor committed his aggression and the victim played his victim's role; it only catches up with the after-effects, and provides a forum in which the essential situation is not corrected but repeated. We would reply: 'Of course, positive law cannot morally prevent. It can only provide redress; it addresses itself to overt acts and deals with motives only after they have first been revealed in acts.' But Antiphon's target is not positive law; else his objections would not make sense. He is attacking the unwritten and written laws which comprise the ethos of an acquisitive and aggressive society. His target is total. It is not so much that the laws sanction aggression as that they expect it; they indeed invite it, in so far as they urge a citizen not only to hate an enemy, but to guard his own rights against infringement and condition him to a perpetual posture of semi-hostility. Perhaps Antiphon goes even deeper. The initial act and the posture of its victim are each created by personal motivation arising out of the nature of each man, a nature healthy in one case, perverted in the other. But law, just because it is a social thing, a series of group attitudes, cannot touch the heart, the natural feelings at the seat of action. It is not present in the initial act at all; it lacks a private imperative, a personal morality. And so in court; the process as it continues to impel itself to its conclusion is unable to recognize the private innocent man. He stands there only in his social guise, a legal opponent of the other party.

After this fashion Antiphon poses the problem that we have called the Vulnerability of Innocence. His vision of society is painted in the darkest colours. It is a machine in which the natural man of friendly impulse and quietist preference gets caught; he, the innocent, walks in a jungle of lurking enemies, society itself being the one big enemy.

There is a passage in Plato's *Republic* which reflects a similar gloom: society is inherently vicious and hostile to goodness; all the philosopher can do is to withdraw, if he can, and seek shelter from the mortal storm behind some sheltering wall. Plato's definition of goodness is not Antiphon's; they are philosophically in rival camps. But for both thinkers the bottom had somehow dropped out of things. No hope or confidence was left in Athens, apparently, or in people as they found them. One wonders if, sharing this common feeling of revulsion, they had shared also a common experience which had produced it. One can say: Yes, this was that Athens defeated in war and disrupted by faction. But the curious precision of Antiphon's picture of the innocent defendant, who leaves it to others to prefer sworn testimony against himself, is also reminiscent of the last act in the drama of the life of Socrates. Was Antiphon's vision of the natural man and his fate derived from a perception of the Socratic life and its conclusion? There are arguments which could support the inference of some link between the two men. We remember that Socrates himself straddled a philosophical position between idealism and naturalism; one which reconciled hedonism with the claims of moral virtue. On no other hypothesis can we explain the divergence between the Socratic schools which later claimed to expound the master's teachings. Tradition associated Antiphon with Socrates as a rival rather than as a disciple, and did not count him among the Socratics. It is easy to see why. His pessimism was too profound, and his method too destructive, to form the basis of a doctrine which could find and win proselytes. Even the Cynics exploited a personal arrogance that he lacks. But his conception of human nature finding its salvation by refusing to engage in the competitive practices of politics and the courts has a fairly close analogue in the Socrates of Plato's *Apology*, who defends his political quietism by arguing that it was necessary for his survival in a society which would not have tolerated his principles. What Antiphon does is to isolate and abstract from the Socratic life certain attitudes which he then treats out of context and converts into all-inclusive principles. But so did others who fell under the master's spell. Even his double standard, which counsels observance of convention in the presence of reporters, has some parallel in what we know of the historic Socrates.

It is of more significance for the history of political theory that the sheer destructiveness of Antiphon's attack on legal process as understood in the city-state of his own day could only be answered in the long run by introducing into the public domain new conceptions of how that process should be administered. The essence of his critique is that there is no jurisprudence, in our sense of the term. The courts, those substituting the force of words for the spear and sword, are still arenas for public combat. Antiphon demands that the criteria which determine innocence and guilt should be built on 'nature'. He perceives the main difficulty, though his mind is not powerful enough to formulate the solution. Society in the course of time proceeded to the task of formulating such criteria, but only as it met one condition: a certain area of private behaviour and moral opinion was excluded from the province of law; it came to be regarded as not a proper subject for legal process or punishment. The precise limits of this area still vary somewhat in different civilized societies. Totalitarian governments wish to narrow them as much as possible; liberal democracy seeks to extend them. But that the area came into existence is due to the kind of protest in defence of the private man and his natural needs that Antiphon made. It is noteworthy that he even anticipates the fact that difficulty of public enforcement will turn out to be a good practical reason for leaving the vagaries of nature alone. As he well says, there are so many acts of nature which do not require witnesses; that is, are not social in their effects. It is well to make this case for Antiphon, if only because the better-known and more respectable political systems of Plato and Aristotle show no sign of any willingness to draw the distinction. Their conception of *nomos* in this respect rested on the past rather than anticipated the future.

When under Rome the building of a legal system really began, one whose principles Europe has ever since found serviceable, it could advance to the status of a system with some hold on the allegiance of all men and minds only so far as the combat conception of legal process was abandoned, and a conception of natural law formulated and recognized as, so to speak, sovereign, independent both of courts and of parties in the courts. This answered Antiphon's criticism theoretically by eliminating the arbitrary and accidental character of law as mere local custom, or a given public opinion, or the cultural attitudes of a given group. It sought to replace the *mores* of a human group by principles akin to those of mathematics. However limited the success thus attained, however vulnerable the systems of St. Thomas Aquinas or Hugo Grotius, the idea itself was the only way to answer Antiphon. His natural man, oppressed by a competitive and custom-ridden society, is rescued from his sudden fears and arbitrary insecurities by an equally natural law.

Those papyrus fragments which have preserved portions of Antiphon's argument in its original form are now exhausted. They have been enough to reveal the outlines of a man's mind. Other testimonies to his teaching can furnish a supplement, but only a supplement, to this outline. They are so scarce and disconnected that it is safe to interpret them, if at all, only by standards which conform to the papyrus. We here pass over his metaphysics and epistemology. As a political theorist, it is plausible that he founded himself on some sort of anthropology. This has been the indication of the papyrus, and the record confirms it by reporting a few scraps of a cosmology, of a human embryology, of a history of technology and perhaps of a comparative ethnology of primitive tribes. It also preserves Antiphon's statement [*FVS*^{6} 87 B48] that man

was an animal, the most godlike.

The cosmology would then conclude with the formation of the earth, and was plausibly followed by a zoogony which described the origins of life, plant and animal upon the earth's surface, and then of man as one of the animals. After laying these physical and biological foundations, Antiphon proceeded to construct some account of technological civilization, achieved, we may be sure, by natural and gradual stages. Conceivably he even entertained the task of including the comparative customs and usages of man as a specific aspect of evolving human culture. This is guess-work, but it would provide a suitable historical basis for the support of that critique of *nomos* which is attested by the papyrus. We have suggested, however, that he may not have been a very systematic thinker. The most that can be safely argued is that the vein of his naturalism must have persisted through any historical account of the universe and man that he attempted.

What are we to make of another set of testimonies [*FVS*[6] 87A2; B44a] which state that he wrote a treatise on 'Consensus' (*Homonoia*)? Here, briefly revealed, is perhaps a portion of his doctrine which might amount to a whole edifice in itself, yet an edifice pivoted for us upon the report of a single explosive noun. Standing as the title, it may represent only the catalogue label of Alexandrian scholars. But as a topic of a manuscript which bore this attribution, it was surely conspicuous. This is where critical control over our conjectures has to be established by the light of the testimony of the papyrus already examined. 'Consensus' in its traditional significance was political. It described that happy condition of the *polis* which prevented party strife [Xen. *Mem.* 4.4.16]. 'Oaths of consensus', it is alleged, had been required of the citizen body by lawgivers. There is a tradition which even associated the teaching of Heraclitus with such themes. Democritus, as we have seen, formulated a rationale of those conditions leading to civic consensus.

Yet it is difficult to see how Antiphon's use of the term could have been political. His spiritual renunciation of society and its *nomos* would surely prevent him from envisaging social concord as even valuable. But his doctrine of the uninhibited natural man, thwarted by a competitive society, and seeking to live in spontaneous amicable relationships with other men, might lead to a notion of private consensus [cf. Iambl. apud *FVS*[6] 2.356.23-4] as available to individuals who allowed themselves to get clear of the artificial attitudes imposed by *nomos*. This is one attested meaning of consensus in the lexicographers, and Antiphon may have invented it somewhat in anticipation of the Epicurean doctrine of friendship in a later epoch.

This speculation can gather some indirect support from Aristotle. Books 8 and 9 of his *Ethics* form in effect a separate treatise on the topic of personal friendship. He owes here, as always, a good deal to Plato's inspiration. His own premises require him to present friendship teleologically as achieved completely only in relationships between two completely good and virtuous men, who seem to bear a strong resemblance to Aristotle himself.

However, the Greek term *philia* could apply to other relationships besides personal ones. Aristotle narrows it down, so to speak, as he becomes progressively involved in his thesis of the fellowship

of good men, but here and there he feels compelled to notice
fellowship in its more diluted forms, as it inheres in various kinds
of social, legal and political partnerships. Consensus, a classic
term, is included in his over-all review. Now, he specifically
admits that the term is political. But he goes on to try and
accommodate it to his own present perspective by arguing that it
could also apply to a personal relationship. It could be suggested
that he only takes the trouble to make this accommodation
because a previous thinker had already given to consensus a very
personal and intimate sense, a union of hearts, rather than the
common mind of citizens or parties.

To this union of hearts Aristotle adds his own strongly moral
colour. The different colour of Antiphon's doctrine would not of
course have been acceptable to him and this may be why he
suppresses it by substituting his own – a characteristic of Aristotle's
non-historical method. For Antiphon, consensus would have been
a natural and spontaneous relationship between two human beings
which could occur only outside the conventional patterns of *nomos*.
For the latter forces men into unnatural relationships which replace amity by tension. For Aristotle, on the contrary, the traditional
conventions would be indispensable for achieving the same goal.

Aristotle in any field of investigation which preoccupied him at
the moment always kept an eye on rival theories which were
pertinent. If Antiphon did indeed teach some doctrine of spontaneous personal amity, a union of affinities, so to speak, the 8th
and 9th books of the *Ethics* would be the place to look for any
echoes of it. In a passage cited already to illustrate Antiphon's
concept of the importance of 'just being alive' and being conscious
you were alive, Aristotle goes on to remark as follows:

> One should have a fellow-consciousness of the existence of
> one's friend [*E.N.* 9.9.10].

This is a conclusion which his own reasoning has pursued but the
terminology is here naturalist, as though the bodily senses were
capable of extension into the sensations of a fellow man. Is this how
Antiphon developed his own characteristic notion of consensus?

In an earlier context, Aristotle's treatise had turned to notice
the sexual relationship and observed:

> Between man and woman it is held that amity subsists by
> nature.

and then he adds most surprisingly

> That is, a human being is by nature a pairing animal rather than a political one [*E.N.* 8.12.7; cf. *Politics* 1.1.2].

The reason with which he at once supports this statement is unexpected in the author of the *Politics*; it is an anthropological reason, not a teleological one: the household is prior to the city and therefore more 'essential'. This echoes the language of all the naturalists. Was the doctrine of the natural amity of the sexual pair, as constituting the nexus of a household, exploited by Antiphon?

This conjecture would not arise, were it not prompted by a comparison with a paragraph preserved in the anthology of John of Stobi, and attributed to Antiphon. All the material in 'Stobaeus' which bears this attribution – there are twelve citations under Antiphon's name [*FVS*⁶ 87 B49-51; 53-54; 57-62] – rest under grave suspicion. None of it can be used without qualification to fill in an outline of Antiphon's mind. There may have been confusion with other Antiphons, and the deep social pessimism of our Antiphon has been edited out of its original idiom and colour by excisions and additions. However, a few sentences in the longest cited paragraph, when considered in their nakedness, seem to give a rather affirmative response to the conjectures we have been making. The sentences run as follows:

> However
> assume the years of life proceed,
> assume you form a desire for marriage and wife . . .
> should she turn out to be really unsuitable,
> how shall the catastrophe be handled?
> painful it is to divorce her
> > to make enemies out of friends
> > who feel and think in the identical medium that you do,
> > who draw the identical breath that you do.
> > You accepted them
> > and they accepted you.
> Yet painful also to have appropriated a property of this character.
> You thought you were appropriating pleasures,
> you really married pains.

However . . .
assume supreme suitability
and what is more pleasurable for a human being than a
woman after his own heart?
What more delicious, not least when he is young? . . .
However
assume the birth of children next
and at once come the crowding cares
and the youthful heartbeat dances away
and the smile on the face is lost [*FVS*⁶ 87 B49 with omissions].

Greek literature is not free from the occasional diatribe against
wives, and the anxiety and expense they cause, and the difficulty
of controlling them. It is not even free from hostility to women as
such. The charms of Aphrodite in a woman's glance and carriage
can be a trap for fools. This seamy tradition is as old as Hesiod,
and its prevalence bespeaks the unflattering status which women
enjoyed under the custom-laws of classic Athens. But the present
passage is rather different, though it has been contaminated (in
the excised portions) with sentiments which better reflect the
tradition. First, we observe characteristics of Antiphon's style, as
revealed in the papyrus. Alternatives are proposed, and then
subjected to the criticism of a hedonistic calculus. The human
beings comprehended in the author's vision all enjoy a common
humanity, they still draw in the same natural resources, and
breathe the same air. But here, what aspect of custom-law is
subjected to criticism? Clearly it is in the first instance marriage
itself, as an institution which organizes the mating of human
beings and arranges matches between them without regard to the
dictates of what Antiphon calls 'suitability'. This would be a
natural suitability, either a meeting of common tastes and
interests or a biological harmony in which the springs of sexual
feeling flow together. Moreover, Antiphon has his eye on more
people than just the sexual pair involved in mating. A separation
or divorce which could be arranged means a split not only
between two people but between two families and further tension
and hatred are created which (as in the papyrus) inevitably
replace natural amities.

Beneath the surface cynicism there lurks a quite different conception of mating as a union of natural spontaneous affection.

We have seen how criticisms made by Antiphon against other institutions could be met only by a totally new conception of jurisprudence. Is he here, in effect, demanding that the Greek mind accept a totally new conception of romantic love between the sexes as the proper condition of mating? This would then fit the reference in Aristotle to a theory of man and woman as mating animals rather than as political ones. Antiphon has no attention to spare for the larger social relationships.

His concentration is on the workings of the heart, and the natural unfettered emotions. If he launched an attack on the custom laws of Greek marriage (*gamos*) we can understand why it was so necessary to suppress him, more especially as his polemic continues to consider the birth and the nurture of children within the marriage tie, and condemns the anxieties and cares that it brings. We have seen that his attack on the family takes the form of a defence of children against parents (above, p. 284). Here he comes to the rescue of parents against their children. His target is not personal in either case. He is attacking the institution of the Greek family as understood in his day. Nor can he have been so very eccentric in this, for Democritus had noticed the burden that children bring to a middle-class family though he had accommodated this burden to his overall philosophy of acceptance (above, p. 122). Antiphon, whether or not he had any solution to offer (it would be unlike him to offer a solution, as in Plato's communism of wives and children) is determined to point the finger at another abrogation of nature's benign rule. For under the burden of supporting and raising and educating children, the 'youthful heartbeat dances away'. This semi-poetic phrase confirms the strong impression gained from the papyrus that Antiphon's law of nature is an impassioned plea for the rule of spontaneity. Presumably the family as an educational institution training the children in the *nomoi* of society is for him a straitjacket which destroys spontaneous relations between parent and offspring and so increases pain and decreases pleasure for both.

The twentieth-century note in his teaching is there. It sounds almost uncanny. Was he an apostle of the new education? Would he have approved a progressive school? Is it possible that in his Greek we catch, across the centuries, the accents of Sigmund Freud?

CHAPTER XI

THE EMASCULATION OF LIBERALISM
IN ARISTOTLE'S *ETHICS*

PLATO'S conception of himself as the philosophic Homer of
his day, and of his philosophy as a sort of cultural index to
Hellenism, impressed itself powerfully on the mind of his
chief pupil, giving him the conviction that this did indeed express
the proper task of philosophy. Aristotle's own originality, however, made it impossible for him to become merely Plato's
commentator. He therefore formed a similar ambition for himself,
and produced a system even more encyclopaedic. This meant
that both men, so far as they wished to report predecessors and
contemporaries, shared at bottom a common attitude toward
such a task. It was relevant to them only as a function of their
own philosophizing; it was less a matter of agreeing or refuting
than of mastication or digestion. However, Aristotle shows differences of method in his reporting which reflect the more empirical
cast of his temper. At bottom he had a little more respect for
what 'they say' or 'what some believe'. With a less exacting
standard of literary form, he was also less arrogant. Committed
as he is to the notion that the efforts of all previous thinkers unite
in himself, he in effect tells his public: 'I can say better what they
try to say'; while Plato asserts: 'What they say is relevant only as
corrected and reformed by my own system'. It is, therefore,
characteristic of Aristotle that on the one hand he likes to support
his treatises with the reports of other men's opinions, which he
puts into the prefaces, and also interlards here and there in the
text; and on the other, that he often avoids giving names in his
reports. Though a poor historian, he had like Hegel a conception
of philosophy as an historical process which reached finality in
himself. All previous opinions are therefore part of a tradition:
they have a certain partial inevitability, part-truths that make
sense only as they come to rest in his own system. But since he is
committed to the effort of absorption, he has perforce to correct

what he reports. If the report itself is given anonymously, the reader is liable to get the impression that it is not a report at all but a dialectical exchange which Aristotle conducts with himself. As compared with Plato, the chief practical difference is that his pages are full of suppressed contradictions. A rival philosophical position to his own is summarized briefly, but often justly, and then paraphrased or interpreted or emended and so rendered digestible by his own omnivorous system. In the field of physics, because he more often names his authorities, and because some of their opinions are independently known, critics have been able more easily to catch up with the methods he uses and to expose the lack of historicity in his emendations and paraphrases; which, indeed, are plainly accommodated to the tenets of his own metaphysics. But in politics and morals, perhaps because some of his sources were close to him and still living, he almost never names names. His empiricism, which grew on him with age, not only made his reporter's conscience a little less Platonic, a little more sensitive, but perhaps encouraged in him a more genuine sympathy with that descriptive naturalism with which the liberals sought to explain human beings. Thus, though he no more than Plato will accept the notion that society's law is the result of a compact, he is willing to report the reasons which have induced others to think that it is; and he shows something less than Plato's hostility to their belief in human equality and natural philanthropy.

He shares, then, with Plato the determination to interpenetrate other men's systems, but he sets out to do so piecemeal. Therefore from his text it is a little easier to separate out alien statements which he intends to emend. Naturalism and idealism, or rather that version of teleological idealism which he made his own, fight a running battle with each other over many pages of his *Ethics* and *Politics*, often producing ambiguities which are better digested in the *Politics* than in the *Ethics*. These two treatises form the leading source for our knowledge of the liberal doctrines of the fourth century.

The *Ethics*, despite its name, is professedly an account of ethical man only as an introduction to political man. It deals extensively with human nature in the context of social rather than personal behaviour. Aristotle's felt need to relate himself to the liberals is therefore quite considerable. But he has different priorities. The focus of liberalism is on the natural universal man, to be taken and trusted as you find him: essentially a democrat, a utilitarian, a hedonist, non-aggressive and even philanthropic; architect of a society which allows his lively energies to discover a basic community of interest through mutual and peaceful communication. Aristotle's own system demanded a reverse emphasis. Intelligence and force of character have priority as political principles. His concept of society is hierarchical: he, more even than Plato, is haunted by the figure of the paterfamilias, the authoritarian. The spontaneous is suspect; communication without control is meaningless. Affection, philanthropy, love are extras, a special dividend declared upon the operations of the virtuous and intelligent life. His treatise feels it has to solve the problem of moral choice (Books 2 and 3) and of justice between human beings (Book 5) and of moral prudence (Book 6) before ever it is allowed to reach the topic of affection and amity (Books 8 and 9). When he does reach it, he gives it the surprising honour of two whole books of exposition more extensive than that accorded to any other single topic in the treatise. The disproportion has rightly intrigued the curiosity of critics, who however can make little more of it than a tribute to the supposedly superior quality of Greek social life in the city-state, among gentlemen of leisure. But a different explanation is possible. Suppose that liberalism, by the time that the *Ethics* was composed, had constructed a doctrine of human equality and philanthropy so fundamental and so challenging that Aristotle felt compelled to give to the same topic a compendious, albeit very different handling? This is the hypothesis we shall proceed to test, not without some support already furnished in previous chapters.

If Books 8 and 9 do contain a report of a doctrine of equality and fraternity, universal, spontaneous and normative, they take care to embed it in a surrounding context which assumes that significant amity is not social but personal. This way of controlling what Aristotle reports is followed even in the first chapter. Teleology demanded that amity, like any other aspect of human relations, should reach its final form only when actualized in emotion between two completely 'good' men, leisured intellectuals whose personalities bear a striking resemblance to that of Aristotle himself. In this form, philanthropy is converted into an intimate personal 'friendship', the common English translation of the topic to which the two books are formally devoted.

But his reporter's integrity, and perhaps his fastidiousness about terminology, compel him almost literally to digress in order to give some account of the quite different conception of friendship as a biological and social fact. It becomes that spontaneous feeling of sympathy or goodwill which all members of a species are supposed by definition to feel for each other, and which expresses their recognition that they have common traits. Beginning perhaps as a herd instinct, it becomes the basis for that co-operation which creates and supports human society.

The collision between this social amity and personal friendship is minimized, and the terminology of the social school is interpreted and corrected to bring it into line with that of the personal school. If the ideal of personal friendship succeeds in dominating Aristotle's mind, this is probably due to the Platonic influence of the doctrine of *eros*, itself in essence a homosexual rather than a heterosexual conception as Plato uses it, and therefore socially exclusive rather than inclusive.

The stamp of this exclusiveness is printed deep upon the pages of these two books. One has difficulty in thinking of Hellenic friendship except as Aristotle has memorialized it – a civilized, intimate understanding, a meeting of minds and matching of characters. Yet the other is there too – the deep organ note of a universalism prophetic rather than personal, and a science of society more catholic and compassionate. The philosopher's method of piecemeal analysis allows some exactitude in the untangling and tabulation of the reports, to the first of which we now turn.

I

Report disguised as discursive introduction, controlled by teleological context
[*E.N.* 8.1.1-5]

1. The next topic is amity
2. which is a species of virtue or [at least] accompanied by virtue
3. as well as being one of the essentials for living.
4. Who would choose to live without friends, though in possession of all other goods?
5. Even men who enjoy riches or power would seem to feel the need of friends . . .
6. In poverty, etc., friends, we think, are our one refuge . . .

7. The young need friends to keep them straight
8. and the old to help and assist them in their feebleness . . .
9. and the mature to cooperate in noble deeds: 'the twain that go side by side'. [8.1.1]

Thus it is that Aristotle prepares his readers for that topic which is to grow and dominate two whole books of his treatise. His first sentence reads innocuously enough, till it is realized that it propounds an axiom which is to guide and control everything he says on the subject. Whatever other aspects of amity he may be prepared to discuss, these will be subordinated to a teleological conception of it; amity, being in the context of 'virtue', is the symbol of a fixed habit of character or a result thereof, the end-product of selective cultivation and training. Equally, then, whether viewed as an emotion or as a relationship, it will be a matter involving individual decision and personal choice, and its quality will match the quality of the persons involved. Only completely virtuous persons will, by definition, be capable of expressing perfect amity. Hence, though he does not cover all this distance until later, his initial illustrations all view amity in the context of a purely personal relationship, ending with a phrase quoted from Homer (item 9) which aptly illuminates the close connection between Aristotle's teleology of virtue and the heroic tradition of Greece – a tradition which, in its aristocratic form as persisting in the city-state, his moral philosophy sought to rationalize. Later he finds occasion to quote a saw from Hesiod, and then to cite the ancient myth of the marriage of heaven and earth. His thought is in a traditional and almost antique groove.

But once fully embarked on his real subject, it is safe for him to steer briefly up a side-channel, its direction plainly marked by an initial signpost.

1. By nature
2. amity inheres between parent and offspring
3. not only in human beings
4. but in birds and the majority of animals
5. and between members of the same 'ethnic group' mutually
6. particularly the human group
7. which is why the 'philanthropic' are approved.
8. Travel [books] show every human being is familiar to every other, and amicable.

9. Amity also appears to be [the principle] cohesive of cities.

10. Legislators concentrate more attention on amity than on righteousness

11. for consensus would appear to be something resembling amity

12. and consensus is the particular aim of legislators: passion, which implies hostility, they are particular to expel.

13. If men are amicable, there is no need of righteousness

14. whereas if they are righteous they still need amity

15. and of right or moral [principles] the most part seem to consist in amity. [8.1.2.]

These positions, though tabled by Aristotle summarily in compressed Greek, have only to be spelled out to reveal a conception of amity in the first instance anthropological, with biological roots; and in the second philanthropic, with universal application (a theory supported by comparative ethnology); and in the third social-political, as Protagoras and Democritus might define it, taking shape in that practical consensus which enables a group to function as a socially effective mechanism; fourthly, the last sentence broadly hints at a theory which made natural philanthropy prior to (artificial) justice and perhaps derived the principle of correct justice from it.

1. However [Aristotle continues], amity is not only an essential but is a moral ideal ['a noble thing'].

2. We approve [not only of lovers of human beings but] of lovers of friends

3. and intensity in friendship is held to be one of the ideals.

4. Furthermore, we think that a man who is 'your friend' means also a 'good man'. [8.1.5.]

In these four propositions appended to the previous fifteen we see how Aristotle, after voyaging briefly up his naturalist side-channel and sighting landmarks which look dangerous, hastily backs out. The concept of the (biologically) essential is corrected and replaced by the concept of the morally ideal embodied in ideal persons; and so he returns to the point of view of the initial paragraph of the chapter. Thus, though he is committed by his method to reporting all doctrines relevant to the topic amity, he manages to bring them under teleological control by embedding them in his own context. Likewise, he denatures his reports by refusing to identify their ideas as specific doctrines, preferring instead to marshal them as possible points of view. The only common denominator of impression which he wishes to carry over to his reader is that, after all, amity is a very significant topic, or so many people would not have bothered with it. This allows him to treat the term as a blank cheque which he can fill in himself.

2

Report denatured and reduced to level of commonplace
[*E.N.* 8.1.6]

1. Several controversies have arisen over the topic of amity.
2. One [school] posits it as a similitude, so to speak, and posits that the amicable are 'similars'
3. which is why they say that like is as like and 'birds of a feather' and so on
4. while another [school] says that potters are the opposite with other potters, etc.

Aristotle, having concluded one part of his introduction, opens up another by disclosing a conflict of opinion relevant to his theme. This conflict is to be presented as a dialectical device which will lead into a statement of his own theory as the 'inevitable' solution. In this way he seeks to imitate the methods of a Platonic dialogue, but does it in greatly compressed form. Now, the main liberal doctrine which he needs to overthrow is not that amity is 'natural' (for he has his own special brand of nature which he wishes to include in his own moral system), but that it is spontaneous and inevitable between human beings as such, because of their generic similitude as members of the same animal species. This argument, whether regarded as scientific or as utopian, is already implicit in Antiphon. Hence it is also the position which, after he has hinted at it in his general introduction, he now selects as controversial. However, no sooner does he do this than he prepares artfully to sidestep the consequences of following through what was a perfectly serious philosophical proposition. For he promptly places it in a context not of scientific reasoning but of proverbial commonplaces. And since one proverb can always be found which will cancel another, he then cites Hesiod on the theme that 'two of a trade never agree'. This device enables him to conclude that the dialectical problem: Does human amity depend on similitude? is unprofitable. It can be as easily contradicted from experience as supported. So, having pretended to raise it, he can now drop it. He has thus denatured the strength of his opposition by misrepresenting the context in which their doctrine had been offered. If the Greek language was still not relatively poor in technical terms, he would not be able to accomplish such feats of legerdemain so easily. The key term 'similitude' appropriated by the natural philanthropic school and used in a technical sense he simply transfers backwards into its non-technical usage. He is guilty, one would say, of a certain historical frivolity. But as philosophical propaganda, it is of its kind as effective as Plato's methods.

3
Report disguised as a question mark and disposed of dialectically
[*E.N.* 8.1.7-8.3.1]

1. Problems [about amity] raised in a physical or cosmic context are not relevant.
2. Anthropological problems are relevant, for they are referable to human character and emotions.
3. Does amity, for example, inhere in all [human beings?]
4. Or are vicious human beings incapable of amity?
5. Is there one generic form of amity?
6. Or more than one?
7. The view that there is only one
8. with differences confined to degrees of intensity
9. must be wrong. [8.1.7]
10 The problem is cleared up
11. once it is recognized that amity can be directed not on all objects indiscriminately
12. but only on 'that-which-is-amicable'.
13. The amicable must be either (a) good or (b) pleasurable or (c) useful. . . . [8.2.1.]
14. These are formal [and fundamental] differentiations
15. and hence there are three generic forms of amity. [8.3.1.]

The preamble (items 1 and 2) to this analysis is noteworthy for the hint it gives that aside from the pre-Socratic speculations about physics (i.e., metaphysics of matter, etc.) there was also a field of anthropological speculation, which came into Aristotle's purview. He then selects from it precisely that premiss which in another form he has already touched on. Is amity a generic, biological thing characteristic of our species? Do we all have it? Should it, descriptively speaking, be viewed as a single natural instinct which, in the actual diversity of human relations, is seen to be operating only at differences of temperature, so to speak? This puts us in a position to guess, if we choose (and a later testimony will support the guess), that the philanthropic school was not content simply to identify a loose, generic, instinctive emotion in human beings but was prepared to describe its modes of realization in different degrees of intensity: Diverse forms of association, ranging from the loose and unconscious to the close and co-operative, could be brought under a single formula controlled by a single calculus; such would reconcile our basic common humanity with our evident variety of social and personal preferences. If this, or something like it, was the full version of the theory, Aristotle had no desire or intention of getting involved in it. It would be too attractive and too dangerous. He therefore treats it dialectically, as thought he had indeed thought of it, but of course it creates problems only soluble by substituting his own method of formal classification of amity into fundamentally distinct species. This has the advantage of dissolving the great hypothesis of the amity and brotherhood of mankind before it has had a chance to stake its own claims.

There is a second advantage for him. The original doctrine had treated the good, pleasant and useful as overlapping labels, symbols of a single value system; it had assumed no conflict between biological hedonism, social utilitarianism and morality. Aristotle carefully sets out to distinguish these as quite different motivations of amity, thus by implication confuting an opposing theory without naming it explicitly; yet thus also reporting it for posterity, should posterity choose to look beneath the surface of the argument. He himself has now adequately prepared the ground for his triumphant dialectical conclusion that

1. Amity between good men is specifically different from other types.
2. It is teleologically complete according to nature. [8.3.6.]

4

Report cut to size and disguised as introductory to Aristotle's own theory
[*E.N.* 8.2.3-4 and *E.N.* 9.5]

When, in the opening of the second chapter of Book 8, Aristotle
distinguished good, pleasant and useful as three quite different
motivations for amity (see above, p. 302), he shows his awareness
of previous discussions of the problem, and that he knows the
context in which they have been held. The liberals had grounded
humanity in biological hedonism. You felt a spontaneous philanthropy because this was naturally pleasurable; when it took
co-operative form in societies, this result, they argued, was
equally supported by the principle of social utility. Aristotle is
determined to come to grips with the hedonism and the utilitarianism and to render them innocuous as quickly as possible.

He is therefore at the outset disposing of fundamentals in the
theories of his rivals and, because this is his initial aim, he also
comes, in the course of his formal analysis, quickly upon a piece
of basic terminology, namely, human 'good will' (*eunoia*).

1. There are then three motivations for amity [viz. goodness,
pleasure, utility].
2. The term amity is not applicable to our feeling for inanimate objects which we may happen to 'like' [e.g. wine],
3. for an inanimate object cannot reciprocate
4. and furthermore our liking it is not inspired by a wish for
its 'good'.
5. However, 'the view is held that' any object of our amity
is such because we 'wish good' for it
6. and 'it is further held that' those who 'wish good' in this
way are 'good-willed' whether or not there is reciprocity.
7. When the good will is reciprocated you feel amity.
[8.2.3.]
8. But no: surely we should add that this feeling has to be
conscious on the part of both parties.
9. Many people can be 'good-willed' towards those they have
never seen, whom they assume to be nice or useful people.
10. Such can be only 'good-willed' but not amicable in the
absence of conscious awareness of reciprocity.
11. To have amity you need to have mutual good will plus
the wish for mutual good plus conscious awareness. [8.2.4.]

To interpret this little sequence, it is of assistance to know that in a passage of the *Politics* Aristotle admits that the liberals denounced slavery and all similar despotic relationships on the ground that they violated the moral principle of mutual good will between human beings. In the present context, items 1, 3 and 4 are directed at Plato's *Lysis*, where the discussion tried to connect our 'liking' for things, e.g. food, with our liking for people. In Aristotle's commonsense view, the two are not connected at all. But this refutation brings him to the question in item 5: How important is the factor of 'wishing good' in human relationships? That is, what place has altruism in the scheme of moral values? And then we learn of a school of opinion that identifies this altruism as the expression of good will in men, which operates independently of reciprocity and is apparently an unconscious or instinctive urge. To be sure, Aristotle does not say so positively: he confines himself to denying that this kind of good will is important unless it is consciously reciprocated; then, he concludes neatly (item 11), it becomes full amity in his sense.

This is an example of indirect reporting of a doctrine of others where his denials are as important as his positive statements. His own theory is working up to a final determination of amity as a personal, intimate fellowship between two perfectly good and wise men. Hence it must express the consciously chosen moral relationship. But he prepares *en route* to accommodate and digest as a sort of elementary preface to his own conception the quite different liberal concept of a good will native to human beings, instinctive and universal, always potentially operative between human beings, who become fully amicable and consentient whenever there is full reciprocity. (If there were not reciprocity, the fault, according to Antiphon, should be laid to some effect of custom-law, not to personal failure, which by definition was impossible, since the emotion was instinctive.) The theory omitted precisely that element which is so vital to Aristotle's own construction: namely, personal moral choice; which is why he rightly raises the problem of conscious awareness so early in his treatise.

The ninth book of the *Ethics* (or the second of the treatises on amity) seems to have the design of tidying up his whole account of the subject, initially by disposing of several problems connected with friendship, and also by settling accounts with items of terminology germane to the topic and employed by other schools of thought. Among these he takes up again the formula of 'good will'.

1. Good will has resemblance to amity without being amity.
2. It can relate itself to men unknown and involve no conscious recognition.
3. It does not involve strong psychological desire; it can operate casually and superficially. [E.N. 9.5.1-2]
4. It is the initiation [arche] of amity
5. as visual pleasure is initiative of erotic passion.
6. You have to be good-willed to be amicable but that does not mean that good will necessarily involves amity.
7. Good will means you wish good for the object of good will
8. but this does not necessarily involve co-operation on your part.
9. One can say it is equivalent to 'quiescent amity' which becomes natural amity through active temporal association,
10. not the amity created through pleasure or utility
11. for good will is not conditioned by these factors.
12. Good will is that which the favoured recipient of benefit renders back to the bestower
13. which then becomes 'morally right'.
14. If A wishes B to fare well
15. because A has expectation of A's own 'provision of need' through B
16. then A feels good will not to B but to himself
17. nor can A feel amity to B if his cultivation of B is motivated by some use-or-need. [9.5.3]
18. Generally speaking, good will in A is generated by virtue of some sort in the character of B;
19. if, for example, B creates the impression in A that B is a fine man or a courageous one, etc. [9.5.4.]

These items form a very interesting supplement to the previous and much briefer treatment of good will. In that earlier instance, Aristotle had lifted the curtain briefly on the doctrine of social amity, of which the basic element is a universal propensity to good will, which in turn issues in altruistic desire in A on behalf of B; this being instinctive and not initially dependent on reciprocity, though it needs reciprocity to be actualized as fully formed amity.

As he here repeats and amplifies his account, we can see more clearly what he means to do with such a hypothesis; he converts good will the basic natural instinct into good will the colourless general tendency. This twist of the naturally basic into the elementary and formless is characteristic of the semantics of his own thought system, which always posits value or significance in the end product at the expense of the raw material. So he indeed accepts good will as the initiation of amity (No. 4) where his opposition would say to him: You are using the word *arche* here merely as initiation. Why don't you admit, as you usually do, that it is also the first principle? He even echoes the language of naturalist psychology, by allowing the parallel between good will as the sensory medium of amity, and vision as the medium which kindles passion. He also repeats that good will means instinctive altruism (No. 7).

But then, to keep the conception under control in his own system, he has to deny that it involves psychological depth or drive (No. 3) or leads to co-operative action (No. 8) or has any connection with hedonist or utilitarian motives (Nos. 10, 11). These three negatives are, reportorially speaking, statements of positives; they are positions upheld in the liberal theory; instinctive amity is strong, it issues in action, and it does so because it obeys the motives of pleasure and utility working in parallel.

Then items 12 and 13 take up without warning the relation of good will to benefaction, and we are told that the relationship and the emotions between benefactor and benefited are disparate; good will is the label for that attitude which the benefited has for his benefactor, but not vice versa. This, we suggest, bespeaks an intention to deny the contrary view that (a) good will as altruism issues automatically in benefaction and (b) that it tends to evoke reciprocal benefaction and (c) that good will is then evenly balanced between the two parties in such a relationship. Why this would offend Aristotle is seen in items 18 and 19. Human beings for him are by definition disparate in their moral states, and hence in their material status. Good will is that moral emotion which the inferior is able to feel to his superior, considered as his benefactor (12 and 13) or simply as his model for virtue (18 and 19). It is close to reverent admiration. Aristotle must insist on the importance of finding some room for this kind of emotion in his moral system, for it is so appropriate to relationships which are, morally speaking, unequal. How deep the cleavage here is, between his own idealism and the materialism, if that is the word, of his opponents, he reveals in items 14 to 17. Here what he denies is crucial for understanding liberal theory. The good will and altruism of A have no masochistic roots. They exist as instinctive drives, because based on the (equally instinctive) supposition that A will through them win provision of his own needs from B. Of course this means that A 'wishes good for himself'. Aristotle proposes this as the antithesis to wishing good for B. For the liberals, the antithesis is false; it simply does not exist. Had their doctrine been allowed to prevail and influence the mind of Europe at a crucial stage in its development, who is to say what happier and sunnier societies would not have in time arisen on the plains of Gaul and Germany?

If our inferences are correct – and they can be supported by other contexts – they make clear that the philanthropic school was not utopian: it viewed material interests between men as, at the natural level, either identical or interchangeable or complementary, fulfilled through the exchange of goods and services. Therefore they preached neither altruism nor selfishness, but tried to describe human motivation in a calculus which comprehended and superseded both. Aristotle's thought is committed to quite alien conceptions, which can be described as the absolute 'ego-demands' of the theoretically good man and the absolute 'group demands' of the theoretically ideal state. These two coincide only when the ideal forms in both instances also coincide. Otherwise, his practical ethics, for ordinary men, is shrewd, narrow and authoritarian. It can digest philanthropic liberalism only by first destroying its essential shape.

5

Reports cut to size and disguised as supplements to Aristotle's own theory
[*E.N.* 9.7]
[*E.N.* 9.6]

Three chapters of the ninth book (5, 6 and 7) are respectively devoted to the three topics of good will, consensus and benefaction. They have the air of a desire on Aristotle's part to cover the ground completely before he winds up his treatise on amity. We have suggested that they were, in fact, written to dispose of

three leading conceptions which liberalism had applied in exploring the role of human altruism. Chapter 5 having dealt with 'good
will', as the instinctual basis for altruistic behaviour, chapter 6
turns to 'consensus' as the social and political condition which
results when this human instinct takes organized form in a community, and chapter 7 treats of benefaction as that concrete
method by which it operates between human beings. If in chapter
5, then, Aristotle takes over good will and makes it a kind of
elementary preface to his own system of intimate personal
friendship, in chapters 6 and 7 he treats other elements of the
original theory as supplemental additions or footnotes to his own.
Whether treated as introduction or as supplement, the original
doctrine has, as always, to be reduced and pared to those dimensions which will fit. Since the issue of benefaction has already
come up in connection with good will, let us now consider its
fuller treatment in Chapter 7.

1. Benefactors feel amity for objects of benefaction rather
than vice versa.
2. This is regarded as a paradoxical problem
3. explained popularly on the analogy of the creditor and
debtor; the debtor would abolish the existence of his creditor,
while the creditor seeks to protect the security of his debtor.
4. Some authorities [the poet Epicharmus] say this maligns
human nature, but it is like human nature, most men being
forgetful. [*E.N.* 9.7.1.]
5. Actually the analogy is a poor one. [9.7.2]
6. The benefited is, as it were, the product called into
existence for which the benefactor feels an intimate affection.
[1167b31]
7. This emotional relationship is natural because based on
our desire to exist and to call into existence. [1168a5]
8. On the other hand, the object of benefaction feels only
'interest' in the deed, not pleasure [1168a11]
9. and his utility is impermanent while the moral nobility
of the benefactor is lasting and so leaves a lasting pleasurable
memory in him. [1168a15]
10. Again, to express amity resembles positive action, but
to experience it is negative and those who have the advantage
in action have the advantage in amity. . . . [1168a19]

11. And again, products which cost effort evoke greater affection, whereas to be the object of benefaction costs nothing, which is why mothers are fonder of their own children, they being more conscious that they are their own, and this feeling relates to benefaction too. [9.7.7]

The interest of the argument lies in the persistence with which it isolates benefactor and object of benefaction as two quite different moral species of human beings and treats the benefactor as the morally superior and as conscious of it. To support this he uses the analogy of artist and product. It is not without significance that this implies a reduction of the status of the object of benefaction from a human being to a thing. The same method of reasoning, as we shall see, is used to support the institution of slavery in the *Politics*. The fact is that Aristotle's conception of benefaction is deeply rooted in a premiss he does not here express; namely, that relations between men are rarely egalitarian. Society is hierarchical: benefaction is that mode of action open to the powerful and the rich, as he has already said in the opening of Book 8. He therefore refuses even to consider how a benefaction might operate as *mutual* altruism between *equal* human beings. Instead he takes care to eliminate any such notion. But his insistence on the moral difference between agent and object is, we suggest, an answer to an egalitarian theory which argued the opposite. He has therefore abolished the significance of benefaction as a universal principle operating between human beings, and he does this by confining it within the dimensions of a one-sided operation available only to the superior party in a disparate human relationship. Only so can he accommodate the conception to his own moral scheme.

The liberal concept of consensus as an application of good will at the political level offers a more stubborn problem of accommodation, and he is unable to deal with it without some contradiction:

1. Consensus belongs to the amity category
2. therefore it cannot be congruence of opinion
3. which would be available to men who were mutually unaware [ignorant] of each other
4. nor does it apply to congruent decision about any and every topic [e.g. astronomical problems].

5. It is held that cities enjoy consensus
6. when common sentiments prevail covering [common] interests
7. and when these are made [voted] into declared preferences
8. and embodied in action
9. which reflects opinions reached in common. [9.6.1.]
10. I.e., consensus occurs in the realm of important action
11. involving two parties or all parties.
(12. Examples: unanimous opinion to have the offices elective, or form an alliance with Sparta, or that Pittacus should hold sole office
13. [versus] a division between two parties as to which should hold office, which means faction.)
14. Now consensus does not mean that both parties 'think the same thing', whatever that thing may be
(15. but only when they think of it as being in the same hands
16. e.g., when the *demos* and the upper classes agree that the aristocrats should hold authority.)
17. In fact, consensus is 'city-state amity'.
18. It does pertain to [human] interests and what affects livelihood. [9.6.2.]
(19. Now you get such consensus only in upper classes. . . . They wish for what is morally right, and of interest, and aim in common thereat . . . [9.6.3.]
20. The inferior classes are incapable of consensus. They aim to grab something selfishly from among the utilities . . . so that faction is their normal condition since they refuse to do what is morally right.) [9.6.4.]

It may be doubted whether any passage in Aristotle more unblushingly uncovers the narrow partisanship of his political ideals. It is more to our present purpose that he does this by correcting a previous usage of the term 'consensus' which he thinks improper. It had been a traditional term with a traditional significance which predated democratic theory, and to this he seeks to return, but with a difference, even so. Loosely speaking, the earlier legislators had advocated consensus as a 'harmony of parties'. Aristotle brushes this aside with his own brand of cool and clear logic: there can be no real harmony between aristocrats and lesser breeds; there can be a common acceptance of the fact that the superior elements must rule (15, 16) which may be called consensus; but, properly speaking, unanimity is possible only among the aristocratic elements themselves, who have the sense to hang together against the rest (19). Here he offers a virtually Platonic conception of the closed ranks of a governing class, and if he were asked in what terms to describe the over-all condition of the united community, it would seem that in place of consensus he would prefer the Platonic substitute, 'discipline' (*sophrosune*).

However, while merely amending the old traditional view of consensus, he sharply corrects the democratic conception of it which had begun to emerge, as we have seen, in Democritus, and which, it is to be inferred, was further pursued by the later liberals.

If we take his negatives as revealing positives, we learn:

Consensus is congruence of political opinion (2)
reached impersonally among any group of human beings (3)
and reflects capacity of human beings to reach operative opinion about anything after conference (14)

To these planks Aristotle adds several more in the form of positive admissions. Consensus, he proceeds to confess, is indeed a congruence of political opinion reached in common (9). This seems to be a flat contradiction of item 2 and indeed it is. Aristotle begins by overhastily denying what he is later, with honest reporting, obliged to admit.

In fact, items 5 to 11 seem to constitute an isolated paragraph of faithful reporting. They state, perhaps by inadvertence, the true liberal theory of consensus; it is simply a rationalization of what we today call the democratic process, in which argumentative discussions end in common agreement and in common decisions implemented in the form of legislative enactments. Nor is this rationalization, practical though it was, unconnected with liberal first principles. Aristotle includes the topic in the context of amity. This gives us a hint that the account of the democratic process, so strongly reminiscent of the formulas by which Protagoras and Gorgias accounted for the formation of opinion, sought to base itself on what were viewed as psychological realities. This was the way in which basic human philanthropy works itself out to practical effect in the joint action required of organized groups.

But Aristotle's objection to such a notion is so fundamental that it provokes him to an unusually explicit statement of reactionary politics. First he brushes aside the operation of opinion formation on any and every issue. The only important issues to agree on, he assures us, are constitutional, i.e. who holds power (12, 13, 15, 16). And then, the role of the *demos* in forming opinion is simply abolished. Instead, the upper class unite in a congruence not of opinion but of moral conviction, of which they have a monopoly (19 and 20). Thus he disposes of what was perhaps his most influential and dangerous opponent in the whole body of liberal political theory; namely, the presumption that the actual working of a democracy could be analysed and described cogently and rationally as a meeting of minds. This was dangerous, because it had epistemological arguments to bring against the *a priori* doctrine of both Plato and Aristotle; and it was dangerous, because it described an actual working system, the municipal democracy of the fourth century, to which they remained studiously indifferent or actively hostile. To describe is also to defend, which is why they dared not allow liberalism the privilege of a proper description.

Report dismembered and denatured piecemeal
[*E.N.* 8.9-12]

If we return from the ninth to the eighth Book of the *Ethics*, we find that by the time Aristotle has reached the end of Chapter 8 of that book, he had defined with sufficient clarity his own teleological conception of human amity: it should reach its perfected form as a moral friendship between good men (8.3); this is its most valid form; those brands which reflect pleasure or utility are inherently inferior and occur between inferior men (8.4-6); since society is composed of human beings who are unequal both in social and in moral stature, friendship must be adjusted to suit these differences; it will be expressed in attitudes and services proportionate to the respective grades of the two parties (8.7-8). Thus it submits to a calculus not unlike the calculus of proportionate justice in Book 5.

This brings him to the relation between amity and justice (Chapter 9); and to what might be called the social context of amity. Now, early in his introduction, as we have seen (8.1.2ff.), he had shown awareness that his own brand of personal friendship was not the only possible conception. There was the view that amity was a generic or biological emotion characteristic of the human race as such; it was responsible, perhaps for the formation, at least for the cohesion, of political society, and in this guise it was proclaimed to be the fountain from which men drew, or should draw, their criteria of what is right and just. These propositions open up radically new perspectives – new, that is to say, when judged by the light of Aristotle's system. But the view offered has been tantalizingly brief. The historian would like a further report on a school which had evidently felt the influences of the anthropologists, of Democritus, and of Antiphon, but had combined these in a new synthesis, a new constructive theory of morals and politics. The report is forthcoming, when in Chapter 9 Aristotle returns to the social context of amity, by asking: What is the connection between amity and justice? And in fact chapters 9 and 12 form a sort of excursus. A treatise consecrated to ideal personal friendship is interrupted by a consideration of amity as it might be conceived taking institutional form.

Since this fundamentally reflects the whole liberal attitude to amity, as inclusive rather than exclusive, a conception of philanthropy in the large rather than of personal friendship in the intimate, these four chapters contain many echoes of liberalism. Aristotle is not interested in refuting them for their own sake; they must be defeated and digested into his own system of concepts. It is therefore characteristic that as he allows himself the luxury of digression into a field potentially dangerous to his own teleology, he does this only after he had first established his reader firmly in Aristotelian views of what friendship really is. The four chapters are enclosed and contained within a context which helps to control them, and which assists the reader in glossing over those elements of liberal ideology which briefly intrude.

Nor does Aristotle allow this report on social amity to be made as a whole. Its over-all pattern, if perceived, might appear too convincing; its own inner logic must be concealed. So to deal with it adequately he dismembers it, and brings up items in the liberal account piecemeal, so that they can be corrected piecemeal. No doubt he did this without conscious deliberation. It is the way his mind works and, as a philosopher bent on substantiating the different logic of his own system, he was perfectly justified in so doing.

To clarify what has happened in these four chapters, it will be easiest first to abstract and to represent the various liberal items contained in them, before describing the context in which they have been placed and which is used to denature them. They emerge in four distinct portions, which we shall for convenience identify as A, B, C, D. These occur not in the order that the original authors would have chosen, but according to that connection required by the logic of Aristotle's own treatment.

A

'It is held' that in every [type of] community there inheres a principle of right
and also amity.
For instance, in our language, 'adventurer-companions' and 'soldier-companions' imply that the members are amicable, and the same applies to other types of community.
The degrees of amity correspond to the degrees of community, as does the degree of moral right.
The proverb 'Common are the things of amicable men' is correct
for amity inheres in community [8.9.1.]

B

All types of community are like departments of the civic community;
for instance, companions in adventure join to achieve some [common] interest,
i.e. to make provision for some of the needs required for livelihood.
The city-state community, 'it is held', originally was combined to serve interest
and persists for the same purpose.
Thus legislators made this their aim by asserting that [moral] right is the community interest. [8.9.4.]
The [smaller] forms of community aim at interest departmentally.
For example, merchant voyagers for economic gains of the voyage,
soldier companies for money, victory or booty gained in war;
clan members and deme members operate on the same principle.

Besides interest, 'it is held', pleasure is another motive for other types of community

such as cult societies and social clubs,

for cult proceedings, beside providing honour for divine beings,

ensure provision of relaxation plus pleasure to the human beings concerned.

Indeed, primitive sacrifice and assemblage would appear to have accompanied harvest

when leisure was most appropriate. [8.9.5.]

C[a]

'It is held' that there inheres a principle of right between any one human being and any other

who is capable of communal participation in custom-law and compact.

Hence also amity inheres as well between human beings *qua* human beings. [8.11.7.]

Amity and moral right are found at a minimum in despotic relationships.

They are maximized in democracies.

For between human beings [treated as] equals, communal [interests] are maximized. [8.11.8.]

C[b]

Amities which are city-wide or clan-wide

or merchant-adventurer-wide

are closer to community-type amity

than is kin-group amity,

for they owe their existence, in a sense, to man-made convention (*homologia*)

and can include international amity [8.12.1.]

D

Male and female, 'it is held', enjoy an amity according to nature.

The human being is by nature not so much a *polis*-living animal as a mating animal

since reproduction is the common property he shares with all animals.

However, whereas the purpose of animal mating is confined
to this,
human beings mate also for purposes of general livelihood.
[Male and female] suffice for each other's need
contributing individual resources to a common stock
whence, 'it is held,' in this type of amity
there inheres both utility and pleasure. [8.12.7a.]

That Aristotle is indeed citing other men's doctrines can be
perceived in the reiteration of the reporter's verb 'it is held
that . . .'. But even without this signpost, the liberal origin of
these items is plain. Though buried in an alien context which
helps to disguise their flavour, the coherence and clarity of that
philosophy of politics and society which they represent becomes
unmistakable when they are isolated and viewed in sequence.
The gulf between Aristotle and his source lies not only in conclusions but in method. These statements approach man and
society descriptively and historically, without *a priori* judgment of
value; they view the human group in all of its manifestations
coolly and dispassionately. No type of group is excluded; all are
equally significant, for all are based on the urge to satisfy material
needs and interests at different levels of integration. They begin,
perhaps, with the mating pair, which comes last in Aristotle (D),
but first in a properly genetic account. Inadvertently, perhaps,
the reporter here discloses his own distance from what he reports:
man is by nature a mating animal and not a civic animal. This
flatly contradicts the position which is later to be assumed in the
Politics. And at this primary level, man's two urges are pleasure
and utility, for himself even more than for his children. This
point of view, however 'selfish' it seems, can be paralleled in the
teachings of Democritus and Antiphon; the latter, we have
suggested, may have gone further and insisted on a spontaneous
mating as against conventionally arranged marriage as alone
fulfilling man's inner need for personal and intimate consensus.
Taken as a whole, however, the views of man and society here
recorded in all four sections are Democritean rather than Antiphonic; or rather they reflect a sort of synthesis of both; a mature
liberal theory which accepts society but insists it must express
Antiphonic values.

The formulas of sections A and B make systematic use of the

concept of 'community' or 'partnership' (*koinonia*). The liberals may have been the first to apply this term in the context of social theory. It crystallizes the idea of 'society' formed at all levels of integration. It was the term used by Plato in his descriptive account of the origins of the *polis* in the *Republic*, and is commonly applied by Aristotle in both *Ethics* and *Politics* to various types and levels of social organization, but in particular to the family and city communities. Now, it is significant of the temper of liberalism that the kind of 'community' which here seems to be cited as typical of the workings of all community at all levels is the commercial company of merchant adventurers or the hired band of mercenary soldiers (A). For here can be seen the unifying effect on human beings of the organized pursuit of common material objectives. Again, these types of association subsist by virtue of a 'convention' or common agreement (C[b]). Is this to be a foundation argument for the theory that law and justice themselves are created by human compact? It is characteristic of the descriptive method that, rather than start with the city-state and work backwards, it should start with precivic types of community and work forwards. Thus the clan and deme are included (section B), and we hear another echo of the method and language of Democritus. Indeed, we are treated to an anthropological footnote (B sub fin.) in which we are reminded that historically speaking religious festival is a first-fruits festival, serving the purpose of physical recreation. This purpose explains its timing, for it coincides with that agricultural leisure available in the late fall. The footnote also reminds us that material need includes pleasurable satisfaction as well as utilitarian services. Indeed, the two do not conflict but march parallel.

But though descriptive and naturalist, this embryo science of society is not materialist. It keeps its gaze focused on that species of philanthropic amity which, latent in all men as an instinct, emerges actively at an organized level in organized communities. This, and not superior intelligence controlling distributive apportionment, is the fountain of morals and justice between men. So we get the striking statement that any two men, *qua* men, are capable of full community and partnership inspired by amity and expressive of basic justice and right (C). It is in that egalitarian society created under democracy that human beings maximize these potentialities (C). Once more we hear an unmistakable echo of Democritus. Aristotle, it could be said, here lapses by inadvertence into straight reporting of a doctrine which he is going to have to contradict in his *Politics*.

But, on the whole, effective contradiction and correction are managed within the compass of these four chapters themselves, if one now considers the setting, the frame of the picture, so to speak, which has been designed to control the perspectives which it contains.

This pattern of control is highly significant for the understanding of Aristotle's own inspiration; it reveals the unconscious assumptions and the archaic prejudices on which he erected his own system of politics. Each section of reporting is followed up by a section of Aristotelian argument designed to bring the report into line. These four passages of teleological control we will for convenience identify as P, Q, R, S.

P

Blood-brothers and comrades have complete community.
Other combinations enjoy definable types of community in varying degree
since amities vary in intensity.
Hence also the principles of right involved vary in application.
For example, from parent to children,
versus from blood-brother to blood-brother,
versus from comrade to comrade,
versus from citizen to citizen.
The same applies to all types of amity
with corresponding differences in degrees of moral wrong
with the wrong increasing as the tie of amity gets closer;
e.g. it is more awful to rob a comrade
than to rob a fellow citizen,
or to refuse to help a blood-brother
than to refuse a man outside the kin group,
to kill your father
than to kill anyone else.
In fact, the degree of moral right and wrong increases proportionately with the degree of closeness of the tie of amity.
[8.9.2-3.]

These few pregnant sentences draw upon that reservoir of archaic prejudice which clings to two social ties conceived as

THE LIBERAL TEMPER IN GREEK POLITICS

prior to all others: firstly, the blood-group, identified as the patriarchal unit, the household plus the clan of households, and secondly, the heroic band of peers, young fighting men who exchange oaths and operate as comrades in a group sworn to protect and defend each other. These are mobilized here with great effectiveness as a battery with which to demolish the intellectual universalism implicit in that liberal position just stated in section A. It is going to be essential to Aristotle's own hierarchical social system to assert a formal differentiation between different types of community, which shall correspond to moral and social differentiation. So, in effect, he is preparing to bring in the family and its values in order to destroy and obliterate the liberal vision of universal community and undifferentiated philanthropy.

Q

The next piece of purely Aristotelean doctrine occupies all of Chapter 10 and most of Chapter 11. Because it opens abruptly with a constitutional analysis, it wears the air of a digression, but, before it is concluded, the analysis has returned to the kin group and we realize that Aristotle, so far from relinquishing his thread, is knotting it more tightly. To counter the liberals, he has already started to probe what he considers to be the fundamentals of any community, and he here continues the task:

The three fundamental types of normal polity [constitution] and their aberrant counterparts,
monarchy *versus* despotism
aristocracy *versus* oligarchy
timocracy or polity *versus* democracy. [8.10.1-3.]
The corresponding three fundamental types of community in the household
patriarchal – father's rule over sons
marital – husband's rule over wife
sibling – blood-brother's equality with blood-brother. [8.10.4-6.]
The corresponding three fundamental types of amity and of moral right [which runs parallel]:
(a) monarchic benevolence towards political subjects [8.11.1.]
plus patriarchal benevolence towards children

[Aristotelean footnote: by nature the father is the ruling element over
the son, and ancestors over descendants, and monarchs over subjects
[8.11.2.] hence the corresponding amities and justices are proportionate];
[8.11.3.]
(b) aristocratic [patronizing] amity of husband for wife
as of the morally superior for the inferior; [8.11.4.]
(c) timocratic amity of free-born equals
corresponding to blood-brother amity of siblings. [8.11.5.]
The aberrant type known as despotism contains least amity
and implies least moral obligation
where there is a minimum of common interest between
despot and subject.
Compare craftsman *versus* his product or tool,
soul *versus* body,
master *versus* slave.
You cannot enjoy a moral relationship involving amity
with an inanimate object
or a domestic animal
or a slave *qua* slave.
The slave is an animate tool
and a tool is an inanimate slave. [8.11.6.]

Now, section P had already indicated his intention of dis-
rupting an egalitarian and universalist conception of society by
advancing, so to speak under cover, the alternative type of human
relationship exhibited in the kin group. Here he brings it out into
the open. For it is not always sufficiently noticed that the paradigm
of constitutions, a variant on Plato's schematism, although he
begins with it, really emanates from and is controlled by the
paradigm of household authority which follows it. He is going in
his *Politics* to argue that the *polis* is the family, writ large. Here he
is already preparing that position. Now the skill of the section as
a piece of interpretation – and misrepresentation – of liberalism
lies in this: it enables him to resume the concept of 'community'
(*koinonia*), but in a radically altered form. It suddenly appears as
equivalent to the authoritarian relationship between the (all-
wise, all-benevolent) ruler and his subject, between the patriarch
and his children, between the husband and his (obedient) wife.
Egalitarian associations, as a type, are limited to that which is
found between a band of blood-brothers, a thinly disguised clan
of predatory Homeric warriors.

Are these normative types of constitution to be taken seriously as three forms of ideal state? It is difficult to say. For the paradigm, while it seems to intend a classification of states, is really directed to a different end and a subtler purpose. He wishes to insinuate and to substantiate what in his view is the basis and purpose of any community: namely, the organization of human beings under authoritarian regulation, which recognizes degrees and types of moral and social status but is always authoritarian. This he thinks he can do if he can prove it for the kin group, for this he takes to be the prototype of all groups. True, the kin group recognizes a sibling comradeship, but (though he does not explicitly say so) this kind of equality is not its central characteristic. Armed with this paradigm of kin-group relations, he can then proceed to the second stage of his attack on liberalism. He can dissolve the concept of a universal philanthropy between human beings as such by splitting it into three different emotional patterns of amity: that of authoritarian benevolence; that of aristocratic guidance; and that of blood-brother loyalty.

He has now eliminated from liberalism not only its universalism and its philanthropy but its egalitarianism also. To complete this last stage of demolition, he then enlarges on that relationship found, according to his analysis, in the despotic form of state (8.11.6). Now this is or should be an aberrant form of political constitution, yet in this appendix it creeps back into a semi-respectability. Why? Because it is needed to rationalize the ownership of slaves within the household group. This shows how his constitutionalism is only a means to other ends. His eye is all the time on those formal elements of the patriarchal household, all of them authoritarian, which he deploys with more finality and clarity in his *Politics*. Thus he needs to rationalize and justify one kind of so-called human relationship in which amity does not appear at all, nor even moral obligation. This type is accommodated neatly to that element in the household so far unaccounted for – the slave. In a master's despotism over his slave there is strictly speaking no room for mutuality or community. So, to explain this, the slave must be depersonalized into a 'living tool', over which despotic authority can be exercised with complete propriety.

That this is meant seriously is evident again from the *Politics*, with its fuller and more frank disposition of the human slave in this handy category. Indeed, as we have said, throughout this digestion and conquest of liberal doctrine, he is laying the ground for the fundamental positions taken up in the later treatise.

But there follows section C of the liberal report already given, an item perhaps unique of its kind in Aristotle's writing. For instead of being a piece of testimony carefully controlled by context, it reads more like an angry protest against what he has just said. Indeed, he here reverses himself: all human beings are members one of another; they communicate in amity and in moral obligation. Therefore, if a slave cannot be a human being, should a slave exist at all? As we know from the *Politics*, the complete liberal position denied that he should. Aristotle knows it and is determined to settle this heresy. But all he can do here is to cover the yawning gulf between the heresy and his own formula for man by glueing them together with a sentence which simply recognizes the gulf and expresses it in the form of a logical dichotomy; he splits his victim down the middle; *qua* slave he is a thing, *qua* man he may still enjoy the status of a human being. It is thus that philosophers can sometimes employ the resources of language to evade a moral issue. His device, whether regarded as philosophic or propagandist, proved effective for many weary centuries, till at last liberalism could be revived and the philosophic defence of slavery abandoned, but without benefit of that Hellenic insight of long ago, for that had been effectively denatured in these pages.

R

The liberal doctrine presented in section C had concluded with the suggestion that a distinction should be made between the kin group and other forms of community, commercial, social and the like. These latter, created by 'agreed convention', more effectively express that social principle represented in amity. The distinction seems to be drawn to the disadvantage of the kin group, as not involving human compact and as narrowing the emotional possibilities of philanthropy too much. But this is speculative. Liberal theory may simply have noted the kin group as having special features. What is certain is that Aristotle, reversing the emphasis, converts this separate identification of the kin group into an excuse for dwelling on the closer and more significant forms of amity which, from his point of view, inhered in that relation. The absence of agreed convention is for him a moral advantage. So his own corrective commentary follows:

> Kin group community, despite its variety, depends ultimately on the patriarchal role.
>
> Parents love their children as parts of themselves and vice versa.
>
> The progenitor knows his offspring and has more familiarity with it
>
> than the reverse.
>
> For example, he recognizes the teeth, hair, etc.
>
> and has a head start in time, since he begins conscious loving right away,
>
> hence the reason for more intense love shown by mothers. [8.12.2]
>
> In sum, progenitors feel amity for offspring as though for themselves
>
> but offspring feel amity for parents only as derived by nature from them,
>
> and blood-brother for blood-brother as they derive from the same source.
>
> It is their common relation to the parent that makes for identity between themselves,
>
> hence the phrase 'same blood,' 'same root,' etc. [8.12.3]
>
> Common nurture and contemporary ages contribute a good deal to amity,
>
> hence blood-brother amity has a similitude to comradeship.
>
> The cousins and other relations enjoy familiarity by the same principle,
>
> that is, by derivation from the common ancestor.
>
> Proximity or distance of relationship to the patriarch (*archegos*) governs the degree of familiarity. [8.12.4]
>
> Now the amity of children towards parents
>
> like that of men towards gods
>
> is that felt for an ideal which surpasses ours.
>
> Those who have 'fathered well' deserve the 'biggest things'.
>
> The ancestor is the greatest benefactor,
>
> being the author of being, nurture and education. [8.12.5]
>
> This amity also includes pleasure and utility
>
> more than that felt for members outside the kin group

in proportion as the community of living (-pattern) within the kin group is closer . . . [8.12.6]

The antique bias is familiar, for it persists to this day, in the face of contrary experience, in all communities where the liberal values of a commercial-exchange society exist in competition with an agricultural and patriarchal condition. The hold of these conceptions on Aristotle is too often ignored by his interpreters. As offered here, they clinch the argument in favour of the blood group as the basis of significant politics, in place of the exchange economy featured in Plato's *Republic* and described elsewhere in both *Ethics* and *Politics*. Plato had, it is true, launched his society out of a household, but, more faithful to his source, he had not treated this household as a kin group. The relations of parent and child, husband and wife, owner and slave, had never emerged in the description as relevant to social development. Aristotle with an unfaltering hand sets the clock back. In place of the theoretic household, used as the mere matrix for a society of divided labour and exchange of products, he puts in very truth a flesh-and-blood household. Nor is his purpose confined to the negative objective of interpreting the liberal idea of community out of its original shape. He is, we repeat, laying the groundwork for his *Politics*. Now, one of the two central premisses of that *Politics* will prove to be that all human relations are by nature authoritarian, and that politics, therefore, deals primarily with the problem of the correct definition of political power and rule. To support this premiss, he fathers an anthropology of his own to displace the universalist anthropology of his rivals. In his version, the earliest society already recognizes a rule of father over children, husband over wife, master over slave. And this supplies the moral archetype for all societies. The pattern must be preserved, then, in all healthy types which have emerged from the primitive mould. Thus and only thus can he deal a death-blow to liberal egalitarianism and total democracy. Here in the *Ethics* he is taking up his stance for the delivery of that blow.

S

His analysis of the kin group has suggested, in defiance of Plato, an authoritarian relationship between the sexes, without, however, clearly defining or defending it. A last desperate honesty then made him add, as we saw, a liberal passage (D) suggesting that the mating relationship between the sexes reflects a quite different kind of amity from his, one conferring a completely mutual pleasure and utility on its members, independent of reproduction.

To this, too, he is now forced to add a final correction:

If the partners are virtuous, the amity will reflect virtue combining their respective virtues.
Children also are a great bond.
Childless matings are more liable to disruption.
The children form a common good
and the common good is a uniting principle.
The problem of how a man should conduct his life in relation to women,
as of any relationship involving amity,
is simply the problem of [estimating] the moral rights involved.
These vary in the various amities which subsist
between close friends
versus between men unrelated by blood
versus between comrades
versus between club members. [8.12.7b.]

That image of a spontaneous, sympathetic mating union, which might have become the germ of a doctrine of romantic love in Greece, vanishes like smoke before the patriarchal severity which demands a union of virtues, a joint responsibility in reproduction and (he broadly hints) a system of moral rights which assumes that the male patriarch is the superior. For are not all relationships (he implies) varied, and only rarely built upon a basic equality between partners?

7
Report perhaps preserved intact

The fifth book of Aristotle's *Ethics* is devoted to the single topic of 'justice' (the usual English translation, though the Greek includes 'moral right'), that most ambitious of virtues and, as he says himself, the most comprehensive. His definition of the subject, the main distinctions he wishes to draw and the main applications he wishes to make, are established by the end of the seventh chapter (out of a total of eleven). Within these seven chapters is contained a good deal of indirect testimony bearing on the liberal view of justice. But the chapters make hard reading; Aristotle's own thread of connection is often difficult to establish, and there is good reason for this. His argumentation, taken as a whole, only makes sense if it is regarded as composed of parts or sections which compete with each other. On the one hand, they seem to defend two different conceptions of justice; and on the other, to describe two irreconcilable views of the proper legal relation between human beings.

First, as to the two conceptions of justice: the teaching of the previous books has been constructed so as to culminate in an analysis of the virtues, taken one by one, as illustrations of his formula of the ethical mean. This means that he now wishes to discuss justice as a personal state of character (*hexis*) primarily identifiable as a condition within 'me', or as resulting in a series of actions 'I' perform and for which 'I' personally am responsible. This he calls 'that justice which is a department of virtue'. He also calls it, misleadingly, 'absolute' as against that brand which operates 'in relation to others'. Its correct label would be the Greek *dikaiosune* or 'righteousness'.

But equally he wishes to include within the same purview an analysis of another 'justice', as the symbol of the correct regulation of social relations. This he calls 'relative to another' and 'political' and 'complete'. Clearly the Greek tongue would have been better equipped if it could have supplied him with distinct terms. (We ourselves, however, still speak of personal morality *versus* social morality.)

Righteousness as a personal state of character built up by deliberate choice and measuring its behaviour as a mean between extremes is a concept adapted from Plato and specifically worked up into its Aristotelian form. On this he spends the major portion of his attention and space. When he turns to consider 'political' justice, we feel not only that by comparison his treatment is brief and summary, but that he is speaking in terms alien to the rest of his presentation. He raises more problems about it than he solves.

The second main contradiction within his treatment cuts even deeper: it lies between two irreconcilable views of human nature and human beings. Either they are to be viewed as morally unequal and requiring therefore to measure themselves by a 'proportionate' justice or morality, which recognizes wide degrees of moral worth and merit; or else they are for practical purposes to be regarded as equal, and the inequalities lie not in the persons themselves but in the things they have or the things done to them. Justice will then consist in 'restoring equality' of things or conditions in order to match the presumed equality of the human beings involved.

Of each of these pairs of positions, the latter alternative was the liberal one. The liberals (a) by-passed the problem of inner moral character, which they presumably regarded as not amenable to the descriptive method, and addressed themselves to the proper regulation of men's external relations with each other; and (b) felt that social regulation should conform to the principle that human beings, for social purposes, are equal. If these two liberal postulates had been reported clearly by Aristotle and then denied or brushed aside, he would have written a clearer exposition of his own doctrine as well as of that of his rivals. But on the rule, to which he is always faithful, that you must not confute and reject but absorb and digest, he does two things which utterly confuse the issue.

Firstly, while still engaged in the presentation of a personal moral justice as a virtue – to him the prior commitment – he works in two applications of justice in the fields of legal administration and economic exchange, which, properly speaking, should belong to political justice, if anywhere. That is, he tries by extension of context to extend the sway of his personal moralistic conception over areas where it does not rightfully belong. And, in both these cases, he gets into the field of liberal theory, both political and economic.

Secondly he is determined not to allow the liberals to arrogate to themselves the propagandist advantage of claiming the gospel of 'equality' for themselves. For this had a great hold on the Greek mind. So he constructs his famous formula of 'proportional equality' in place of actual personal equality. This, in human terms, is simply a piece of double-talk. It consists in assuming that persons A and B are fundamentally unequal: therefore their deserts or rewards, as enjoyed in the community, represented by C and D respectively, will also be unequal. He then proposes the truism that since C corresponds to A and D to B, A is to C as B is to D: which of course is correct and proves nothing. But it gives him a specious pretext for claiming that he too believes in 'equality' – namely, a correspondence of proportion. Only his brand is more sophisticated and 'educated'.

Given this kind of manipulation of the term 'equal' (*ison*), it can be imagined that his notices of the liberal doctrine can become dangerously corrupted. However, in one chapter, the fourth, which he devotes to the topic of how the legal process works, he drops his own special brand of proportional equality altogether and reverts to the normal meaning of the term equal. And here, perhaps, he reports the liberal view of legal process unadorned by teleology.

The clash between Aristotelian and liberal notions of equality, when perceived, is very striking, and can be demonstrated from his text rather easily, as follows:

The third chapter proceeds to set forth that form of the doctrine closest to his heart and most typical of him. Justice is envisaged not primarily as the negative correction of injustice, but as that formula which arranges the positive status of the just. He postulates that the relative virtue and personal moral worth of a man can be ascertained: it is definable, whether you call it a quantity, a quality or a status. Has he not spent many pages telling us how virtue operates in measured form? If it measures, it can be measured (a proposition which he assumes without proof). Hence the 'estate' – shall we call it? – that is, the money, honour or status appropriate to such a human being can be estimated in proportion to his worth; and the justice which regulates this proportion is called 'distributive' (5.4.2). This seems pretty theoretic, unless an all-wise ruler is to dole out estates. It is more to Aristotle's purpose that he then seems to argue that the different estates of different persons can be relatively estimated and defended as representing 'proportionately' their relative moral merit. Thus the analysis has anything but a theoretic purpose. It is designed to give philosophic respectability to a society of orders and stations, and ranks and privileges. No chapter in his works reveals better than this the direction in which the bias of his social thinking tended.

The fourth chapter (beginning at 5. 4. 3) brings Aristotle to the more conventional topic of corrective or legal justice, that is, the kind which most people, and most Greeks, would think of as characteristically enforced by legal machinery. Now here, as we have said, the striking thing is that he drops the previous assumption that men are fundamentally unequal. The law, as we would say, is 'no respecter of persons'. Punishments or correctives, for murder, theft, and tort of all descriptions, are assigned regardless of the position or status of the persons involved (at least formally speaking). He is forced to realize that in any egalitarian system of justice, such as was growing up in the Greek city-states of his day, this was true. Hence 'the laws deal with men as equals' (5.4.3; cf. 5.4.10) and for a while we hear no more of 'proportionate equality' (i.e. personal inequality).

In the process of corrective justice, not only are persons treated as equals, but the application of redress is treated as one of 'equalization'. How is this to be made to apply? The answer is, by using a conceptual device which regards the offender in a tort as having acquired unjustifiable advantage or 'gain', and the victim as having suffered a loss or diminution (5.4.4-5). Justice redistributes the situation, subtracting from one man's gain to add to another's loss and so restoring the two individuals to their previous equality.

This rather striking theory may be liberal doctrine which has been retained in the pages of Aristotle virtually unchanged. For, as a rationalization of the legal process, it would reconcile that process with the supposition that all men are naturally equal. The courts merely restore such an equivalence which has become disarranged. And it would therefore also reconcile the need for the existence of law, viewed as a social compact, man-made, with those supposedly natural philanthropic relations proper to human beings. For positive law would exist simply to protect these relations or to restore them if abrogated.

This speculative inference that we are being really treated to a report on liberal theory is supported not only by the contradiction with the anti-egalitarian philosophy of the previous chapter, but by the curious appendix:

These terms, loss [or penalty] and gain [or advantage]
are derived from voluntary exchange
for example, in buying and selling
and in all other matters where law has provided social security (*adeia*) [5.4.13].

Now in terms of traditional usage, this derivation would seem artificial. The average Greek would think of 'loss' or penalty as meaning personal injury to honour or life, rather than economic 'damages'. But the artificiality of the transposition may suggest the economic and materialist bias of liberal political thinkers, who would look for the model of justice not in heroic tradition nor in *a priori* concepts but in the process of commercial exchange, and apply what they found to be the working principle of exchange as the working principle of social justice also. This kind of genetic approach to political justice would assume that historically the problem of adjusting material needs had to be solved before men reached the finer points of moral virtue. This would fit the bias of the anthropologists which, as we have seen, regularly envisioned the first communities as formed under material pressure to gain and to preserve food, etc., before they ever thought of morals in a civilized sense.

This facet of liberal theory, as thus reconstructed, remains, we repeat, speculative, but it leads right into the analysis of how the exchange economy works, and here developing contradictions within the heart of the report itself disclose an original which has been emended.

8

Report subjected to distortion by interpolation
[*E.N.* 5.5.6-16.]

The fifth chapter, under the heading of 'reciprocity' as a facet of human behaviour, proposes an analysis of 'that type of justice which gives coherence in communities-of-exchange'. Now, it is vital to notice that his context is not political. He still thinks he is involved with moral justice as a personal virtue of character. Thus, in the definitions of chapter 2, which were intended as introductory to his whole treatment, he included economic operations (buying, selling, lending, deposit, etc.) in the same category with illegal acts like theft, adultery, assault, robbery, and the like. The combination looks quaint, and has rightly provoked the curiosity of commentators. But it is quite strictly enforced on Aristotle by his moral teleological approach to all problems of society. He does not mean that communal transactions are also illegal transactions; he means that buying and selling and theft and robbery are alike examples simply of trans-actions, of active human relations in which men become involved, voluntarily in the one case, involuntarily in the other. And a science of moral justice exists to supervise all human relations in a moral manner. Thus his classification ensures that the economic side of life will not get out of hand and run away with itself to furnish a type of calculus and a type of justice which would cope with purely material necessities. It is men that have to be regulated (he says), not things.

In line with this classification, then, when he comes to describe how the exchange-economy aspect of society works, he weaves into a purely descriptive account of the exchange of goods and services a teleological assumption that the men exchanging them are themselves morally unequal, and that we must construct a formula for commercial activity which will satisfy this moral inequality. But his basic account, we repeat, is descriptive and came from the liberals, who assumed equality or likeness of persons, and variety or unlikeness of material resources at the disposal of persons, and hence a variety (or inequality) of needs. Exchange and division of labour, currency and the like, were devised to assist in the redistribution of resources as evenly as possible, to match the equality of the human beings who wished to use them. Aristotle reduces this perfectly understandable theory to confusion by interlarding here and there both inequality of persons and proportional exchange of goods and services. The two strands in the account can be unravelled and presented separately. They are so ingeniously interwoven that it will be convenient to tabulate them side by side in descending parallel columns.

ARISTOTLE	THE LIBERALS
A return which is proportionate is represented by a cross-conjunction.	
If A is the builder, B the cobbler, C the house, D the shoe [5.5.8]	
	the builder must receive from the cobbler his product and vice versa.

LIBERALISM IN THE *ETHICS*

<table>
<tr><td>ARISTOTLE</td><td>THE LIBERALS</td></tr>
</table>

ARISTOTLE

Provided you start with the principle of proportionate equality and follow it up by reciprocity, you get what I mean

but otherwise you don't get [true] equality, nor can it stand up.

There is nothing to prevent the product of one party being superior to that of the other.

THE LIBERALS

These two products, then, must be equated

and so in the case of all the technologies.

ARISTOTLE

The basis of the technologies would be undermined if the type, amount and quality of the object did not correspond exactly to the type, amount and quality of the effort put into it [5.5.9].

THE LIBERALS

For a community is not created by combining two doctors, but by combining a doctor and a farmer;

in fact by combining different types of workers

ARISTOTLE

and unequal types of workers who must however be equalized [5.5.10].

THE LIBERALS

Therefore all products put into exchange must somehow be made comparable

for which purpose currency came on the scene.

For currency is a measure of everything,

ARISTOTLE	THE LIBERALS
so that it measures also the [personal] excess and defect,	
	that is, how many shoes are equal to a house or a man's food.
Now, as is the ratio of the builder to the cobbler, so must the number of shoes be to the house or the food, etc.	
	If you don't have this universal measure, you don't get exchange or community.
You don't get [measure?] unless things are equated somehow [5.5.11].	
	All things, then, to repeat, must be measured by some one thing.
	Fundamentally, this is demand-and-use (*chreia*),
	by which the whole [system] coheres.
	If men did not have wants, if these wants were not similar, you would not get exchange, or at least not uniform exchange.
	Currency has arisen as a substitute for the pressure of demand and is so constituted by compact.
	This is the reason for the term 'currency', since it exists not by nature but by 'current law'.
	It is in the power of human beings to alter [the material of it] and put [a previous currency] out of use.

ARISTOTLE	THE LIBERALS
In short, you get reciprocity with equalization. Thus: as is the farmer proportionately to the cobbler,	
so the product of the cobbler is proportionate to that of the farmer.	
Don't apply the figure of proportion to them when exchange is taking [has taken?] place.	
If you do, one extreme will have both the excesses;	
Apply it when they each hold their own.	
If they are equals, it is because this kind of [proportional] equality can be applied to them.	
A is the farmer, C the food, B is the cobbler	
D his product, which has been equalized.	
If reciprocity did not occur on this basis, you would not have community [5.5.12].	
	The fact that it is by demand-and-use (*chreia*) that the whole thing coheres as one, is revealed by the fact that when, of two men, either one or both find they have no demand on the other, exchange does not take place. [5.5.13]
	As to future exchange, assuming there is no present want, currency is as it were our 'guarantee' that this will take place when wanted.

ARISTOTLE	THE LIBERALS
	It is assumed that if you bring it, you must be able to get what you want.
	Now currency too can fluctuate [like demand]: it does not maintain complete equality [of value].
	But it tends more to retain this [than anything else]
	which is why everything must be priced, which makes exchange possible, and with exchange you get community.
	Currency, like a measure which brings other items into commensurability,
	equalizes all products.
	Without exchange you would not have community:
	without equalization you would not have exchange:
	without commensurability you would not have equalization.
Strictly speaking, such deep differences [in demand or in persons?] cannot be made commensurable	
	But in terms of demand-and-use it can be done well enough [5.5.14].
	You need to have one thing created by human assumption.
	That is why it is called 'currency' [current law].
	This makes everything commensurable, i.e. everything is measured by currency.

LIBERALISM IN THE *ETHICS*

ARISTOTLE	THE LIBERALS
	Example: A is a house
	B is ten minas
	C is a bed
	Now A, if a house is worth five minas, or equal to five minas, is half of B.
	C, the bed, is a tenth of B [i.e. worth one mina].
	This makes it clear how many beds are equal to one house, namely, five [5.5.15].
	It is evident that exchange went along these lines [viz. direct barter] before you had currency,
	since it makes no difference whether you exchange five beds for the house or the money which five beds are worth [5.5.16].

The right-hand column gives a straightforward and continuous description, albeit quite simple, of how an exchange economy comes into being and of the mechanism by which it operates. The Aristotelian supplements in the left column, supplements which are interlarded to control and alter the spirit of this description, are obviously alien to it. Even the syntax of the Greek is interrupted, suggesting that an original report has been interpolated by a running commentary in a teleological vein. The main difference in spirit and method is revealed at the beginning. Aristotle prefaces a proportionate calculus, which assumes that the technicians as men have to be measured as well their product; so you get a four-sided equation – though he never shows how it would work out in practice. The descriptive account knows nothing of inequality of persons. It is preoccupied with the exchange of a variety of disparate things, which need to be equated by money. The A, B, C figure which concludes the account is correctly applied to describe different values of objects only, which are rendered commensurable by money. Aristotle's

THE LIBERAL TEMPER IN GREEK POLITICS

earlier attempt to apply A, B, C, D to the different worths of the people simply makes hash of the whole analysis. It is to be noted that the descriptive account contents itself with observing that technicians are 'different', that is, make different products, and that an exchange community is necessary because they are different, while Aristotle slips in the word 'unequal' alongside 'different' (5.5.9). This gives the measure of his failure to understand the point of that economic analysis which he is determined to alter and absorb into his own moral system.

The economic analysis itself is not without its refinements. Currency is not treated as a *deus ex machina* or given magical properties. The limitations of its function are clearly perceived; it is not one of those miraculous inventions which develop a behaviour-pattern independent of human relations. Human demand is the basis of all exchange, and therefore of all value; currency accelerates exchange but does not create it. It can itself fluctuate in value. It is, however, recognized that currency can also take the form of capital. Besides being spent, it can be withdrawn from circulation temporarily; then it becomes your 'guarantee' that you will be able to exchange when you want to. It is still at the service of future demand even when hoarded.

There is also more here than just economics. Exchange of products is the basis of 'community' – the statement is repeated (5.5.10 and 14). No doubt Aristotle is thinking of Plato's use of the same formula to create society in the second book of the *Republic*. But both are drawing on a common source. Plato included currency which was needed. Aristotle's reporter's instinct is strong enough to enlarge on it. Currency, we learn, is created by compact; it represents an agreement or 'supposition' on the part of society; it is also a guarantee of future exchange, and finally it is by its very name a facet of 'law' (*nomisma-nomos*).

It is possible to deduce from these links that the liberals used currency as perhaps their primary model to illustrate the character, origin and application of all law; not a set of religious sanctions, nor ancient and unquestioned traditions, nor *a priori* imperatives; but a set of working compacts, instruments of social flexibility and prosperity; almost automatic in operation and certainly indispensable in effect; but still man-made, the servant of human demands which begin with the biological needs of human beings all fundamentally alike.

CHAPTER XII

THE REJECTION OF LIBERALISM
IN ARISTOTLE'S *POLITICS*

ARISTOTLE in his *Politics* presents the end result of that complex thinking process which is still being dialectically conducted in the *Ethics*. His own conclusions are solidified. He is concurrently less inclined to make accommodation with the liberals. Their theories where mentioned are more boldly refuted or incontinently dismissed. The quality of the reporting is more dogmatic.

The treatise is composed in a kind of tug-of-war between his metaphysics and his empiricism, the two contending but not discordant aspects of his philosophical method. It abstractly states and firmly develops his basic theory of the state in teleo-logical terms, and seeks to apply it to the delineation of an ideal constitution. Equally it devotes space and energy to collecting, classifying and evaluating a good deal of concrete data about the constitutions of existing states, and a great many examples of how they actually behave politically. The empirical material is embedded between sections of the metaphysical, which has tempted critics to alter the traditional order of the books or rearrange their content. But the order of the manuscripts accurately reflects a basic truth about the whole. Its empirical descrip-tions are always tightly controlled by the underlying premises of the political teleology, which can be compressed into two pro-positions: first, that human society in all its varieties of size, shape and organization exhibits one unique form, which is alone capable of constitutional perfection. This is the Greek *polis*, or city-state. In its perfected form, this supplies that standard by which the relative imperfections of other forms of association can be judged. Second, the social structure of any human society at any stage of its development, and, of course, of the city-state in its perfected form, is built upon the natural principle of authority. Nature everywhere exhibits the relationship of ruler and ruled, and there are few if any political problems which are not reducible to this measure.

These two presumptions are treated in the two opening chapters as twin foundation stones to be shaped and laid in position with precision and care. Here is no loose assortment of general opinions, but the firm assertion of architectural motifs on which some stylistic pains have been expended. Since the two chapters are written in a spirit teleological, to be sure, but also in part genetic, it will be no surprise if they prove on examination to be a skilful amalgam of his own principles plus as much naturalism and historical description as suits him. But the interlocking composition is closer and more cunning than anything in the *Ethics*. Forming as they do the historical introduction to his treatise, they can be said to constitute Aristotle's 'anthropology' and, as such, they were deployed for inspection at the conclusion of the fourth chapter of this work.

The *Politics* is an arid treatise, intensely condensed and codified, the work of a mind that has now perfected its own self-analysis and brought every one of its prejudices and moods to total abstraction.

Basic theory is covered in the first and third books. Book I asserts that all society is moral: it culminates in that most moral of all forms, the Greek city-state. Its origin lies in the moral patterns of the patriarchal household. These are authoritarian, and supply the archetype for the organization of the government of any state. They must control in the first instance the purely material aspects of human life. The provision of goods and services must obey that law of limit which operates in all self-sufficient and perfect types of human organization. Hence many kinds of economic activity which civilized states are prone to develop in overcomplicated form must by definition be excluded from the normative pattern of society as Aristotle sees it.

To assert dogmatically that all society is moral, and that the city-state is the most moral of all possible forms, is to propose not a description of the life of man, but a programme for its con-solidation and guidance. So Book 3 continues: there is a perfectly moral man; he is a citizen of a city-state. He does not live in a vacuum; he enjoys a precise relationship to his society. But all significant relationships in a society are, as we have seen in the original household, authoritarian, and turn on the disposition of

LIBERALISM IN THE *POLITICS*

power. So the citizen is definable by the way he is related to this problem. There is in fact only one problem of politics, essentially speaking: Where is the sovereign power located, and how is it divided and distributed? All societies, whatever their shape, must begin by including at least two elements formally distinct, and maybe more than two, the rulers and the ruled.

The power-pattern becomes the constitutional pattern. The citizenship of the citizen, who is such by virtue of his relation to power, becomes definable only as the constitution is defined. Monarchy, now treated as the archetype of constitutions, is such only because it is also the archetype of all authority. It is a government; and a state, before it is anything else, is a system of government. Monarchy happens to be that system which is closest to patriarchy, the original constitution of the authoritarian family.

One can say that the above propositions, as argued in Books 1 and 3, define the limits within which all subsequent discussion of politics is conducted. And this helps to clarify the over-all logic of the treatise, and even to justify the traditional order of its component parts. Books 4, 5 and 6 consider actual oligarchies, democracies and despotisms, the causes and the forms of their instabilities, their devices for distributing legislative, judicial and executive authority. He is looking at states as they are, in all their variety and unpredictability, before turning back to consider the state as it should be. Books 7 and 8 conclude with a memorable portrait of his own small-town vision – the city-state of his ideal, in which he would like to live and in which his conception of educational and civic training would prevail.

If, then, there is a conflict in the treatise between empiricism and idealism, it is more apparent than real. The shift from one to the other is in method rather than in perspective. There is not an observation nor an idea which is not confined within the walls of the small town; and very few which do not pertain to the problem of who rules whom within those walls. The Greek *polis* is the place where history stops; and its orders and priorities of command and obedience are the measures of the stature of the men within it.

That is why the second book, regarded as the *locus classicus* for constitutional theories which competed with Aristotle's, is not a source which sheds any light on liberalism. For though it reports and criticizes at length several utopias, including two historical

341

specimens widely admired as models, Aristotle can afford to report these precisely because they still stay within the limits of the city-state as a closed system. His polemic allows them to assume form and substance, he names names and itemizes details, because they belong in his field and can be attacked without exposing vistas which would threaten to dissolve the fixed form within which, for him, social history and behaviour are confined. Indeed, placed where they are, as classified examples of the city-state and its officers and offices, they assist in riveting upon the reader's mind the presumption that there is nothing else that can be usefully classified, even before the theoretic examination of principles is completed, as it is in the third book.

If, then, liberal political theory gets into the *Politics* of Aristotle at all, it can do so only as the rumble of thunder offstage, at those points where he is building his own small-town defences as high as possible. For the liberal opinion which is most relevant to what he has to say constitutes itself a direct assault on the limits of those walls and upon the little systems of authority inside them. Since it is in the first and third books that he builds them, there also the signs, if any, of his repulse of liberalism are to be expected. There is the likeliest source for any testimonies, however indirect, to doctrines so wholly at variance with his principles. But as we have seen, he has moved on since he wrote the parallel passages in the *Ethics*. The political dialectic is over; his conclusions are crystallized; he is ready to be dogmatic. When he does report, it is more often to contradict. The tone is firmer and, if the testimony he gives is clearer, it is because it is communicated so often as the direct negative of his own ideas.

I

Liberal doctrine rejected and destroyed by use of pseudo-liberal methodology
[*Politics* 1, Chapters 3-5.]

The twin foundations having been exposed in the first two chapters, it becomes necessary at once to defend and stabilize that one of them which is the more vulnerable: the premiss, briefly introduced in Chapter 1.2, that power relations inhere in the natural order and are the substantial reality of all human relations. This was vulnerable because it was exposed to attack from the twin articles of faith claimed by the liberals: men are genetically or biologically equal, demanding a relationship in law

and justice which conforms to this equality; and they are moved
in all their relations by a fundamental goodwill, which is dangerously blocked when confined by pressures which recognize
superior force. Of the many practical issues provoked by the
application of these principles to human affairs as they were,
none was more acute than the question of slavery in Greek
states. Accordingly, Chapters 3 to 5 address themselves to a
defence of authority in general and of the master's authority
over the slave in particular; and Chapter 6 defines the limited
role assigned to philanthropy and goodwill in an authoritarian
society.

Having broken the city-state down into the primary parts
out of which it is composed
and having reached the household
our first problem is its 'economy'.
The household has its own primary parts,
basically the two-fold groups of free and slave,
but more precisely master *versus* slave,
husband *versus* wife,
father *versus* children [1.3.1].
[One school holds
that the definition of household economy is different,
viz. it is so-called 'business activity'.]
First, then, the relation of master and slave must be analysed
both in order to visualize the machinery for meeting essential
demand
and to achieve a theory of the relationship better than other
theories at present held [1.3.3].
One school holds the exercise of mastery to be a science
comprehending all economy and politics.
Another holds that to exercise mastery is contrary to nature,
custom-law being responsible for the status of slave and free,
whereas in nature there is no difference
which likewise makes the relationship not morally right
[just]
since it is induced by pressure of force [1.3.4].

The structuration of Aristotle's thought is firm and the contrast
with his method in the *Ethics* is already plain. He has his own ideas
of what economy is to mean – the regulation of moral and

authoritarian relationships between persons within the household. Such a conclusion has been prepared dialectically in the *Ethics*. Here he states it must have priority over all other problems of human activity. In an aside he notes a contrary opinion to the effect that economy means business activity; this it is safe to attribute to liberal thinkers, but he reserves it for later attack in Chapter 8 following. Of the relationships in the household, that of master and slave is selected for primary treatment. Once this has been disposed of, it will turn out later that parental and marital relations can be dismissed much more summarily. The reason is that while all three involve the exercise of some degree of authority by persons over persons, the question of the moral basis of authority is posed in its most acute form in slavery. Settle this, and you have settled everything. So after noting briefly a Platonic position on mastership (that it is a science), he boldly confronts the liberal doctrine that men are by nature equal. Stating it, as he does, in its negative form – that the relationship is unnatural, and not right, and created only by the application of force sanctioned by custom law – he documents the position more explicitly and clearly than in the *Ethics* because he now intends a more explicit and exhaustive refutation.

Provision of essentials is necessary for mere living, let alone good living.

Hence property and its acquisition are a department of economy.

Economic science is like any other technology

it requires its specific tools to carry out its task [product] [1.4.1].

and tools are some inanimate

and some animate.

Example: a pilot uses both rudder

and a look-out.

Any human servant ancillary to a technique is classifiable as a tool.

Thus property being a tool for living

but really comprehending a plurality of tools,

one of these is animate – the slave

[and in fact every ancillary servitor is a tool substituting for other tools a living automaton, in fact] [1.4.2].

LIBERALISM IN THE *POLITICS*

A slave, however, is the ancillary servitor of the means to action
rather than to production [1.4.4.1254a5ff.].

This famous, indeed classic, defence of slavery is not addressed to industrial conditions, though its logic would appear applicable even there. Although it assumes the provision of material essentials as a starting point for discussion – and this is common ground which he holds with the naturalists – his conception of the slave's function is that of an ancillary to maintaining the personal relationships within the household – an ancillary of action, as he says, rather than an instrument of sheer production. Nevertheless, when it comes to the crucial definition, it is the procedure of technology in production that is taken as the analogue: the slave is like a spade or any engine; he is not a person, for all his animateness. It shows to what lengths the Socratic use of technological procedure as an instrument for the analysis of human behaviour can be carried.

And, to make it quite clear what he means, Aristotle continues:

A piece of property is like a part taken from a whole,
it is completely the property of the whole
whereas the converse does not hold;
so that a slave is his master's property in an absolute sense,
whereas the master cannot belong to the slave in any sense
[1.4.5].

The only possible inference from this piece of moral logic is that the slave, to function properly, must be wholly in his master's power. Authority in the relationship is absolute; it has no degrees.

Is such a relationship grounded in nature?
Or is it good or right?
The theoretic answer is clearly affirmative [1.5.1].
The relationship of ruler and ruled is found
(a) as one of the primary essentials
(b) as one of the natural interests of man
(c) immediately on the birth of any animal
the ruler-subject distinction is evident.

There are many species of these,
and that authority is superior
which is exercised over superior beings
e.g., over men as against animals [1.5.2].
(d) and the product of superior agents is itself superior
and wherever you have the ruler-subject relation
you have a product created by it.
(e) Again, in all compounds
where there is a single community formed
you find revealed the ruler and subject [1.5.3].
(f) Animate nature exhibits this *par excellence*
as well as inanimate. . . .
(g) For instance, an animal is composed initially
of body and soul, subject and ruler [1.5.4].
(h) even though in debased or aberrant specimens
the relationship be reversed [1.5.5].
(i) Thus primarily and in the animals
you see the principle of despotic authority
[soul over body, etc.]
and civic authority
[mind over desire]
and monarchical authority
(j) and these relationships are obviously in line with interest
as well
and the converse of them is injurious [1.5.6].
(k) Similarly, of animals, the domestic types, themselves
superior in nature,
find it better to come under the authority of men.
This achieves security for them.
(l) Equally in nature the male-female relationship
is one of superior to inferior
and hence authoritarian.
(m) This principle applies to men taken as a whole
[1.5.7].
(n) That part of men which is distinct from all other
men as body is from soul, or as animals are from men,
are natural slaves.
(o) The function of the slave is the performance of the use of
his bodily labour [1.5.8].
This function is the best [appropriate] function

and the slave's submission to authority is the best [appropriate]
role [1.5.9].
(p) It is nature's intention that this distinction be incorporated
in the actual bodies of free men and slaves
but the intention often miscarries [1.5.10].

Previous accounts of Aristotle's method in the *Ethics* have
supplied examples of his determination to defeat the liberals by
transplanting, so far as he can, their concepts into the context of
his own. The present passage supplies a crucial instance. For in
order to substantiate his authoritarian pattern, he argues that it
is founded in biological facts and anthropological history. It is
truly natural as nothing else is. Probably the addition of embryology to the argument (item c) is his own, for it shows up elsewhere and is characteristic of him. For him, man starts as an
infant, the helpless subject of his parents, and in his adult status
he remains as subject of law and of the educator who informs him
in law. To this extent his own geneticism is a sort of parody of
the liberal formula, which took as its norms the homogeneity of
the species and the adult condition of its members. Nor will
Aristotle let the factor of self-interest slip from his grasp (j and k): it
too is served by authority, precisely as the infant's interest is served.

But with this sop to liberal geneticism, his argument combines
elements drawn from a psychology which he derived from Plato
and Socrates: the control of soul over body is also a material
analogy for the control of man over man (items g and n): and it is
the argument which proves the clincher, for it enables him to
classify the slave, and the whole caste of slaves, as the mere
'body', obedient to the 'soul' of that society of other men in which
they live (n and p). If the slave is no longer a tool, at least the
fragment of personality which he has acquired is fairly minute.

Natural human equality is now safely reduced to a shibboleth.
But there remain amity and goodwill and natural self-interest to
dispose of. These tenets are not going to be destroyed, we find,
but altered and absorbed into his dialectic of power. The sixth
chapter undertakes this task.

2

Liberal doctrine emasculated by partial confusion with its opposite
[*Politics* 1.6.1-4]

1. The 'opposition' [viz. who deny existence of natural slave]

2. are in one sense correct.
3. There is a 'lawful' [conventional] slave
[as opposed to a natural one]
4. as seen in the law which sanctions the practice that
5. in war
6. the conquered become the property of the victors [or superior and stronger].
7. This is a kind of convention (*homologia*) [1.6.1].
8. This also is a so-called 'moral right' [principle of 'justice']
9. which is indicted as illegal [unconstitutional]
10. by many of those 'whose field is the laws'
11. who argue that it is a terrible thing
12. if, when A can exert the pressure of force on B
13. and is the superior and stronger in power,
14. B, the victim of the pressure,
15. should be a slave ruled by A.
16. Some think this, some think that;
Even philosophers disagree [1.6.2].
17. The disputation arises
18. and the two positions overlap
19. because there is a sense in which it is precisely excellence
20. when in possession of means
21. which can exert forceful pressure.
22. The superior and stronger element
23. always inheres in an excess of some 'good'.
24. Hence the view that the fact of forceful pressure
always implies the presence of excellence.
25. Hence also the disputation created
26. turns solely on the question of moral right. [1.6.3].
27. Hence one side holds moral right is goodwill
28. the other holds moral right is the rule of the superior and stronger.
29. If these two positions are placed in clear antithesis
30. neither position is strong or plausible
to confute the view that the better in excellence should rule and be master [1.6.4].

This is an astonishing feat of legerdemain. A piece of adroit verbalization is employed almost like patter to allow the fundamental humanitarianism and egalitarianism of the liberals to be slipped quietly under the table and disposed of. But they are still there, even under the table. The 'opposition' theory (i.e. that slavery is against nature) had been supported by the practical argument (so we infer from the report of it here) that in fact slaves are created by capture in man-made war, and not by nature at all. We learn further of the horror with which the liberals repudiated the idea that just because B is subject to the forceful pressure of A, he should be ruled by A permanently (items 4 to 15).

Nor were they content with negative protest. They raised the positive issue of what is right (as against what is merely conventionally lawful) and answered: 'Right is goodwill, and not the rule of the stronger' (items 27, 28).

The accents of Antiphon (and Hippias?) are unmistakable. Forced relations between men, as against spontaneous ones between free men, are the work of artificial convention and contrary to nature. War is a conspicuous example of an enterprise undertaken to achieve such relations; war is one of the artificial lawful conventions; so far as it achieves enslavement of the defeated, it carries the violation of nature to its extreme conclusion.

But there is a natural right or morality which is not found in such conventions. It is a morality of goodwill, based upon the philanthropy between human beings. We have heard of this already in the *Ethics*. So far, the position as extracted from Aristotle's disjointed admissions is clear-cut.

But what he does with it is to juxtapose it against its extreme opposite, the crude doctrine that might is right, and then present the two positions as both confused and as part of a confused argument (items 16 and 17). Hence he subtly associates them as though for logical purposes they can be treated alike. And then he virtually identifies them with each other by arguing that of course they share a common premiss (item 18) – that excellence, by definition, always prevails and is stronger (items 19 to 23). Thus they differ 'solely' over the problem of 'what is right'.

This 'solely' is a barefaced piece of semantic deception. For of course the issue of right is the main, the crucial, the irreconcilable issue. It always was, and it always will be. And the moral dilemma as posed by Aristotle is painful. He evades it by a process designed to suggest that the real trouble is logical confusion – the two opposites really agree on the fundamental issue of defining 'virtue', and the issue left to settle is only, so to speak, something 'extra', something minor – namely, 'which is right?'

Thus he can cut down the moral problem to manageable size and, having obscured the irreconcilable gulf in moral theory between the pro- and anti-slavery schools, he can further pretend that his position is not quite that of either. For neither extreme is able, he says, to refute his own doctrine that 'the better in excellence should be master' (item 30). This, though he does not say so here, is how he would express in his own words the far too crude principle that might is right. Natural authority is for him the basis of all moral relations. His position, in fact, is far closer to the might-is-right school than it is to the philanthropy school. In given cases he might demur that the might in question is an accident, without relevance to real moral merit. But it is hard to see that this objection would arise very often in the society which he viewed. However, he is determined to avoid identification with that school – traditionally represented in the 'Thrasymachus' and 'Callicles' of Plato – and probably fears the danger that, if he refutes the philanthropists in open fight, he will indeed be so identified. Hence the somersaults performed by his logic in the present passage. It is strictly a case of a liberal philosophy entombed and devoured by dialectical mastication.

3
A fragment of diluted (Isocratean) liberalism
[Politics 1.6.5-9]

After completing the process just described, the argument of Chapter 6 proceeds continuously to determine who concretely are the actual persons, if any, who fit the theoretic category of natural slave. The answer given by Aristotle, while not pertinent to the straight liberal record, is certainly pertinent to the history of liberalism's diluted influence.

> One school without reservation makes the issue turn on what
> is right
> and posits slavery resulting from war to be right
> because it is a lawful convention
> and law is a form of right.
> Yet they are contradictory.
> The origin of a war may not be right,

and hence any resulting slavery would be undeserved,
that is, if you refuse to admit that men of high spirit and reputation
will turn out to be slaves
supposing they be captured and purchased [1.6.5].
When this school mentions slaves
they don't really mean these
but the barbarians,
which automatically means they are looking for the natural slave
along the lines laid down above.
Essentially one has to admit that some are slaves wherever they are
and some are not slaves anywhere [1.6.6].
Good birth follows the same rule
[Greeks] assume they are themselves of good birth not only at home
but everywhere
whereas barbarians enjoy good birth only at home,
Greeks being well born and free without qualification
and barbarians with qualification . . . [1.6.7].
We have now established the reason for the disputation
namely, not all slaves are such by nature
nor all free men such by nature,
and we have also established
that this natural distinction does hold
in cases where it can be said that
it is to the interest of A that he be a slave
and of B that he be a master
and that it is right that this should be so
and that it is necessary for one to be ruled and the other ruler
on the lines of that kind of authority which is natural [to their relationship]
and this may involve that kind which is [despotic] mastery [1.6.9].

Our heading describes these conclusions as 'Isocratean liberalism'. Some would add, pseudo-liberalism. Negatively they declare that for practical purposes the non-Hellene is the natural inferior and slave of the Hellene. Positively, they imply a concept of all Hellenes which forbids enslavement of fellow-Greeks. Admittedly this is not spelled out explicitly. But it seems to be the inference suggested by (a) a distinction between just and unjust wars and (b) the assertion that Greeks are free-born everywhere. 'Unjust wars', then, would be wars between Greeks, which are always bound to produce enslavement of persons who are not natural slaves. Elsewhere Aristotle seems prepared to accept the notion that Greek cities may fight each other. Here, true to the more theoretic spirit of Book I, he seems to be attuned to Panhellenism as a political policy. If it deserves the name pseudo-liberalism, it is because it took the liberal conception of universal brotherhood and exploited it to unify the Greeks at the expense of the foreigners, whom the Greeks were then invited to conquer and enslave in the interests of their own unification. Alexander's ultimate policy turned out to be closer to true liberalism than this diluted version. If true liberalism has had any effect on this section, it shows perhaps in Aristotle's curious reluctance to assume personal responsibility for the relegation of all barbarians to the status of inferior beings. Here, as occasionally elsewhere, when he comes to the crude concrete application of his authoritarian philosophy, he will swerve aside a little, as though to avoid the odium of criticisms to which he should logically have been indifferent.

4

Liberal doctrine stolen and misapplied
[*Politics* 1.6.10]

If the mastery exercised is bad
it violates the interest of both parties.
The interest of the part and of the whole is identical,
of body and of soul.
The slave is a given part of his master
as it were an animate part of his body,
which however is distinct from it.
Therefore slave and master in their mutual relations,
if their respective status has been acquired according to nature,
enjoy a certain common interest
and amity.
But if it has been acquired under pressure of force
according to custom-law
then you have the opposite.

These are only six lines of printed Greek, yet they say enough to expose with clarity the difference between Aristotle in his *Ethics* and Aristotle in his *Politics*. The corresponding passage in the *Ethics* (above, pp. 320-321) had pursued a dialectical schematization of the primary relationships in the household, in order to accommodate within them the despotic relationship between master and slave. In the conclusion, the slave was reduced to a thing, the animate tool of his master, and between a man and a thing amity was impossible. Then had followed the angry liberal correction: human beings are not things, but by definition partners in some community of right and law which gives formal expression to their common interest and which springs from their natural equality and spontaneous philanthropy. Aristotle had merely sought to reconcile these disparate philosophies of human beings by a logical dichotomy, which split the object owned into part slave and part human being.

Here, on the contrary, a bolder and more dogmatic absorption of the liberal position is carried through. The concepts of 'amity' and 'interest', interwoven with equality in the liberal philosophy of man, are appropriated and, one might say, stolen, severed from the concept of equality, and placed in the context of a wholly Aristotelian philosophy of power relations, where they do not belong. To make the transposition possible, the figment of the animate tool, though already used in the *Politics*, is dropped in favour of a substitute, the figment of the 'animate part' of the master's body. The advantage of this is that the slave, conceived as part of another man's body instead of merely the tool or stone he holds in his hand, now retains a fragment of personality, just enough to make plausible that amity and interest he is supposed to share with his master. This surely is the classic example, in the works of either Aristotle or his master, of that maxim which enjoins that in order to defeat your philosophical enemies, you go through the motions of joining their ranks.

5

An economic theory of real wealth embedded in a context of pure agrarianism
[*Politics* 1, Chapters 8-11]

In *Ethics* 5, apropos of his own theory of 'just distribution', Aristotle had briefly disclosed some genuine economic analysis undertaken by his anonymous competitors (above, pp. 332-338).

Preoccupied as he was with the proportionate rendering of reward for moral merit, he limited his report to an account of how exchange develops with the aid of currency, and how currency itself, as a substitute for demand, assists in maximizing the division of labour and the accumulation of real wealth. The effect of this description, we recall, was cancelled out as much as possible by the interpolation of a theory of unequal persons who exchange, or should exchange, in proportion to their respective moral merits.

Four chapters of the first Book of the *Politics* are devoted to the same general topic of economic activity, described here variously as 'acquisition' and 'business'. But the perspective has now enlarged to include the process not only of exchange but of production. He never considers factory production, but his terms 'acquisition' and 'business', though perhaps imperfectly understood by himself, do identify the gaining (through applied labour) of that material substance by which the community lives. The topic of exchange, therefore, while it recurs in these chapters, occupies a more subordinate position.

Here is the *locus classicus* for a teleological or moral exposition of the problems raised by material wealth and its proper role and limits in moral society. But it is not easy reading. For one thing, the terminology employed, including the term 'business' itself, proves to be unusually slippery, suggesting different senses of the same word in different contexts. In fact this reflects that fundamental ambiguity of the Greek language which allowed the same word to mean both money and material goods (*chremata*). But the confusion is compounded by what Aristotle is trying to do. It should never be forgotten that he had already defined household economy as the conduct and regulation of the personal relationships basic to the household. In the larger area of the state, economy is another name for politics. Politics is economy writ large – the rules for the conduct and regulation of offices and responsibilities of governors and governed. But he has also admitted that another school of thought identified economy with business exclusively. That is, a school of theory had already arisen which had used and perhaps coined the term 'economy', or 'household disposition', to mean the disposition of goods and services that accumulated around the household. Plato's report on 'Protagoras' may indicate that this development was already under way in the fifth century. It recognized the basic fact that

Greek production and commerce were still executed largely in family units by the members of the household, including the slaves, trained and untrained. But equally, in the teaching of the naturalists, 'economy' could indicate that area of theory which would formulate rules for the behaviour of 'things' rather than men. Men admittedly do the producing and exchanging, but a theory of production and exchange has to ignore their moral sensibilities and inequalities, their varying abilities and merits, and assume they are theoretically each and all alike; that is, in the modern jargon, they are producers and consumers. As we saw in the *Ethics*, this was exactly the working hypothesis which liberal economic theory adopted. Aristotle will have none of it. Not only does he reject equality as a working hypothesis, he will not admit the propriety of recognizing the existence of an independent economic theory as such at all. Yet he cannot ignore the genuine economists altogether. His terminology alone, which is in fact borrowed from them, forbids. So he follows the familiar method and embeds a liberal account of the accumulation of real wealth between two layers of purely moral theorizing on how to limit the economic activity and keep it under rigid control, in what turns out really to be an agrarian community.

The chapters make better sense if they are first read with the omission of his report on (true) economic theory. Then they render a quite positive and clear statement of his own position on the proper role and purpose of economic activity in the good life. What that position will be is partly predictable, we repeat, from the way he has defined 'economy' as early as Chapter 3 (above, pp. 344-345): its raw material, so to speak, is composed of three human relationships, all authoritarian; these include the slave, that animate tool which he also defines as a piece of property before he has yet defined what property is. Thus, when he opens up the topic of property as part of the over-all problem of economic activity in the eighth chapter, he says he does so because of the fact that a slave is a piece of property; and so, would it not be pertinent to consider property in general? That is, he reasons from persons to things, not vice versa. Goods and services, we may say, do not constitute in their own right one of the essentials of politics. They are only incidentals. So after dealing with them in Chapters 8 to 11, he reverts in the twelfth to those personal relations which they serve. He reasserts these relationships all over again: the patriarch, his wife, his children, his slaves; in order that, at the opening of Chapter 13, he may reach the complacent moralist conclusion:

It is clear that economy, properly regarded, deals with human beings, not with the acquisition of inanimate objects. Its vision is fixed upon
the moral virtue of men, not the [functional] virtue of that acquisition which is termed wealth [1.13.1].

This then is his postscript to the four chapters which do pretend to deal with the 'virtue' of property and the acquisition of wealth. And the ambiguous semantics show the trick which his teleological temper is playing. For the 'virtue' of property-acquisition would mean, for a descriptive writer, the best way to increase wealth: Aristotle converts this into a sneer at the illusory virtue of mere money-making contrasted with the real morality of virtuous men.

These chapters, then, make room for economics only unwillingly, and exhibit a determination to treat the subject morally, as follows.

[*Politics* 1.8]

Mere business activity
has the purely subordinate function of providing goods
which the economic manager [i.e. the householder] puts to [human] use.
Basically this means the provision of a food supply [1.8.1-3].
From an anthropological standpoint
the modes of provision of food supply can be said to condition
the pattern of men's livelihoods [1.8.4-5]
which fall into three main categories,
that of nomads,
hunters,
agriculturalists, [1.8.6-7]
all of them doing business with self-grown products [1.8.8]
which constitute a natural form of acquisition
achieving self-sufficiency [and stopping there],
unlike commerce and exchange,
meaning a livelihood which does not deal with nature [1.8.9].
The facts of embryology, lactation and so forth

illustrate the principle governing a natural food supply
[1.8.10].
Do not the plants exist to feed animals
and plants and animals to feed man?
And even lesser breeds of men
to provide slaves by capture in war
for superior races? [1.8.11].
In fact nature does nothing in vain [1.8.12].
Hence there is that level of business activity and acquisition
which is natural.
It achieves the storage of essential products for the household and citizen [1.8.13]
and this is true [Aristotelean] wealth
a measure of limitation
self-sufficient,
opposed to wealth otherwise understood
envisaged as unlimited and without measure [1.8.14-15].

[*Politics* 1.9.14f.]

True economy does have a limit
but business does not,
and so business properly speaking is not a function of economy
at all.
Indeed, all wealth in my sense has an essential limit.
We can, however, look at the way of the world
and see the exact opposite taking place.
Business people increase [their supply of] current coin
without limit [1.9.14].
People are confused by this.
True acquisition deals with real wealth
and money-making seems to, also,
which encourages men of the world to think that
mere accumulation is a proper objective to spend their lives
on [1.9.15].
This is a universal human disposition
caused by failure to distinguish
between mere living
and virtuous living.
The psychological cause
lies in unlimited desire [1.9.16]

which seeks unlimited means of meeting desire,
and even those who have virtuous aims
also aim to get bodily satisfaction,
spending all their lives on business activity.
So we have men undertaking all possible types of business
and so the other [false] type of business
has invaded society
since the goal of satisfaction involves excess [1.9.17].

The principles of his pseudo-economic dogma are now plain.
They have been deployed in obedience to the inner logic of his
moral system. And he sums them up as the chapter ends as

Business which is essential,
truly economic,
based on natural foundations
rooted in the [provision of] food supply
a limited [pursuit of limited] objectives. [1258a16-19].

[*Politics* 1, Chapter 10]
The next chapter merely spells out the practical consequences:

True business activity plays the role of the supplier of raw
materials
which the householder disposes of
[in service of moral ends] [1.10.1-3].
Since the raw material required is sustenance,
the preferable form of business is the natural one,
namely agriculture [1258a34].
The commerce and exchange type of business
is rightly deplored [a38],
and, still more, investment for interest [b2].
Currency at least serves exchange
but usury simply breeds currency out of currency [1.10.5].

[*Politics* 1, Chapter 11]
But he then decides to add an appendix. His *Politics* is to be a
handbook for statesmen; it must therefore be written not only
as a guide to theoretic principles, but to equip them also to deal
with situations as they find them. Empiricism may be allowed to
supplement moral science and the ways of the world may be

exploited with certain accommodations, provided all is done in the spirit of the previous principles:

> The above is the theoretician's analysis and evaluation;
> the practical householder and statesman ought in addition
> to have some practical business grasp [1.11.1]
> primarily of agricultural problems [1.11.2],
> secondarily of exchange economy problems,
> i.e. trade, usury and wage-labour [1.11.3],
> and thirdly of that intermediate type of economic activity [1.11.4-5]
> seen in mining, lumbering and the like
> [i.e. raw material production] [1258b28].
> Activity in business and factory establishments
> can in its effects induce technological precision,
> or vulgarity,
> or slavishness,
> or ignobility [1.11.6].
> See the books on agriculture by various authors [1.11.7]
> and the scattered instances told of successful monopolies,
> which should be compiled [1.11.8-12].
> Cities may require an income of this kind
> which is why some men of affairs [politicians]
> specialize in the subject [1.11.13].

Such is Aristotelian economic theory as finally and forcefully crystallized in his *Politics*, in a form which was to exert an influence both far-reaching and disastrous over historians and theologians of succeeding centuries. It has been unfolded in its full length to exhibit its structural coherence, and so to bring out the formidable strength of his leading ideas. Two convictions pervade the whole analysis. First, man's proper interests are moral, concerned with human relations. Second, any business activity is a regrettable distraction, or an ancillary occupation; it is what goes on in the kitchen to supply meals to those who sit in the front parlour to discuss politics, give orders to slaves, guide their women-folk, and educate their children.

This being so, business activity is better confined to the essentials and the 'naturals', which means, in the first instance, food supply. So farming is the ideal type of 'business', and, next to it, the extraction of raw materials other than food. Do they not still

come from 'mother earth'? Commerce of any kind comes a very
bad third, for it is removed from nature and the soil. As for
finance, it is unspeakably artificial and so bad. This theoretic
rationale supplies the occasion for a sort of lament for the estate
and the mind and morals of the worldly business man, who is
seen (rather in the face of the facts) as the embodiment of bound-
less desire, taking measureless material satisfactions. The concluding appendix on the need of business experience in the
householder and statesman implies no break with these previous
premisses. Agriculture still remains enthroned. The statesman, as
a practitioner of applied politics, will use human knowledge of
other kinds also to earn income – even monopoly income – but it
will be for the service of (the good life of) the citizens. Aristotle's
empiricism is always contained within the limits of his teleological
and moral assumptions.

But the excursus on liberal economic theory is something else
altogether, and to this we now return.

[*Politics* 1.9.1-13]

There is a second type of acquisition and business activity,
indeed, the one generally so recognized.
Indeed, it may even be admitted to have connection with
'Aristotelian' business.
It, however, has no limit.
It is not a child of nature
but of experience and technique [1.9.1].
It has a genetic origin as follows:
you can use a thing in one of two ways,
directly [to wear or eat]
or as barter for something else.
Barter begins as a natural thing;
men vary in their possession of sufficiencies [1.9.2-3].
[But commerce and trade, adds Aristotle sadly, are not a natural part
of business, because they carry exchange beyond sufficiency] [1.9.4].
In the original society, i.e. the household, maybe, you did
not even have barter,
but as the society enlarged
and the possible exchange patterns became dispersed and
various,
so barter arose

and persists to this day among barbarian nations [1.9.5].
[But barter, repeats Aristotle, with another admonitory headshake, involves no break with nature, and is not really a species of that debased thing called business, for it is confined to self-sufficient purposes] [1.9.6].
From the practice of barter you pass to monetary exchange.
The mutual material assistance between men
stretches to include foreign communications
and so import and export [1.9.7].
This needs an easily transportable medium
to replace barter
and so leads to the choice of certain standard materials
useful *per se*
but transportable and measurable
like iron and gold.
Finally they are stamped
to avoid the necessity of weighing and measuring the amount
of exchange involved in a given transaction.
Coined money, therefore, arises out of 'essential' exchange
[1.9.8].
and leads to trade and commercial activity
[this is our second species of business activity]
which acquires its own degree of technique
a technique aimed at multiplying gain [he should say 'real wealth']
through exchange [1.9.9].
This leads to certain further results, as follows:
1. There is the view that business technique operates mainly in the field of currency;
2. that its function is to review the means for the maximization of 'things' [wealth? or money?].
3. It is that technique productive of wealth and things.
[Yes indeed, adds Aristotle, shaking his head again, men often assume that the accumulation of currency is wealth] [1.9.10].
4. There is the simultaneous 'reverse' view,
that currency is merely a front,
a lawful convention,
which by nature means nothing
since the human users can make it valueless overnight
by choosing to change the raw material of currency.

[The material itself, adds Aristotle, being futile as a means of sustenance—cf. Midas] [1.9.11].

5. This leads to the view that

true wealth and business must be of a different sort from currency,

[And how right this view is! adds Aristotle; of course they mean my brand of true business, meaning agriculture.]

commerce and trade being productive of business goods [things? money?]

not *per se* but in the course of exchange;

hence the view that business operates 'in the field of currency', currency being the 'element'

and also the 'limit'

employed in exchange [1.9.12],

but wealth produced by this type of business

is itself unlimited.

This follows the rule of all arts and sciences

where the objective is, in degree, theoretically unlimited

[you want all the health you can get]

whereas the means employed are limited.

The end in the case of business activity is wealth

and the acquisition of 'things' [money? or things?] [1.9.13].

It is impossible to mistake the descriptive objectivity of this account. The head-shaking moral qualifications and comments inserted, as it were, *sotto voce* by Aristotle, which we have placed in brackets, offer only feeble opposition to an analysis which in effect proposes the following:

(a) Production of real wealth is properly unlimited, the infinite objective achieved by the use of an instrument wholly limited and finite, namely currency.

(b) Although not rooted in nature (meaning primitive practices), this activity calls for great experience and science.

(c) It has a natural historical genesis in barter, still observable in pre-civilized peoples (if you use comparative methods).

(d) The genesis of barter lay in the enlargement of society (beyond the household), and the multiplication of exchange patterns (i.e. through increasing division of labour, though Aristotle omits this here).

(e) Barter, in turn, gave way to the employment of currency

(f) when the exchange economy had become international.

(g) This development has given rise to a school of thought which argues that

> Business activity operates to maximize real wealth and in this sense operates like any other practical science (e.g. medicine).
> The means used (again imitating science) are a finite and limited tool
> which, in this case, furnishes only the 'field of operation' for business activity (Aristotle omits the 'only').
> Currency, in fact, is a peculiar thing, for although the material is chosen for some intrinsic value,
> yet its actual value depends purely on a social convention, a compact, and would vanish tomorrow if the compact were changed.

If the original Greek text is not so nakedly descriptive as it is made to appear here, if its non-Aristotelian bias does not spring so automatically to notice, this is for the double reason that (a) as we have said, the report is artificially embedded in the middle of that long Aristotelian discourse on pseudo-economics already reviewed; and also that (b) the qualifications inserted in the liberal report itself, those little items we have placed in brackets, go far towards blunting the edge of the analysis and so help to bring it into line with Aristotelianism. There are very good though subtle reasons why he should make every effort to accomplish this. For one thing, this liberal account not only described various degrees of economic activity as evolving through increasingly complex techniques; it implied that various social forms became outmoded under the pressure of expansion to meet human needs. Thus you get barter because the household bursts its seams, so to speak, and you get currency when the city-state bursts its seams, and its inhabitants find themselves living in an international exchange economy. Aristotle cannot cling to his axiom that the forms of patriarchal household and aristocratic city-state exist *a priori*, and still make his peace with this view of history.

And this brings us face to face with those two economic formulas for which he has most repugnance. One is the conduct of commerce by the use of currency at all. Barter is natural – currency gets out of hand. He is suspicious of the invention from the start. He shows a mental malaise in dealing with it which, we suggest, is a symptom of a mind that never really understood what currency was, and what its possibilities and limitations were, and what the liberal analysis meant. We have seen in the earlier report in the *Ethics* that the liberals were not afraid of currency. They did not magnify its importance. At bottom it is merely a convention, a representation of demand. And here in the present account it is posited as a limited, definable thing, quite different from the real wealth which it helps to increase. But the second thing Aristotle dislikes is precisely this prospect of indefinite increase of real wealth. His ideal man is a limited person with a limited desire and a limited way of life in a limited society. The economic doctrine of multiplication of goods and services filled him with repugnance.

Now what he does is to confuse these two dislikes. Whereas the actual account shows that wealth and money were by liberalism sharply distinguished, the one being unlimited and the other limited, he keeps trying to identify them as both equally unlimited and obnoxious. Thus he actually tries to interpret a theory of the acquisition of real wealth as a theory of the acquisition of mere currency. The community's capacity to command goods and services becomes for him the miser's obsession with his strong-box. It is all the easier for him to do this because of the ambiguity, as we have said, of the Greek word *chremata*, which means both things and money. It looks as though the liberals spent some pains on defining the distinction: he continually refuses to recognize it.

The present report, therefore, gives a more complete picture of liberal economic theory than the report given in the *Ethics*. We can now see that, besides giving a correct analysis of the function and character and behaviour of coinage, it had the beginnings of a working concept of real wealth, to increase which the process of division of labour and exchange of labour products is only the means. This was not a bad start on the road towards reason and common sense applied to the difficult problem of economic processes. Gone is all the musty furniture of Aristotle's economic museum – the cows and horses on the farm, the patriarch with his wife, his ox, and his slave, the small town, spiritually isolated and self-contained, the cautious homespun moralities, the peering contempt and fear of the city fellow, the trader, and the business man.

Unfortunately these weeds and nettles clustering in the same text managed to choke the liberal doctrine at its birth. Aristotle's primitivism and ruralism triumph, to dominate historians, of Rome, for example, who lament *ad nauseam* the decay of peasant farming as the supposed cause of republican decline, but hardly spend a page on the analysis of the commercial and financial patterns which made the republican political machine unworkable. It dominated the medieval mind of Christendom, supplying an ideological prop for feudal practices and placing a block in the path of the intellectual acceptance of the commercial revolution which gathered momentum during the Renaissance. Machiavelli, for all his pretensions to iconoclasm, feels the paternal hand of Aristotle as heavy on his shoulder as Livy had long before him.

It is on our shoulders still, touching even educated people with an inherited reflex of uneasy suspicion of the urbanized qualities of a complete civilization. Stagirus proved to be the most influential small town of antiquity.

But the liberal record is there too – a large and rather indigestible piece of the Hellenic mind, a descriptive system of economic theory with speculative overtones, left for Aristotle to handle as best he may. It certainly contributes to the ambiguous effect of these famous chapters, even as it also affords striking testimony to the sweeping power of the Hellenic intellect.

6

Some fragments of a descriptive [positivist] theory of citizen and state
[Politics 3.1.3-4, 3.2.2, 3.3.3. 3.5.2, 3.6.4-5]

Book I has involved Aristotle in keen if subterranean controversy with liberal theories which passed the boundaries of his own city-state. One may say this was inevitable, so far as he permitted himself in this book to consider problems basic to all society and community as a preparation for defining that community which he considers to be normative.

In the third Book his vision narrows towards its appointed goal: the city-state of his dreams, a little community where moral control is effective and, therefore, where practical government is neat, tight and orderly; a community of ranks and classes and privileges and functions, morally regulated; a community aristocratic or middle-class, depending on one's perspective.

He still has a little way to go to reach it, and part of the distance to be travelled can be conveniently laid out in the following brief paradigm of the first six chapters.

We want to be able to define city-state constitutions ['polities'], but since the citizen is the unit of these,

we need to look at what is a citizen in order to help us find out what is a polity.

A citizen is a human being definable by his relationship to or participation in power.

In fact, the primary or absolute definition of a citizen turns upon the degree of his participation in legislative and judicial authority [3.1].

Practical definitions, it is true, depend usually on who your parents were,

but this raises many difficulties, as contrasted with the view that a citizen is definable in terms of some given degree of authority held [3.2].

Take for example the problem that arises when the seat of authority itself is changed through some revolution or constitutional change,

which in fact also raises the problem of what is a city's real identity,

and we can only conclude that its identity depends on the character of its polity or government,

and this in turn is definable by the disposition of the centres of authority in it ['offices'] [3.3].

Next there is the [Platonic] question:

there is the virtue of a solid citizen

there is also the virtue of the morally perfect man:

are these identical? [3.4]

The answer would be, Yes,

if you excluded from citizenship

the vulgar sort [mechanics, etc., traders] [3.5].

So now we return from the citizen to his constitution

and conclude that a polity is definable by the disposition of its centres of authority

and primarily by the sovereign authority [3.6.1-2].

What then should this disposition be?

The question temporarily makes us return to basic problems.
What is the purpose of any community?
And what is its basic or natural form? [1278b16].
See my first book [3.6.3]
where the three types of household authority are defined.
All of these are organized to achieve the interests common to
rulers and ruled [3.6.6.].
We conclude that the correct polity has the same common
interest as objective, while an incorrect is one that serves only
the interests of its rulers,
whether they be despots, oligarchs or democrats [3.6.11].

In trying to describe the effect conveyed to the modern reader
by Aristotle's political method, words like 'formal' and 'teleological' inevitably tend to recur. They apply here in these six
chapters, so much so that one gets the impression that as Aristotle
looks out on society and social behaviour, there is always present
in his mind, before he looks, a vividly etched picture, a shape,
concrete in his imagination, which partly describes what he is
looking at but much more describes what he thinks he ought to be
looking at: a medieval walled town, and its citizens' register,
and its little hierarchies of guilds and officials. He is still keeping
it in the background, he has not yet fully exposed his dream, but
everything he says is guided by it.

So his description of what he sees is only partly descriptive:
he selects for emphasis, he also ignores or lightly skirts. The shape
in his mind is geographic: there are the town walls, the definable
limit in space. And it is also moral: there are the offices held,
the powers shared or denied to the people within these walls.

His vision, we say, is steadily narrowing down to its finite
determination. Just here and there, then, in this contracting
context, he allows himself to make a few notes which touch less on
rival theories of state and citizen than on a wholly altered perspective on human beings, as such, and as members of any
society. These notes disclose theories which described the inhabitants of Greek cities as they found them, just as inhabitants.
They are truly descriptive, not teleological, and, for what they
are worth, can be exposed as follows.

(a) A citizen does [not] become such merely by inhabiting a
place.

Aliens and slaves have community and common habitation.
(b) Citizens are [not] definable as those who partake in a [system of] rights
i.e., who are liable to legal process
and also competent to administer it.
This attribute is available to those whose community is derived from commercial relations (*symbola*) [3.1.3-4].

These negatives indicate the existence of a political theory which in the purely historical positivist manner viewed the social context of the human being as determined primarily by his geographical situation. This view inevitably drew no theoretic distinction between slave and free man and alien; all are 'citizens' in so far as they derive their livelihood from a common area. Here we hear overtones – which have now grown familiar – of doctrines derived from an anthropological conviction that men belong to an identical species.

Theory (b) gives a different but equally descriptive approach to the problem. Societies, besides being topographical, represent organized legal processes, procedures for redress of injury and protection against injury. These could be viewed as examples of social compact; the ultimate standard of reference is the individual and his need. As a subject of legal process, however, he is also its arbiter. There is no theoretically useful distinction to be drawn between rulers and ruled, the judge and the judged.

Both these theories, therefore, are rebutted by Aristotle's doctrine that the nexus of all society rests on the organization of authority.

Gorgias of Leontini, perhaps realizing the difficulty [of defining citizen],
perhaps in irony, said
'Mortars are things made by mortar-makers,
Citizens of Larissa are people made such by the 'public craftsmen' [magistrates] of Larissa [3.2.2].

This is an interesting fragment of documentation. The Greek sophist may or may not have been a constitutional theorist, but this sally of his, in whatever context, seems to be made at the expense of all moral, teleological and even patriotic conceptions of citizenship. Whatever it is, it is a man-made convention; this is at least implicit in what he says.

> When, if ever, are you to say that the identity changes?
> The most superficial approach to the problem
> concentrates on the topographical situation and the human beings in it.
> For instance, you can have two localities join together
> along with the human beings in them,
> the two groups [really] inhabiting different locations [3.3.3].

This returns us to the topographical definition of citizenship already reviewed, with perhaps the interesting addition that topographical identity can be (artificially) created by human agency. Is this an echo of a defence of Athens and Piraeus as forming a single genuine community? Such a defence by the commerce-minded liberals against the agrarian idealists would be plausible. But it is speculative.

> [Apropos of the exclusion of the vulgar from citizenship]
> It is surely true that
> you must not posit as citizens
> all those [human beings] without whom you could not have a city [3.5.2].

This may be an indirect quotation from the liberals who, if they advanced to specific theories of citizenship in existing states, would inevitably have argued for the premiss that all topographical inhabitants and all whose labour constitutes or contributes to real wealth should by definition have a right to all the benefits which co-operation in a community creates.

> [A political community is one formed to achieve the good life]
> This is by definition the purpose and end of community.
> However, men combine just for the purpose of sheer living.
> Perhaps mere living has a touch of the ideal in it.
> Men maintain the city-state community just in terms of living alone
> unless disaster in their lives and livelihoods proves over-balancing.
> It is evident that the majority of human beings
> hang on, and endure great hardships

in their yearning for just being alive,
the assumption being that, in just being alive,
there is something genial,
some natural savour. [3.6.4-5]

The severity of Aristotle's political morality relents. Men are not wholly confined to his authoritarian objectives and functions. It can be allowed that they also want just to live and enjoy themselves and love and laugh. The echo of Antiphon, of the hedonists, of the philanthropists, is unmistakable. Perhaps in the reference to the dissolving or suicidal effects of occasional catastrophe, we hear also an echo of a mournful but compassionate commentary upon the political despair to which Greek communities were sometimes exposed in eras of war and pestilence. The pages of Thucydides can bear witness.

7
Liberal doctrine destroyed by logical corruption
[Politics 3.9.1-5]

If the quarrel between Aristotle and the liberals is irreconcilable, it is because its dimensions are moral rather than logical. The gulf opened in Book 1, as he confronted the question of slavery. He admitted even then that the issue at bottom was over 'what is right', even though he strenuously sought to disguise how fundamental this was.

The topic of democracy in the last half of Book 3 brings on a crisis of equal dimensions. He has just classified the main types of constitutions. But what, he now asks, more particularly, are the formal pretensions surrounding oligarchy and democracy respectively? Critics have noted that his attention, despite his previous classification, seems focused on these two particular types. The concentration is inevitable, for it is these two that illustrate most obviously the basic moral collision between the doctrines of human equality and inequality.

What is the principle of right
recognized respectively by oligarchy
and by democracy?
All [theorists?] have made a point of having some principle of right

but fail to pursue the principle to its logical conclusion
or to state it in its entirety
and in its sovereignty;
e.g. it is held
(a) that the principle of right means equality [and indeed it is,
but only in the sense of equality for men already equal] [3.9.1];
(b) that the principle of right means inequality
[and indeed it is, in the sense of inequality for men who are unequal]
but [theorists] omit the relevant qualification
and so their judgment is incorrect [3.9.2].
[Degree of] right is determined by relation to the parties
concerned;
it has rules of distribution
which apply to the matters [to be distributed]
and to the persons [who receive distribution]
as I have said in the *Ethics* [3.9.3].

This could be called an example of philosophic cannibalism.
A serious theoretic position – that men are historically equal and
should be socially organized in such a way as to reflect this – is
not rebutted in open fight, but turned inside out and then, in its
more palatable form, swallowed into the system of its benevolent
host. The tactics followed resemble those applied in a previous
passage in Book 1 (above, pp. 347-350). First range the doctrine of
human equality against its exact opposite. Then pretend that
both are confused or imperfect formulations. This has the
dialectical advantage of blurring both, but particularly of blunting the integrity of the egalitarian school. Then Aristotle supplies
his own particular piece of legerdemain to clear up the supposed
'difficulty': both are right, of course, 'in a sense'.
Now this concession of his really applies only to one side. For
the position of the egalitarian school depended upon making no
compromise. Once allow a modification, and the whole position
collapsed. But the oligarchic side could tolerate qualifications of
its doctrine of inequality, provided the main thesis was left alone.
The degrees of inequality can vary. The gulf between them is
deliberately concealed by as dishonest a piece of interpretation
as can be found anywhere in his pages. It was noticed, when Book
5 of the *Ethics* was considered, how important to Aristotle was his
semantic trick of inventing an 'unequal equality' applied to

unequal persons. The present context confirms the view that the dialectical conclusions of the *Ethics* are designed to furnish the dogmas of the *Politics*.

8

The liberal theory of society disguised as negative of the teleological theory
[*Politics* 3.9.6-11]

In this, the ninth chapter of the third book, Aristotle, as we have said, reaches a crisis in his exposition. For the last time, as he brings his own politics to their crystallization, he feels the need of a supreme defence of them, and a supreme dismissal of the historical naturalists, the egalitarians, the humanitarians; of liberalism, in fact.

If we reach forward to the last paragraph of the chapter, we came upon his own statement, not less impressive for being tersely worded, of his own formal and unalterable conclusions:

> It must be pointed out that the city-state community exists to serve moral acts, and not simply living together [3.9.14].
> Therefore those who contribute most to a community of this kind should have priority in the distribution of [what] the city [can give]
> over those who may be 'equal' in terms of free birth and blood
> or who may be superior
> but are not equal in terms of the morality [virtue] of the city-state
> and over those who have the advantage in wealth
> but are at a disadvantage in terms of this morality [3.9.15].

Now, a democrat may readily admit that in practice individual rewards turn out to be unequal, and perhaps should be so. But Aristotle insists that this be rigidly recognized as a political principle, and expressed in the state machinery. That is why, as we retrace our steps to the beginning of the chapter, we find our philosopher, as he faces the moral claims of equality and inequality, compelled to stabilize his own position by rebuilding that axiomatic community, final, complete and good, of which he laid the foundations in the first two chapters of the *Politics*. But he now has to define it more explicitly, in opposition to the historical and liberal account of society. He says emphatically what it is not, as well as what it is. And these negatives, if extracted from his statement and rendered positively, present the following system of ideas:

> Any form of society is just a pattern of living, a vehicle for expressing needs which originate in man's biological nature; a society of animals is conceivable,
>
> and societies include slaves [as human beings];
>
> descriptively speaking a society is a defensive alliance formed by its members to prevent mutual wrong doing,
>
> and is stimulated by relations of economic exchange;
>
> an international commercial alliance between Carthage and Etruria
>
> illustrates factors basic to any society [3.9.6]
>
> through its commercial agreements
>
> which are compacts to prevent wrongdoing
>
> and limited to this obligation
>
> plus an alliance the terms of which are documented [3.9.7];
>
> for it brings out the fact that custom-law is indeed a compact, a guarantee of mutual rights, as Lycophron said [3.9.8].
>
> Another international example would be the federation of two city-states
>
> which brings out the fact that societies, while topographically conditioned, can extend their locale,
>
> since society [essentially] exists as a medium of exchange and a vehicle of protection [3.9.9-10]
>
> and contains individuals who otherwise have their own lives and purposes,
>
> their politics being confined to that mutual assistance which they render each other [3.9.11].
>
> Summary of the three conditions which create community: geographic contiguity, legal protection, economic exchange [3.9.12].

For collectors of 'fragments' of lost thinkers, the reference by name to Lycophron furnishes a useful morsel. But the surrounding context is no less relevant to a reconstruction of that body of theory which Aristotle is repudiating. No item here is new, though many, otherwise occurring in scattered testimonies, are here combined. Even the description of the social compact as a guarantor of rights has been partly anticipated in the *Ethics*, where currency, that conspicuous example of man-made convention, is described, when hoarded, as a guarantor of future exchange. Apparently the anticipatory calculus was one of the Promethean facts recognized by the liberals as a creative factor in shaping social machinery.

At the uttering of words and ideas like these, the walls of the city-state fall down. Did the liberals deliberately choose international treaties of various kinds to illustrate the growth and purpose of law, in order to break the Greek mind free of its purely civic preconceptions? They may have been no less interested in the commercial quality of such agreements, as an illustration of the fact that social community is a response to material need for goods and services. Some of the postulates are Democritean – the link connecting men historically with the animals, and the view that society's purpose is to attain security, achieved by mutual assistance rendered between members. Some of the language recalls Antiphon – the hint that just to live, securely and happily, and protected but otherwise unregulated, is man's simple but supreme goal; that once the social machinery of security has been won, he can be left to himself. But the most conspicuous contribution belongs to those – perhaps Lycophron was the chief, but we may never know their names – who took Antiphon's bitter rejection of compacted law and turned it into an acceptance, and made their own synthesis of law and nature into a complete descriptive account of how human beings continually combine, without benefit of the 'natural ruler', into tribes and cities and states for mutual advantage and material happiness, the measure of which is still untold.

But these, in Aristotle's written pages, all appear as denials; these are what a state should not be, and cannot be, in order to remain a state. His negatives so easily beguile us into agreement with him, for negatives are a very powerful propagandist weapon. Over against them, interlarded with them, come those positive moral statements which are so much more convincing just because they are positive, which sound so respectable because they are so uplifting, and which sound so typically 'Greek' because of course Aristotle is the only Greek in this field we have had the pleasure of knowing. It is pertinent, as we here conclude our account of his method as a reporter, to summarize these positive assertions of his also, and let him have the last word, as he always does:

Society is formed to promote [not biological needs but] the good moral life

and slaves and animals could not share in it, since they are not purposeful creatures seeking happiness [3.9.6.]

A true society is constituted by agreement over a single sovereign power or authority [3.9.7]

and by a common concern to promote citizens of a given moral character,

preventing personal immorality and not simply overt aggression,

and by a continual moral investigation of its members to determine their degree of vice and virtue.

Custom-law is [not a convenient compact but] a moral force which makes citizens good [3.9.8].

These conditions are met in the self-sufficient and perfect life of the city-state [3.9.12-14].

CHAPTER XIII

GREEK LIBERALISM – THE
FULL FLOWER

ARISTOTLE has exercised over the Western mind a moral authority not unlike that which has been wielded by the Old Testament and for essentially the same reasons. His moral code is ambiguous: it approves the ethos of power-relations, but tempers it with concessions to the wholly different standards of equality and fraternity. This ambivalence between aggression and love makes it possible for many sorts and conditions of men to feel at home in an atmosphere of compromise which, as it is antique, is also respectable, and seems to validate the similar condition of moral ambiguity which is characteristic of the mixed motives, the realism and the idealism, of modern man or at least of modern Western man. For it could be claimed that hypocrisy, considered as a method of conserving the morale of civilization, has been one of the West's specific contributions to cultural development. The modes of Aristotle's ambiguity in his *Ethics* and *Politics* have been uncovered. It is not characteristic of the Greek mind to be quite as ambivalent as he manages to be and it is legitimate to look for explanations, as we have done, in the disparity of his sources of inspiration. His own convictions, which the early Platonic indoctrination only strengthened, required a moral and political system which was teleological and author-itarian. But he tried to make this system elastic enough to accom-modate the pieces of a materialist, historical, and egalitarian system which he has dismembered in order to make them innocuous.

The order in which they have been reviewed is that of Aristotle's treatment, an order controlled by the logic of his own system, which is necessarily hostile to them. Do they have a logic of their own, and can it be expounded? Can they, in fact, be reorganized to present a liberal system of political philosophy as it obtained in the first half of the fourth century? It does not follow that any one thinker or group of thinkers ever made themselves responsible for documenting all of these ideas together, and placing them in systematic order. It can be argued that liberalism shows a developing logic: that the known positions taken by Democritus and the Elder Sophists and Antiphon respectively must have led to some revaluation and reassembling of the naturalist theory in the fourth century. It can be argued that the political planning and the humanist conceptions of Alexander the Great imply the guidance contributed by a corresponding type of political theory, which existed before his conquest began. It can be argued that the philosophies of man and of society propagated by Stoics, Epicureans, and Cynics, if cross-compared, point to a common stock of sociological conceptions, lying outside the classic control of Plato and Aristotle, a stock from which the schools diversely drew what suited them. But in the end, if the historian is to attempt any synopsis constructed out of these pieces, his best guide is that thread of inner logic which seems to run through them as they exist in Aristotle's text. All these scattered affirmations and denials, rebuttals and corrections, bespeak a philosophical opponent whose utterances however various and apparently disconnected have a consistency of temper. There is a recurrent terminology of equality and good will, pleasure and utility and common interest; of security and leisure and wealth, of commerce and reciprocal exchange and federation; and a brooding sense of the natural justice between men, which is no respecter of persons. Can it be an accident that some or all of these have emerged in Europe at all times of social aspiration, of reform or revolution? One thinks variously of the Levellers, the Utilitarians, and the Liberals of England; of the Encyclopaedists, of the Physiocrats, and the Revolutionists of France. Are they just slogans pragmatically devised to appeal to ephemeral discontents, or do they derive their power over men's minds from the fact that they are integrated into a coherent vision of human nature, of history, of society, morals, and law?

The vision, if it be such, had nothing visionary about it. At the bottom of the glass stands the human being who eats and drinks, breathes, sleeps, and requires of his environment that he be allowed to survive. Though his cosmic ancestry on the earth's primeval surface is not now the main question, it is evident that this man is still being measured and estimated as a member of a biological species, his behaviour as a social and moral creature

– his specifically human and humane characteristics – still viewed as derivable from that law of his being which just requires him to live. Survival means security, but if he wants to live well he also needs pleasure; and pleasure is what he inevitably seeks and realizes. The relish of food and drink comes to him privately, but that of sex is available to him only as he forms association. As for his recreation, luxuries and comforts, none of them is practicable without economic co-operation through division of labour. And finally there is one specific pleasure – as native to him as eating and drinking – which inheres in the fact of association itself; it is the pleasure of good will and amicable feeling.

If survival, security and pleasure are viewed as essential drives which animate the human being and control his behaviour-pattern, it is evident that association with his own species is essential. For none of the primary goals is realizable without it. Survival means security from attack and this originally meant co-operation – man being physically weak. This motive has now become 'historical', for man is no longer among the weakest of the animals. But it is powerfully reinforced by the secondary motive to obtain security against his fellow men. For this, unlike the first, is a reciprocal requirement which can be managed only by organizing a give-and-take system. It needs an association which is not only co-operative but legal with its primary rules of order. Even sexual desire leads to the association of the mating pair, perhaps permanently, while the urge to obtain goods and services in variety and surplus tends to generate a community of economic exchange which is not casual but regulated; nor can man's amiability be satisfied by merely casual acquaintance and meeting. In short, it is native to him to require not only association at various levels but relatively stable association. He needs organized community, and the task of moral and political philosophy is simply to describe and make explicit the processes and patterns of community constructed to satisfy these needs.

However, an association generated from these roots and dependent on them for its validity can never be a state with a metaphysical or ideal identity. It exists as a vehicle of the common good, a convenience, no more. It is a pattern of process, not a thing in itself. It is not even formally definable; the only reality with properties or capacities amenable to formal definition is the human being and his membership in a society. That membership can be described in three different ways: as in the first instance geographic propinquity to others, without which any conscious association is impossible; or as a legal community with others which makes him a partner in a group system of established usage, custom-law, rights, and penalties; or as an economic partnership in which his labour and his consumption-habits are geared into the corresponding labour-habits of an exchange community. This last may be widely dispersed, yet it obeys the same laws of organization which the human drive for society always requires. Organized community is therefore definable only as topographical or legal or economic. These are descriptive categories. They prescribe no ideal limits; the community may call itself a state from time to time but, in fact, it is historically and descriptively a fluid and relative thing.

Nor can any one form of society – the city-state for example – be viewed as theoretically final, complete, or correct. If such existed, it would represent the completion of man's hedonist drives; but these are still evolving. Man is a historical animal, not a fixed quantity; he lives in process; even his capacity for producing material wealth is unlimited. In short, then, liberalism required that no peculiar honours be paid to the city-state at the expense of other types of association smaller or larger. Man is not a *'polis* animal'. The liberal theory is one of human society, not of statehood. And it was Aristotle's vigorous and successful purpose to kill this theory and replace it by one of statehood. For statehood and state are definable in terms of permanent patterns of power; while 'society' for the liberals was ultimately something different, something in which power-patterns existed pragmatically and temporarily.

In the liberal vision, all human beings, whatever their varieties of endowment or temper, were equal partners in the societies they formed. This egalitarianism did not mean that 'one man was as good as another'. The identity between human beings lay not in technical capacity or in moral character but in the common drive for safety, for sociality, and for pleasure. Men were in fact all 'equal in the law' rather than 'before the law'; because law merely represented the usage of that form of society which happened to be the one that all members had collectively formed to satisfy their needs. Aristotle's text, even if unwillingly, preserves a stirring assertion of this principle:

THE LIBERAL TEMPER IN GREEK POLITICS

It is held that there inheres a principle of right between any
one human being and any other who is capable of communal
participation in custom-law and contract. . . .
Amity and moral right are found at a minimum in despotic
relationships.
They are maximized in democracies.
For between human beings treated as equals communal interests are also maximized [*E.N.*8.11.7].

This conception of equality was not invented in the fourth
century. We know from other sources (Herodotus and Thucydides) what a grip it had obtained over the Greek mind in the
fifth. It responded to the Greek capacity to view reality – in this
case the human reality – in mathematical terms. It had also
controlled the thinking of the Elder Sophists, who rationalized
the democratic process of government. Perhaps they did not even
choose to argue it, simply because in their day it was accepted as
self-evident. Aristotle's semantic contortions undertaken, in his
Ethics, to construct a system of 'proportional equality' show how
even he never dared to dismiss the notion – which he logically
should have done – but was compelled instead to keep it and
render it as innocuous as possible.

Though the principle of equality was identified with that of
moral right (*dikaion*) it was never linked with any inalienable
rights theoretically possessed by any and every human being.
Indeed, the whole doctrine of natural rights (in the plural) is
modern; and while in spirit and temper it recalled Greek liberalism, the form in which it was cast reflected the long influence of
the doctrine of the independent existence of the soul of man,
a doctrine which grew up outside the circle of liberalism, but was
afterwards mated to liberal theory, as for example in Locke.
Greek naturalism relied, instead, on a more generalized and
scientific perception of the human being. He is a member of a
species and between him and his fellow members the natural
similitudes are therefore basic while the personal differences are
incidental. The similitudes take effect in the common drive to
survive, to enjoy oneself, and to express amiability. The instruments, social and technical, which make survival, enjoyment, and
amiability possible are all genetically identical and procurable
only by co-operation. Therefore, society exists only as the

framework of supply, each and every man having an equal vested interest and at bottom a biological interest in the maintenance of its mechanism. His biological demand upon it for services is identical with that of any other man. It follows, said the liberals, that while his personal function in operating the machinery, his kind of work, may have special characteristics, there would always be others resembling him – he is never alone – and the inherent value of his contribution is identical with that of any other man's. It must be, because all contributions are evoked only by response to basic needs and these are all identical. No room here for moral hierarchies within the community membership.

The accents of Antiphon are discernible: 'We all breathe the same air . . .'. His fierce naturalist rejection of classes and orders in society must have sharpened the focus of egalitarian theory in the fourth century. At the level of daily politics, it found increasing practical application. With the passing of the Athenian empire, the legal relationships of all free Greeks with each other tended to become formally identical. In municipal government, a democracy of equals was the norm. Tyrants might seize power, but classes, principalities. and powers validated by the state apparatus tended to disappear. The Athenian decree of circa. 330 B.C. forbidding purchase of free Greeks captured in war is significant of the growing temper. Hence it is that, when Aristotle includes a working account of the legal system as it actually operated, he is forced to drop his 'proportional justice' and describe a situation in which 'the laws deal with men as equals' and in which law operates to 'restore equality' between persons. His own report, that is to say, testifies to the growing influence of liberal temper upon administration and to his own personal distance from what was actually going on in the cities of his epoch. He, like Plato, lived mentally in a political vacuum which for him was partial and for Plato total. The vigour of their preoccupations with problems of education and of intellectual authority robbed them of any interest in or feeling for the actual democratization of the Hellenic society of their day.

Equality as a working principle of politics may have had an important influence upon the kind of anthropology preferred by the liberal theorists. Plato, as Homer long before him, proposes as the prototype of all society the family unit, the patriarchal household. This, offered in myth in a semi-historical guise by

Plato, becomes converted in Aristotle's politics into a fixed historical and moral principle; so that the authoritarian relations between man and wife, father and children, master and slave are treated as fundamental to the anthropological process and as the prototype of the present civic and social relations proper between men. To this the liberals might object, with simplicity and common sense, that the familial relationship of parent to child depends on the child's temporary helplessness and cannot possibly be a prototype of a state composed of adults. They might add that, since this parental relationship forms the basis for the claim of all authoritarians that power-relations are rooted in nature, the argument that authority is 'natural' falls to the ground with it. For in nature the parental care is only a preparation for an adult existence in which equality replaces authority. And so the analogy from nature applied to defend patriarchal control over women and slaves is destroyed also.

Whether or not they so argued, it is fairly clear that, in the theorizing over the genesis of social forms, they rejected the familial household as a meaningful prototype. There are a few hints to the effect in Aristotle's pages. The rejection must have begun in the fifth century. There is indirect proof of it already in the plays of Aristophanes: the controversy provoked satirical portraits of the relation between parents and children. Democritus himself said some things on this subject which, from a traditional standpoint, read very subversively. It remains true to this day that the supposedly sacred prerogatives of the family in the natural and divine scheme of things are always evoked by political authoritarians.

The liberals were committed to dealing with historical processes at the expense of formal classifications. The latter might pragmatically be useful to assist description but no more. They maintained a persistent fluidity of outline. Any 'fixed quantity' in the human being was represented only by his drives to manufacture the means of security and so forth. Societies were social shapes moulded and remoulded to satisfy these drives at increasingly complex levels. The historical process was unlimited in time and perhaps in invention. It could not be arrested and neatly pinned down between the two extremes, the household on the one hand and the city-state on the other. Accordingly, to answer the questions: What is society, and what if any are the norms of its behaviour? What are the proper relations between society and its individual members? – liberalism tended to become purely descriptive and to cast around for any and every observed sample of meaningful association. By 'meaningful' was meant relatively stable – not necessarily historically permanent, but demonstrably forming at some time and for some purposes a working partnership.

The schematism of anthropology had noticed and exploited the linguistic and ethnic group as one of the elementary stages in social growth. The theory of Democritus and the sophists had focused on the existing possibilities of the Athenian city-state democracy, but without letting the concept of such a *polis* dominate their historical thinking. Antiphon had noticed the fundamental search and the natural need of men for sociality, expressed in the mating of the sexes and also in the desire to escape from aggressive relationships. Fourth-century liberalism gives closer scrutiny to the variety of types of corporate association, the existence of which is observable either historically or in the present. Thus the clan and the deme are selected from history and present practice as examples of 'society'; and so are the cult society and the social club. But to show that even historical institutions represent man-made choices for material and natural ends, the list is also made to include companies and corporations formed for professional or business purposes. Finally there were those types of association which united cities in pairs or groups composing commercial federations.

It is surely significant that Aristotle's report here includes two observations which, to say the least, are not made in an idealist or teleological spirit. The proceedings of cult bodies, despite their professedly religious purpose, derive their raison d'être from the human need for recreation and amusement; this was originally true of all primitive religious assemblages held at harvest time when the seasonal rhythm provided material opportunity for recreation. This is a fragment of 'natural religion', a piece of descriptive science taken from the anthropologists. As for the commercial types of association formed for material profit these in fact, he reports, are more representative of the real character of human society and its aims than are the kin groups (including the household), for they forcibly demonstrate the effect of human compact (*homologia*) in forming community. Here is a fragment of positivist sociology. Both observations, so alien to Aristotle's own teleological method, stem directly from the working principle that society's business is simply to provide the mechanisms of human welfare and pleasure, and can take many forms to accomplish this.

But aside from observing the variety of types of association already institutionalized within the framework of Greek society, liberalism focused an increasing share of its attention upon the developing range of commercial exchange. It was prepared to recognize the 'exchange society' as a going concern, an operative and meaningful conjunction of human beings to form a definite type of social system. It is even probable that in this kind of association it sought the typical models of law and justice as functional principles of human community.

For Plato, as for Aristotle, the developed commercial community, which is well enough organized to produce a surplus for at least part of its population to enjoy, represented a condition of social disaffection or abnormality. If the liberals were able to estimate it without benefit of moral prejudice, this was due not only to their descriptive method but to their initial conception of what made any human animal tick. If the animal requires security, pleasure and amity, all three of which can be comprehended under the rubric of pleasure, and if society comes into existence to pursue the means to this, clearly a society which tends to expand the supply of goods and services is not something to be afraid of, but a logical consequence of the historical development. Man *qua* man cannot go wrong in it; for he is still pursuing the drives of his elemental nature, and these are not to be feared but accepted.

It was assumed, apparently, that an exchange-economy of itself tended to expand the supply of goods. This was true so far as goods were available in a raw state on the earth's surface, but the theory tended to ignore the importance of production. However, in a sense the earlier anthropology of the fifth century had looked after this omission, by stressing the vital role of the various material technologies in the development of culture. These included the productive ones like agriculture and metallurgy. And then, anthropology, as we saw, correctly estimated the labour-value of a pair of hands. Plato's account of the growth of a commercial society in *Republic* II, written perhaps before 380

B.C., accordingly stressed production of goods and services and its acceleration through the division of labour. The two economic accounts of Aristotle, in the *Ethics* and *Politics*, pay little attention to production, and much more to the mechanism of exchange. They can be combined to produce a descriptive theory as follows:

The original human societies operating with a minimum of invention were essentially land-locked, inasmuch as land contact requires less technique than maritime intercourse. They were groups of contiguous human beings who carried out some elementary exchanging of raw materials and products. This level of co-operation evoked its corresponding pattern of usage and social regulation. Society, however, showed a natural tendency to enlarge (presumably in principle to increase the field of man's sociability and the means of his happiness) and the extension of numbers and territory (into ethnic and linguistic groups?) called into existence a system of barter. We say system, for even this level of exchange required the invention of weights and measures, standards which differed in different communities, and represented the invention of different social groups. These inventions became conventions, locally disposed in a variety of patterns representing an important extension of social custom and 'law'.

A further extension took place when society ceased to be land-locked. Technical mastery of shipbuilding and navigation moved parallel with the growth of import and export trade at the various coastal centres. The sea-born traffic in turn prompted the invention of an improved technique of exchange – that of coinage or stamped tokens or money. Money like the weights and measures of an earlier stage is simply another token of measurement. But perhaps, like them, it created its own system of exchange. It became itself a vehicle for further maximizing community and hence we may say created new levels of society and sociality. Yet itself it is only another example of man-made compact or law. This invention, like the previous one, becomes a convention, none-the-less binding and legally enforceable for being the result of human compact, which theoretically can be changed at the will of the same human beings who made it. Indeed, the metal of which it is composed has two 'natures'; as metallic raw material and as a token of value and price. The latter 'reality' is man-made by the historical process.

That it behaves, however, in conformity with the rules required by the fundamental nature of human beings is seen in this: that as between human beings who are equal, and resources which are unequally distributed over the earth's surface, money tends by its common measuring-rod to facilitate through exchange the removal of these geographic inequalities. Of itself it tends to accelerate the flow which adjusts and equalizes things. (The theory could not by definition deal with how money behaved if monopolized by the more powerful; for the theory refused to recognize that in nature more powerful persons existed).

Lastly, the money can be withdrawn temporarily from the exchange process, and stored, hoarded and kept. This does not withdraw it from the system as such. The holder merely retains it till he wishes to spend it. But in a sense its man-created nature has undergone a further Protean development. It has temporarily ceased to act as a token of exchange and becomes a sworn guarantee, a 'surety' held by the owner against future exchange. We would say it represents his future 'claims' on the community in conformity with that tendency of modern economic theory to speak the language of moral and natural rights. In short it has become, at least potentially, 'capital'. Whether the theory went on to rationalize the process whereby such hoarded guarantees could be transferred to others who had immediate use for them – the process of lending capital at interest – we do not know. For Aristotle's moral objections to usury intervene to prohibit any further reporting of what must have always seemed to him an objectionable theory.

For the liberals, history remained open at both ends. It presented a continuous recital of process and development. It was therefore open to them to conceive that the increase of goods and services, of things, of real wealth, might continue to accelerate as exchange systems became larger and more complex. The money supply would also have to increase in proportion, not as the essence of real wealth, but as the measure of the increasing quantity of goods and services. This double calculus whereby money and real goods have to multiply in parallel to maintain stable prices may be responsible for the confusion in Aristotle's account between money-hoarding and wealth-increase. But the suggestion is speculative. What is at least clear is that the liberals envisaged the production of material wealth as a proper goal of community, and that they could abstract goods and services as a significant factor in human life and that they traced a parallel between increasing integration in community and increasing production of wealth.

Their firm grasp of the theoretical importance of these insights is shown by the fact that they were ready to admit them as the material of a new discipline – that of 'wealth-making' or 'economy' (*chrematistike, oikonomike*); an applied science historically invented in the manner of all of the technologies, and employing currency as its finite tool. Such a science Aristotle was inclined to reject as properly speaking non-existent. Instead of wealth-making he prefers to substitute agriculture and for economy in the liberal sense he preferred economy in his own sense, namely the study of moral and constitutional relations within household and state.

When the liberals accepted the social dynamism of economic exchange as inevitable and normal, they shattered the walls of the Greek city-state. Monetary systems, they argued, were the creation of 'import and export'. The *polis* was not a self-sufficient unit. Plato, we saw, recognized the fact, but had refused to allow it any significance beyond the economic level. Morally the *polis* remained for him 'complete'. It is important to realize that for the liberals, just as economics and morals are not conflicting sciences, so the existence of an area of exchange which includes several cities presupposes an area of true community which theoretically supersedes the respective city administrations. This follows not only from their theoretic willingness to recognize all exchange societies, and name them as societies, but from their emphasis on political federation and commercial alliance between different cities. These exemplify a partnership of human beings united in the observance of a common system of commercial law; they therefore illuminate the general process of society-formation under the aegis of law, which is always going on. Aristotle would not have felt it so necessary to condemn such a conception as erroneous, if it had not gained acceptance. Nor did liberal theory at this point, dazzled by the mere mechanisms of international trade and banking, succumb to a crass materialism. The progressive dynamic enlargement of previously narrow societies was felt to represent a historical principle of social growth. For, so they argued, the instinctual amity of men was thereby given enlarged opportunity when existing units of human settlement attempted federation or amalgamation. No doubt their eye here was focused primarily on combinations of Greek cities, but the theory could apply to any type of social shape or system. Presumably a social configuration which might include Persia with Greece would not be theoretically obnoxious, if it achieved a net increase both of economic exchange and of human fellowship. Thinking of this kind pointed simultaneously towards world citizenship of equal and amicable human beings, and a world economic system in which products obtained from the ends of the earth were exchanged with facility, to the advantage of such human beings. Whether or not such a vision was made explicit before the conquests of Macedon made it feasible, and the power of Rome made it a fact, is open to question. But it is not open to question that the vision, when compared with the historical logic of the liberals, wears an air of inevitability.

So man is not a 'political animal' after all – meaning in Aristotle's quite specific language a 'city-state animal'. The ambiguous extension of the modern word 'political' has served to cover up and hide from view the essentially static and rigid character of his moral and social thinking. To the liberal mind, the condition of man is determined by those energies, biological and psychic, which at once seek satisfaction and devise means to find it. It is a process at once dynamic, flexible and continuous. It is precisely its 'unlimited' character which Aristotle seeks to destroy, by erecting a system of classifications imposed upon the variety and the inventiveness and the restlessness of human behaviour. These categories have the effect of breaking up the continuity of process and also enable him to omit large elements which fail to fit into his teleological scheme.

Thus, for example, in the liberal historical view a barter system developed by the inner logic of the social process into a monetary system, and the same logic required that agriculture be supplemented by commerce. Aristotle's theory sunders bartering from monetary exchange and agriculture from commerce. He approves of the two former; he morally rejects the two latter as though human history could be thus parcelled out into lots, marked 'accept' and 'reject'. Similarly he refuses, in defiance of the history of his own time, to allow social development to pass beyond the walls of the small town. In this last instance, the character of the limitation he proposes is not essentially geographic but moral. He wants a community which taken as a whole has a significance denied to its individual parts and members. It is vital to recognize this motive, rooted as it is in a temperamental preference for power and authority over equality and amity. For this '*polis* idea' rules over all its members, just as the superior among the members rule over their inferiors, the artisans and workmen. As thus conceived, the city-state doctrine was the ancestor of the modern doctrine of statehood and of the absolute sovereignty of the nation-state. The transition from the Greek word *polis* to the English word 'state' is not a mistranslation, for it retains the metaphysical and authoritarian flavour, and merely enlarges the geographic boundaries. What disasters for men have been bred by the influence of this rigidity we do not yet fully know. The liberalism which was devoured and destroyed deserves to be rescued from its entombment, if for no other reason, at least to put it on record that Hellenism had larger conceptions of man's social destiny in which the fateful power of the state played no significant role.

The limits of Aristotle's political horizon had, however, one advantage; they left his mind free to concentrate upon the actual civic machinery by which city-states were administered. His perception, as it was narrow, was also concrete. There were other types of sovereignty and administration in the world, but none of them were easily available to Greek inspection. Even his liberal opponents had to live lives conducted under the aegis of laws framed, and of orders given, by officials and assemblies of small towns. The era of experiment in leagues and federations had dawned. But none of them touched the sovereignty of the *polis*. They might assist the liberal vision to embrace the logic of societies other than the city-state, but presumably liberalism was inspired in the first instance by those foundations previously laid in general anthropology.

When it came to describing actual systems of administration, the liberals like Aristotle were confined in practice to models provided by the city-state. It is therefore plausible that they gave less attention to government than he did, and made relatively little contribution to constitutional theory. Their business was with a general theory of society not with the niceties of constitutional apparatus. But the general theory itself made it inevitable that at least the apparatus had to conform to democratic principles. Legal sovereignty and administrative act, however they might be executed, must harmonize with the fact that any society is created by the needs of all the human beings composing it, and that, since these needs are equal, and the energies which seek to fill them are equal, the framing of law and usage required to effect this must somehow grow out of the equal participation of all members.

1. The view is that cities enjoy consensus
2. when common sentiments prevail
3. covering common interests
4. and when these are voted into declared preferences
5. and embodied in action
6. which reflects opinion reached in common [E.N. 9.6.1].

Whereas items 1, 2, and 3 simply approve a condition of political harmony and give it its appropriate label, items 4, 5, and 6 are the echo of an operative theory of democratic government in which common agreement is not a happy moral achievement, dependent on the motives of superior persons or 'good citizens', but a process in which the opinions of the human beings forming the society are by debate and discussion integrated into a 'common opinion'; the process would be necessary as well as dynamic, because the very existence of the group presupposes a set of common interests which calls it into existence. When Aristotle adds a denial that consensus can mean 'both parties think the same thing whatever that thing may be', he is replying to the egalitarian view that the generic similitude of human beings and their needs will guarantee that their opinions about their own interests will issue in joint decision which serves the common interest.

The process of debate, negotiation and calculation by which this issue is reached is omitted in Aristotle's text. Otherwise there is little more here than a repetition in abbreviated form of that kind of rationale of the democratic process already carried out by the Elder Sophists, and described above in Chapter Eight.

There may be something over-spontaneous, over-optimistic, over-facile about this account of the formation and execution of group decisions, but it reflects still that tenacious belief in the continuity behind all forms of human behaviour, at all historical stages, which might be called the liberal version of natural law. The generic identities between men are more important than their differences; their life-drives, to find security and well-being, can therefore without difficulty coincide in common group decisions; their needs, physical and spiritual, for amity and fellowship with their own species guarantee some basic readiness to explore and find agreement; the democratic consensus, however approximate, is therefore a natural and historical condition by which all societies operate and function to greater or less degree.

'It is in democracies that amity is maximized.'

But Aristotle applies the classifications of moral hierarchy to break up this dynamic continuity. Verbally retaining the concept of consensus, he limits it to the state of mind of a governing class; below them is a second category and a different state of mind. This second category 'grasps at something selfishly from among the utilities', so that its moral condition is factional, since it refuses to do what is morally right. In this way the organic conception of liberalism – in which the human social instinct, and the utilitarian aims of political groupings, and the humane morality of all the group members, were conjoined in a single system – was completely destroyed.

The conception of the common interest as the principle properly served by all societies and their governments has today become a commonplace. Exactly what it means depends on how the common interest is defined. Greek moral theory, however, had to create the conception before it could be even debated; it is a sophisticated abstraction which represented in the fifth century a considerable effort of generalization. Greek political and moral science is haunted by the three terms *sympheron, chresimon,* and *ophelimon*; the first corresponding to expedient-interest, the second to what is serviceable, and the third to what helps or assists or benefits. All are appropriate in general to that pattern of thinking which one would call utilitarianism, and the pattern is already visible in the first half of the fifth century.

No Greek moralist, whatever his preconceptions, was afraid of these terms. He simply imposed his own context on them. They are indigenous to Socratic idealism as to liberal materialism. A basic split between the moral or ideal and the expedient or selfish did not develop until Christian other-worldly influences had begun to affect the vocabulary and the mind of the West.

The precise context in which liberal political theory viewed these terms has, of course, to be disentangled from the way in which they are employed in Plato and Aristotle. And, since the vocabulary of evaluation, approval and preference to which they belong is notoriously slippery, the task is not easy. The anthropologies had established the achievements of technology as 'useful'; this signified their historic role in the life of man: they assisted his development; they enlarged his stature; they made him happier. The adjective was also employed by medicine and reinforced by a second adjective 'expedient' (*sympheron*) to identify those forms of diet and regimen which 'fitted' or 'were appropriate to' the human biological mechanism. This notion of biological appropriateness gave an early precision to the words, and the Socratic method, seeking to define the procedures and objectives of the techniques and crafts, added another shade of precision, for which it employed the word 'serviceable' (*chresimon*), meaning that which is functionally correct and effective.

Perhaps the most characteristic application of these criteria by liberal political theory occurred when it constructed a rationale of the exchange community. Here was an actual form of society evolving out of the pressure of human 'use and need' (*chresis* and *chreia*). Its goal therefore could be logically identified as the serviceable and the useful. But the goal inhered in the exchange system; it is in virtue of demand-and-use that society coheres at all. What is serviceable and useful is here identified mainly with material goods and their provision (*poros*), itself a perfectly proper and indeed inevitable principle of community.

Plato and Aristotle could recognize such economic utilitarianism, while relegating it to a minor role in the human equation. The liberals were unique in insisting that it drew from the fundamental and urgent springs of all life. And they made their point by placing equal and parallel stress upon pleasure and expediency as proper human motivations. They argued, in fact, that between these and social utility there is no essential difference. The union of pleasure and expedient and useful is prominent in Antiphon. Presumably the liberals who reconstructed social theory after his attack on law had to insist that whatever was socially useful had always to be also pleasurable and expedient.

The significance of so insisting was more than verbal. For pleasure was the label placed upon the egoistic and personal and even private sensations of the individual human being. The fact that his identity with his species made his pleasures similar to those of his fellows did not alter the fact that they had to be his personally. Hence the common interest on which the liberals insisted as the goal of community had to emerge as a harmonization of all the individual interests of all its members. And this harmonization was such as to confer direct pleasure on each and all. This allowed the economic objectives of society, in the production of goods and services, to assume equal importance with the moral ones – in fact they *were* the moral ones or part of them. The other part was represented by the increased opportunities in society for expressing the equally hedonistic urge to amity and fellowship. For this, too, was part of the urge to live and to live well. In short, the citizen of a liberal society was properly a hedonist and a philanthropist and an egalitarian all in one.

That this or something like it was the way in which the liberals worked out the conception of the common interest is visible from the way in which Aristotle goes about rejecting the theory in favour of his own. Thus he reports in his *Ethics* the view that all kinds of society and indeed all forms of justice are designed simply to achieve the common interest; he admits that the degree of interest increases with the degree of amity. But he is at pains elsewhere in the same treatise to deny that true amity has any connection with motives of pleasure and utility, and also that there is really any common interest uniting the doer of good and the recipient thereof. Thus, by classification, once more he proceeds to disrupt a dynamic continuity between pleasure and expediency, social utility and amity. Where this takes him becomes clear in the *Politics*. He has prepared the ground to assert a new form of human 'interest', namely, that interest which ruler and subject, or master and slave, respectively, have in their mutual relationship. He could only have pulled off this piece of double-talk by first dissevering (in the *Ethics*) interest from pleasure. For he would be asking too much of his readers to believe that the subject or slave savours his subjection with any personal relish. Thus, having removed the conception of an egalitarian harmonization of all personal interests, he proceeds to construct his own version of the political 'common interest' as that condition of discipline in which ruler rules and subject obeys. He denies emphatically that this interest is that of the governing class alone. Then whose is it? One can answer in effect; the interest of the city-state as a whole. That is, the conception of interest is placed finally at the service of an intellectual abstraction – the 'good of the state'. From this semantic manipulation of terms, originally defined with biological and scientific precision by the liberals, came all those ambiguities of the patriotic and public good which have served so often in the West to cloak the actual interests of social minorities.

It is not fashionable to count human affection among man's political principles. Its inclusion sounds both unscientific and sentimental. Yet as the account of Greek liberalism proceeds it conveys an increasing and inescapable impression that the concept of philanthropy was central and that it was intended to describe not how human beings should feel and behave if only they were good enough but how they actually did; surely a bizarre perspective to take upon a society divided by faction and rent by war.

The topic acquires prominence from its place in two books of Aristotle's *Ethics*. Though these are addressed in the first instance to personal friendship, they include notices of a general philanthropy, either as background or as supplement to the philosopher's own theory. It was suggested earlier that if Aristotle thus felt compelled to devote so much space to personal and virtuous friendship, this was because the notion of human affection had already been exploited by contemporary thinkers in a different context, and that Aristotle felt compelled to displace the effects of their kind of teaching by substituting his own. In short, Books 8 and 9 of *Ethics* form one more extended example of that running warfare which he conducted with liberalism. But what proof is there that the case was not in reverse? There may have been some vague notions of general philanthropy abroad. Was it not Aristotle's own and very specific obsession with philosophic friendship, a theme inspired by Platonism, that was responsible for giving them artificial prominence?

The answer lies in those passages of the *Politics*, few but significant, where amity on the one hand and force on the other are noticed as political principles, in contexts which connect them with problems of justice and equality. But the answer lies also in a retrospect, which carries back as far as the *Prometheus Bound*. That play afforded some evidence that philanthropy (a term hitherto unknown in Greek) and good will had already got into the anthropologies, and played there some role descriptive of the evolution of human civilization. The hint was partially confirmed in Democritus, who stressed compassion as a social-psychological mechanism operative in mature political situations. The Platonic myth of civilization, as attributed to 'Protagoras', described justice and shame as 'bonds of amity' among men. The theorizing in support of democratic procedures, attributed to Prodicus and Hippias, seemed to place some reliance on both amity and good will as providing a biological support for reaching agreed decisions. Antiphon, fiercely repudiating the tyranny of existing 'law', did so in the name of non-aggression. Such a chain of testimonies, when linked with the parallel reports in Aristotle's *Ethics*, justify the contention that human amity had come to occupy an organic position in the liberal account of man, society, and morals. The conception was neither as sentimental nor as simple as it sounds. It was elaborated and applied somewhat on the following lines:

Association, to achieve security, and secondarily to manufacture the means of plenty, being the visible law of man's historical development, the human being involved in this process must by definition possess some capacity for permanent association. This at its lowest common denominator shows itself as an inclination to feel 'good will' rather than 'ill will'. For ill will and suspicion and enmity are the concomitants of mutual separation and isolation. Since man commands both emotions, the growth of community and society involves an increasing capacity for one at the expense of the other. Amiability is therefore built into the biological structure of the human being, and its presence and function in him are defined by the conditions of the similitude which obtains between members of a common species. This generic similitude allows a human being to 'recognize' his neighbour as familiar (a touch retained in the Diodorus anthropology), and, since the familiar is more pleasant than the unfamiliar, we enjoy consorting with our similars. The sexual relation, though limited to pairing, exhibits the same biological inclination in intense form. For, in this relationship, the physical disparities are incidental; the welcome given by like to its like is essential. Ethnic cohesion and the sense of 'nationhood' demonstrate the tendency of human amity to increase in intensity in proportion to the increase in similitude; for to the generic human similitude is added, in this case, identity of spoken language. Greek linguistic usage itself betrays the operation of the instinct in smaller associations formed within the larger unit, for when we address certain of our neighbours as 'fellow voyagers', 'fellow soldiers' and the like (a usage of wide application), we use a means of expression which is, so to speak, performative. It identifies a sphere of association in which we operate with others in the eternal endeavour to serve our human interest and utility.

If pleasure then be the name of that drive which requires biological satisfaction, and utility, or interest the name of any means devised to serve either protection or pleasure, amity falls under both heads. It serves use and interest as providing the right atmosphere for legal and economic co-operation; it is fundamentally pleasurable because it expresses the instinctive inclination to greet and welcome and live with our human neighbours. It 'inheres in human beings as such'. But human history is a process, and man is not entirely a fixed quantity. Sociability has to enlarge as the physical area and the content of society enlarge and as its mechanisms of exchange become more complex. Pleasure itself is, therefore, not a fixed quantity either; our capacity for it increases with our historical development. Our original amity was perhaps nothing more than an erratic and unreliable instinct. Since its intensity increases in proportion to the growing intensity of community, it is possible to discern different levels in its development.

What may be theoretically true in historical retrospect is concretely demonstrable by an analysis of the levels of relationship that obtain between two present individuals, A and B, who encounter each other, not fortuitously, but are already members of some associative unit – civic or commercial or social – which is likely to bring them into some relationship of exchange. A, confronting B, and before any exchange of feeling or service has taken place, is basically 'well minded' towards him: he possesses an instinctual attitude, receptive but not active, which is independent of reciprocity. He could feel something akin to this even towards men unknown and invisible, for it is a generic attitude. But the feeling is stirred into some mobility by the specific situation. He is still however hardly aware he has it, and since B is in the same condition, a situation of incipient and unconscious good will pertains between the two of them. They like looking at each other. The liking is a form of pleasure as specific as the pleasure of beauty which kindles the glancing eye. It can lead to something more definite, just as the simple visual pleasure can lead to love. As the feeling is reciprocated, however, a measure of co-operation begins between the two parties. Each undertakes motions towards the other which are activated with the idea of mutual 'good performance'; that is, some service is offered by A to B and by B to A: the services may be quite dissimilar in form but the psychic operation which energizes them is common. At this level, the instinctual good will has mobilized itself into the full consciousness of an amicable relationship. Presumably a close affectionate relationship would be a step further along the road which may or may not be taken. And at this level of mutual service is also demonstrated the organic connection between human amity and human interest and utility. A will himself be served and benefited by the interchange of 'good acts'. He has expected that instinctually from the beginning; he expects 'provision of his own need' even at the moment when he makes some move to meet the need of B and vice versa. Hence no tug-of-war between altruism and selfishness is involved. The biological human good will, at all its levels, is a good will towards others and towards one's self simultaneously. And doing good and having good done to one are different facets of the continuous dynamic process which comprises association and forms society. Altruism and egotism are complementary aspects of man's natural endowment. It is equally obvious that they are functions of his egalitarianism. The generation of amity at extending levels through increasing exchange between A and B presupposes an equal generic capacity for it in the parties involved, and an equal interest in the services rendered. If there is inequality (of legal or social status) the function of amity is thereby inhibited: 'it is maximized when conditions are equal'.

If the field of our example be now transferred from the personal to the social, it can be seen that the actual employment of amity, descriptively speaking, increases with the rate and complexity of social integration. It deploys itself and energizes itself in close connection with the technical and material advance of culture. For example, in the commercial sphere it could be said that the coinage which accelerates exchange is one of amity's own invented instruments. In the political, it is mandatory that all legal relationships between men be such as will facilitate its expression. Since amity is expressible only in egalitarian exchange of services, legal relations must therefore be egalitarian; nothing else corresponds to the fundamental psychology of man. Ruler and subject, master and servant, owner and slave, considered as such, are cut off from amity with each other, for their status inhibits or forbids the full co-operative relationship. Such disparity of status is, therefore, in the deepest sense 'unnatural', and always implies that forceful pressure is being artificially applied to inhibit and prevent natural pleasures and sympathies. And therewith also the human interest, personal and communal, is prevented also. For the community is robbed of that provision of 'good work' which co-operative energies could supply.

To the modern mind, criticism of this kind of philosophy comes easy, long skilled as we are in exploiting the classic position that the differences between men are more significant than their similarities, and that society should operate by the rule of observing classified distinctions not philanthropic exchanges. Even Plato's embryo economics shows the difference, stressing as it did the division of labour necessary to production, rather than the mutuality of exchange necessary to consumption. What Aristotle did to the theory can be forcibly appreciated in his treatment of the relationship between the hypothetical persons A and B.

One of them, he says, has to be benefactor and the other the benefited and therefore one is in the superior, and one in the inferior position. He never even stops to consider the possibility of a mutual give-and-take. Thus, while B responds to the motive of self-interest and feels the brief faint good will of gratitude tinged with resentment, A, who is able to render service, has the power thereby to confer genuine amity and to derive a creator's (smug?) satisfaction from his product. He is in fact the 'better man' and he has 'made something' out of the other man. Aristotle's facile and fatal habit of correlating human beings with things comes in again. The social psychological continuity of the amity process is split by classification into two divergent types of emotion: a vague sense of good feeling *versus* conscious moral friendship. And the whole perspective is placed under the close control of a completely authoritarian conception of human relations. None other is possible unless among the rare members of the philosophical and virtuous élite. Transferred to a level of social and legal relationships, this same analysis is used to justify the notion that even master and slave can enjoy a form of amity which expresses the 'true interest' of both. From these semantic manipulations there derived in long descent our later notions of virtuous charity and its proper reward of humble gratitude. The clarity and vigour with which these corrections made by Aristotle are pressed home is unmistakable and one can only speculate on the fateful consequences which they may have had for the temper of Western man and society. Even admitting that co-operative amity on the one hand, and competition for superior power or influence on the other, are equal rivals for the allegiance of man's emotions (an admission which liberalism would never make) it was surely disastrous for man to be taught by his Greek masters that scientific politics must ignore the former and base itself on the latter. Such teaching, reinforced by all the splendour of an antique tradition and a great language, swung the balance too heavily one way. Even the very different intuitions of primitive Christianity were not powerful enough to overcome it. For practical purposes it placed the weight of moral and metaphysical authority behind the use of force, and principalities and powers have not been slow to take advantage of such schooling. There were voices in antiquity which could have warned us, but they were extinguished.

Many as were the areas of conflict between Greek political liberalism and the classicism of Plato and Aristotle, no debate divided them so keenly as that which was held over the origin and character of law and justice. Even to name these names is to accord the honours to classicism. For law and justice inevitably evoke in the modern mind concepts of a majesty and authority which is imposed on common men for their good, even in their own despite, rather than of a kindly convenience invented by men to serve their own deepest impulses. In the liberal language, custom-and-law (*nomos*) remained hyphenated and tied to social usage and convention. 'Law', as a set of principles independent of time and place, was a concept forbidden by the very structure of liberal thinking. Nor could 'that which was right and proper' for men to claim from each other in given situations ever be moulded into the shape of an abstract and unchanging 'justice'. Yet so profound has been the influence of Platonism, so successfully has it seized on notions of usage and right dealing, and converted them into the shape of eternal verities above and beyond history and not to be elicited from the historical process, that it becomes almost impossible to describe the liberal doctrine of *nomos* and *dikaion* except as a reflex of its metaphysical rival.

Yet liberalism was in the field first. The beginnings of an historical critique which traced the roots of law in social usage are already perceptible in Democritus. For him, lawful action is primarily a device – perhaps the main one – invented by human beings to serve their need of security. He sees it in its grim primitive beginnings – the agreement to kill 'the enemy'. He is aware of its historical varieties, its growing complication, as the exceptions to killing multiply. He recognizes that it can have a positive quality in releasing human energies and benefiting the historical process – if men consent to be benefited. But this insight is not pursued far. At least, the growth of complex political partnerships involving compassion and consensus is not linked with 'law'.

Antiphon's impassioned attack upon 'lawful usage' produced a turning point in the development of liberal theory. In effect he fastened precisely upon that one of its functions which Democritus had viewed as historically effective – its power to bring social pressure upon the members of the group. While in the thinking of Democritus this pressure was directed to prevent aggression, in Antiphon's it becomes a compulsion to commit aggression. Law for him is the legal system of a civilized state, with its apparatus of litigation and judicial process and its perils of imprisonment and fine, exile and execution, its opportunities for manœuvring for position, its encouragement of enmity, its fundamental principle of fending off aggression by aggression. And Antiphon detests it. The court of true justice to which he appeals against it is 'nature', meaning the biological hedonism and the fundamentally amiable instincts of individual men. Law, he cried, is only a compact (*syntheke*) and a convention (*homologia*) man-made, artificial, temporary, a violation of nature to whose spontaneous impulses it applies cruel and forceful pressure (*bia*).

Liberalism after him, as is clear from Aristotle's testimonies, so far from being content with this negativism, set about reconstructing a theory of custom-law which would stand up to this attack. First the historical analysis of Democritus is reaffirmed and amplified. An operative society is recognizable by the fact that it has a system of law and legal rights in which all its members 'partake'. This indeed, for practical purposes, is what their citizenship in the community amounts to. Any two human beings can enter into a relationship which becomes a 'law, a system of rights'. They create it by their association, and their essential humanity is guaranteed by their partnership in it. Law is an arrangement entered into with the initial purpose of furnishing them with 'freedom from fear'. It also identifies that machinery which allows mutual wrongs to be righted.

This keeps the character of law at a purely descriptive level. Its modes of regulative operation were then clarified further, in the light of those egalitarian convictions which had been exploited by the Elder Sophists. Law, negatively speaking, as a protective device is an 'equalizer'. For various reasons (what they are is not explained) the mutual equality of men is disturbed by unequal distribution of advantage; meaning the subtraction of a natural benefit from A and its addition to B. Law through equalization restores the original relation. Thus it is not properly designed to punish for the sake of punishment, but only to correct and to restore the previous equilibrium of nature.

But then, turning to Antiphon's assertion that law is only a non-natural compact or convention, the liberals accepted this, but deleted the qualification 'non-natural'. For, with a more thorough historical method, they were prepared to see the growth of compact and convention as itself inherent in the historical process. Democritus had said: 'Men form social shapes'. And perhaps the notion of shape gave him a special interest in the city-state. Liberalism of the fourth century said: 'Men form covenanted agreements', and these become society.

How firmly they applied this insight can be seen from the treatment of the example of weights and measures and of money. These illustrate social instruments, invented it is true, but dependent for their existence and substantiality on human compact and convention. If you change the agreement, the instrument dissolves back into its primal formlessness. Even so is law itself an invented instrument, wholly substantiated by human agreement and negotiation. The analogy is not accidental. Just as currency, rightly named as 'current convention' (*nomisma*), maximizes association through the acceleration of exchange, so does all lawful convention (*nomos*). The degrees and intensities of 'law' are like those of amity. Both increase with the increasing socialization of relationships. Again, a currency when stored becomes a 'guarantor' of future purchase that future need will be met. Even so, law is our general 'guarantor' that our rights will be always met. Its validity, therefore, for us lies in its capacity of temporal extension into the future. Society rests not merely on topographical contiguity but on expectation of future stability.

Yet this stability must never be over-played, till it becomes a monolithic and unchanging set of principles. Since law is human convention historically applied, there is no one unique law or set of laws, but only an unending series of arrangements and integrations. These must retain flexibility, for they have work to do as yet unforeseen, and their shapes may change as the needs of men require. Positive written law, therefore, as increasingly made by vote and decree in the fourth century, takes on a new historical importance, as against the unwritten law of conservative custom and past tradition. Plato and Aristotle, with the unerring instinct of metaphysical conservatives, gave their preferred allegiance to unwritten law.

Lastly, when law is named a 'com-pact' (*syntheke*) and a common agreement (*homologia*) this naming is true to its nature, for law is really valid only as it is an emanation from the common communication held between equal and similar human beings. There can, strictly speaking, be no law that is not democratic law. For it represents that coincidence of real interest and that joining of natural amity which emerge in joint thinking, joint opinion, and political consensus, the last stage of which is that decision which implements, and so adds to, the legal pattern.

Yet are all human conventions and all civic law formed in accordance with this process? The liberals must have had an answer to this – some critical weapon by which to disentangle apparent law from true. What they had to say here is largely hidden from us. Yet there is a hint. A crucial passage of the *Politics* calls attention to that custom-law which allowed the victors in war to enslave free men. If Aristotle's own mind had not been so ambiguous on this point, the report of how the liberals met the problem might have come through more clearly. But it can be inferred how they would have met it. Behind all laws of men stands the rule of 'natural right' (*dikaion*) or natural justice. This it is which supplies the criterion of their validity. How then, if they should violate this *dikaion*, can they be true 'conventions' of human beings, true 'agreements'? We suspect the liberals said that they were not, and that they failed of being true compacts because they were maintained only by superior pressure applied by one party to another. Such would be the kind of spurious usage which recognizes slavery itself, as well as hierarchies of privilege, wealth and power.

This would mean that the positive and historical methodology of the liberals led them into a stringent social criticism of some aspects of contemporary society. They could never reject society as Antiphon did. The great meaning of their reassertion of the historical logic of law is that they did not turn away into a theoretic Utopia of saints. But they could not have escaped some necessity of passing moral judgment upon slavery and war. And it is to be expected that precisely for this reason did the classic thinkers find liberalism so disagreeable that it had to be ignored.

We say 'moral judgment', even though their method was so descriptive, because they too, like Plato and Aristotle, had their standards of natural or true justice. But while classic philosophy identified these standards with the disciplined social guidance exercised by the superior over the inferior, liberalism named them simply the rule of 'amity'. Now, this is not just an inspirational statement. The emotion of amity and the behaviour pattern we call justice are both processes, not fixed quantities: they have evolved in parallel, as historical mechanisms, psychological and social, which mark the growth of the 'civility' of our race. 'The most part of justice is held to be amity: indeed amity is enough without justice, but what use justice without amity?' And again: 'As the integration of society increases, so do justice and amity.' And again: 'When one is maximized, so is the other.'

This kind of formula is not aspirational in the sense that it seeks to find the laws of human decency written in the geometry of the heavens. But is it any the less grandiose for being woven out of those uncounted years of human invention which came slowly to terms with elemental swamp and primeval forest in order to prepare a place of habitation, and a society of men, which would be gracious and kindly and good?

APPENDICES

CHAPTER II

THE conception of 'History as Regress' is here argued without prejudice to the view that in fact many regressive versions may have been included in an overall formula which was cyclical. This while obviously true of the myths of *Statesman* and *Laws*, as also of Empedocles' version, may be implicit also in Hesiod (*W.D.* 175). The issue as it affects a basic philosophy of human history and morals is whether we *at present* are living in a regress or a progress. Thus even those committed to the conception of 'History as Progress' (caps. III and V), who viewed the present as an evolutionary period, may have retained this within the framework of a cosmic cycle: cf. Anaximander (*FVS*[6] 12A10, I, p. 83, l. 31), and Xenophanes (*FVS*[6] 21A33, § 6).

The combination, in the myth of *Laws* 3, of 'a revulsion to the old Hesiodean doctrine' with 'the theory of Ascent' was noted by Sikes, *The Anthropology of the Greeks* (1914), p. 41, and analysed by Uxkull-Gyllenband, *Gr. Kultur-Entstehungslehren* (1924), pp. 28-30, who attributed the *kulturgeschichte* embedded in the myth to Democritus (though it need not have been exclusively atomist; see below, appendix to cap. V) and went so far as to argue (correctly, as I judge) that Plato 'die atomische lehre unterbricht, ja diese damit eigentlich aufzuheben oder mit ihr mindestens mit unverkennbar ironie die spitze abzubrechen sucht'. I cannot, however, follow him (p. 29) in viewing the Platonic account of the familial origins of State and law as also atomist; see my text.

CHAPTER III

I HAVE used, in caps. III and V and elsewhere, the term '(scientific) anthropology' to characterize any speculations covering the biological origins, the present technical equipment, or the present institutions of man, provided that these (*a*) deal with man generically as a single species, and (*b*) reflect the control of an overall historical perspective. This rules out most of the comparative material, on race and customs and the like, contained in Herodotus, as well as the 'archaeology' of Thucydides, for concrete observations, however acute, do not themselves lead to anthropology unless they are used to support some generic schematization. It also rules out that perspective towards cultural history which views it as the achievement of individual 'inventors', human or divine; this kind of schematization, treated exhaustively by Kleingünther, '*ΠΡΩΤΟΣ ΕΥΡΕΤΗΣ*', *Philol. Suppl.* 26 (1935), reflects the teleological methods of the peripatetics, who systematized the earlier mythic usage of the motif; cf. Sikes, *op. cit.*, p. 100, and Kleingünther, *op. cit.*, pp. 135-151.

The *kulturgeschichte* problem, in whole or part, has received attention from S. Dickermann, *De Argumentis quibusdam . . . e structura hominum et animalium petitis* (1909); K. Reinhardt, 'Hekataios von Abdera und Demokrit', *Hermes* 47 (1912), pp. 492-513; Sikes (*op. cit.*) (1914); Uxkull-Gyllenband (*op. cit.*) (1924); J. Dahlmann, *De Philosophorum Gr. Sententiis ad Loquellae Originem Pertinentibus* (1928); A. Kleingünther, *op. cit.* (1935); Lovejoy and Boas, *A Documentary History of Primitivism and Related Ideas in Antiquity* (1935), cap. VII; J. S. Morrison, 'The Place of Protagoras in Athenian Public Life', *C.Q.*, 35 (1941), pp. 1-16; G. Vlastos, 'On the Prehistory in Diodorus', *A.J.P.* 67 (1946), pp. 51-59, and 'Ethics and Physics in Democritus' (Pt. 2), *Phil. Rev.* (1946), pp. 53-54; cf. also the literature on the Protagoras myth in the next appendix.

Reinhardt's argument, that Diodorus I. 7-8 was Democritean, first put the importance of pre-Socratic anthropology in proper perspective, but the subsequent literature became entangled in narrower issues, as, for example, that the cosmology in Diodorus was actually pre-Democritus, or alternatively that it was after all Epicurean, or that the history of civilization was not Democritean but Protagorean, that its language theory was either 'natural' or 'conventional', and the like. In particular, the role assigned to cult figures in early accounts of the origin of civilization has attracted an attention which seems disproportionate (cf. Kleingünther, pp. 66-94 and Uxkull-G., pp. 25-27). No one, so far as known to me, has carried out an exhaustive comparison of *all* the terminology and doctrines of those passages of the *Prometheus*, *Antigone* and *Supplices* cited in the text, and compared these in turn with *all* relevant materials in the first seventeen chapters of Diodorus' first book. Once this is done, it may become evident that Diodorus' material is not the private property of Xenophanes or Anaxagoras or Protagoras or Democritus or any other single thinker, but is an epitomized amalgam of pre-Socratic speculations in this field, and one that (in the Egyptian sections) has been manipulated by that kind of teleological use of the gods as benefactors already apparent in Plato's *Statesman* and *Laws*, whether or not its intermediate source was Hecataeus of Abdera.

The formal character of the schematization lying behind the *Prometheus* passage has perhaps been obscured by a reluctance to interpret ll. 442-450 as referring specifically to man's pre-human

APPENDICES

condition, to his development of consciousness and of language from animal cries, and to the non-social nature of his savage state. Line 442 has even been amended to delete a reference to the wretchedness of the primitive condition. It is surely one of the anomalies of scholarship that, while critics have been loath to accept the figure of Prometheus in Aeschylus as a dramatic fiction (which would mean accepting the play as a play and not a religious tract) they have *per contra* been almost as reluctant to view the divine apparatus of Plato's myth in the *Protagoras* (see next appendix) as philosophically serious (which would mean accepting a Socratic dialogue as indeed Socratic, and not as an essay in entertainment).

At the other end of the cultural scale, ll. 367-375 of the *Antigone* have been punctuated and interpreted (in Jebb's edition) so as to sever their sense from the preceding *kulturgeschichte*, and convert them into a corrective and pious commentary on it, on the assumption, apparently, that (in the poet's view) a naturalist humanism can contribute nothing to the secret of the true nature of political institutions and human morality; to this end, line 368 has also been amended; the sense of the MSS. reading νόμους παρείρων χθονός can, however, be supported by reference to the weaving analogy in the *Statesman*, if one assumes that Plato converted a pre-Socratic metaphor for joint collectivist weaving into a monarchical operation.

The account in Lucretius, Book 5, while nearly contemporaneous with that of Diodorus, reflects too much Epicurean influence for it to serve as independent documentation of pre-Socratic speculation.

Translations of excerpts from the *Prometheus Bound* are taken from my version of that play published in *The Crucifixion of Intellectual Man*, Boston Beacon Press, 1950.

CHAPTER IV

THE myth spoken by 'Protagoras' in Plato's dialogue has had its share of critical attention, with opinion as to its authenticity deeply divided and, it would seem, unguided by any firm criterion which distinguishes between the *a priori* assumptions of the Platonic dialectic and the historical-genetic method of other schools of thought. Probably the largest group of critics are those who would identify the myth as wholly the work of Protagoras – (W. Nestle, in Zeller, *Phil. der Griech.* I[6] p. 1387, n., and *Vom Mythos zum Logos* (1942), pp. 282-289; K. Bitterauf, 'Die Bruchstucke des Anonymus Iamblichi', *Philologus* 68 (1909), p. 508; S. Dickermann, *op. cit.* (1909), pp. 73-92; Wilamowitz,

THE LIBERAL TEMPER IN GREEK POLITICS

Platon I (1920), pp. 80-1; J. Kaerst, *Geschichte des Hellenismus* I³ (1927), p. 62, n. 3; J. Mewaldt, 'Fundament des Staates', *Tub. Beitr. z. Alter.* 5 (1929), p. 72; A. Menzel, *Hellenika* (1938), pp. 86-7; M. Untersteiner, *The Sophists* (Eng. trans., 1954), p. 72, n. 24; T. A. Sinclair, *Hist. of Gk. Pol. Thought* (1951), pp. 57-8;) – or at least as a fair imitation of his style and thought (cf. F. Blass, *Die att. Bered.*² I (1887-98), p. 28; C. Gunning, *De Soph. Gr. praecept.* (1915), p. 76; K. Freeman, *Companion* (1946), p. 352). The decision of Diels, in the *Frag. der Vorsok* (1st edn., 1903, p. 521), was to treat it under the heading 'Imitation', which has encouraged uncritical users of the collection to do likewise.

At the other extreme, Grote in 1865 (*Plato* II, pp. 46ff.), Stewart in 1905 (*Myths of Plato*, pp. 220-2), Th. Gomperz in 1910 (*Die Apol. d. Heilk*, pp. 103, 105), and Shorey in 1933 (*What Plato Said*, p. 124) have regarded it as a wholly Platonic composition.

Between these two poles, a large though not united chorus, while reluctant to jettison altogether what seems such a useful addition to our meagre store of testimony on the great sophist, express uneasiness in varying degree over accepting it as it stands, mainly because of its religious apparatus, which becomes philosophically effective in the sentence (322a): ἐπειδὴ δὲ ὁ ἄνθρωπος θείας μετέσχε μοίρας, πρῶτον μὲν διὰ τὴν τοῦ θεοῦ συγγένειαν ζῴων μόνον θεοὺς ἐνόμισεν. Some have sought compromise by viewing this apparatus as merely a formal convenience suitable to the mythic form in which the theory is cast. For this explanation cf. Uxkull-Gyllenband, *op. cit.* (1924), pp. 16-20 (who, however, admits 'diese partie ist bei Plato etwas verschwommen'); A. Kleingünther, *op. cit.* (1933), p. 103; D. Loenen, *Protagoras and the Greek Community* (1940), pp. 87-9; G. Vlastos, *Plato's Protagoras* (transl. Ostwald) (1956), Introd., p. ix, n. 11.

But another group perceives that the apparatus is essential to the structure of the myth, and yet cannot have been Protagorean. This was simply stated fifty years ago by Alessandro Levi, 'Contributo ad un'interpretazione del pensiero di Protagora' (in *Atti del Reale Istituto Veneto di Scienze, Lettere ed arte* 45, 1905-6), when he said (parte 2, p. 878): 'But, to be truthful, we have not a single proof of the trustworthiness of the Platonic testimony. . . . If . . . the famous saying about the gods is Protagorean . . . it seems to us that it offers evidence against the authenticity of the myth of the *Protagoras*'; cf. the parallel pronouncement by Adolfo Levi, 'The Ethical and Social Thought of Protagoras', *Mind* 49 (1940), p. 290, n. 1: 'The myth, in so far as it attributes the first origin of civilization to the gods, was bound to assume their existence; while Protagoras, on the contrary, declared he knew nothing about them. It is therefore clear that we cannot here find an expression of the ideas of the sophist . . .'; cf. also Cherniss in *A.J.P.* 71 (1950), p. 87. O. Gigon, in 'Studien zu Platons Protagoras' (*Phyll. f. P. Von der Mühll* (1946), pp. 124ff.) seems alternately to suggest that the Greek sentence quoted above cannot represent a Protagorean original (p. 127-8) and yet that perhaps it may (p. 129).

The unworkable character of any compromise has been forcefully stated by P. Friedländer, *Platon* I² (1954), p. 346, n. 7: 'For although one may well concede to W. Uxkull-Gyllenband . . . that a mythical dress is possible for Protagoras, yet one can reckon for himself approximately how the development of religion must have looked to him. And now let us read from Plato: "Man because he is related to divinity alone among all living creatures believes in gods and builds altars and likenesses of gods." . . . When one recognizes how un-Protagorean that is, one will then have his doubts whether the divine origin of ἔντεχνος σοφία and πολιτικὴ ἀρετή can really be regarded as mythical dressing. It is bound up, according to the sentence ἐπειδὴ ὁ ἄνθρωπος θείας μετέσχε μοίρας, with the origin of religion. There thus remains very little left for Protagoras of what Uxkull, *loc. cit.*, vindicates for him, least of all the "Foundation of the science of the history of human origins".'

It is perhaps not surprising that a generally sceptical judgment has been expressed by M. Pohlenz, *Staatsgedanke und Staatslehre der Gr.* (1923), who says (p. 36) '. . . we know Protagoras' viewpoint unfortunately only through Plato's intentionally inexact reproduction', and by P. Frutiger, *Les Mythes de Platon*, I (1930), who calls the myth (pp. 183-4) 'a tissue of obscure and contradictory thoughts'; while W. C. Greene, *Moira* (1944), Appendix 33, p. 414, takes refuge in total ambiguity: 'The substance of the myth owes much to sophistic discussions in which Protagoras may have taken part, and preserves something of his style and point of view; but it is shaped by Plato's literary art, and is used by Plato in the sequel as a stepping-stone to a point of view that Protagoras could not have held.'

It should be added that the treatment of Gomperz over forty years ago (*loc. cit.*, p. 105) had the great merit of perceiving the crucial significance of the way in which the term τέχνη is used in the myth.

CHAPTER V

THE design here attempted is that of assembling those testimonies bearing on *kulturgeschichte* in the pre-Socratic period, together with those bearing on 'zoogony' and 'anthropogony', where these seem pertinent to a connected anthropological theory. By the light of this criterion, five thinkers, Anaximander, Xenophanes, Anaxagoras, Archelaus, and Democritus emerge as successive contributors to a genetic conception

THE LIBERAL TEMPER IN GREEK POLITICS

of general human development which is historical, whether or not it be labelled evolutionary. Empedocles, whose regressive attitude to his own epoch may have inhibited any interest in *kulturgeschichte*, is excluded. The remains of Protagoras, Prodicus, Critias and Antiphon demonstrate the influence of anthropology on their thinking, but it seems best to exclude them as a group, in order to clarify the original and separate existence of anthropological theory as a department of early science. If it be asked why the existence of such a theory should have been eclipsed in the record of later antiquity, I believe that Heidel (in 'Anaximander's Book . . .', *Proc. Am. Ac. Arts Sci.*, vol. 56, 1921), discussing the similar eclipse of what he calls the 'historico-geographic tradition' has pointed in the direction of the correct answer, when, apropos of the control over the doxographies exercised by Aristotle and Theophrastus, he says (*op. cit.*, p. 281) 'a considerable field of early scientific thought and interest lies partly or wholly without the scope of the doxographic tradition', and again (pp. 282-3): 'It is unfortunate on all accounts that Herodotus is the only extant representative of this branch of literature from the sixth and fifth centuries—in fact down to the time of Diodorus; all the really representative authors of this kind being known solely through detached quotations or fragmentary reports.'

The pertinent items have been numbered consecutively to a total of thirty-seven. Of these, the existence of fourteen seems to have been recognized by Sikes (*op. cit.*): Nos. 1 and 2 (Anaximander), 14, 15, 17 (Anaxagoras), 21 (Archelaus), 24, 25, 26, 29, 30, 33 (Democritus) – all in Chapter III of his book – and Nos. 6 and 10 (Xenophanes) – in Chapter II, a different context. Lovejoy and Boas (*op. cit.*) noticed only nine: Nos. 2 (Anaximander), 6 (Xenophanes), 16, 17, 19 (Anaxagoras), 21 (Archelaus), 30, 31, 33 (Democritus), and of these five were cited to illustrate a supposed 'primitivism' and five 'anti-primitivism', with Archelaus featured in both camps (*op. cit.*, caps. 13 and 7). Even Uxkull-Gyllenband (*op. cit.*) recognized only ten: Nos. 6 and 7 (Xenophanes), 19 and 20 (Anaxagoras), 21 (Archelaus), 27, 28, 30, 31, 33 (Democritus). A comparison of omissions and inclusions shows that only Sikes recognized the structural continuity which links zoogony and anthropogony with the subsequent history of culture. Lovejoy and Boas, seeking to impose on the material certain post-classical schematizations like primitivism, anti-primitivism, animalitarianism, and the like, disrupted it and destroyed the overall perspective. Very different, but hardly less arbitrary, seems the schematization imposed by Uxkull-G., viz. the 'anthropocentric theory' (Anaxagoras and Archelaus) the 'sophistic theory' (Protagoras) and the 'constructive theory' (Democritus). The first of these depends for its validity on the assumption (which seems to me untenable, as also to others: cf. Döhring,

Die lehre des Sok. als soz. ref. syst. 59ff., and Lincke, *N.J. f. kl. Alt.* IX, 673ff. and Vlastos 'Ethics and Physics in Democritus', *Phil. Rev.* (1946), p. 53, n.3), borrowed from Dickermann *op. cit.*, that Xen. *Mem.* 1.4 and 4.3, which argue teleologically that man has a special place and character assigned by divine Providence in the universe, represent at least in part a position held not by Socratics of the fourth century but by Anaxagoras and his disciple in the fifth; support for this is sought in items 19, 20, and 21 combined with ll. 332-3 of the *Antigone* (Uxkull *op. cit.*, pp. 10, 11), a structure too frail to bear such weight. The second depends on the assumption that Plato's myth in the *Protagoras* is strictly Protagorean (on which see previous appendix). Once these two assumptions are removed, the schematization attempted by Uxkull-G. falls apart, though scholarship remains in his debt for asserting and proving the structural importance of *kulturgeschichte* in Greek science. Doctrinal differences surely existed between the five pioneers, but I have preferred in this place to stress the character of their work as a joint enterprise cumulatively achieved.

Item 2: This testimony from Censorinus can be supplemented from the paraphrase of A's doctrine in Theophrastus' epitome (*FVS* 12A10 *sub. fin.*) – '. . . originally (κατ'ἀρχὰς) man was generated from animals of another species (ἀλλοειδῶν), this being inferred from the fact that while the others quickly look after themselves, man alone needs prolonged nursing, so that if this was his original (κατ'ἀρχὰς) condition, he could not have survived (διασωθῆναι).' Conceivably, the recurrent κατ'ἀρχὰς echoes A's description of a κατάστασις ἐν ἀρχῇ; cf. Democ., *FVS* 68B278 (item 27b below) and Protag., *FVS* 80B8b; with διασωθῆναι cf. the emphasis on survival in the Protagoras myth (cap. 5 above). The same testimony can also be expanded by a statement in Plutarch (*FVS* 12A30 *sub. fin.*) which however may reflect only Aristotelian improvements (*H.A.* 6.10, 565biff. and *G.A.* 3.3, 754b; cf. Sikes, *op. cit.*, p. 49).

Item 3: I follow Heidel (*op. cit.*, pp. 257-260), as against the doubts of Diels (*FVS* 12C, note *ad. loc.*) and the certainty of Jacoby (*F. Gr. H.* I, p. 480, n. 3) in attributing this testimony to Anaximander 'the elder'; its congruity with items 1 and 2 becomes apparent, once it is realized that a similar pattern of speculation is followed in A.'s successors.

Items 21-23 and 27: For my translation of *nomima* ('lawful usages') and *nomos* ('custom law') and *nomizon* ('custom usage') cf. next appendix. With my argument that Archelaus himself is unlikely to have exploited the formal antithesis between *nomos* and *physis*, cf. Heinimann *Nomos und Physis* (1945), p. 113. Correspondingly, *nomizon* in item (27g), while superimposed on *physis* (27a) is not discontinuous with it. I cannot here agree with Heinimann (*op. cit.*, p. 144) – 'Der grundgedanke dass die naturgesetzlichkeit für alle gelte, der mensch sich aber anschauungen bilde, die nicht auf der physis beruhen, stimmt mit Antiphon und dem Adikos Logos überein.'

Item 28: I have isolated this sentence from the rest of the citation in Sextus, and have referred it to human, not atomic, agglomeration; so also Uxkull-G., *op. cit.*, p. 31; cf. also *FVS*, note *ad. loc.*

Item 29: Proclus attributes to Democ., not three but four types of demonstration (ἐπιχειρήματα) designed to prove the anomalous character of language. But he then adds: καλεῖ δὲ ὁ αὐτὸς τὸ μὲν πρῶτον ἐπιχείρημα πολύσημον, τὸ δὲ δεύτερον ἰσόρροπον, τὸ δὲ τέταρτον νώνυμον. Instead of inserting (with Diels *ad. loc.*) in the appropriate place (τὸ δὲ τρίτον μετώνυμον), I prefer to view this last list of three as alone authentically Democritean, so that the third of the four earlier cited cannot be his: it reads: τρίτον ἐκ τῆς τῶν ὀνομάτων μεταθέσεως. διὰ τὶ γὰρ τὸν Ἀριστοκλέα μὲν Πλάτωνα τὸν δὲ Τύρταμον Θεόφραστον μετωνομάσομεν, εἰ φύσει τὰ ὀνόματα; This type of specific illustration, attached only to the third *epicheirema*, is patently not Democritean, and casts dubiety on the text it is supposed to illustrate. I would for good measure also view as post-Democritean the antithesis (drawn twice in Sextus) between *physis* on the one hand and either *thesis* or *tyche* on the other, here agreeing with Vlastos *A.J.P.*, 67.1 (1946), p. 53, n. 14, especially his statement 'τύχη or θέσει refer to different aspects of language', which I take to be an accurate estimate of Democ.'s whole position on this subject, though whether he actually used the term *thesis* I would not feel safe in asserting (cf. Steinthal, *Gesch. d. Sprachw.*, cited by Vlastos, *loc. cit.*).

Item 31: interpreted by both Lovejoy and B. (*op. cit.*, p. 391) and Uxkull-G. (*op. cit.*, p. 30) to mean man is inferior to the animals, a view plausible only on a non-empirical definition of what the principles of intellection are.

Item 36: I would defend my translation of *logioi* here – 'human beings with power of expression' – by reference to Hesiod *W.D.* 3-4, combined with Herod. I. l., Pind. *P.* 183. Democ. views the early bards as formulators of Greek theology, much in the manner of Herod. 2.53.

CHAPTER VI

WHILE the floruit of Democritus as established by Apollodorus (420 B.C.) seems to be based on an unreliable computation (forty years after Anaxagoras) critics have continued to assume that Democ. was younger than Protagoras. Whether or not this be true – and the style of Democritus at least bespeaks his reliance on oral methods of

APPENDICES

publication – the difference cannot have been great, and I feel person-ally convinced that the structural and systematic analysis of the human condition carried out by the atomist must have supplied the intellectual foundation for the sophistic communications-theory. Hence the order of treatment in chapters VI, VII and VIII.

That group of statements treated in this chapter seem to have been largely by-passed by historians; a clue to indifference may lie in the myopic statement of Burnet, *Thales to Plato*, p. 201: 'What we have of him has been preserved mainly because he was a great coiner of telling phrases, and these have found their way into anthologies. That is not the sort of material we require for the interpretation of a philosophical system, and it is very doubtful whether we have some of his deepest thoughts at all.'

Reluctance to accept Democritean material in Stobaeus (*FVS* 169-297) as authentic (cf. Sinclair, *op. cit.*, p. 65, n. i, where however the cross-reference to the admittedly spurious Pythagorean material appears scarcely relevant) seems to derive mainly from failure to under-stand it. I hope my explication may help to settle the matter, on grounds of (*a*) vocabulary: e.g. could any post-Platonic writer have described a given social grouping as *cosmos* or *rhuthmos*, rather than, say, *sustema*? (*b*) continuity with pre-Socratic anthropology; (*c*) close attachment to political events in Athens from Solon to Pericles. This Stobaeus material (in contrast to the 'Democrates' material) is free from that kind of moralizing characteristic of Peripatetic and Stoic editors; cf. the very different fate that befell 'Antiphon' (below, appendix to cap. X).

Items nos. 1 and 3 in my series (*FVS* 68B257, 258), which seem crucial for establishing the continuity, in Dem.'s thought, between the defence of the human species against its rivals and the development of the primary social sanctions, are unluckily omitted in the useful collec-tion of W. Kranz, *Vorsok. Denker* (1949), pp. 204-208.

Items 4, 9, 10, and 13: *nomos* in these contexts, as generally elsewhere when used in pre-Platonic authors (Sophocles, Archelaus, Antiphon), I have sought to render by linking the ideas of 'custom' and 'usage' with that of 'law'; *nomos* is admittedly usage which is 'solemn', but on the other hand is never wholly hypostatized as 'law' in the absolute, until enclosed in the context of the Socratic search for universals. Lines 450-457 of the *Antigone* are often translated as if they did describe Kantian universal imperatives (cf., e.g., Sinclair, *op. cit.*, pp. 49-50 and 89), but they refer, as both the Greek text and the dramatic context reveal, specifically to the solemn usages surrounding the treatment of the dead, especially when they are blood-kin. Similarly, *Oed. T.* lines 863-872 refer to the equally solemn usages (also familial) which forbid patricide and incest, crimes which the chorus forebode may be in the offing, though not yet revealed. Both passages could in fact provide text for Democritus' own approach to *nomos* as social usage, which, because it represents stages of historical growth responsive to social need, is not thereby any less essential or sacred. Aristotle's interpretation (*Rhet.* 1.13.2.) is unhistorical.

Items 2, 4, 8, 9, 12, 13, 16, 17, 21-29 correspond to only 7 distinct entries in Stobaeus, which I have sub-divided into the separate aphorisms of which they seem to be composed. Such combinations, often formed with scant attention to the logic of the original, are characteristic of editors of *florilegia*; sometimes a connective γάρ or δέ is inserted, sometimes not. Hence in (*FVS* 68B265) I take καὶ γὰρ δίκαιον οὕτως to be an editorial addition, with no lacuna after it as imagined by Diels.

CHAPTER VII

THE learned literature on Protagoras tends to assume that sophistic viewed the operations of opinion, speech, and judgment (*doxa* and *logos*) as personal, not political; which means that they are interpreted in relation to those logical problems which preoccupied Plato. It is a little as though a figure of Hume were propped up on a platform and made to memorize and apply the logic of Kant to defend his own. Sinclair (*op. cit.*, pp. 53-5) is a sympathetic exception, who stresses Protagoras' 'strong social sense', arguing that in the *Theaetetus* he appeals to τὸ κοινῇ δόξαν, and that the *Protagoras* supplies a social-political foundation for τὸ δίκαιον; cf. also Loenen (*op. cit.*, cap. 4).

The 'Defence of Democracy' could of course be illustrated from the Funeral Speech, where the influence of Democritus and the liberals is patent. But its documentation there, as also in the Corcyra episode and the Mytilenean and Melian debates, is an intricate business, better reserved for a separate treatment; the powerful mind of Thucydides, while accepting many of the concepts of contemporary thought, also remodelled them.

CHAPTER X

THE single name Antiphon is cited by ancient authors in a variety of contexts. It is today usually assumed that the orator of that name, the author of the 'tetralogies', is to be distinguished from all other

APPENDICES

Antiphons, and identified with the politician admired by Thucydides (8.68). In later antiquity this distinction was not observed by the author of the *Lives of the Ten Orators*, by Hermogenes, and by Philostratus. Even if it is observed, the record continues to connect the name Antiphon with the following intellectual activities: sophistic (Xenophon, *Mem.* 1.6.1; Aristotle, *On Poetic* fr. 75; Hermogenes, *de id.* B399, 18Rff.; Suidas, *sub voc.*); drama (Aristotle, *Rhet.* B2; *Lives of Ten Orators* 1.833c; Athenaeus XV.673f.; Suidas); geometry (Aristotle, *Phys.* A.2; Simplicius, *Phys.* 54.12; Themistius, *Phys.* 4.2); metaphysics (Aristotle, *Phys.* B.1); divination and interpretation of dreams (Aristotle, *On Poetic loc. cit.*; Lucian *V.H.* II.33; Hermogenes, *loc. cit.*; *Gnomol. Vind.*, 50 p. 14; Suidas); and finally psychiatry (*Lives of Ten*, *loc. cit.*, and Philostratus, *V. Soph.* 1.15.2). Aside from these activities, the following titles are by late authors attributed to 'Antiphon': (1) *(On) Truth* (by Hermogenes and, inferentially, Lucian) (2) *On Consensus* (by Hermogenes and Philostratus) (3) *Statesman(ship)* (by Hermogenes) (4) *On the Judgment of Dreams* (by Suidas) (5) *Handbook for Removal of Pain* or *Lectures to Lull Pain* (*Lives of Ten* and Philostratus). The later existence of three of these treatises in MS. form is attested by citations mainly lexicographical which actually name them and their author 'Antiphon,' as source: The *Truth* is cited in this way (from either one of two books) twenty-five times in Galen, Origen, Pollux, Hesychius, Suidas, Harpocration; the *Consensus* fourteen times in Harpocration, Suidas, Photius, and *Anecd. Bekk:* the *Statesman(ship)* five times in Athenaeus, Harpocration, Priscian and *Anecd. Bekk.* Finally, and as if to compound the confusion, the Anthology of Stobaeus contains twelve quotations, of varying length, attributed to an 'Antiphon'. Their content is moralistic and on the whole conventional, dealing with the topics of the hazards of marriage and parenthood (*FVS* 87B49), the shortness and uncertainty of life and the need to enjoy it actively while you can (B50, 51, 53, 53a, 54), the true nature of temperance (B58, 59), and the importance of education (B61, 63).

Such being the character of the tradition covering the name and works of 'Antiphon', critical scholarship has sought to come to terms with it by concentrating in the main upon the supposed authors of the *Truth* and the *Consensus*, generally assumed to be the same person. To the former Galen had assigned two consecutive sentences (text doubtful) on epistemology (B1 and 2) and two more on meteorology (B29). The same 'Antiphon' was identified, on the strength of cross-comparison with a citation in Harpocration, as the metaphysician cited in Aristotle *Phys.* B1, and hence also as probably the geometrician of *Phys.* A2. These testimonies were harmonized with the lexicographical notices to constitute a 'portrait of an author', in the moulding of which, it is clear, the actual word *Aletheia*, or rather its implications, exercised considerable influence. Thus on the one hand his treatise was assumed to represent Eleatic interests (cf. Parmenides *FVS* 28B1) and on the other to represent also a rebuttal to a work of Protagoras supposedly bearing the same name. That this 'Antiphon' accepted Eleatic doctrine is maintained by H. Diels, 'Ein antikes System des Naturrechts', *Internationale Monatsschrift*, 11 (1916), p. 85; J. Stenzel, art. 'Antiphon', *P.W.* Supplementband 4 (1924), c. 37; W. Aly, 'Formprobleme der frühen griechischen Prosa', *Philologus* Supplementband 21 Heft 3 (1929) pp. 115 and 141-2; K. Freeman, *op. cit.* (1946), p. 395; J. H. Finley, Jr., 'Origins of Thucydides' Style', *H.S.C.P.* 50 (1939), pp. 69, 72; W. Nestle, *op. cit.* (1942), pp. 372-3; F. Heinimann, *op. cit.* (1945), pp. 133, 139. That the same author must have combated the doctrine of Protagoras is held by F. Pfister, 'Zu den neuen Bruchstucken des Sophisten Antiphon,' *Phil. Woch.* 45 (1925), p. 205; E. Bignone, *Studi sul pensiero greco* (1938), pp. 77. 218-221; O. Regenbogen, review of Bignone in *Gnomon*, 16 (1940), p. 99; W. C. Greene, *op. cit.* (1944), p. 236.

As to the *Consensus*, a title cited to be sure in antiquity, but without enough quotation to give the work substance, it assumed a corporeal existence for scholars when in 1892 F. Blass (*Antiphontis Orationes* et *Fragmenta*, p. 139, n. to fr. 125) identified it as the source of the moralistic excerpts from 'Antiphon' in Stobaeus. This identification was assisted by one definition (among others) of 'Consensus' supplied by Iamblichus, namely that it represents a harmony with oneself. (*FVS*, vol. II, p. 356, ll. 20-21 and 24-30). Here again, the supposed implications of a single word have influenced the portrait of that author who is supposed to have used it as a title. This 'Antiphon' has been credited with that kind of ethical psychology which would anticipate or imitate features of Platonism. For this point of view see G. Altwegg, *De Libro* περὶ ὁμονόιας *scripto* (1908), p. 58-9; J. Stenzel, *loc. cit.*, c. 40-41; F. Altheim, 'Staat und Individuum bei Antiphon dem Sophisten', *Klio*, 20 (1926), p. 267; Finley, *loc. cit.*, p. 68. Regenbogen, *loc. cit.*, p. 100, calls the *homonoia* of the individual with himself 'an essential Antiphontic trademark'.

In 1915 Grenfell and Hunt in *Ox. Pap.* XI 1364, items A and B, published a text which on the suggestion of Wilamowitz was attributed to that 'Antiphon' who was the author of *On Truth*. The ascription depended on the fact that the words τοὺς νόμους μεγάλους ἄγοι in the papyrus are quoted by Harpocration as from this treatise (*FVS* ii.346, l. 20, note). Publication was followed by an extended analysis and interpretation of the text by H. Diels, *loc. cit.*, pp. 82-102. Since item A appeared to contrast law with nature and since this same sophistic antithesis purports to be treated by Plato in his *Gorgias*, the English interpreters, Ernest Barker, *Greek Political Theory* (2nd edn.,

APPENDICES

1925), pp. 66-9, and G. C. Field, *Plato and his Contemporaries* (1930), p. 90, seized upon the preconception thus supplied to view 'Antiphon's' work as a rather trivial exercise in the kind of *Realpolitik* for which Plato's 'Callicles' has become notorious. Thus their treatment of the problem presented by the papyrus relegated its author to the stock role of a sophist as portrayed by Plato, in stark contrast to that portrait of 'Antiphon' hitherto constructed. Item B, which seemed written in a different vein, was relegated to the status of a footnote and tacitly ignored.

After Diels, the next extended treatment of Antiphon (apparently unknown to Barker and Field) was that of J. Stenzel (*P.W. loc. cit.*) who correctly saw that in some respects the interpretation of Diels had been superficial. He also wrestled with the problem of reconciling the author of the papyrus with the supposed authors of the works *On Truth* and *On Consensus* and their supposed preoccupation respectively with epistemology and psychology. But presumably his article had been composed without knowledge of a second papyrological contribution. For in 1922 Grenfell and Hunt had published *Ox. Pap.* XV 1,797, which on grounds of vocabulary, syntax, and content was immediately attributed to the author of the previous papyrus. The attribution was examined and defended by F. Pfister, *loc. cit.*, pp. 201-5, with arguments which seem to be irrefutable, and also to reach successfully toward the inner meaning of the text. Subsequent studies have on the one hand delved more deeply into the specific meanings of terms employed, and on the other have returned, not very successfully, to the problem of reconciling terminology and content with the supposed doctrines of the supposed treatises *On Truth* and *On Consensus* (E. Bignone, *loc. cit.*, pp. 87ff., F. Altheim, *loc. cit.*, pp. 262ff., and J. Mewaldt, 'Fundament des Staates', *Tübinger Beiträge zur Altertumswissenschaft*, 5 (1929), pp. 69ff). In general, it can be said that one detects a steady tendency to treat the 'Antiphon' of the papyrus more and more seriously, as a thinker of profound if rather unique moral convictions. Thus Diels' notion of the triviality of his thought (Diels, *loc. cit.*, pp. 92, 97) was corrected by Stenzel's analysis. And Barker's and Field's caricature of the sophist subverting law with nature has given way to far more circumspect examinations, as in W. C. Greene's careful study, *op. cit.*, pp. 232-240, and the sympathetic account in Sinclair, *op. cit.*, pp. 70-71 (who however reverses Antiphon's position in one vital respect, when he says: 'A. meant to reject the statement that justice means doing injury when you have received none, but the sequel does not appear to say this'; the contradiction could have been avoided by noting the force of νομίζεται (*FVS* II 354.1.5) which identifies not what A. himself believes, but what he rejects).

Merely to tolerate this 'Antiphon' by viewing him as a moderate

THE LIBERAL TEMPER IN GREEK POLITICS

whose views were carried to their logical extreme by Callicles and Thrasymachus (Heinimann, *loc. cit.*, p. 140, n. 52: Callicles' position is merely a '*radikalisierende Weiterbildung*' of Antiphon's; cf. Greene, *loc. cit.*, p. 240) is not enough. (Cf. Jaeger, *Paideia*[3], II, p. 327: 'Antiphon's ingenuous naturalism and rationalism with respect to equality are an extreme contrast with Callicles' passionate belief in inequality.') For a determination of the philosophical position of the author of the papyrus, item B of *Ox. Pap.* XI 1,364 is crucial, a point perhaps appreciated by Bignone, 'Antifonte sofista ed il problema della Sofistica nella storia del pensiero greco', *Nuova Rivista Storica*, I (1917), pp. 489-90, when he remarked on what appeared to be a difference in attitude between item B and item A.

My own treatment, formulated in the light of this previous scholarship, relies on the following methodology: (1) the two papyrological finds are themselves adequate to define in firm outline the mind and philosophy of a man who can be called 'Antiphon'; (2) in forming this definition, all speculations relevant to this 'Antiphon' which had been entertained previous to the discovery of the papyri should, at least in the first instance, be discarded, and the attempt to read the terminology of the papyrus in the light of these speculations, raising as it does formidable difficulties, should be abandoned; (3) in particular, previous conceptions of the meaning of the terms Truth and Consensus, as supposedly used by this 'Antiphon', should be dropped, remembering that titles attributed to pre-Platonic thinkers are in an evidential sense likely to be worthless, reflecting as they do the librarianship and mental preconceptions of men trained in the Academy, Lyceum and Museum (cf. Heinimann, *loc. cit.*, pp. 133-4); (4) hence one cannot begin by placing this Antiphon in the context of Eleatic problems of epistemology or Platonic doctrines of soul-harmony, still less in the context of that kind of controversy over law versus nature which Plato for his own purposes conducts in the *Gorgias* and *Laws*; (5) but a suitable context for him does exist, if it is sought in the naturalism of the anthropologists and of Democritus, provided that the first clues to his position are sought not in item A but in item B of Pap. XI 1,364, which commits him to the double premiss of human equality and human community. The relegation of this item to the status of a kind of afterthought seems to have been the result of its publishers' whim; (6) the rejection of *nomos*, and the emphasis on non-aggression, are consistent with the assumption that this 'Antiphon', if he used the term Consensus, applied it to spontaneous or 'romantic' relations between human beings friendly by nature. The assumption can be supported, though scarcely proved, by those later references to this kind of relationship which I have noted in Aristotle (above, pp. 281, 291). I would here in the main agree with the conclusion, though

418

not necessarily all the argument, of Bignone, *op. cit.*, that for Antiphon *dikaion* and *homonoia* were identical and that it is gratuitous to join with Kranz (*FVS⁶*) and Regenbogen (*loc. cit.*) in suspecting the papyrus reading, μηδὲν ἀδικεῖν μηδὲ αὐτὸν ἀδικεῖσθαι (*FVS⁶* II 355.20).

The style and substance of the papyrus, both of them highly individual, supply a criterion by which to estimate the genuineness of the Stobaeus excerpts, and make their rejection inevitable (Sinclair, *op. cit.*, pp. 72-3, notes the incompatibility) but with one curious exception. The longest of them (*FVS⁶* 87B49, on Marriage) contains some formulaic phrases which seem to be embedded in a text otherwise discursive, and which exhibit that type of tight parallelism and antithesis characteristic of the papyrus. Three of these also read like echoes of corresponding sentiments in the papyrus. I give references according to page and line in volume two of the *Vorsok*: (1) 358.2: τοὺς φίλους ἐχθροὺς ποιῆσαι – cf. 355.8ff., ὡς ὑπάρχει γ'αὐτῷ ἐχθρὸς τοιοῦτος κτλ.; (2) 358.2: ἴσα φρονοῦντας ἴσα πνέοντας – cf. 353.28ff., ἀναπνέομεν τε γὰρ εἰς τον ἀέρα ἅπαντες κτλ.; (3) 358.4: δοκοῦντα ἡδονὰς κτᾶσθαι λύπας ἄγεσθαι – cf., 350.17ff. ἔνι τ'ἐν αὐτοῖς ἀλγύνεσθαί τε μᾶλλον, ἐξὸν ἥττω, καὶ ἐλάττω ἥδεσθαι, ἐξὸν πλείω. . . . A second curious fact about the same excerpt is that its pessimistic view of the family relationship is echoed, sometimes verbally, in the sentiments of Democritus concerning the hazards of parenthood, hazards which seemed to him so strong that he advocated adoption in preference to the begetting of children (*FVS⁶* 68B275, 276, 277, where Diels-Kranz, notes *ad. loc.* observe the Antiphontic parallels in the first two): (4) 357.16: τί γὰρ τύχοι μὴ ἐπιτηδεία γενομένη (of the wife) – cf. 202.8, ὃς ἂν δοκῇ ἐπιτήδειος εἶναι κἂν μάλιστα κατὰ φύσιν ἔποιτο (of the adopted child); (5) 358.3: χαλεπὸν δὲ καὶ ἐκτῆσθαι κτῆμα τοιοῦτον (of the wife) – cf., 202.1ff. οὐ δοκεῖ μοι χρῆναι παῖδας κτᾶσθαι ἐνορῶ γὰρ ἐν παίδων κτήσει πολλοὺς μὲν καὶ μεγάλους κινδύνους, πολλὰς δὲ λύπας κτλ.; (6) 358.6: τί γὰρ ἥδιον ἀνθρώπῳ γυναικὸς καταθυμίας – cf. 202.10 . . . ἔστι τὸν παῖδα λαβεῖν καταθύμιον ἐκ πολλῶν κτλ. (7) 360.1: φροντίδων ἤδη πάντα πλέα κτλ. – cf. 201.16: τεκνοτροφίη σφαλερόν· τὴν μὲν γὰρ ἐπιτυχίην ἀγῶνος μεστὴν καὶ φροντίδος κέκτηται κτλ. In three of these four instances, the 'Antiphon' of Stobaeus applies to the wife language which Democritus had used of the child. Lastly, the formula: (8) ἀξιώσαντα καὶ ἀξιωθέντα, which occurs in the Stobaeus excerpt (358.3) can perhaps be compared with Xenophon's description (*Mem.* I.6.11) of a conversation in which 'Antiphon' uses the adjective ἄξιος four times in a single statement of seven lines.

These eight pieces of phraseology from the Stobaeus excerpt are embedded in a context which has been put together out of moralizing reflections borrowed from the *Medea* and the *Phaedo* (cf. Diels-Kranz

footnotes *ad. loc.*) and from the *Choice of Hercules* as worded by Xenophon (*Mem.* 2.1.28). I have concluded that our 'Antiphon' must have
discussed mating and marriage in the context of that naturalism
attested by the papyrus, and that in his discussion he borrowed and
improved upon certain radical views of the family relationship already
put forward by Democritus. This conclusion is incorporated in the
text I have printed on pp. 292ff. I would further conjecture that
his discussions of these and perhaps other matters were later edited
and garbled, to suit conventional prejudices, perhaps by the Peripatetics (cf. *FVS*[6] 87A4) before they reached the pages of Stobaeus.

INDEX

INDEX

INDEX

427

INDEX

INDEX

goods, 142, 212, 213, 250, 298, 332, 340, 354-356, 364, 374, 378, 384, 385, 386, 393

goodness, 173, 203, 206, 287

Gorgias, 160, 164, 165, 195, 213, 245

Gorgias, 19, 123, 156-158, 165, 195, 213, 245-249, 251, 368, 416, 418

governing class, 312, 391, 393

government, 41, 42, 44, 50, 93, 98, 124, 125, 140, 149-153, 155, 171, 231, 234, 235, 246, 248, 272, 341, 366, 389

gradualism, 46, 48, 69, 76, 77, 83, 85, 91, 93, 106, 111, 119, 123

grain, 83, 86, 204

gratitude, 120, 398, 399

Greece, 161, 205, 214, 223, 227, 388

Greek, 117, 118, 120, 144, 155, 162, 328, 329, 351, 354, 367, 374, 380, 381, 389, 399

Green, 16, 19, 143

Greene, 409, 416, 417, 418

Grenfell and Hunt, 416, 417

Grote, 408

Grotius, 14, 155, 289

group, 79, 81, 86, 90, 94, 103, 106, 107, 118, 124, 128, 130-139, 143, 146, 170, 172, 173, 175, 178, 180, 187, 189, 191-193, 220, 223, 228, 230, 235, 246, 254, 260, 269, 277, 278-280, 282, 286, 289, 300, 308, 312, 317, 379, 383, 390, 391, 400

grudge, 136, 137

guarantee, 335, 338, 373, 374, 386, 401

guardians, Platonic, 96

guilds, family, 98, 189, 367

guilt, 153, 174, 288

Gunning, 408

gymnast, 159, 179

habit in Democritus, 116, 117, 118, 119, 121, 122, 138, 144; in Protagoras, 70, 152; in Antiphon, 272

habitation (cf. topographical), 44, 368

Hades, 57

hair, 204, 324

Hammurabi, 129

hands, 77, 90, 106-108, 110, 111, 113, 117, 119, 275, 277, 384

happiness, in Plato, 41, 44; in Antiphon, 124, 286; in Aristotle, 375

harbour, 247, 253

hard *versus* soft, 196

hardships, 115, 369

harm, 102, 261, 262

Harpocration, 415, 416

harvest, 83, 316, 383

hatred, 235, 261-263, 286, 395

have nots, 142

health, 96, 116, 253, 266, 362

heart, 141, 275-277, 293, 294

heat, 89, 112

Hebrew, 13, 14, 30, 31, 54, 137

Hecataeus of Abdera, 406

Hecataeus of Miletus, 104

hedonism, 265, 266, 279, 281-283, 287, 293, 297, 303, 304, 370, 379, 393, 400

Hegel, 15, 16, 19, 146, 295

Heidel, 410, 411

Heinimann, 411, 416, 418

Hellas, 211

Hellene (in Antiph.), 256, 257, 278

Hellenism, 389

Hellenistic Age, 29, 33, 126

hemerosis, 79

Hephaestus, 42, 53-55, 89

Heraclitus, 127, 290

herd, 102, 103, 109, 115, 118, 298

Hermes, 84, 90, 93

Hermogenes, 415

hero, 26, 28, 31, 39, 54, 55, 74, 86, 93, 119, 123

Herodotus, 73, 120, 135, 137, 147, 158, 170, 171, 225, 269, 380, 405, 410, 412

heroic tradition, 257, 280, 299, 320, 331

Hesiod, 31, 35-40, 43, 44, 47, 53, 54, 56, 58, 61, 66, 71, 75, 76, 92, 100, 120, 136, 147, 214, 265, 293, 299, 302, 405, 412

Hesychius, 415

hexis, 327

Hippias, 156, 157, 159, 164, 194, 207, 216, 218, 221, 223-229, 236, 349, 395

Hippocrates, 161, 210, 243

Hippolytus, 112

historical method, 14, 26-28, 30, 32, 91, 98, 99, 101, 113, 117, 118, 121, 123, 129, 130, 140, 161, 167, 168, 171, 172, 176, 193, 238, 273, 317, 368, 372, 376, 379, 388, 391, 401, 405, 410

history, 36-103, 108, 147, 197, 233, 386

history of Greece, 18, 19

history of philosophy, 34

Hobbes, 147, 149, 150, 155, 156, 258, 262

hold dialogue, 208, 211-216, 222, 239, 242, 245

hold discourse, 217

holiness as part of 'virtue', 195, 196, 198, 201

Homer, 39, 54, 57, 114, 132, 141, 187, 245, 280, 295, 299, 321, 381

homo sapiens, 26, 27, 36, 57, 60, 69, 72, 79, 92, 105

homologia, 272, 383, 400, 402

homonoia, 235, 290, 416, 419

homosexual, 298

honey, 119

honourable (*kalon*), 112, 114

horses, 106, 119, 204, 253, 364

hospitality, 39

INDEX

INDEX

Moses, 13
mother, 310, 324
motion (cosmic), 41, 42
motive (Democ.), 136, 151, 152, 392
mountains, 45, 50
mouth, 195, 257, 261
mud (cf. swamp), 115
mule, 116, 119, 121, 122
municipal government, 381
murder, 330
Museum, 418
music, 100, 116, 119, 120, 179
mutation, 30, 105, 119
mutual (relationship, etc.), 46, 74, 76,
  79, 82-86, 89, 94, 95, 134, 142, 185,
  215, 217, 232, 236, 239, 242, 292, 299,
  304, 305, 310, 322, 326, 347, 361, 373,
  374, 393, 398
Mycenae, 38
myth in Aristotle, 299
mythos, 129
myths, in Plato, 41-51, 120, 168, 223, 381,
  395, 405, 407-409, 411
Mytilene, 225, 414

names (in language), 118, 120, 193
nation (cf. state), 16, 73, 76, 79, 395
nation-state, 389
native growth (Antiph.), 271
natural, 114, 222, 251, 268, 287, 348,
  352, 356-359, 367, 370, 377, 391, 402
natural justice, 403
natural law, 13-17, 94, 137, 269, 289,
  390
natural rights, 380, 402
naturalism, 19, 25, 26, 34, 44, 45, 70, 76,
  77, 82, 83, 86, 87, 89, 97, 101, 106,
  110, 117, 118, 124, 132, 154, 156, 168,
  185, 257, 290, 296, 307, 340, 345, 372,
  380, 381, 407, 418
nature of man, 25, 28-30, 44, 95, 155
navigation, 48, 59, 60, 66, 67, 70, 71, 95,
  120, 385
necessary and necessity, 28, 115-122,
  132, 194, 200, 217, 263, 269, 390
need, 30, 32, 42-44, 55, 62, 63, 65, 68,
  77, 81, 82, 94, 95, 100, 116, 123, 128,
  130-133, 143, 167, 185, 199, 249, 251-
  253, 259, 266, 288, 306, 308, 315, 317,
  318, 331, 332, 363, 375, 378, 379, 381,
  383, 390-392, 401, 414
negligence (public), 148
negotiation, 20, 32, 145, 157, 212, 222,
  223, 225, 229-231, 239, 241, 390, 401
nemesis, 40, 174, 235
neo-idealism, 16, 19
neo-Platonism, 111
nest, 119
Nestle, 407, 416
New Testament, 259

Newton, 15, 155
nightingale, 116
Nile, 83
noema, 81
nomad, 356
nomima, 411
nomisma, 338, 401
nomizon, 122, 411
nomos, 81, 83, 98, 122, 137-139, 181, 269,
  270, 278, 288-290, 294, 338, 399-401,
  411, 413, 414, 418
non-aggression, 260-262, 264, 267, 274,
  284, 285, 297, 395, 418
non-interest, 265, 275, 279
norm, 31, 114, 193, 260, 266, 340, 365
nose, 195, 204, 257, 261
nostalgia, 36, 37, 43, 47, 100, 188
novelty in history, 45
numerals, 58, 60
nurture, 115, 324

oath, 39, 67, 69, 128, 131, 282, 290
obedience, 138, 171, 178, 220, 277, 278,
  283, 393
object of act, 282, 283, 285
obligation, 321-323
Oedipus, 25-28
Oedipus Tyrannus, 25, 413
office, 145, 147, 149, 151, 152, 182, 183,
  248, 311, 342, 354, 366, 367
official, 150, 389
oikonomike, 387
oikumene, 74-78, 83, 84, 112
old age, 37, 41, 43, 44, 96, 299
Old Comedy, 157, 158
Old Testament, 376
oligarch and oligarchy, 140, 143, 147,
  162, 234, 255, 320, 341, 367, 370,
  371
olive, 204
Olympia, 225, 226
omission (cf. negligence), 150, 203
'one thing' (Protag.), 198, 201
onta (cf. 'is'), 228
operational and operative, 132, 134, 203,
  265, 272, 312, 390
Ophelimon, 391
opinion, 16, 20, 32, 105, 124, 156, 157,
  167, 171, 175, 191, 193, 194, 201, 202,
  207, 209, 213, 216-222, 230, 231, 236,
  237, 239-241, 244, 247, 250-254, 258,
  270, 271, 279, 289, 310-313, 390, 402,
  414
opposition (parliam.), 211, 215
oral publication, 126, 214, 215, 276,
  412
oration (sophistic), 209, 211, 215, 216
orators, 158, 247, 248, 250, 251
order (social), 90, 128, 129, 131, 139,
  140, 141, 151, 154, 177

435

INDEX

retail, 159, 161

retribution (cf. punishment), 174-176, 275

revelation, divine, 13

revenge, 174

reverence in Protag. myth, 90, 91, 93, 195, 201

reverence for life (Antiph.), 280

reverence for superior (Arist.), 307

rewards, distribution of in Aristotle, 328, 372

rhetoric, 48, 193, 206, 230, 240, 245, 246, 249

rhuthmos, 139, 140, 153, 413

rhythm taught in school, 179

rich and riches (cf. wealth), 47, 144, 162, 183, 239, 298, 310

right and rights, 39, 44, 47, 67, 69, 83, 85, 90, 91, 93, 102, 112-114, 128-136, 143, 151, 154, 171, 175, 179, 180, 184, 185, 187, 201, 231, 245, 247, 250, 252-254, 260-266, 271, 274, 277, 283, 286, 306, 311, 314-316, 318-320, 326, 343-345, 348-353, 368, 370, 371, 373, 379, 380, 386, 391, 399-401

right-redress, 134, 283, 285, 286, 330

right way, 138

Rights, Natural, 17

Rights of Man, 15

righteous, 39, 47, 49, 62, 258-260, 264, 268

righteousness, 94-96, 102, 103, 169, 170, 176, 177, 185, 195, 196, 198, 199, 201, 267, 282, 300, 327

ritual (origins explained), 59, 60, 83

robber, 141, 319, 331, 332

romantic love, 294, 326, 418

Rome, 229, 269, 288, 365, 388

roots of plants, etc., 108, 116, 121, 204

Rousseau, 20, 144, 262, 273

rudder as tool, 344

ruler and ruled, 101, 149, 150, 180, 182, 272, 312, 321, 325, 339, 341, 345-351, 367, 368, 374, 393, 396

uralism, 365

sacrifice (ritual), 59-62, 84, 316

St. Thomas, 187, 289

Salamis, 135, 146

sanction (social and legal), 68, 91, 92, 128-130, 140, 141, 173, 175, 178, 252, 259, 260, 267, 272, 276, 413

satire (cf. parody), 207, 215, 223, 224, 267, 382

satisfaction, 217, 358

savage, 26, 31, 32, 54, 70, 78, 83, 86, 91, 92, 102, 106, 131, 139, 141, 153, 170, 172, 176, 186-188, 407

savour, 109, 370, 393

schooling, elementary, 179, 183

science, 343, 344, 363

sculpture (art), 100

Scythians, 118

sea, 104, 105

seasons, 25, 26, 89

security, 14, 37, 39, 79-81, 88-90, 128, 130, 131, 133, 134, 136, 143, 144, 152, 175, 178, 180, 185, 188, 235, 252, 286, 330, 346, 374, 377, 378, 379, 382, 384, 391, 395, 396

seeds (Anaxag.), 108, 109, 113

self-consciousness, 281

self-contradiction (Socratic method), 209, 296, 310, 350

self-direction, 121

selfish, 308, 311, 317, 391, 397

self-sufficiency, 340, 356, 357, 361, 375, 387

selling, 330-332

semantics, 199, 203, 264, 307, 356, 371, 380, 394, 398

Senate, 219

Seneca, 242

sensation, 108, 110, 250, 251

sense (mind), 38

senses, 228, 291, 307

sententia, 126

separating out, 109, 112, 116

servant, 344, 398

Sermon on Mount, 259

serviceable (*chresimon*), 391, 392

services (economic), 332, 340, 354, 355, 364, 374, 378, 381, 384-386, 393

Seven Wise, 276

sex, 36, 42, 112, 113, 117, 122, 291-294, 325, 326, 378, 383, 395

Sextus, 105, 115, 116, 412

'shame' (cf. reverence), 395

shape, social, 106, 109, 115, 139, 140, 151, 153, 177, 382, 388, 401, 402

share (cf. participation), 67, 90, 91, 170

ship (of Hippias), 226

shipbuilding, 385

shipwright, 246

shoes, 89, 90, 332, 334

shoots (of plants, etc.), 204

Shorey, 408

'short form' and 'short style', 211, 213, 224

short-lived, 112

sibling, 320-322

Sikes, 405, 406, 410, 411

silver, 38, 47, 59, 82

similarity of humans, 97, 223, 256, 301, 302, 332, 338, 380, 390, 395, 398, 402; of virtues, 196-200

simplicity in utopia, 95, 99

Simplicius, 105, 109, 111, 415

Sinclair, 408, 413, 414, 417, 419

skepsis, 237

439

skill (cf. technique), 25, 45, 47, 48, 56, 67, 71, 72, 79, 89, 92, 108, 111, 116, 118, 119, 163, 176, 184, 186, 189, 200, 205, 219, 243-245, 249, 253

sky, 108, 109, 120

slave, 98, 101, 305, 310, 321-323, 325, 343-353, 355-357, 359, 364, 368, 370, 373, 375, 382, 393, 398, 402, 403

slime (cf. swamp), 112, 121

small town, 341, 342, 364, 365, 388, 389

snub-nosed, 106

sociality, 81, 135, 383, 385, 396

society, 12-14, 26, 29, 40, 60, 68, 77, 79-82, 87, 91, 97, 99, 103, 105, 114, 120, 124, 129, 133, 134, 141, 149, 153, 154, 166, 168, 170-173, 175, 177, 178, 184, 190, 228, 237, 259, 261, 265, 268, 282, 283, 287, 314, 317, 318, 340, 347, 360, 362, 367, 373, 375, 378, 379, 382-395, 397, 400-403

Socrates, 62, 91, 93, 95, 112, 113, 119, 121, 157-161, 164, 168, 197-200, 206-210, 213-216, 237, 256, 259, 263, 268, 287, 288, 345, 347, 391, 392, 407, 411, 413

soft *versus* hard, 196

soldier, 315, 318

solitude (cf. isolation, dispersion), 46

Solon, 135, 145-149, 151, 153, 158, 174-176, 181, 182, 248, 258, 278, 279, 413

sophia, 89, 111, 153

sophists, 18, 19, 21, 64, 87, 88, 124, 155-165, 181, 229, 240, 244, 383, 417

Sophist, 159, 161

sophistes, 158, 159

sophistic, 160, 162-168, 174, 175, 191, 193, 194, 197-199, 203, 205, 207, 210-215, 218, 220, 221, 223, 226-228, 233, 237, 238, 241, 247-249, 251-254, 414, 415

Sophocles, 26, 33, 35, 66-70, 72, 79, 82, 110, 413

sophrosune, 312

soteria, 92

soul, 12, 14, 15, 94, 159-161, 163, 193, 197-199, 205, 217, 220, 239, 259, 321, 346, 347, 352, 380, 418

sovereignty, political, 149, 150, 153, 156, 272, 341, 366, 375, 389

space *versus* time, 49, 112

Sparta, 228, 234, 258, 311

speaker (cf. chairman), 227

specialization, 93, 95, 97, 98, 149

species (human, etc.), 30, 31, 41, 52, 53, 66, 74, 76, 88, 91, 97, 103, 104, 106, 109, 111, 113, 115, 117, 118, 124, 129, 141, 154, 184, 188, 205, 257, 298, 301, 303, 346, 347, 368, 377, 378, 380, 391, 393, 395, 405, 411, 413

speed of animals, 88

Spencer, 17

sphinx, 25, 28

spider, 116

spirits (daemons), 44

spontaneous (cf. automatic), 12, 33, 41, 43, 44, 75, 76, 91, 109, 115, 117, 118, 262, 274, 280, 283, 290, 291, 293, 294, 297, 298, 301, 304, 317, 326, 349, 400, 418

stability, social, 142, 146, 402

stamp (currency), 361

starvation, 77

stasis, 133

state, Greek, cf. city, *polis*

state of mind, 220-222, 391

state of nature, 15, 49

Statesman, 19, 40-43, 87, 100, 101, 405-407

statesman (Plato and Aristot.), 166, 171, 359, 360

Statesmanship, On, 415

statues of gods, 107, 121

status, 307, 322, 329, 330, 352, 397, 398

Steinthal, 412

Stenzel, 416, 417

Stephanus Byz., 242

Stewart, 408

Stobaeus, 105, 115, 116, 125, 239, 292, 413, 414, 416, 419, 420

stockpile, 77, 109

Stoics, 11, 13, 115, 137, 175, 229, 377, 413

storage, 77, 357, 386

straighten out, 179, 180

strength of early men, 38; of animals, 88

strong (i.e. superior) man, 144, 148, 262, 285, 348, 349

subject *versus* object, 283

subject *versus* ruler, 320, 321, 346, 347, 393, 398

subterranean genesis, 88

success, 148, 151, 166, 233

succour, 134, 272

sufficiency, 102, 360

suggestion (i.e. model), 77, 82, 84, 86, 119

Suidas, 113, 415

suitability of wife, 293

sun, 109, 116

superficial, of goodwill, 306

superior, 40, 148, 149, 153, 167, 176, 183, 248, 250-252, 254, 307, 310, 312, 321, 326, 333, 343, 346, 348, 357, 372, 389, 390, 398, 403

Suppliants (Eurip.), 33, 70-73, 96, 406

supply (cf. food), 358

'support' from laws, 283

'supposition' (social), 338

surplus, 116, 120, 121, 384

surety (cf. guarantee), 386

INDEX

survival, 30, 43, 53, 58, 70, 71, 92, 118, 136, 377, 378, 380, 411

suspicion, social (cf. enmity), 47, 262, 395

swallow, 116

swamp (cf. slime), 83, 105, 106, 113, 403

swarm (cf. herd), 103, 115

swift, 257

syllogism (dialectic), 210

symbol, linguistic, 76, 102

symbola, 368

sympathy, 52, 151, 298, 398

sympheron, 76, 391, 392

synetheia, 116

synistanai, 114

synoikia, 94

'synonymous' (Democ.), 116

syntaxis, 74

syntheke, 150, 400, 402

system, 102, 112, 177, 203, 388, 391

systema, 51, 76, 413

Tartarus, 56

taxis, 102

teach and teacher (cf. instruction), 42, 64-68, 81, 161, 168, 176, 212

technique and technology (*techne*), 25, 28, 31, 36, 41-50, 54, 55, 58, 60-63, 67, 68, 72, 77, 78, 82-100, 105, 108-119, 122, 144, 159, 164, 169, 184-193, 200, 230, 240, 245, 247, 266, 281, 289, 333, 337, 338, 344, 345, 359-361, 384, 385, 387, 392, 397, 405

teeth, 324

teleology, 11, 16, 19, 33, 34, 101, 102, 118, 123, 139, 143, 152, 274, 290, 292, 296-300, 303, 313, 314, 319, 331, 332, 337, 340, 354, 356, 360, 367, 368, 372, 376, 383, 384, 388, 405

telos, 102

temperance (cf. discipline), 121, 169, 201, 202, 415

temples in Egypt, 84

terpis, 122

territory of *polis*, 96, 385

testimony (cf. report), 267, 287

tetralogies, 414

text books, 154, 189, 216, 219, 358

Theaetetus, 158, 195, 249-254, 414

Thebes in Greece, 25-28, 39, 258

Thebes in Egypt, 84, 85

theft, 330-332

theism, 43, 71, 72

Themistius, 415

Themistocles, 247

theocratic, 13

Theogony, 36, 120

theology, Platonic, 92, 412

theology in Hesiod and Democ., 120

Theology in Xenoph., 107

Theophrastus, 108, 410, 411

Theseus, 70, 72

thesis, 412

things, 228, 310, 323, 328, 332, 334, 337, 353-355, 361-364, 386, 398

thinker (*sophistes*), 158, 160

thought (i.e. consciousness), 67, 81

thought (i.e. reflective) in Thrasym., 232, 236, 237

thought, Promethean, 56, 65

Thrace, 106, 107, 225

Thrasymachus, 156-157, 165, 195, 203, 231-239, 241, 350, 418

Thucydides, 73, 147, 212, 225, 233, 255, 370, 380, 405, 414, 415

thunder (cf. lightning), 116-120

timber (cf. lumber), 46, 57, 60

time, 49, 61, 74, 75, 88, 105, 112, 231-234, 382

timocracy, 320, 321

titles of books, 418

toleration, sophistic, 175, 201, 277

tongue (in Antiph.), 275-277, 280

tool, 26, 38, 45, 46, 60, 69, 84, 85, 95, 110, 119, 184, 321, 322, 344, 347, 353, 355, 363, 387, 397

topographic (cf. locality, territory), 80, 368, 369, 373, 379, 386, 388, 402

tort (cf. crime), 330

totalitarian, 271, 288

town, 67, 68, 81

town hall, 226, 227

trade and trader, 95, 97, 159, 161, 162, 164, 205, 302, 359-362, 365, 366, 387

tradition, symbolized in *nomos*, 277-279, 285, 402

tragedy, Greek, 174

tragic flaw, 27

transaction, 331, 332

transgress, 271

transmission of excellence, 178, 179, 189, 231

transport, means of, 46, 48, 58, 60

trapping game, 67

travel-books, 299

Tree of Knowledge, 36

trees (cf. shoots), 204

tribe, 114, 374

Trojan War, 147

Troy, 39, 50

truce (Democ.), 131

'true' and 'truth' in Protag., 249-250; in Antiphon, 259, 261, 262, 266, 271

trustee, 149

Truth, 415-418

'twin discourses', 243

tyche, 412

typoi, 76

tyranny of *nomos*, 223, 270, 381, 395

INDEX